The Moral Circle and the Self

The Moral Circle and the Self

Chinese and Western Approaches

Edited by

Kim-chong Chong
Sor-hoon Tan
C. L. Ten

OPEN COURT
Chicago and La Salle, Illinois

To order books from Open Court, call 1-800-815-2280 or visit www.opencourtbooks.com.

Open Court Publishing Company is a division of Carus Publishing Company.

Printed and bound in the United States of America.

Library of Congress Cataloging-in-Publication Data

The moral circle and the self : Chinese and Western approaches / edited by Kim-chong Chong, Sor-hoon Tan, C.L. Ten.
    p. cm.
Includes bibliographical references and index.
    ISBN 0-8126-9535-6 (trade pbk. : alk. paper)
  1. Ethics, Comparative. 2. Ethics–China. I. Chong, Kim Chong. II. Tan, Sor-hoon, 1965– III. Ten, C. L.
    BJ69 .M66 2003
    170—dc21

                                        2003010937

Contents

PART III
IDENTITY: INDIVIDUAL AND SOCIAL

PART IV
RIGHTS AND CIVIL SOCIETY

PART V
SELF: THE NARRATIVE OF THE *Analects*

Acknowledgments

Most of the papers in this volume arose out of a workshop on "Self, Family and Community: Aspects of Chinese and Western Ethics," organized by the Department of Philosophy, National University of Singapore, on May 12–13, 2000. The workshop was partially funded by the National University of Singapore (Research Project R-106-000-004-112). Additional funding came from the following organizations in Singapore: Kwan Im Thong Hood Cho Temple, Lee Foundation, and Tai Pei Yuen Temple. We gratefully acknowledge the generosity of these organizations. Dr. Tan Choon Kim, Chairman of the Board of Trustees, Kwan Im Thong Hood Cho Temple, deserves special mention for his support of this and other workshops/conferences undertaken by our department.

We thank the following: Our colleagues in the Philosophy Department for their participation and support during the workshop; Rosna Buang, Mabel Tan, Isabelle Yapp, Mislan bin Paiman (Hassan), and the students for their help in administration and organization; Kwong-loi Shun for his subsequent assistance in procuring one of the papers in this volume; and Adrian Kwek Sui Kion for his help in preparing the manuscript.

Two of the papers in this volume were previously published. We thank the editor of *Philosophy East and West*, Roger Ames, for permission to reprint Herbert Fingarette's "The Problem of the Self in the *Analects*," *Philosophy East and West* 29, no. 2 (April 1979); and Blackwell Publishers for permission to reprint Cecilia Wee's "Descartes and Mencius on Self and Community," *The Journal of Chinese Philosophy* 29, no. 2 (June 2002).

Finally, we are grateful to the editors at Open Court, Kerri Mommer and Cindy Pineo, for the care that they have taken in helping to see this project through.

Introduction

The aim of this volume is to probe some conscious and unconscious assumptions in both Chinese and Western ethics as well as to call into question some of the ways in which both forms of ethics are commonly distinguished. The eighteen contributors (two essays are jointly written) are all professional philosophers, albeit with different interests and backgrounds. Together, they address issues at the interface of Chinese and Western ethics. The mutual engagement of the two ethical traditions brings in fresh perspectives and demands a deeper understanding of both.

The impetus for the essays is provided by the overarching question: If ethics encompasses not just a concern for self and family but also for a wider circle of others, what resources do both Chinese and Western ethics have to motivate and to guide this expansion of concern? Arguably, the Confucian emphasis on hierarchical ethical structures does not seem to encourage the development of a common humanity. On the other hand, many Western and Chinese ethicists take it for granted that the concern for self and family can expand, as if there is a unitary motivational and justificatory basis for all relationships. Some of the contributors question how such an expansion is possible and analyze the motivational resources that are said to be available in the ethical theories of both Chinese and Western ethics. Others show how philosophers like Descartes and Mencius have tried to account for the expansion of concern through their analyses of emotions like pity and compassion. The Chinese philosopher Mozi is another example of one who believed in the possibility of an expanded concern through the idea of impartial caring, and this idea is also analyzed.

Certain relationships may hinder the expansion of concern, while other relationships and social structures serve to encourage it. Friendship, for instance, may subvert wider moral concerns. On the other hand, the educational, ritualistic, aesthetic, and normative resources of a community provide the means of a wider concern. These resources include what are recognized as moral authorities. Many people are skeptical about the notion of a moral authority. However, an investigation of both Western and Chinese contexts reveals that the notion may have been misconstrued. Moral authorities play an important role in various areas of our lives, and it may well be that we have taken it for granted.

If our identities are both personal and social, one cannot know how one should live without also answering the question, "How should *we* live?" Family and other relations play an important part in ethics. Examinations of how personal identities are formed in both Chinese and Western cultures undermine the crude assumption that Chinese moral and social systems are "collectivist" in nature, while Western moral and social systems are "individualistic." Questions of identity and community cannot avoid the issues of rights. Thus, what kinds of rights are required for ethical life in a community? The concept of rights serves both as a guide and a limit to ethical expansion. In this volume, it is discussed in the contexts of the treatment of children, the possibility of a Confucian civil society, and the sociopolitical treatment of minority populations. Finally, analysis of the *Analects* reveals a sophisticated vocabulary of the moral circle and the self, indicating a rich concern with personal identity, autonomy, and self-cultivation.

The contributors address issues from a comparative perspective, engaging different cultural-philosophical traditions to illuminate the issues from more than one angle. Comparisons provide mutual criticisms as well as mutual reinforcement. Similarities show us concerns that cut across cultural and temporal boundaries; differences cause us to question what had hitherto been taken for granted. Agreements and disagreements properly understood are both valuable. They not only enable us to understand each tradition better in the light of another, but also create conditions for further improving one's own tradition. We hope that the questions that are raised about both Chinese and Western ethics in this volume will help the reader to make sense of the various complexities in both the Chinese and Western ethical traditions. Making sense of these complexities of the moral circle and the self becomes more important as cultures increasingly come into contact. Some of the essays raise provocative questions, as can be seen from the summaries below. It is hoped that these questions will lead other scholars to respond in such a way as to lead to a clearer and deeper understanding of the issues.

The book is divided into five parts. In what follows, we first describe the general issues that are addressed in each part. This is followed by a summary of the individual papers in each of the sections. The essays in part one, "Community: Expanding Love and Concern," discuss the following questions: Does the hierarchical structure of Confucianism ignore the thought of the contingencies of life and the artificiality of civil distinctions, and is this why notions of equality and democracy do not seem to fit Chinese society? Certain Western and Chinese ethicists talk of the necessity of "expanding" the concern that one has for family and loved ones to encompass a wider circle of strangers, community, and beyond. Do they assume that there is only one kind of motivational and justificatory basis for our actions? How is such "expanding" or "extending" possible?

In "Golden Rule Arguments: A Missing Thought?" Martha Nussbaum first examines the work of the Sinologist and philosopher David Nivison on "Golden Rule Arguments in Chinese Philosophy." The concepts of *zhong* and *shu* play a central role in these arguments. The former could be rendered as "loyalty" and is associated with reliably carrying out one's duties toward superiors or equals. The latter refers to an attitude of "sensitive consideration" and humaneness toward inferiors that could involve the amendment or the suspension of certain ritualistic rules. Golden rule arguments in the early Confucian texts (the *Analects*, *Daxue*, and the *Zhongyong*) that employ these concepts have a hierarchical structure: one is asked to consider what one expects others to do, or how one is to act, in the position of either a superior or an inferior. Contra Nivison, Nussbaum finds no sense of common humanity here, especially when she compares it with examples from the Greek tradition, for example, from Homer's *The Iliad*, and *The Odyssey*, Sophocles's *Philoctetes*, and Diogenes Laertius's *Lives of the Philosophers*. These examples reflect an awareness of the vicissitudes of fortune, making one consider what it would be like for one to be in the vulnerable and suffering position of another. The idea of a common humanity strips away all civil distinctions, reinforcing the idea that people are at bottom equal. It is a thought which permeates the Western tradition. Rousseau in the *Emile*, John Rawls in *A Theory of Justice*, and even former President Clinton in his First Inaugural Address all exemplify this thought, something that seems to be missing in the Chinese—or at least the central Confucian—philosophical tradition. The link between the idea of the vicissitudes of fortune and the fundamental equality of persons on the one hand, and democracy on the other, is one of mutual support: the thought is an essential prop for democratic institutions and these institutions in turn contribute to this mode of thinking. The Confucian philosophical tradition, on the other hand, with its emphasis on the fixity and appropriateness of hierarchical distinctions, would tend to impede the perception of a fully common humanity and in this regard would not encourage the public articulation of thinking about the vicissitudes of fortunes, with all their political ramifications. Nussbaum asks: "I would like to know whether what I have . . . said is true, and whether there are examples of this missing thought in other parts of Chinese culture." She also wonders whether there is a real and profound cultural difference here. Her ascription of a "missing thought" in Confucianism is deliberately provocative. If she is right, it can provide some explanation of the anti-democratic tendencies in Chinese ethical thinking. It would require some argument to prove her wrong. But it is precisely such challenges and responses that are necessary to the deeper study of central aspects of both Confucian and Western ethical thinking.

C. L. Ten's "The Moral Circle" questions the common assumption in both Chinese and Western ethics that there is only one ultimate value and/or one motivating force behind all our moral concerns. This ethical monism can be found in the Western theories of Utilitarianism and environmentalism as well as in Confucianism. Typically, they speak of expanding the concern or love we have for family and friends to an ever-wider circle. (In the case of Utilitarianism, this could include animals, and in environmentalism, this includes inanimate objects.) Given that the ultimate value for Utilitarianism is the maximization of utility, this theory could disagree with Confucianism over the issue of filial piety: in the classic hypothetical dilemma of whether one should save the Archbishop Fenelon or his chambermaid—who happens also to be one's mother—from a burning building (assuming that only one can be saved), the Utilitarian answer would be based on the calculation of utility. The answer of William Godwin, who posed this dilemma, was that one should rescue the Archbishop because this would produce the higher utility or better consequences. This is of course contrary to the Confucian priority of love and concern for one's parents over the concern shown for others. Despite this fundamental difference of priorities, however, both Utilitarianism and Confucianism would seem to share the assumption that love and concern is of a unitary kind. The motivational basis of this love and concern is variously described as sympathy, compassion, benevolence, or reciprocity. Ten points out, however, that even though we may have reason to limit self-interest—and people in general do have the capacity to express love and concern for strangers (sometimes at great risk to themselves)—the justificatory and motivational reasons we apply to different objects of love and concern may not be similar. The personal relationships we have, for instance, would not be what they are if described in terms of compassion, sympathy, benevolence, or reciprocity. The Confucian philosopher Tu Wei-ming, for example, holds that it is the principle of reciprocity that underlies the basic relationships. But this cannot account for all relationships because some relationships are asymmetrical. Ten also takes issue with the Confucian belief articulated by Tu, that one who does not care for close relatives cannot be expected "to understand universal love in a real and experiential sense." Saintly people like Gandhi who love all humanity may have difficulty in sustaining the love involved in personal relationships, given that they may not be prepared to run certain risks that these may imply. A public figure such as Arthur Koestler may have acted courageously in public or performed his public duties admirably, but behaved badly in his personal life. Conversely, the fact that the Confucian ruler shows affection for his family is no reason in itself to believe that he will necessarily care for his people.

Although Ten does not discuss this, it is stated in the *Analects* (1.2) that filial love and respect is the root of benevolence. Mencius too asserts that one first has affection for parents before being benevolent toward others. This could refer to both a developmental and an ethical priority. Ten's argument would force Confucians to rethink the basis on which filial piety can be expanded or extended. At the same time, it would be fruitful to see whether Confucianism does have the resources to deal with different motivational and justificatory bases of action and to explore how it would deal with dilemmas that could arise when they conflict.

Ten's challenge to show how, say, compassion can be extended to others is nicely taken up by Cecilia Wee in "Descartes and Mencius on Self and Community." Most of us have the image of Descartes as an individualist and solitary thinker. Wee's essay therefore comes as a refreshing surprise, telling us that Descartes too was concerned with moral motivation, and the problem that he faced here was not very different from one that exercised Mencius. Descartes holds that the interests of the community must be prior to an individual's interests. One is a part of a number of wholes: the universe, the earth, state, society, family. In each case, one's own interests must always be subordinate. The justification for this is that it is a virtue to subordinate one's interests to that of the whole. Descartes qualifies this by adding that this is to be done with measure and discretion, through the use of practical reason. But given the recognition that one should act in the wider interest, how does one ensure this? Descartes acknowledges that there may be a gap here. As he says, if we lack a "firm habit of belief," we may not do what we ought. The passions may lead us astray, but they are not for that reason to be rejected: they are "by nature good," for instance, fear may steer us away from danger, courage may move us to fight. Reason tempers the passions to the extent of helping us to "reprogram" or redirect them so that we are not led astray. But how exactly does this work? Here, Wee draws an interesting parallel between Descartes and Mencius. For both, there is no cognitive/affective divide. Pity and compassion, for instance, are object directed, they are modes of awareness that allow us to perceive the objects as being in a certain way, not something added onto a cognition. Cecilia Wee brings in the example of Mencius and King Hsuan in *Mencius* 1A:7. The king had felt compassion for an ox being led to slaughter and had asked for it to be spared. Mencius says that he can extend this compassion to his people. In evoking the sense of compassion in the king, Mencius believes that the king would be moved into alleviating the suffering of his people. Cecilia Wee suggests other examples of how we might evoke similar feelings. Thus, one's passions can be "reprogrammed" by relating it to the relevant situation.

In "A Response to the Mohist Arguments in 'Impartial Caring'" Bryan Van Norden discusses the debate within the Chinese tradition between the Confucians and the Mohists on extending love and concern beyond the immediate family. Although the Confucians did argue for the extension of love, they accorded priority to love of family over love of others. The Mohists questioned this, through their concept of *jian ai*. Van Norden translates *jian ai* as "impartial caring" and takes it to mean that "one should have equal concern for, and has equal ethical obligations toward, promoting the well being of every person, regardless of any special relation a person might have with oneself." According to Van Norden, the Mohists may be attacking a straw man if they interpret the Confucians as partialist in an egoistic sense. In this regard, a more appropriate target may have been the followers of Yang Zhu who could more justifiably be labeled as egoists. In any case, Van Norden finds the Mohist arguments to be weak. In the "caretaker" argument, for instance, one is asked whether one would leave one's family with a partial or an impartial person, should one go off to war? The Mohist answer that one would surely opt for the latter is not obviously true. Under certain circumstances, one could imagine that it is the partial friend who would do more for one's family. The Mohist characterization of the partial person as one who would not care for his friend, whereas the impartial person would, is also surprising. The impartial person is characterized as someone who would help his friend, whereas the problem as stated earlier is caring for others as a whole, and not just friends. In the "filial piety" argument, the Mohists argue that given one's love for one's own parents, one can ensure that they are well looked after by looking after the parents of others. In other words, reciprocity would help to ensure the welfare of one's own parents. Van Norden argues that reciprocity is not invariably ensured. But there is also a questionable assumption behind the Mohist argument. Even if in a lifeboat situation I would look after my family first, it is false to assume that partial or graded love will lead to the harming of the families of others. The reciprocity argument begins with the assumption that we would all want to look after our own parents or families, and to ensure their welfare. This does not ensure impartiality and in fact endorses our actions in lifeboat scenarios. The Mohist advocacy of impartial caring and its rejection of graded love are in the end impractical. In their belief that people are malleable to the extent that they can be influenced by the rulers to behave as they liked, the Mohists seem to have the view that there is no human nature. Perhaps it is this rejection of any human nature that is at the bottom of the idea that one can have impartial caring.

The essays in part two, "Friends, Authority, Family, and Self-Cultivation," raise questions about specific kinds of relations: Is friendship subsumable under role morality or is it morally subversive? Is moral authority a suspect notion, or does it have an important role in our lives? What qualifies someone to be a moral authority? Does the concept of filial piety lead to authoritarianism and oppression within the family? What is moral cultivation and why do the Confucian texts talk of music in conjunction with it?

In "Friendship and Role Morality" Dean Cocking and Jeanette Kennett resist the attempt to place friendship alongside certain professional roles that may call for acting against some general moral requirement in the interest of the client or out of loyalty for the client. In these cases, professional considerations constitute a source of moral good. Similarly, a parent might tell a lie for a child, say, to her schoolteacher, but there is some moral justification insofar as she does so out of wider considerations for the welfare of the child as a parent. In contrast, there are no such considerations in what is properly characterized as friendship. And in this regard, friendship may be regarded as morally subversive. A good friend may tell a lie for her friend without any moral justification or without seeing the act in terms of any role. She just does so in view of its being in her friend's interest. There is a "mutual drawing" and contribution to the other's self-conception that is not role-governed in any way. In this regard, friendship can be held to be "minimally structured": it is not just that it is ungoverned by any role or institutional conception, but even such agent-relative features as mutual affection, trust, loyalty, a disposition to promote the other's serious interests and well-being and so forth, are also features of other roles, especially familial ones. These would not (by themselves) account for the kind of engagement involved in close or companion friendships. What distinguish such close friendships is the fact that "close friends are especially receptive to being directed and interpreted and so in these ways *drawn* by each other" and the way in which they "contribute to each other's self-conception." These are unique features of friendship. In this regard, friendship poses a challenge to the idea that moral reasons override all others. Quite evidently, Cocking's and Kennett's thesis poses a challenge also to Aristotelian and Confucian conceptions of friendship of the highest order as being based on the virtuous qualities of the friend.

In "Pluralism and Moral Authority" John Kekes discusses a relationship of another kind. He reminds us that in our everyday lives, we do legitimately accept the moral authority of exemplary others. This is the case even in a pluralistic society. The political model of authority has raised the question of why people should subject themselves to authorities, placing the discussion in the context of the primacy of autonomy and the reality of power relationships between individual and state. This makes one tend to forget that authorities are not just states and institutions, but individuals as well. There are all kinds of authority relations in our lives: parents and children, teachers and students, physicians and patients, coaches and athletes, and so forth. Authorities may be *de facto* or *de jure*. The right question to ask is how to tell real from spurious authorities, rather than the politically inspired question of why reasonable people would subject themselves to authorities. An acceptance of moral authorities is based on an appreciation of their deep knowledge of the moral tradition and their ability to see through the complexities that bedevil others. The subject matter of moral authority is a good life. Beside knowledge, moral authorities show commitment and are reflectively aware of evil and pluralistic conceptions of the good life. All these enable them to cut through the moral complexities caused by changing conventions. They are able to judge the adequacy of conventions in the light of the underlying moral vision that they were meant to express. If there is a pluralism of conceptions of the good life, why should one live only according to one of them? The answer is that one can only live according to a conception of something that inspires and motivates one, that engages one's feelings and imagination. It is the moral authority that can make vivid this conception of a good life through the living of his or her exemplary life.

A. T. Nuyen's "Love and Respect in the Confucian Family" complements John Kekes's essay. The anthropological evidence seems to show that the authoritarian structure of Confucianism does great physical and psychological damage to subservient people within the Confucian family structure, especially in view of the role of the father as a strict authoritarian. Nuyen argues that a distinction has to be made between politicized and philosophical Confucianism. The three-bond doctrine of the subservience of the minister to the ruler, son to father, and wife to husband is something that is taken from the *Han Fei Tzu*, a legalist text. In the *Mencius* itself, however, we find not the three-bond doctrine but the five relationships: affection between father and son, righteousness between ruler and minister, the separate functions of husband and wife, proper order between young and old, and fidelity between friends. These do not support the strictly "authoritarian" view of Confucianism. Nuyen provides a description of the roles of the concepts of *ren* and *li* in Confucianism which parallel love and respect. Drawing upon Kant, these can be said to be linked to the need for affection and distance, respectively. The social and emotional manifestations of *li* are respect and reverence, while for *ren* they are love, affection, and benevolence. Pyschologically, *li* and *ren* tend to pull in different directions. This is because respect tends to inhibit love and love tends to dull respect. Yet both, with their cognate feelings such as affection and benevolence on the one hand and reverence and deference on the other, are necessary in human relationships, and living well require a proper balance between the two. In the *Doctrine of Virtue*, Kant compares the forces of love and respect with the forces of attraction and repulsion in the physical world as described in Newtonian mechanics. Extending the analogy, we may say that both *li* and *ren* must be in balance for there to be order and harmony. In the absence of harmony, the human world will be a brittle aggregation of beings without deep and meaningful relationships. As stated in the *Zhong Yong*: "When [the] passions awaken and each and all attain due measure and degree, that is *harmony*, or the moral order." Thus, to interpret filial piety as purely a demand for respect, reverence, and obedience is to misunderstand the dynamics between love and respect. While love and respect, or *ren* and *li*, can be considered separately, they are always joined together in a dynamic harmony. The traditional Confucian family may well be authoritarian and totalitarian. However, it does not follow that the Confucianism that underlies the traditional structure is *ipso facto* authoritarian and totalitarian. It is true that Confucianism emphasizes *li* in the family context, but only as a counterpoise to the love and affection that naturally exist. Nuyen disagrees with those who predict the disintegration of the traditional Confucian family structure in modern society. For, given the Confucian emphasis on the harmony of opposing forces, the general Confucian structure is most likely to survive into this millennium.

Karyn Lai's "Confucian Moral Cultivation: Some Parallels with Musical Training" develops the theme of harmony and cultural refinement in Confucian moral self-cultivation. Various Confucian texts talk about the necessary role of both music and *li* in self-cultivation. Karyn Lai draws parallels between the two. In musical training, one begins clumsily with the acquisition of musical knowledge and technical skills that require continuous and rigorous practice. Similarly, one begins learning and practicing the ritual rules of *li* within the family. In this beginning context, the rules are conservative and somewhat inflexible. As the musical beginner develops, however, one is expected to become expressive. Similarly in the context of *li* one is expected to express humanity or *ren* in the ritual performances. In both contexts of music and *li*, technical perfection is necessary but not sufficient for a good performance. In this regard, *ren* and *li* are interconnected, each a necessary component of the other. The cultural and traditional background of *wen* has to be taken into consideration here. *Wen* connotes a civilizing refinement. The acts of *li* are refined and cultivated acts that have a cultural and traditional background against which they have a communicative meaning. No musical performance can be understood independently of a cultural background. Similarly, the practice of *li* requires a shared communal and cultural context. It is only within such a context that a *li* action allows for self-expression. Socialization does not preclude self-expression and improvisation, but instead, it is precisely such a socialization that makes them possible. A further parallel with music is that the refinements of *li* make self-cultivation an aesthetic process. Lai explicates another concept: *yi* or righteousness. This is seen as what is fitting or appropriate in relation to *li*. There is no fixed idea of what is right independent of context. Still, Lai is concerned to show that there must be room for independence here. She sees it as a basic disposition, *zhi* (*Analects* 15.18) as opposed to *wen*, acculturation. Where *yi* would play a role in the modification of *li* is in the application of moral intuition to various *li* practices, to judge whether these might be contradictory or inconsistent with one's innate sense of right. According to Lai, *yi* is an "innate moral sensitivity to what is right."

The essays in part three, "Identity: Individual and Social," raise the following questions: Upon what does my identity hang and to what extent can I break free of the structures upon which it hangs? Is it accurate to say that Western ethics extols individualism whereas Chinese ethics extols collectivism?

In "Personal Identity and Family Commitment," Alan Montefiore describes personal identity in social terms, instead of as a metaphysical self that persists through physical and psychological changes over time. We are all socially entangled, and the ability to speak meaningfully about oneself or anything else is essentially bound up with the ability to speak to and to be understood by others. Wittgenstein's argument against private language has emphasized this. Any person's ability to structure even her own thoughts, including those about her own identity, is inextricably bound with the possibility of encountering other speakers of the same language incorporating the same conceptual structures. In this regard, the fact/value distinction does not apply. One's identity brings with it a role and corresponding responsibilities and obligations. For example, one finds oneself occupying a certain role within a family structure. In Montefiore's own case, this role "to some variably important degree may be seen to interact with that which my family has been taken and may still be taken to occupy within the wider Anglo-Jewish society and beyond." There are limits to one's freedom to maneuver in relation to given roles and responsibilities.

But how far can one free oneself from any given role? One can only do so by reference to some other role, which one cannot in principle escape. How we see ourselves depend on the conceptions available to us, and we are also structured by how others regard us.

John Greenwood's "Individualism and Collectivism in Moral and Social Thought" argues that the common characterization of Western and Chinese moral and social systems as respectively "individualist" and "collectivist" in nature seriously distorts understanding of the relation between the individual and social forms of being that underlie *any* system. To begin with, the conception of oneself as a physical and psychological individual with a distinct history and biography is universally shared. However, the contents of any particular conception of individuality are the product of certain culturally and historically shared social representations. As such, all conceptions of individuality are *collective* in nature. How individuality is valued varies across culture and historical periods. Thus, the liberal-democratic and laissez-fare tradition of John Stuart Mill and Jeremy Bentham represent only one example of an *individualist* conception. Other conceptions can be found among the Chinese themselves: Yang Zhu's egoistic conception of life and even the Confucian protection of errant members of the family from legal or state action are far from "collectivist." Paradoxically, the communist vision of a collectivist state in China was presaged by a radical rejection (by Tan Sitong and Kang Youwei) of all social conventions and principles and led to a "borderless" society of homogeneous individuals. In the West, the picture is no less complicated. The *laissez-faire* individuality of Mill and Bentham is only a relatively recent and contested position (even within the West). Greenwood traces the origin of the term "individual" to show that in medieval times, it meant "inseparable," being employed to individuate "a member of some group, kind, or species." Persons were thus defined as individuals by reference to the groups of which they were members, and their identity was thus determined by their membership in a group. The Renaissance and the Reformation, and the tradition of social thought from Hobbes, Locke, and Smith to Bentham and Mill, gave rise to a conception of the isolated, egoistic individual. But the medieval conception is still maintained and continues to play a significant role through the moral and social thought of thinkers like Rousseau and Hegel, and idealists like Bosanquet and Green. More recent thinkers like William McDougall, Dewey, Cooley, Baldwin, and Mead regard sociality not as a threat to individuality, but as the very source and medium of individuality. MacDougall in fact traced this idea back to the Greek city-state. Western and Chinese systems share a similar problem: how to extend motivation for caring about others beyond a wider group. There are psychological difficulties in extending love and concern for humanity as a whole. Any system, Eastern or Western, works better if it begins by evincing a concern for those nearer to one.

The essays in part four take up the following social and political issues: Is the notion of rights disruptive of family and communal relations? What is the relation between rights and autonomy and why are these important? What role can the concept of civil society play in helping along the process of democratization in China? What underlying social and political conflicts exist between Liberalism and Confucianism when the question of the assimilation of minorities is addressed?

In "Regulating the Family," Margaret M. Coady and C. A. J. Coady analyze the supposed conflict across cultures that many (for instance, Huntington) see or foresee. But there seems to be little that is conflictual about, say, the rights of the child to protection, as evidenced in the League of Nations and the United Nations *Declaration of the Rights of the Child* in 1924 and 1959 respectively. In this regard, there would seem to be no cultural difference: all would agree with the principle that the child needs protection from harm although differences may arise over what constitutes harm. The 1990 UN *Convention on the Rights of the Child* incorporated autonomy rights (qualified in many ways) and at the same time recognizes the importance of the family. The Coadys canvass "the view that there is a sense of autonomy which can be applied to children and which is not incompatible with their membership of a community, or more likely many communities, including their families." The Coadys address two issues related to this view: (1) the role of rights in a community, and (2) an account of the kinds of autonomy which children, including young ones, may be said to have. With regard to (1), they challenge the narrow view of rights as claims we are making *against* others. "Far from being destructive of community, rights can help build communities. We often feel a common bond in exercising and enjoying rights. Critics of rights may claim they are destructive of community and solidarity but the joint exercise of rights is often creative and restorative of community." With regard to (2), the Coadys argue, "The assumption is often made that the ideas of atomistic individualism—independence, separateness, self-determination, and autonomy—are interchangeable or at least always conceptually connected. But autonomy is clearly not necessarily the same as . . . individualism. . . . Clearly, a sensible notion of autonomy, for adults or children, cannot be encumbered with too rigid an understanding of independence or self-determination." The Coadys provide the metaphor of a child as a participant in a conversation: "The child establishes its identity through being involved in an active manner in the discourses, social structures, and practices of its world." This metaphor "allows for the evolving nature of cultures rather than suggesting that cultures are static. It conveys a view of autonomy which is not the Kantian exercise of the capacity for universalizable second order reflection on one's first order preferences, but is that of an individual human being actively constructing its identity." This framework of rights and autonomy fits any culture including the Confucian and gives the lie to Huntington's thesis of an inevitable "clash of civilizations."

In "Can There Be a Confucian Civil Society?," Sor-hoon Tan questions certain assumptions implicit in the dominant Western conception of civil society, which are problematic in the Confucian context. She reconstructs the concept of civil society to fit into the framework of a Confucian democracy; this concept of Confucian civil society also offers some insight into the erosion of public life in some Western liberal democracies. In the Confucian context, for example, the boundaries between family and nonfamily associations and between social and state organizations are fluid. Although formal institutions need to be formed for democratization to work, there is also the need for the "regeneration of communities that would rebuild social identities and a sense of social responsibility." The recognition of a communitarian framework for civil society as opposed to a liberal one should not mean that individuals would necessarily be oppressed. Instead, the "individual-society relation should be mutually enhancing rather than parasitic or antagonistic in a civil society, whether Confucian or Western." Another dichotomy that needs to be modified when applied to the Confucian context is that of the "public" and the "private." In Chinese, *si*, or "private," is often synonymous with selfishness. In the West, however, the private has moral value. It is not surprising if most Confucians view the Western emphasis on individual rights, and the interest group politics it is associated with, as a kind of selfishness. In Confucian thought, *gong* ("public") and *si* ("private") are not simple dichotomies, but form a complementary polarity. The conception of civil society as something opposed to the state should also be modified. Interdependence and not dependence should exist between civil society and state. Tan agrees with some writers that trust is a necessary condition for both civil society and democracy. In this regard, Confucianism could be valuable in reconstituting the problem of civil society to focus on the problem of trust. A Confucian civil society is one where ritual practice fosters and nourishes the growth of trust. In such an atmosphere of trust, individuals not only compete but also cooperate in voluntary associations united by common interests. It is easier to trust fellow citizens in a society where ritual practice reigns. Such trust makes it easier to participate in social action and to build a vibrant civil society.

Baogang He's "Minority Rights: A Confucian Critique of Kymlicka's Theory of Nonassimilation" is a comparative study of the underlying political philosophies of Liberalism and Confucianism, applied to the question of minority rights and assimilation. The Confucian framework is characterized by duty, goodness, compassion, and the principle of humanity, which teaches love for all peoples regardless of ethnicity. A Confucian notion of justice prioritizes order and stability, and values collectivity, political authority, and the unit of the nation. Confucian policies dealing with the minority question feature paternalistic benevolence, cultural assimilation, autonomy, and intermarriage. By contrast, Kymlicka's conception of justice adopts the perspective of the least advantaged group and takes seriously the value of cultural diversity. Kymlicka's normative structure of justice contains three main ideas: equality, the honoring of historical agreements, and the value of cultural diversity. It stresses individual rights as against obligations, entitlements as against benefits given. While the Confucian communitarian approach can support the state's provision for the protection of minorities, it can also be used to justify the suppression of minorities, or to camouflage the exercise of majority power. It tends to be paternalistic and can lead to repressive measures. Despite its attractions, however, Kymlicka's theory of nonassimilation on liberal principles cannot work in practice. Thus, for example, the liberal policy of internal restriction (no internal violation of human rights) may itself be seen as a violation of the self-governing principle by minority groups because such internal restrictions may reduce the power of minority communities to maintain their cultures. It might also be argued that internal restriction is a sort of liberal "imperialism" that does not take seriously the desire of some minorities to maintain their illiberal elements and customs. Paradoxically, a defense of cultural communities, collective liberty, and communal fate involves a concession to individual liberty that may at the same time require the reduction of individual freedom. For, in defending a cultural community, individual rights are always sacrificed or at least seen as second order.

The title of part five, "Self: The Narrative of the *Analects*," can be seen as a response to those who think that the *Analects* is a fragmented text that cannot compare with, say, Plato's *Dialogues* and the Christian Gospels. In a review of translations of the *Analects*, Owen Flanagan, for example, has said that in comparison to these other two bodies of works, the *Analects* lacks "reasons, arguments, context and motivation for the recommended moral agenda . . . the *Analects* is aesthetically deficient. The sayings of the Master are not embedded in a narrative that might give them life" (Owen Flanagan, "No Talk in Bed," *London Review of Books*, 20: 7, 2 April 1998, p. 30). Readers will have to judge for themselves whether what Flanagan says accurately reflects the *Analects*. Perhaps the three papers in this section will disabuse the reader of the notion that the *Analects* is, for example, "aesthetically deficient," or lacks "context and motivation for the recommended moral agenda." The three contributors discuss concepts of self in the *Analects*, each with a different focus. The first essay shows how the psychical self is related to bodily self-expressions. The second contribution discusses the sense of an autonomous self in the *Analects*, in terms of the notion of self-directedness. The third essay is concerned to show that whereas self-cultivation is intensely personal, the actions required are impersonally grounded in the *dao*. It is in this sense that the self-cultivated person is "selfless."

Yuet Keung Lo's "Finding the Self in the *Analects*: A Philological Approach" finds in the *Analects* "a deep underlying concern with the problem of human self-identity." For Confucius, the idea of human nature is more of a construction than it is of biology. Lo examines several self-referential terms. *Wu* and *yu* function as a first-person pronoun, grammatically marking self from others. However, *yu* is also used by Confucius to refer to himself in such a way as to "display a vague ring of idiosyncrasy that intimates a sense of self." Lo mentions two incidents in which the term *yu* occurs, and where Confucius perceives himself uniquely as a "Heaven-ordained transmitter of culture." In these and other cases, Confucius has a sense of self that is "personal and cosmic at once." Another first-person pronoun, *wo*, "can also be used as an adjective that characterizes one's ego or egotistic thought. As such, *wo* is the most versatile self-referring term in the *Analects*; it can refer to any dimension of the first person, marking its somatic boundaries as well as presenting its psychic existence." Lo mentions certain instances where Confucius, in using *wo* to describe himself, "clearly indicates that Confucius is aware of himself possessing a personal identity," for instance, in terms of his love of learning and teaching, and his personal integrity. But *wo* also has a "psychic dimension." For example, when Confucius "declares that humaneness is not far away and it is within reach as long as I have a desire for it, he might be referring to himself in contradistinction to others, but it is more likely that he is actually referring to *any* individual self and emphasizing it as an autonomous willing subject." Lo discusses terms like *shen*, *gong*, and *ji* "that may signify the human person as a distinct entity, physically, psychically, or morally." The term *shen*, though literally referring to the body, is something that can be killed in order to fulfill humaneness; offered for the service of one's ruler; forgotten in a fit of anger; the medium through which one does good or evil deeds; humiliated; examined for self-reflection; rectified as a moral example; purified and resists defilement. In other words,

> *shen* refers to the person of an individual which normally follows the conscious conduct of its owner. It is the agent of good deeds and recipeint of self-inflicted humiliation. Only when one loses control such as in a fit of anger will one become careless with it. No doubt *shen* marks the individual person as a moral being with clearly demarcated boundaries; it is a personal domain over which one should keep constant guard. It is both physical and nonphysical; the nonphysical is expressed through the physical whereas the physical defines the nonphysical. This is one reason why the Confucians are so keenly concerned with rituals, because rituals can regulate our personal expressions of what or who we are in our core of being. Once our person is properly regulated, people will be inspired to follow our example.

Lo investigates *ji* with its strong element of self-directed self-worth and compares it to *shen*:

> *ji* signifies the inner psychic self that makes the decisions that define what and who we are, and the endless process of decision-making ultimately constitutes our personal

identity, while *shen* performs all the self-defining decisions from the inner self and ultimately embodies the inner self and gives it a personal, bodily expression. But self and person form an organic holism; the inner-outer dichotomy is a heuristic one that can only fool the purely analytical mind.

Kim-chong Chong, in "Autonomy in the *Analects*," describes certain features of Confucius's ethics, namely, the expression and development of aims and aspirations, their establishment and maintenance throughout one's life, an integral sense of self, and the effort required for self-directedness. Following Isaiah Berlin's distinction between the "negative" and the "positive" conceptions of liberty, there are two corresponding senses of autonomy. Under the negative conception, autonomy is the absence of constraints on individual action. This freedom is to be curbed only when it causes harm to others. While the negative conception is concerned with the *area* of control, the positive conception is concerned with the *source* of control. As moral agents, we have a desire for directing our own lives. This gives rise to a sense of autonomy called self-directedness, which can stand independently of institutional arrangements, no matter how wide the area of freedom they may allow. In the *Analects*, the effort and commitment required to live according to the ideal of *ren* comes from a conception of self oriented toward the ideal. This ideal is in turn conceived through a shared ethical practice with a set of like-minded individuals. The ideal may, for various reasons, be elusive. Nevertheless, it is a goal that sustains one, especially with the guidance and influence of a charismatic teacher. Commitment to a goal and its maintenance, leading to identification of one's self with the goal, can come about only through a process of socialization. The social and developmental process is therefore necessary for self-directedness.

Herbert Fingarette's book *Confucius: The Secular as Sacred* (New York: Harper and Row, 1972) made a tremendous impact when it first appeared, and continues to be discussed. It is a good example of what can be done when the tools of Western philosophy are sensitively applied to a close reading of Chinese philosophy. Fingarette's work has inspired many philosophers of the Western tradition to turn their attention toward the Chinese ethical and philosophical tradition. His contribution to this volume (which first appeared in *Philosophy East and West* 29, no. 2, 1979) is entitled "The Problem of the Self in the *Analects*." It focuses on the concept of *zhi*, variously translated as "will," "bent," "wish," "set on," "determined," "aim," and so forth. Becoming selfless is a pervasive theme in Asian philosophy. But the *Analects* would seem to be different: it has to do with self-cultivation, not self-loss. The will affirms a commitment toward learning and an ideal way of life involving the realization of concepts like *li* and *ren*, *zhong* and *shu*, in an intensely personal way. Confucius "is insisting that in the respects in which the will is inherently personal it is for us to affirm that will, to exercise it, assert it—and in so doing, of course, to affirm, to assert our self as individual, as unique." This personal aspect of the will, however, is to be distinguished from the *ground* for willing certain acts: "*what I will* is what is called for by the *li*, or by *ren*, or *zhong*, or *shu*, or *yi*, or—to put it most generally—by the *dao*, and . . . my reason for so willing is precisely that this *is* what the *dao* calls for." In this regard, my will is not personal. Fingarette contrasts this with the egoist: "The ego is present in the egoist's will. The *dao* is present in the *junzi*'s will. The egoist's will *imposes* the egoist on affairs. The *junzi*'s will imposes nothing, but it manifests or actualizes the *dao*. In this regard, the "I" of the *junzi* is transparent: "It is a generative space-time locus of will without personal content." Fingarette relates this idea to Daoism and Indian Philosophy, which seems to characteristically emphasize "selflessness." He also relates it to the image of musical performance. What is important is artistic performance and not mere showmanship. It is the musical conception or the *dao* of the piece that is to be brought forth: this "transcends the individual will, and . . . constitutes the ground of the will for each ideal performer."

—The Editors

PART I

COMMUNITY: EXPANDING LOVE AND CONCERN

Golden Rule Arguments: A Missing Thought?[1]

Martha C. Nussbaum

"To a person who thinks," writes Jean-Jacques Rousseau in Book IV of the *Emile*, "all the civil distinctions disappear."[2] A very specific combination of thoughts, which Rousseau has just been describing, will show a growing child the artificiality and, ultimately, the indefensibility of all social distinctions of rank and class. These thoughts will nourish in Emile the compassionate recognition of a common humanity in all his fellow citizens, and a preference for democratic modes of political organization. He will come to want a society in which "the civil distinctions" do not pervasively shape people's life chances and deform their civic relationships.

What is the content of those allegedly proto-democratic thoughts? I shall argue that the complex set of thoughts described by Rousseau has deep roots in the Western tradition of political thought. As he himself indicates by opening this section of the *Emile* with a quotation from Virgil,[3] they derive ultimately from the epic and tragic traditions of Greece and Rome, as well being prominent in many parts of Greek and Roman philosophy. Finally, they are ubiquitous in modern political thought, from John Rawls's *A Theory of Justice*,[4] profoundly indebted in many respects to Rousseau, to examples of popular political rhetoric such as President Clinton's First Inaugural Address.

These thoughts also have at least some resemblance to the thoughts that David Nivison investigates in his fascinating essay, "Golden Rule Arguments in Chinese Moral Philosophy."[5] Some resemblance. But a crucial element of the Greek formulation is absent in its Chinese counterpart, with results that seem to me of deep importance for the political direction of these two traditions. To investigate the significance of that missing element will be my task in this paper.

I write, of course, as a complete amateur in matters Chinese, untrained and quite ignorant. I shall address this defect by simply relying on Nivison to have given an accurate account of the pertinent texts. I shall proceed as follows. First, I shall summarize the argument of Nivison's article; then I shall describe the parallel Greco-Roman tradition. I shall then identify the allegedly missing thought, and I shall argue that, given the absence of this thought from the texts described by Nivison, some of his conclusions about the moral significance of the Chinese arguments should be called into question. I end with a question to Nivison: is the missing thought really missing in the Chinese tradition generally, or only in the specific texts he cites?

Nivison on Golden Rule Arguments

Nivison traces the development, in Chinese philosophy, of a form of argument he calls a Golden Rule argument: to put it very generally, the argument that one should treat another as one would wish to be treated oneself, were one to be in a similar situation. Nivison then introduces two sets of very helpful distinctions. One set concerns the rule itself. Let me summarize:

(a) The criterion announced in the rule may be counterfactual (i.e., how one *would* want to be treated were one in that position), or it may at times be actual (i.e., treat others as if they are oneself right now).

(b) The rule could be taken as a general rule about what acts to perform, or as a meta-rule about what rules of action to adopt.

(c) The rule could be unqualified, or it could invite qualifications (e.g., taking into account ways in which the other person's needs and desires differ from one's own, or some independent standard of right, etc.).

(d) The rule could be stated positively ("Treat others") or negatively ("Do not treat others as you would not wish to be treated yourself").

Nivison's second set of distinctions involve the purpose for which the rule is used:

(A) It may be an account of what it is to act morally.

(B) It may be a counsel of prudence: it's in your best interest to do this, because this disposes others to treat you well.

(C) It may be a rule of thumb, to check on whether something I do is just. (Like Nivison, I am not sure that this is really distinct from [A].)

(D) The rule may be a rule to follow if I want to become a certain type of ideal person, thus hypothetical rather than categorical.

Let us now, with Nivison, consider some examples from the Confucian texts. For convenience I shall simply enumerate them, including all the premodern examples that figure in the article.[6]

T1. *Analects* 5.12 (shortly after 479–77 B.C.E.). Zigong said, "If I do not desire other people to do something to me, then I also desire not to do it to others."
   The Master said, "Oh, Si! This is not something you have attained to."

T2. *Analects* 15.24 (late 4th century B.C.E.). Zigong asked, "Is there one maxim that can be practiced throughout one's life?"
   The Master replied, "Surely, it is *shu* (consideration)! 'What you do not wish for yourself, do not do to others.'"

T3. *Analects* 6.30 (mid-5th century B.C.E.?). The term *ren* (benevolence) means that when you desire getting established [i.e., being received at court] for yourself, you help others to get established; and when you desire success for yourself you help others to succeed. The ability to make a comparison [sc. with the other person] from what is near at hand [sc. from your own case] can simply be called the method of [attaining] benevolence.[7]

T4. *Zhongyong*, Han Dynasty. *Zhong* and *shu* are not far from the *dao* (Way). If you would not be willing to have something done to yourself, then don't do it to others. The ways of the noble person are four, and I [Confucius] have not yet mastered even one of them: What you would require of your son, use in serving your father; . . . what you would require of your subordinate, use in serving your prince; . . . what you would require of your friend, first apply in your treatment of your friend.

T5. *Analects* 4.15 (479–77 B.C.E.). The Master said, "Shen! My way has one [thread] running through it."
    Zengzi replied, "Quite so." The Master went out.
    The other disciples asked, "What did he mean?"
    Zengzi replied, "Our Master's way consists simply of *zhong* and *shu*."

T6. *Daxue*, contemporary with T4. What you would dislike in your superior, do not use in employing your inferior; what you would dislike in your inferior, do not use in serving your superior; what you would dislike in the one who precedes you, do not use in dealing with the one who comes after you; what you would dislike in the one who comes after you, do not use in dealing with the one who precedes you.

T7. *Analects* 12.2 (4th century B.C.E.). Zhonggong asked about *ren*. The Master said, "When you are out of your house behave as though you were conducting a great reception [i.e. by a ruler or official 'hosting' vassals or subordinates]. When employing the common people behave as if you were conducting a great ritual sacrifice. What you do not want for yourself, do not do to others. In this way you will be free from ill will whether [serving] in the state or in a noble family."

T8. *Analects* 5.19. Zizhang asked the following question: "Prime Minister Ziwen was three times appointed Prime Minister, and showed no sign of delight. He was three times dismissed, and showed no sign of resentment. He always informed the incoming Prime Minister of the past administrative business of the Prime Minister's office. What would you say of him?"
    The Master replied, "He was indeed *zhong*."

Zizhang continued, "But was he *ren?*"
Confucius answered, "I do not know yet [from what you have said]
how he would qualify as *ren.*"

Nivison's engagement with these texts is subtle and complex. But let me attempt as best I can to summarize his conclusions. First, although there are some examples of a purely prudential use of Golden Rule arguments in the tradition, these central passages are firmly moral.

Second, there are both negative and positive formulations to be found in the tradition, but it is wrong to link the negative formulations with the attribute of *shu* and the positive ones with the attribute of *zhong* (as was urged by Fung Yu-lan). Instead, *zhong* is associated with reliably following one's duties toward superior or equals, and might be rendered as "loyalty"; *shu* is not strictly required, and is an attitude of sensitive consideration toward inferiors. It is often involved with amending or suspending rules, and is thus associated with *li*, "rites," rules that are flexible and humane, rather than with *fa*, laws, which are neither. The general idea involved in *shu* is to treat inferiors not harshly, but with decorum and civility. In short: one is required to behave with "loyalty" toward superiors; and the really good person will also behave with sensitive "consideration" toward inferiors.

The idea of role reversal comes in the following way: in *zhong* one reasons that what A should do toward B, when B is a superior, is what A would expect an inferior to do for him. In *shu*, one reasons that what A should do to B, where B is an inferior, is what A would find it acceptable for a superior to do to him.

Notice that, as Nivison stresses, the Chinese texts presuppose a fixed structure of familial and social relationships. Distinctions of precedence and authority are taken for granted. Hence an interesting formal difference from other familiar examples of the Golden Rule argument-type. The Chinese forms do not say, "Treat another as you would have that other treat you," but "Treat another as you would have anyone else related to you as you are to that other treat you."

Despite these observations about the qualifications imposed on the argument in the Confucian tradition, Nivison imputes great importance to *zhong* and *shu*, so understood. He ends his essay with a thought that he calls "stirring." The Golden Rule, in China as in other cultures, he writes, is not simply an "affirmation of one's particular mores," nor a basic principle of morality:

> It is something more basic than this: It is the very ground of community, without which no morality could develop at all: it is the attitude that the other person is not just a physical object, or a (possibly hostile) animal, that I might use or manipulate, and that might shove back or bite, but a person like myself, whom I should treat accordingly even in trivial ways, thereby reassuring both that person and myself of our common humanity.

I have my doubts. I am not so sure that we can squeeze notions such as "a person like myself" and "our common humanity" out of these texts, given what Nivison has rightly observed about the presupposition of a fixed hierarchy. What we have is the injunction to treat a subordinate in the way you'd like your superior to treat you; and the injunction to treat a superior with the loyalty you'd like to have from your inferiors. Where precisely is the sense of common humanity here? We might equally imagine an argument that said, "Treat your dogs the way you'd like to be treated by the gods"—a thought that involves, similarly, the idea of a fixed hierarchy, and yet a symmetry of responsibilities running down the ladder. But of course it would be foolish to say that in that case there was any notion of a common humanity, or of the dog's being "like me." To be sure, the dog has to be imagined as the sort of being to whom treatment of different sorts makes a difference, and to that extent is being imagined as not merely inert. That is not without its importance. But the way I myself would understand such an argument, were I to hear it, would involve a notion of the dog's permanently different capacities and needs. I would interpret it to mean not, "Reason with your dogs because you would like the gods to reason with you," but, rather, "Treat your dog according to his own needs and capacities, just the way you'd like the gods to treat you according to your needs and capacities." And there is nothing in that that tends to erode hierarchy in the name of a larger moral community.

The Missing Thought

Let me now turn to the Greek tradition. And let me begin with three texts taken from the literary tradition, which are entirely typical:

T*i*. Homer, *Iliad* 24.503–12 (trans. R. Lattimore).
"Honour then the gods, Achilleus, and take pity on me
remembering your father, yet I am still more pitiful; I have
gone through what no other mortal on earth has gone through;
I put my lips to the hands of the man who killed my children."

So he spoke, and stirred in the other a passion of grieving
for his own father. He took the old man's hand and pushed
him gently away, and the two remembered, as Priam sat
huddled at the feet of Achilleus and wept close for man-
slaughtering Hektor and Achilleus wept now for his own
father, now again for Patroklos. The sound of their mourning
moved in the house.

T*ii*. Homer, *Odyssey* 17.415–23 (trans. R. Lattimore).
"Give, dear friend. You seem to me, of all the Achaians,
not the worst, but the best. You look like a king. Therefore,
you ought to give me a better present of food than the others

have done, and I will sing your fame all over the endless earth,
for I too once lived in my own house among people, prospering
in wealth, and often I gave to a wanderer according to what
he was and wanted when he came to me; and I had serving
men by thousands, and many another good thing, by which
men live well and are called prosperous. . . ."

T*iii.* Sophocles, *Philoctetes* 501–9 (trans. David Grene).
PHILOCTETES: . . . .Take pity on me.
Look how men live, always precariously
balanced between good and bad fortune.
If you are out of trouble, watch for danger.
And when you live well, then consider the most
your life, lest ruin take it unawares.
CHORUS: Have pity on him, prince.
He has told us of a most desperate course run.
God forbid such things should overtake friends of mine.

All three examples involve a type of imagining that is similar to the imagining involved in Nivison's examples. Achilles figures out how to treat Priam
by thinking about how he would like to be treated in a comparable situation.
Odysseus, disguised as a beggar, asks Antinoos to be generous to him by getting him to imagine what he would want were he to become a beggar. (He
does this by telling his own story, thus getting Antinoos into a frame of mind
apt for seeing that a king might be in that lowly position.) Philoctetes asks his
visitors what they would want were they or their friends to be in his situation,
solitary, pain-ridden, rejected by society.

As I say, these examples show a very common structure of thinking, one
that Aristotle describes in his account of the underpinnings of the emotion of
pity:[8] one thinks about what it would be like to be in the position of the vulnerable and suffering person whom one contemplates—and this is supposed
to make one choose generous and considerate treatment. Achilles returns
Hector's corpse. Antinoos spurns the beggar, and the reader knows that this is
an ominous sign—he has transgressed a fundamental moral norm. Philoctetes's
request arouses in the audience, as in the Chorus, a wish to treat him decently,
and thus a discomfort with the callous and deceptive treatment that the leaders
are in the process of giving him.

Now in an obvious way these examples are similar to the Nivison examples.
They involve positional thinking, and an idea of considerate behavior toward
an inferior. But there are two big differences, which I believe to be closely connected. First, they do not presuppose any fixed hierarchy of fortunes and ranks.
Achilles imagines how his own father might be a captive in war; Odysseus tells
the wealthy suitor that he himself has once been a king; Philoctetes reminds his

visitors that they might be brought low. But why is the hierarchy of fortunes not fixed? What is the thought that enters in at this point? The crucial thought is that of the vicissitudes of fortune. All human beings are vulnerable to big shifts in luck. They can turn from kings into captives, rulers into beggars, healthy men into sick men, citizens into lonely outcasts. These things can happen to any human being. Nobody is exempt. The occasions for pity enumerated in Aristotle's account are the accidents that are widely held to be the common lot of all human beings: death, bodily assault or ill treatment, old age, illness, lack of food, lack of friends, having few friends, separation from one's friends, physical disfigurement, weakness, being crippled, having your good expectations disappointed, having good things come too late, having no good things happen to you, having them happen but being unable to enjoy them (Aristotle, *Rhetoric* 1386a6–13).

This thought is, of course, easy to connect to the thought that distinctions of rank and class are artificial. No Greek would deny that there are some merit-based distinctions among men: thus it is necessary for Aristotle to define pity as concerning only those disasters that the person does *not* deserve. But to any normal Greek (and of course Plato here is the non-normal Greek par excellence[9]), it is just obvious that merit makes a small part of the difference, in most cases. They knew what it was to see friends enslaved in battle, to watch children die, to experience a plague that wipes out half your loved ones, to lose a political struggle, to lose all your money when a ship goes down.

In short, the good person can come to grief. The difference between the king and the beggar can be made by a hair's breadth difference of fortunes in war, or on the sea; or by the luck of birth, or the luck of illness. But this really does mean that the "civil distinctions" disappear. Odysseus and Antinoos are equals in a very fundamental way, because of the thought that many of the most important distinctions among human beings are the work of fortune, unconnected to human desert.

This is the missing thought. And although in Homer it gets only to the point of supplying some limits on war, and ensuring that beggars get decent treatment, its deployment in Athenian tragedy is surely not unconnected with that democracy's ideology of the fundamental equality of persons. Indeed, the tragic idea goes in many ways beyond the democracy, by representing the distinction between slave and free as thoroughly artificial, and the distinction between male and female as at least partly artificial. By harping on the miseries of enslavement, and by continually representing enslaved people as dignified, intelligent beings, Euripides in particular takes the side of the more radical critics of that institution in his time. And his sympathy for women—whom he similarly depicts as highly intelligent and as terribly constrained by custom and use—was so notorious that Aristophanes imagines him sneaking into the Thesmophoria in women's garb to find out what women think about their lives. So the idea that a playwright could understand women by inhabiting their situation is an important leitmotif of Greek thought.[10]

Perhaps the sharpest philosophical expression of the missing idea is in the thought of the Greek Cynics, who insisted—often in scandalous and shocking ways—on the total artificiality of wealth, class, power, birthplace, and also sex, as determinants of human fortunes.[11] Diogenes was alleged to have been exiled from his native city of Sinope for defacing the coinage, and this was, at least, an apt metaphor for his philosophical activity:

T*iv*. Diogenes Laertius, *Lives of the Philosophers*, VI.72. He used to make fun of good birth and distinctions of rank and all that sort of thing, calling them decorations of vice. The only correct political order (*politeia*) was, he said, that in the whole world (*tên en tōi kosmōi*).

So convinced is Diogenes of the artificiality of power and rank that he has no interest at all in the things it can give:

T*v*. Diogenes Laertius VI.38. When he was sunbathing in the Kraneion, Alexander came and stood over him and said, "Ask me for anything you want." He said, "Get out of my light."

Here again, we have a radically democratizing metaphor. The gifts of Alexander are of no interest to Diogenes, who sees the total artificiality of all these things, and of the distinctions among human beings based upon them. He asks Alexander only to get out of his light—and this suggests that healthy political life would be like that, a clearing away of all the artificial impediments that stand between human worth and the sun.[12]

Even in the area of gender and marriage, Cynics, emphasizing the artificial character of all distinctions,[13] pursued a radical human equality:

T*vi*. DL VI.96–8. [Hipparchia] fell in love with Crates' arguments and his way of life and paid no attention to any of her suitors nor to wealth or high birth or good looks. Crates, though, was everything to her. Moreover, she told her parents that she would kill herself if she were not married off to him. So Crates was called on by her parents to talk their daughter out of it; he did all he could, but in the end he didn't persuade her. So he stood up and threw off his clothes in front of her and said, "Here is your bridegroom; these are his possessions; make your decision accordingly—for you cannot be my companion unless you undertake the same way of life." The girl chose him. Adopting the same clothing and style of life she went around with her husband and they made love in public and they went off together to dinner parties.

And once she went to a dinner party at the house of Lysimachus and there refuted Theodorus the Atheist, with a sophism like this: "If it wouldn't be judged wrong for Theodorus to do something, then it wouldn't be judged wrong for Hipparchia to do it either; but Theodorus does no wrong if he beats himself; so Hipparchia too does no wrong if she beats Theodorus." And when Theodorus could not reply to her argument, he ripped off her cloak. But Hipparchia was not upset or distraught as a woman would normally be.[14]

An additional feature in this story is that Crates is a hunchback—so the story shows the groundlessness of distinctions based upon beauty, as well as those based upon class and wealth[15] and sex. This Cynic fantasy goes beyond the tragic appeals to pity. It does not simply say, look what fortune can do. It takes a further step: it says, let's build life in a way that curbs the power of fortune to divide and enslave human beings. Let's take off our clothes and walk around in the sun using our reason. But of course that is a logical next step, once one has the missing thought—once one states, that is, that many of the most important distinctions in human fortunes are undeserved and the work of chance.

That is what Rousseau means by saying, "To a person who thinks, all the civil distinctions disappear." To the person who understands the missing thought, the distinctions of society look petty and mean, surely not things to plume oneself on, and not the things to allow lives to be built around. Like the Cynic philosopher, the "person who thinks" will have contempt for these things, and will not think that they create fundamentally different classes of human beings. As Rousseau goes on to say:

T*vii*. Rousseau, *Emile*, book IV. Human beings are by nature neither kings nor nobles nor courtiers nor rich. All are born naked and poor, all are subject to the misfortunes of life, to difficulties, ills, needs, pains of all sorts. Finally, all are condemned to death. That is what the human being really is, that from which no mortal is exempt. . . . Each may be tomorrow what the one whom he helps is today. . . . Do not, therefore, accustom your pupil to regard the sufferings of the unfortunate and the labors of the poor from the height of his glory; and do not hope to teach him to pity them if he considers them alien to him. Make him understand well that the fate of these unhappy people can be his. . . .[16]

The missing thought is true. It could hardly be denied by anyone who really thinks. That is why Rousseau can simply call the person who thinks this thought "the man who thinks." And yet, as he knows well, many many people do not think this thought: they convince themselves that nature has created two or more races of human beings, one high and one low, one invulnerable and one vulnerable. They deceive themselves about their own vulnerability and their prospects. Hence they behave harshly to those beneath them:

T*viii*. *Ibid*. Why are kings without pity for their subjects? Because they count on never being human beings. Why are the rich so hard toward the poor? It is because they have no fear of being poor. Why does a noble have such contempt for a peasant? It is because he never will be a peasant.[17]

Here Rousseau goes straight back to Aristotle, who emphasizes that one will not have pity if one thinks oneself above the common lot of humanity. He calls this state of mind a *hubristikê diathesis*, an overweening disposition of mind.[18]

The missing thought is absolutely central to democratic and egalitarian thought after Rousseau. It has by now been extended to reflections on race and, more recently, on sex. John Rawls's *A Theory of Justice* is, we might say, built entirely around the missing thought—the idea being to imagine a world in which the contingencies of birth, rank, and wealth do not systematically maim and deform human life-chances. And as we all know, almost any politician is likely to pull out such thoughts when addressing a pluralistic democratic gathering. To cite one example from President Clinton: In his First Inaugural he said that the idea of America is "an idea tempered by the knowledge that, but for fate, we—the fortunate and the unfortunate—might have been each other." Here we see the standard combination of a golden-rule appeal to imagination with the missing thought about the vicissitudes of fortune—all in the service of trying to rally people to support some type of social welfare program.

What to Make of This?

How important is it that the missing thought is harped on continually in the Western philosophical tradition, and apparently not harped on in the Chinese tradition, at least not in the parts described by Nivison? Nivison does show us that the missing thought is not absolutely necessary for motivating a type of considerate and sensitive treatment of one's inferiors. But of course that is easy to see all over the world. Not all kings who believe in the hereditary foundations of kingship are harsh to their subjects; not all masters who believed in the natural inferiority of slaves beat their slaves; not all males who believe in the superiority of the male sex treat their wives badly.

To say this, however, does not establish that without the missing thought we have an idea of considerate treatment based on the perception of a common humanity. Most human beings think humans superior to other species, and yet most of them do not mistreat their pets. Nivison's examples show no more than this level of consideration.

Of course it seems difficult to believe that Chinese people did not have the thoughts that my Greek texts record. For, as Rousseau says, anyone who thinks is likely to come up with them. What seems to me plausible, however, is that such thoughts were not supported or affirmed in the public discourse of their society, and certainly not in the Confucian philosophical tradition. Instead, a thought about the appropriateness and fixity of hierarchy is put forward, and this thought, like feudal ideas about rank, enters in, to impede the perception of a fully common humanity and the public articulation of the missing thought about fortunes. I would like to know whether what I have just said is true, and whether there are examples of this missing thought in other parts of Chinese culture.

Surely Rousseau is right in suggesting that people divided by rank and status can come to think of themselves as permanently separate groups, with fortunes radically divergent. Those of us who lived through the birth of feminism in the United States, for example, can probably recall a time when we ourselves did not fully think the missing thought about relations between men and women; we thought there were two different kinds of people, with utterly different destinies fixed in nature, and so we didn't see, until consciousness raising came along, the artificiality of the "civil distinctions" that blunted women's life-chances. Similarly, it is only relatively recently that race has been regarded as an accident of fortune. In general, it is hard to see distinctions as merely accidental, if they structure the entirety of one's society. Thus both Rousseau and Tocqueville suggest that one may not be able to hold firmly to the missing thought if one is not already in a relatively unhierarchical society. Certainly to hold on to such an idea in Confucius's China would have been, despite its truth, difficult: for one would see all around one the evidence of the permanent differences among humans.[19] Thus the relationship between democracy and the missing idea is one of mutual support. Democratic institutions contribute to thinking the thought, and the thought is an essential prop for democratic institutions.

I am therefore inclined to think that we may have a real and profound cultural difference here. Despite the evident human truth of the missing thought, people may not face it if they live their entire lives in a feudal hierarchy. Once again, however, I put this as a question to those who know more than I do: is this actually true?

There are many ways in which such conjectures about the missing thought could be used to reflect about contemporary political events, but I will end with just one speculation. It seems to me significant that it was Marxism that, so to speak, brought the missing thought to China. In Marx we do have, in a way, the Greek tradition's emphasis on a humanity that is ill served by the various contingencies of fortune. Particularly in Marx's early work, that emphasis on a common humanity deformed by hunger and exploitation is clear. There is in Marx a truly Rousseauian commitment to a radical equalizing of fortunes, and the commitment is to some extent grounded in Rousseauian ideas about the common vulnerability of humanity. On the other hand, Marx articulates these insights in a way that might possibly have been more easily assimilated by Chinese traditions than the ideas of Rousseau or Kant, because the basic entities that change places are fixed hierarchical classes; the idea that individual fortunes fluctuate independently of class membership is not so strikingly evident. Could it be that for this reason Marxian class thinking was a more sympathetic place to think about human equality than the thought of the Enlightenment?

In any case, in today's world we urgently need to think well about whether democracy is or is not alien to non-Western traditions—until relatively recently, that is, for we can hardly deny that an idea belongs to a people if they go to their death for it. We also need to ask whether, if the idea of democracy is in some sense alien, meaning a relatively recent arrival, this should be thought to matter at all for normative moral and political purposes. (We do not think this about some of our own recent ideas, such as the idea of the equality of the races or the sexes: we don't think their recentness means that we are not entitled to call them our own and stake ourselves to them.) At a time when we must do our best with these intensely difficult questions, pondering Nivison's profound article, and the contrasts it invites, is an activity of political as well as intellectual importance.

Notes

1. This paper was originally written for a session on David Nivison's work at the Pacific Division Meeting of the American Philosophical Association, April 1999. I am grateful to Bryan Van Norden for organizing the session and to Nivison for his wonderful work. In revising the paper I have profited from comments by Kim-chong Chong.

2. Jean-Jacques Rousseau, *Emile: or On Education*, trans. Allan Bloom (New York: Basic Books, 1979), 225 (discussing the Third Maxim of pity). I substitute "person" for Bloom's "man": French "l'homme" is clearly generic. Bloom knows this, of course, but he simply assumes that "man" is also generic. I think this is less true in 2000 than it was in 1979, if it was true then.

3. *Ibid.*, p. 224: introducing the Second Maxim of pity, Rousseau quotes from *Aeneid* I.630, in which Dido says, "Non ignara mali, miseris succurrere disco," "Not inexperienced in troubles, I have learned how to bring aid to the wretched."

4. John Rawls, *A Theory of Justice* (Cambridge: Harvard University Press, 1971).

5. In David Nivison, *The Ways of Confucianism: Investigations in Chinese Philosophy*, ed. Bryan W. Van Norden (Chicago: Open Court, 1996), 59–76.

6. Throughout I reproduce Nivison's translations, omitting Chinese characters and all diacritical marks. I give his dating of the relevant texts.

7. Kim-chong Chong argues for a different translation of this text. He writes, "The Chinese *li*, which is translated as 'established,' does not obviously take the sense of something like 'being received at court.' Instead, it could take a sense of being established upon the rites, i.e. one has learned how to behave appropriately and in that way, come of age morally."

8. See my fuller discussion of these examples, and Aristotle's views, in "Tragedy and Self-Sufficiency: Plato and Aristotle on Fear and Pity," in *Oxford Studies in Ancient Philosophy* 10 (1992), 107–60, in shortened form in *Essays on Aristotle's Poetics*, ed. A. Rorty (Princeton: Princeton University Press, 1992), 261–90; see also Interlude 2 in my *The Fragility of Goodness: Luck and Ethics in Greek Tragedy and Philosophy* (Cambridge: Cambridge University Press, 1986, reissued with new introduction 2000).

9. Not really, of course: he does not deny that these accidents of fortune occur, or that they pervasively influence life-chances and opportunities. Along with the later Stoics, he simply denies that these things are truly important: virtue is sufficient for happiness. See my analysis in *The Fragility of Goodness* chapter 5, and in "Tragedy and Self-Sufficiency." On Stoic attitudes, see my *The Therapy of Desire: Theory and Practice in Hellenistic Ethics* (Princeton: Princeton University Press, 1994), ch. 10.

10. Contrast the total silence about women in the *Analects*: here I have profited from reading an unpublished manuscript by Bryan Van Norden.

11. An excellent collection of material studying the Cynics and their influence on later philosophy is *The Cynics: The Cynic Movement in Antiquity and Its Legacy*, ed. R. Bracht Branham and Marie-Odile Goulet-Cazé (Berkeley and Los Angeles: University of California Press, 1996); particularly valuable is the introduction, and Branham's article "Diogenes' Rhetoric and the Invention of Cynicism," 81–104.

12. Although throughout I confine my analysis to Confucian texts examined by Nivison, it is worth mentioning that some near parallels to Diogenes's statements can be found in the *Zhuangzi*. Consider, for example, the following:

> Once, when Chuang Tzu was fishing in the P'u River, the king of Ch'u sent two officials to go and announce to him: "I would like to trouble you with the administration of my realm."
>
> Chuang Tzu held on to the fishing pole and, without turning his head, said, "I have heard that there is a sacred tortoise in Ch'u that has been dead for three thousand years. The king keeps it wrapped in cloth and boxed, and stores it in the ancestral temple. Now would this tortoise rather be dead and have its bones left behind and honored? Or would it rather be alive and dragging its tail in the mud?"
>
> "It would rather be alive and dragging its tail in the mud," said the two officials.
>
> Chuang Tzu said, "Go away! I'll drag my tail in the mud!"

(From Burton Watson, *The Complete Works of Chuang Tzu* [New York: Columbia University Press, 1968], 187–88; I am grateful to Kim-chong Chong for bringing this example to my attention.)

13. Again, there are interesting parallels with the *Zhuangzi* that deserve further investigation.

14. Although the previous translations are my own, here I follow the excellent translation of Brad Inwood.

15. Crates is poor because he has previously given away all his money to the poor, inspired, the story goes, by seeing Euripides's tragedy *Telephus*.

16. Page 222 in Bloom's translation; I have modified the translation, substituting "human beings" for Bloom's "men."

17. Page 224; once again, I have changed "men" to "human beings."

18. Aristotle, *Rhetoric*, 1385b31.

19. These differences shape the body itself: nutritional differences make deprived groups smaller and shorter, and one can easily come to believe that they are a different subspecies.

The Moral Circle

C. L. Ten

2

E. M. Forster famously remarked, "If I had to choose between betraying my country and betraying my friend, I hope I should have the guts to betray my country."[1] No doubt to many this comment seems rather dotty, reflecting the Bloomsbury morality with its excessive emphasis on personal relationships, often of unconventional kinds. Perhaps too the choice is seldom as stark as Forster presents it, for the betrayal of one's country could have far-reaching effects, including great damage to one's other friends. The more discerning would also want to have more details about the character of the choice, about what the friend has done, what kind of country one lives in, and what the act of betrayal involves. But my purpose in quoting Forster is only to use his view as one well-known example of the conflict between the demands of family commitments and personal relationships on the one hand, and, on the other hand, the claims of public duty, or more general duties owed to those to whom we do not have close involvements. From this perspective, what is perhaps odd is the ease with which Forster resolves the conflict: he only needs the guts to implement what he clearly sees as the right course of action. But there is nothing unusual about the fact that he sees such a conflict arising.

The literature is full of other examples of similar conflicts, although often they are depicted as involving agonizingly tragic choices. Among the more well-known examples are Agamemnon's sacrifice of his daughter in order to save his army, and the Roman consul Lucius Junius Brutus sentencing his two sons to death for rebellion.[2] In each case the conflict was resolved with the demands of public office prevailing over private affections. But it is not just public officials who face the kind of conflict on which I am focusing. There is Sartre's famous example of the young man tragically torn between leaving home to fight for a cause he believed in and staying at home to look after his mother.

Nor are these kinds of conflicts confined to discussions in Western ethics. Mencius mentions the case of the Emperor Shun, whose father was to be apprehended for killing a man. Shun carried his father away, "casting aside the Empire as no more than discarding a worn shoe."[3] Here the clash of duties arising out of different roles, one public and the other private, was resolved by giving up one role, and literally running away with the other! In another example, when Confucius was told that a man called Upright Kung bore witness against his father for stealing a sheep, he replied that in his country it would be upright for the son to protect the father.[4] And in his account of Chinese bureaucratic behavior in the nineteenth and early twentieth century, C. K. Yang described how the average official was unable to resist the pressure to abandon "the principle of impersonality" which was supposed to regulate his conduct. "But to remain impersonal, he had to combat environmental pressure from a society in which personal relationships were not merely ethically valued but also the only medium the common people had for getting things done."[5]

So both from the West and the East, there is ample evidence to show a pervasive recognition of the kind of conflict of duties I have mentioned. The more fundamental question now is whether the various moral claims arising in different areas of our lives can ultimately be traced back to one ultimate value. There is also a related problem about whether a single motivation can explain our acceptance of the moral demands in different areas. I shall use the term "monism" to describe the view that there is a single ultimate value which underpins all our moral concerns, or that there is a single motivational factor behind all such moral concerns. So monism is in one case a justificatory theory, while in the other case it is a motivational or explanatory theory. I shall consider various examples of monism in Western and Chinese ethics, focusing mainly on monism in its motivational form, and I shall try to show that they are all flawed. A complete answer to justificatory monism is too big an issue to be considered here. I shall not develop an alternative view. But implicit in the rejection of monism is the suggestion that conflicts arise from irreducibly different moral demands whose resolution may be unavoidably tragic. I shall conclude with a brief, more hopeful suggestion that a notion of moral right can be extracted from an account of individual moral development and the limits it places on self-interested conduct.

Monists very often use the idea of an expanding moral circle to explain our developing moral concerns. First, we start with a small circle of very intimate personal relationships, and then we gradually recognize that more and more people have moral claims on us. But the same value or motivating force which accounts for our narrower concerns will also eventually account for our broadest concerns. It is this unitary feature of our moral life which gives monism its simplicity and attractiveness to many. Thus, typically a monist would maintain that we acquire our sense of morality by growing up in a family where we learn to limit the pursuit of our self-interest. In the course of our moral development we acquire various and increasing duties as the circle of our moral concern grows. The obligations to our parents and siblings and other close relatives are extended to our friends, and then we develop shared interests with fellow members of various groups, including those who belong with us to the same political community.

But monists disagree about how far out the expanding circle of moral concern should reach. Confucian ethics is usually interpreted as centering on a few basic relationships, parent-child, husband-wife, sibling-sibling, friend-friend, and ruler-minister. This relationship-based morality is linked with a conception of creative self-transformation which involves the family as the starting point of what the Confucian scholar Tu Wei-ming describes as "an ever-expanding web of human relationships, which we can conceptualise as a series of concentric circles."[6] Utilitarians, on the other hand, are well-known for the suggestion that the moral circle must include not just human beings who are strangers to us without any special relationships, but also all sentient beings, which of course includes nonhuman animals. Thus Bentham wrote:

> The day *may come*, when the rest of the animal creation may acquire those rights which never could have been withholden from them but by the hand of tyranny. The French have already discovered that the blackness of the skin is no reason why a human being should be abandoned without redress to the caprice of a tormen-tor. It may come one day to be recognized, that the number of legs, the villosity of the skin, or the termination of the *os sacrum*, are reasons equally insufficient for abandoning a sensitive being to the same fate. What else is it that should trace the insuperable line? Is it the faculty of reason, or, perhaps the faculty of discourse? But a full-grown horse or dog is beyond comparison a more rational, as well as a more conversable animal, than an infant of a day, or a week, or even a month, old. But suppose the case were otherwise, what would it avail? The question is not, "Can they *reason*?" nor, "Can they *talk*?" but, "Can they *suffer*?"[7]

Singer has also spoken about the need for an "expanding circle" of moral concern, and he gives as the motto of his book, *The Expanding Circle*,[8] the following quotation from W. E. H Lecky's *The History of European Morals*: "The moral unity to be expected in different ages is not a unity of standard, or of acts, but a unity of tendency. . . . At one time the benevolent affections embrace merely the family, soon the circle expanding includes first a class, then a nation, then a coalition of nations, then all humanity, and finally, its influence is felt in dealings of man with the animal world." But even this does not go far enough for some environmentalists. Thus Aldo Leopold sees his "land ethic" as simply an enlargement of "the boundaries of the community to include soils, water, plants, and animals, or collectively: the land."[9]

In spite of these disagreements, monists agree that there is a central unifying value in morality or that there is a single motivating force which can explain all our moral concerns. But monists also disagree about the unitary value or force. I shall focus on one important disagreement among them which relates to how central the family and intimate personal relationships are to our justificatory and motivational concerns. The unreconstructed utilitarian answer is well illustrated by the simplicity of William Godwin's response to what you should do if you arrive at a burning building and have to choose between rescuing an important person, Archbishop Fenelon, and his humble maid, who happens to be your beloved mother. You should rescue Fenelon because better consequences would thereby be produced.[10] So much for the filial piety of the Confucianist! As for the husband-wife relationship, it is also clear, if we use a variation of Bernard Williams's Jim and the Indians example, that Jim would have to kill his wife if that is the only way in which he can save the lives of twenty Indians.[11] Of course as a matter of brute psychological fact, Jim might not be able to kill his wife, but the fact remains that that is what he ought to do, if utilitarians are right.

So the utilitarian's bottom line is always clear, although it might be well hidden by layers of sophistication generated by its indirect versions. It is that personal relationships are ultimately derivative from, and subservient to, the sole ultimate value of maximizing utility. Various contingent reasons may permit or require us to focus on the well-being of close ones, but only because this, in appropriate circumstances, is the best way of maximizing utility. When the relevant calculations can be made clearly, the smaller circles of moral concern, which include family and friends, are simply absorbed or replaced by the biggest circle. We are to be totally impartial between the interests of our loved ones and the similar interests of anyone else within the largest moral circle. The crucial question is whether or not someone, or some being, gets into the moral circle. Once in, its claims are to be recognized on the same basis as those of other members of the circle. There are no privileged members in the circle. Thus Singer describes as "speciesism," on par with racism, the common view that the interests of members of our species count for more than the interests of nonhuman animals which can suffer to the same degree.[12]

We must distinguish between the reason for bringing someone into the moral circle, and the reasons for the various obligations we have to different members of the moral circle. Thus, Bentham may be right that the capacity to suffer, rather than the capacity to reason or to talk, is what makes a being the object of moral concern. But it does not follow that all our moral obligations are ultimately based on the importance of reducing suffering. Consider the debate on the morality of abortion. Much of it centers on the moral status of the fetus, on whether it has the same right to life as a normal adult human being. This question is important because the moral status of the fetus determines whether it is within the moral circle, with interests which must be taken into account. If it is, then it cannot be treated in the way that we may treat an appendix or the tonsils. But it is often assumed that the morality of abortion is settled once we have determined the moral status of the fetus: abortion is wrong if the fetus has a right to life, but right if it does not have such a right, or other claims to be morally considered. But Judith Thomson has challenged the centrality of the moral status of the fetus to the morality of abortion. Although there are considerable difficulties with the details of her defense of abortion, it is one of the merits of her view that it attempts to show that, even if the fetus has a right to life, there are other relevant moral considerations. In particular, she regards as morally central the woman's right to determine what happens to and in her body.[13] This example will help to make clearer my point against monism. It is not enough for the monist to show that there is one general characteristic, be it sentience or something else, which is common to all those who come within the moral circle, and which makes them beings worthy of moral concern. The monist must also show that all the important moral claims are derivable from one ultimate value, or that there is a single motivating force which explains why we will accept these claims.

What motivating force can propel us from the smallest to the largest moral circle? Why would anyone who is embedded in deep and satisfying personal relationships within the family, or among close friends, enlarge her moral circle, in the utilitarian manner, to include total strangers and people in distant lands, let alone countless sentient animals? Sympathy and compassion are usually cited as the sources of our moral development. Certainly they are powerful factors in taking us out of a narrow conception of our self-interest to the recognition that others are like us with similar interests. We can sympathize with and come to be concerned about the welfare of total strangers and even nonhuman animals. There is some evidence, for example, in the activities of those who helped European Jews escape from Nazi persecution, to show that moral concern can be extended to others simply on the basis of their common humanity. And Bentham was effective to some extent when he argued, as we saw earlier, for the better treatment of animals on the ground that they were, like humans, capable of suffering, even if, unlike humans, they could not talk or reason.

However, although sympathy and compassion can generate a large moral circle, they do not take us to this large circle by going through all the smaller circles. They do not provide a common basis for our duties to all who matter. They do not therefore satisfy the requirements of monism because they provide only one of the several different bases of moral motivation. The moral demands based on our intimate personal relationships are not generated mainly by sympathy and compassion. I need sympathy and compassion to respond to the needs of the beggar, who is a stranger to me, but I do not need them to respond to the needs of loved ones. The morality of personal relationships is grounded in particular facts of history, of personality, of shared experiences, commitments, and projects, which bind me tightly to a few others, and give each of us a strong sense of personal identification. Sympathy and compassion are bridges that I do not need in order to be linked with them. We are already joined by those particular facts which mark out my family and friends from others. Sympathy presupposes separateness and otherness. I sympathize with you because you suffer when I do not. But when I am closely identified with others, their suffering is also mine. Close identification removes the ground on which sympathy is built. On the other hand, the demands of general benevolence, on which the utilitarian depends, rest on the most common and general features or capacities which all people have. What matters in personal relationships are the differences between my loved ones and others; but what matters when I extend my circle of moral concern are the similarities between numerically distinct individuals. Moral theorists have been concerned about providing a way out of the small circle of self-interest, which is the common enemy of all morality. But once we succeed in breaking away from the grip of self-interest, there are many different moral paths along which we can travel. Utilitarianism, grounded in universal benevolence, is only one of them. Neither logical consistency nor the deepest emotions of the human heart dictate that we should take that route.

In elucidating the foundation of Confucian ethics, Tu Wei-ming maintains that the basis of relationships in the Confucian view is the principle of reciprocity, a distinctive feature of which is the Confucian golden rule that we ought not to do to others what we would not want others to do to us.[14] But again, reciprocity cannot be the sole normative ground or motivating force of all our moral concerns. We have duties to animals, to the weak who cannot retaliate, and to future generations, who also cannot retaliate if we make the world less safe for them. Reciprocity may be one source of moral claims, but it cannot account for everything because some of our relationships are asymmetrical. The class of moral agents is also not identical with that of moral patients, and some of the beings to whom we owe duties are in no position to reciprocate.

Tu also maintains that, according to the Confucian, "A person who is incapable of caring for his close relatives can hardly be expected to understand universal love in a real and experiential sense."[15] But this is in direct contrast with George Orwell's view in his essay on Gandhi in which he argues that saintly people who love all humanity have difficulty in sustaining loving relations with particular human beings, with all the dangers and uncertainties these involve.[16] Orwell suggests that Gandhi's saintly love of humanity was an escape from the realities of particular friendships. Perhaps this is unfair to Gandhi, but we can at least extract from Orwell's observation the view that there is no necessary correlation between love of particular persons and universal love. Indeed Tu himself acknowledges that the love of a father for his son, something basic in Confucian ethics, is "a primordial tie, charged with strong and persistent human emotions."[17] In that case, it is not duplicated in the less affective, more cerebral, universal love. Why then should we assume that the two would go together? Indeed, we find in some rulers that the source of their public corruption and abuse of power against their people is the desire to enrich their beloved family. So when we see a ruler full of caring concern for his family, we may, in some circumstances, legitimately fear that he will place their interests above those of the general public. Not only is it the case that the ruler's love of his family need not go together with a universal love, but it may even be that one actually undermines the other.

Again, when the bases and nature of the love of family and universal love are so different, it is undesirable to try to bring them closer together. I remember, as a young boy, seeing my father, who was the best doctor in town (there were only two of them around!), pacing up and down in utter frustration while the other doctor treated my mother for a serious illness. My father felt that he could have done a better job, and yet medical etiquette prevented him from directly treating my mother. Of course, that etiquette was designed both to protect him from making uncharacteristic mistakes brought about by his close emotional involvement with his patient, and to protect my mother from the consequences of such mistakes. My father did not appreciate it at the time, but if in fact his love for my mother was simply a reflection of a universal love, then both he and his patients would be worse off. He would confront every patient's serious illness with the same distracting intensity of concern and fear of loss with which he met my mother's illness. His capacity for sound medical judgement would be impaired, and the emotional strain would be so unbearably great that it would soon destroy him.

At another level, we find racists, nationalists, and a few animal lovers who are deeply emotionally attached to one group, but indifferent, or even passionately hostile, to another group that has the same general features, but differs in what are regarded as crucial particulars. The issue is not whether they are justified in making what to us are morally irrelevant distinctions. Rather, it is simply that the kind of unitary moral motivation that monists seek is not found in the actual behavior of very many people, including some whom we admire.

Similar considerations count against Tu's claim that, "The ruler's affection for his relatives is only a concrete manifestation of his broad human concern."[18] This suggestion that if a ruler cannot even show affection to his relatives, then he cannot truly care for his people, if correct, provides a powerful way of bridging our private and public duties. But it must be rejected, not only for the trivial reason that some rulers may have awful, unlovable relatives, but also for the more fundamental reason that our moral life is much more fragmented than Tu seems to think. Tu does not cite any evidence to support his claim, but it is ultimately an empirical claim. The following examples will at least throw some doubt on it.

Consider first the case of President Clinton who, as is now known to everybody, in private life, or at least in the semi-privacy of the White House, clearly violated some Confucian duties. It is arguable that he was a better president than, for example, Jimmy Carter, who in private life only sinned in his heart. Recently, it was revealed that Arthur Koestler, who showed great physical and moral courage in fighting for public causes he believed in, treated some of his women friends badly, including raping one of them.[19] Of course Koestler was not a ruler in the required sense, but he was a public figure, and one may expect the same types of considerations that apply to rulers also to apply to him. I believe that one can multiply these examples. Indeed, as more and more unofficial biographies of public figures are released, I expect that we will find an increasing mismatch between their private virtues or vices and their public ones. In some societies such expectations are widely shared among ordinary people (although not by the more conservative intellectuals or leaders, some of whose own private lives, when exposed, show the hypocrisy of their public views). Thus we notice that the more Starr tried to delve into Clinton's private vices, the greater was Clinton's public popularity.

Monism seems attractive because, as I indicated earlier, moral theorists of all kinds have tried to provide us with a motivation other than self-interest. Once they succeed in establishing that the interests of another person counts, the temptation is to believe that the same non-self-interested motivation can be applied to more and more cases. But this fails to recognize that our relationships to different people may generate different types of motivating or normative reasons. A common enemy may be met by different weapons on different occasions.

My essay has been rather negative in rejecting monism. But let me end on a more positive note. Once it is acknowledged that there are limits, grounded in the interests of others, to the pursuit of self-interest, then I think that we already have the conceptual resources for developing a theory of moral rights, which is vital to the regulation of our conduct to one another. A familiar conception of rights treats rights as constraints on the pursuit of the good, or, as Ronald Dworkin puts it, as trumps over collective goals.[20] If for whatever reasons, a self-interested person learns that other people's interests set limits to his pursuit of his own good, then in taking this first step into the moral world, he has also been provided with the resources for understanding the conception of rights as constraints or as trumps. In that sense rights are conceptually primitive tools in any moral system. A developed moral system will use these tools in order to construct distinctive normative claims, particularly for the protection of the weak and the vulnerable who, unloved and uncared for, are in danger of being left outside the moral circle.

Notes

1. E. M. Forster, "What I Believe," in *Two Cheers for Democracy* (London: Edward Arnold, 1951), 78.

2. Stanley I. Benn, *A Theory of Freedom* (Cambridge: Cambridge University Press, 1988), 44.

3. *Mencius* 7.35.

4. *Analects* 13.18.

5. C. K. Yang, "Some Characteristics of Chinese Bureaucratic Behaviour," in *Confucianism in Action*, ed. David S. Nivison and Arthur F. Wright (Stanford, Calif.: Stanford University Press, 1959), 157.

6. Tu Wei-ming, *Centrality and Commonality: An Essay on Confucian Religiousness* (Albany: State University of New York Press, 1989), 113.

7. J. Bentham, *The Principles of Morals and Legislation*, ed. J. H. Burns and H. L. A. Hart (Oxford, U.K.: Clarendon Press, 1996), 283.

8. P. Singer, *The Expanding Circle* (New York: Farrar Strauss & Giroux, 1981).

9. Aldo Leopold, *A Sand Country Almanac* (London: Oxford University Press, 1970), 204.

10. D. H. Monro, ed., *A Guide to the British Moralists* (London: Fontana, 1972), 187–92.

11. C. L. Ten, "Jim's Utilitarian Mission," *Philosophy* 54 (1979): 221–22.

12. P. Singer, *Animal Liberation* (New York: Avon Books, 1977), 7.

13. J. J. Thomson, "A Defence of Abortion," *Philosophy & Public Affairs* 1 (1971): 47–66.

14. Tu, *Centrality*, p. 104.

15. *Ibid.*, p. 51.

16. George Orwell, "Reflections on Gandhi," in *Collected Essays* (London: Mercury Books, 1966), 455–56.

17. Tu, *Centrality*, p. 41.

18. *Ibid.*, p. 52.

19. David Cesarani, *Arthur Koestler: The Homeless Mind* (London: Vintage, 1999), 399–401.

20. R. Dworkin, *Taking Rights Seriously* (London: Duckworth, 1978), xi.

Descartes and Mencius on Self and Community

3

Cecilia Wee

Not too long ago, the phrase "Descartes's ethics" would have been regarded, as Morgan remarks, as a philosophical oxymoron.[1] Descartes is often thought to have "entered the history of philosophy as perhaps the only systematic philosopher of the first rank who failed to provide any methodical treatment of moral problems."[2] Recently, however, there has been increased interest in Descartes's ethical views, and commentators have argued that there is much that is worth examining in them. This paper aims to discuss one aspect of Descartes's ethics—namely, his views on how a person should relate to her community.

To those who think of Descartes as the individualist and solitary thinker of the *Meditations*, it may come as a surprise that Descartes in fact maintains that one ought to put the interests of the community above one's own interests. In this paper, I will briefly examine Descartes's grounds for maintaining this view. I will then look more deeply into the issue of Cartesian moral motivation. Knowing that one *ought* to put the interests of the community above one's own does not entail that one *will* put these interests above one's own. What is it then that can make us want to put these interests above our own?

I shall argue here that Descartes's views on this issue—perhaps surprisingly—find striking parallels in the views of Mencius. The development of these parallels yields important results. Because of the unusual sympathy between these two philosophers (who at first sight come from vastly different traditions), we are in fact able to appeal to Mencius to supplement the Cartesian account of moral motivation and to fill in what would otherwise be a significant explanatory gap in that account.

I

In a letter to Elizabeth of Bohemia dated 15 September 1645, Descartes writes:

> After acknowledging the goodness of God, the immortality of our souls and the immensity of the universe, there is yet another truth that is, in my opinion, most useful to know. That is, that though each of us is a person distinct from others, whose interests are accordingly in some way different from those of the rest of the world,

we ought still to think that none of us could subsist alone and that each one of us is really one of the many parts of the universe, and more particularly a part of the earth, the state, the society and the family to which we belong by our domicile, our oath of allegiance and our birth. *And the interests of the whole, of which each is a part, must always be preferred to those of our own particular person.* (emphasis mine)[3]

Descartes claims here that it is a truth "useful to know" that one must prefer the interests of the society of which one is a part to one's own interests. This is based on a more general claim: *viz.*, there are a number of wholes (of decreasing size) of which one constitutes a part—the universe, the earth, the state, the society and the family, and in each case, one's own interests must always be subordinate to the interests of the whole in question.[4]

What is Descartes's justification for the claim that the individual's interests must be subordinate to the interests of the whole—in particular the whole that is the community? We must admit here that it is not so easy to reconstruct the justification for this claim, as it is never given directly.

Perhaps the first step must be to consider Descartes's wider account of what counts as goods for the human being. Descartes points out that the goods that will bring inner contentment or happiness to a human fall into two classes—goods like honor, riches, and health, whose attainment are dependent on the vagaries of fortune, and goods like virtue and wisdom, whose attainment is within our control. He maintains that the human agent should concentrate on the attainment of those goods which are within our control—in particular, virtue, which he considers the "supreme good" that is "sufficient to make us content in this life."[5] Descartes is ambivalent about whether this supreme good of virtue is also the final good. In some places, he seems to suggest that the inner contentment which supervenes upon acting virtuously is the final good, in that it is for the sake of obtaining such inner satisfaction that well-judging humans act virtuously.[6] In others, he states virtue is the final good, in that well-judging humans should strive for virtuous ends even if their accomplishment results in our having less happiness than we would otherwise obtain.[7] In any case, his conclusion is that we ought to pursue the virtues (whatever the ultimate goal of such pursuit might be).

Presumably, then, Descartes's justification as to why we ought to place the interests of the community above our own is that it is a virtue to do so. That this is his line of thought is suggested by the following passage, found in the same letter to Elizabeth of Bohemia:

If someone saw everything in relation to himself, he would not hesitate to injure others greatly when he thought he could draw some slight advantage; and he would have no true friendship, no fidelity, *no virtue at all.* On the other hand, if someone considers himself a part of the community, he delights in doing good to everyone, and does not hesitate even to risk his life in the service of others when the occasion demands. If he could, he would even be willing to lose his soul to save others. (emphasis mine)[8]

Descartes indicates that a person who acts solely to promote his own interests is a person who has "no virtue at all." On the other hand, the person who sees himself as part of the community and is prepared "even to risk his life" (and soul) for the sake of others is presumably one who has virtue.

How far does the virtuous agent have to go in subordinating her interests to those of the community? What has been said thus far suggests a rather bleak answer to this. The Cartesian virtuous agent in the above passage seems to be one who always puts the community's interest before his own, for this paragon "delights in doing good to everyone" and is prepared even to risk losing his (immortal) soul for others.

But Descartes does not in fact require that we attain such levels of self-sacrifice. In the passage mentioned at the beginning of the paper, Descartes qualifies his point that the interests of the whole "must be preferred to those of our own" by saying that this is to be done "with measure, of course, and discretion."[9] When Elizabeth subsequently asks him how far she should go in her devotion to the community, he writes back that "it is not a matter on which it is necessary to be very precise" and that she should do enough to satisfy her conscience.[10]

Descartes's reply to Elizabeth here might seem at first sight to be a singularly unhelpful one, and perhaps it is. But it is also possible that he thought the question of the extent to which the interests of the community should take precedence over one's own is a matter for casuistry. The first of three rules of morality that he lists in the *Discourse* and repeats in a letter to Elizabeth is "that [the agent] should always try to employ his mind as well as he can to discover what he should or should not do in all the circumstances of life."[11] In the second rule, he mentions that virtue consists precisely in sticking to whatever reason recommends in these cases. Given such remarks, it is likely Descartes thought that the question of how far an individual should go in placing the interests of the community above his own in any particular situation involves the exercise of one's reason, that is, practical judgment—there is no algorithm that can be employed in these cases.

But suppose that one has, using reason and discretion, recognized a situation as one in which one ought to act for the wider interest rather than one's own? Does such recognition entail for Descartes that one *does* act for the wider interest? Here, Descartes acknowledges there is a gap between the recognition and the action that should result. According to Descartes:

Besides knowledge of the truth, practice also is required if one is always to be disposed to judge well. We cannot continually pay attention to the same thing; and so however clear and evident the reasons may have been that convinced us of some truth in the past, we can later be turned away from believing it by some false appearances. . . . [I]n fact, our failings are rarely due to lack of theoretical knowledge of what we should do, but to lack of practical knowledge—that is, lack of a firm habit of belief.[12]

For Descartes, knowing "theoretically" that one ought, say, to act in a particular situation for the greater good is insufficient to ensure that one will do it. If we lack a "firm habit of belief," we may end up believing that we ought to do something else, because we are seduced by "false appearances."

So doing the right thing doesn't just involve determining *that* it is the right thing through reason, but having a "firm habit of belief" that it is the right thing. Having such a habit of belief obviously plays an important role in the pursuit of the moral or ethical life, but how does one achieve it? In the next section, I shall argue that the passions play an important role in achieving this.

II

At several points, Descartes admits that the passions may, if ungoverned, lead precisely to those "false appearances" which move us to act wrongly:

> Anger, for instance, can sometimes excite in us such violent desires for vengeance that it makes us imagine more pleasure in chastising our enemy than in preserving our honor and our life. . . . The same is true of the other passions. They all represent the goods to which they tend with greater splendor than they deserve.[13]

But although acting in response to ungoverned passions like anger can lead to our harm and dishonor, Descartes does not think that we should therefore extirpate or suppress the passions.

He points out in the *Passions of the Soul* (and also in a letter to Chanut) that "the passions are all by nature good."[14] In an earlier work, the *Meditations*, Descartes argues that God's purpose in endowing him with sensory perceptions is to ensure his survival and well-being *qua* composite of mind and body.[15] Commentators point out that Descartes thinks that the passions have been bestowed on him for a similar purpose. Thus, Cottingham writes:

> [I]n the case of the passions, . . .we are dealing with a psycho-physical system whose operation has a signal utility for our life and health as human beings; thus, [Descartes writes that] "the principal effect of all the human passions is that they move and dispose the soul to want the things for which they prepare the body—for example, the feeling of fear moves the soul to want to flee, and that of courage to want to fight, and similarly with the other passions."[16]

For Descartes, then, our passions are "by nature good" because they are the result of divine institution and meant to enable our physical and ethical well-being as psychophysical substances. When they function correctly, they move us to act in a manner that will attain the various human goods: the passion of fear may move us to flee from (overwhelming?) danger; the passion of courage may move us to fight for our country or personal honor.

How can one ensure that the passions perform their intended role? Firstly, as Gueroult points out, Descartes thinks that they must be brought under "the guidance of reason," which would regulate the passions "through proportioning their force to the real magnitude of the goods to which they are applied."[17] Thus, when one feels great anger and is tempted to seek revenge, an appeal to reflective reason will show that the goods obtained by the outcome are not as great as represented.

Secondly, Cottingham suggests another procedure that might be necessary in order for the passions to play their intended role. He points out that: "Because of the relatively rigid way innate physiological mechanisms and environmentally conditioned responses operate, we may become locked [by our passions] into behaviour that can lead to distress, misery or harm." He suggests that Descartes thinks:

> the appropriate way to cope with such irrational impulses is not to retreat to an austere intellectualism, nor to suppress the passions, but rather to use the resources of science and experience to try to understand what has caused things to go awry, and then to attempt to reprogram our responses so that the direction in which we are led by the passions corresponds to what our reason perceives to be the best option.[18]

In sum, for the passions to play their role in furthering human well-being, we need (occasionally) to moderate their force through deliberate reflection, and also to "reprogram" them so that they do not lead us astray, but will move us to act in accord with what reason tells us. Once we succeed in this, we will possess a "firm habit of belief" in what we had earlier known theoretically. This is because the passions will no longer provide a distorted picture of the goods available to us, and will instead help move us towards achieving the goods indicated (theoretically) by reason.

I have provided above Descartes's views on how the passions could be employed in the furtherance of human well-being. But there seems to be a difficulty with the account. While one can easily comprehend how one might moderate the force of passions like anger or jealousy through the use of reason, the second procedure, outlined by Cottingham, needs a closer look. How precisely does one "reprogram" one's feelings, one's passional responses, so that they are directed towards what reason tells one is the best option?

Descartes himself maintains that one is seldom (if ever) able to redirect one's passions to the appropriate goals simply through an act of will.[19] In that case, an agent could well know through reason what she ought to do, but still be unable to will herself to *feel* a certain way towards the given object, so that this feeling moves her to do what she knows she ought to. (And indeed Descartes's point here is a plausible one: I cannot simply *command* myself to feel pity or love or sorrow in line with the dictates of reason.) But if one cannot directly will one's passional responses in line with reason's prescriptions, how does one bring these responses in line with reason?

Let us bring this issue to bear on the main subject of this paper. Descartes, as I've argued, holds that putting the interests of the community above one's own interests is (at least sometimes) a virtue, and therefore a human good. He also thinks that the passions, when properly regulated, help move one to attain the various human goods—and this of course includes the good of putting the interests of the community above one's own. But precisely how does one redirect one's passional responses, such that they would move one to put these other interests above one's own?

While Descartes does offer some general suggestions as to how one might redirect one's passions to bring them in line with rationally determined goals, they do not seem to be helpful with respect to moving the agent to put the interests of the community above her own. In the *Passions*, Descartes suggests that one can indirectly bring about a change in passional responses by effecting a conditioned response of the sort commonly found in trained animals. Noting that dogs who are naturally disposed to run towards partridges and to run away at the sound of a gunshot can be trained to stop at the sight of partridges and to run towards them upon hearing a gunshot, he suggests that humans can effect changes in their passional responses through the sort of conditioning undergone by the dogs.[20] But even if one allows that it may be possible to effect changes in human passional responses in this way, it is unlikely that one could be conditioned to act for the community by this method.[21]

There is thus an explanatory gap in the Cartesian account: given that it is a good to place the community's interests above one's own, *how* does one reorder one's passional responses so that they will move one to act in the community's interests? I will now argue that this gap in the Cartesian account is best filled by appealing to the views of Mencius.

III

At first sight, an appeal to Mencius to augment the Cartesian account may seem an odd and improbable choice. The two are so far removed from each other both in terms of time and philosophical tradition that one might well maintain that any move to integrate Mencian insights into Descartes's framework must be a risky endeavor.

Admittedly, there are major differences in the philosophical frameworks of the two philosophers. Descartes sees the human person as a composite of mind and body, where the mind and the body are two distinct substances capable of existing independently of each other. The dualism of mind and body is an assumption that Mencius would not accept, and possibly might not even be able to comprehend.

Again, Descartes sees reason as a faculty which is distinct from the passions: the latter are found only in embodied minds (i.e., human beings), while the former belongs to any mind (embodied or otherwise). As one might guess, this distinction between reason and passion does not map easily onto Mencius's views.

The term *xin* in Chinese philosophy is usually translated as "heart-mind," indicating that the distinction between reason and passion commonly found in Western philosophy does not exist here. With respect to Mencius himself, David Wong has argued that this distinction cannot obtain, because Mencius's views on motivation preclude it.[22] Whether or not we agree with Wong's reading, it is evident that Mencius does not explicitly deploy such a distinction. For example, in his celebrated passage in 2A:6, Mencius speaks of the four *xin* of compassion, shame, deference, and right and wrong as the Four Beginnings which, when cultivated, enable one to lead an ethical life. As Wong notes, the first three might reasonably be seen as passional or as containing passional elements. But it is far from obvious that the *xin* of right and wrong is passional—such discernment is usually taken in Western philosophy to belong to practical reason. Yet Mencius clearly treats these four beginnings as equally important foundations for an ethical life, suggesting again that he does not draw the firm Cartesian distinction between reason and passion. One should not minimize the difficulties of incorporating aspects of the Mencian account onto Descartes's views, but I believe that such incorporating can be done and that it can be valuable.

Notwithstanding the differences mentioned above, there are certain fundamental similarities between Mencius and Descartes. One assumption common to both Descartes and Mencius is that there can be a gap between recognizing that one ought to do something and being moved to do that thing. I've earlier dealt with this gap with respect to Descartes. But this gap is also to be found in Mencius—as Nivison writes, Mencius "makes a commonsense distinction between judging that one should do something and actually doing it."[23] (The reasons for this gap and the means by which Mencius thought one could overcome it have recently been discussed by several commentators.[24])

Again, although a major difference between Descartes and Mencius concerns the distinction (or lack thereof) between reason and passion, Mencius's account of how what we would call the passions move us to act has important commonalities with Descartes's account of passional motivation. Margaret Wilson has argued convincingly that Descartes's passions are not objectless affects, but cognitive states involving the representation of an object as being a certain way.[25] For instance, Descartes writes in the *Passions* that "pity is a type of sadness . . . toward those whom we see suffer something bad, which we consider them not to deserve."[26] These cognitive/emotional states called the passions can then move us to act in certain ways towards the object. (Anger, for instance, may move us to act to chastise its object.[27])

Commentators have argued that Mencius holds a similar position with respect to emotions like compassion. Wong and Ihara, for example, both accept that Mencius holds that an emotion like compassion makes salient certain features of the given situation.[28] Using the example of the child in danger of falling into a well in 2A:6, Wong writes that "the reaction is to feel distress and alarm . . . purely from the recognition of the child's endangerment. . . . The intentional object of compassion makes salient the feature of the situation that is the suffering, actual or forthcoming, of a sentient being." [29] As was the case for Descartes, Mencius holds that this cognitive/emotional state can move us to act in certain ways towards the object—for instance it can move us to act to save the child.

Bearing in mind the above similarities, I want now to argue that one can appeal to Mencius to provide an answer to the Cartesian problem of how one can "reprogram" one's passions so that they move us to act in the service of the community. The key to the answer lies in the Mencian account of "extending" (*tui*), as expressed in this passage in *Mencius* 7B:31: "All men have some things which they cannot bear. Extend that feeling to what they can bear, and humanity will be the result. All men have some things which they will not do. Extend that feeling to the things that they do, and righteousness will be the result."[30] What precisely is involved the process of "extending what one cannot bear (or do) to what one can bear (or do)"? I will attempt to explicate this process through a discussion of the exchange between Mencius and King Hsuan of Qi in 1A:7.

There have been a wide variety of different interpretations of what is involved in this exchange.[31] My interpretation of the exchange essentially involves an elaboration and development of some remarks on the issue by Ihara. Defending my interpretation as *the* correct one would of course be well beyond the scope of this paper (and indeed perhaps there *is* no one correct interpretation.[32]) But the interpretation I develop seems, textually speaking, at least a plausible one.

A brief account of the exchange is as follows. King Hsuan had caused great misery to his people because of his territorial expansion. When asked how he could become a true king, Mencius replies that this is achieved only if he brings peace to his people. King Hsuan replies that he does not know if he can do this. In response Mencius says that he had heard that the king had seen an ox led to slaughter. The king had then ordered that the ox be released and a sheep substituted in its place, stating that he was unable to bear the ox's shrinking with fear, "like an innocent man going to the place of execution." Mencius then states that "The heart seen in this [ox-episode] is sufficient to enable you to become a true King."

Ihara's reading of this exchange is as follows:

> According to Mencius, all human beings have a "[heart]-mind" that cannot bear to see the suffering of others. The king's doubt that this is true of himself is shown to be false through Mencius' explanation of the king's behaviour towards the ox. At this point, [what] Mencius is doing is telling the king to see that he has such a [heart]-mind . . . and urging him to experience the suffering of his people as vividly as he did the suffering of the ox. . . . All that is necessary is for the king to perceive his people's suffering, and that will naturally evoke feelings of compassion.[33]

On Ihara's reading, Mencius is not giving here a strictly logical argument of the sort that has been attributed to Nivison, who points out that as the people are as much innocent sufferers as the ox, the king ought as a matter of logical consistency to relieve the suffering of the people.[34] Rather, Mencius is asking the king to *feel* compassion for the people just as he feels compassion for the ox.

How precisely is this feeling of compassion to be extended from the ox to the people? If I am correct, Ihara suggests that this requires an act of imagination on the king's part—he has to *experience* the people's suffering as vividly as he does the ox's. Here it can be noted that the king had substituted the ox whose suffering he had perceived with a sheep whose suffering he did not perceive. One can infer that the king was able to effect this change because he did not experience the suffering of the sheep as he had that of the ox. (Had he done so, he might have been unable to sacrifice the sheep, for he might equally have felt compassion for the sheep.) To extend his compassion for the ox to his people, then, the king would have to somehow experience the suffering of his people, as he had for the ox.

To do this, the king must of course recognize (intellectually) that the ox and the people are similar in being innocent sufferers. But he must go further—he must *emote* or *feel* by vividly evoking in himself the innocent suffering of the people. That is, just as he had vividly evoked within himself the innocent suffering of the ox before him, he must come to evoke vividly within himself the innocent suffering of babies who starve to death, of wives who have lost their husbands, of children crying and lost because their parents have died. Vivid recognition of their suffering and pain would bring with it the feeling of compassion towards the people—and this compassion would move the king to bring peace to his people. Thus, by extending what he could not bear (the suffering of the ox) to what he had earlier borne (the suffering of the people), the king would set himself on the path to humanity (and to true kinghood).[35]

Assuming this interpretation to be correct, the exchange between Mencius and King Hsuan is relevant to our Cartesian problem. King Hsuan theoretically knows at the outset that he ought to bring peace to the people to achieve true kinghood, but thinks he is unable to do it. Part of Mencius's reply is to show him that he is able to do it—he needs to redirect his innate feeling of compassion to the people so that it will move him to act to bring them peace.[36] Our earlier Cartesian question was this: by what means can one "reprogram" one's passions so that they will move one towards what one knows theoretically one ought to do? The answer offered here is that one can do this through the sort of extending recommended by Mencius to King Hsuan, wherein one takes some innate passional response and then relates it to the relevant situation in the manner suggested above.

Let us bring this to bear on the case of the community. Descartes points out that it is a good to put the interests of the community above our own (though how far we go is a matter of rational casuistry). Suppose then that reason shows me that I should minister to the needs of a certain group of people—let's say a group of dyslexic children in a community home who need to learn how to read. (Let's say casuistry shows me that the potential benefits to them far out-weigh the losses to me, so that helping them to read is indeed a rational goal.)[37] I might still be loathe to pursue this virtuous goal, because it means I have to give up a few Saturday afternoons. How do I move myself to do this?

Now suppose that I find in myself great compassion for a lame and partially blind old woman whom I see crossing the busy street alone, and am moved by my feeling of compassion to help her across the street. Following the Men-cian procedure, I would then get myself to recognize that what is true of the woman's situation (viz., she is a sufferer unable to help herself) is also true of the dyslexic children. Just as I had evoked to myself the helplessness of the old woman in the face of fast-paced cars, so I would vividly evoke to myself the helplessness of the dyslexic children in a fast-paced society. These children are after all as disadvantaged by their handicap as the old woman is by hers, and are similarly unable to survive and thrive in a world that moves too fast for them. The compassion that such an evocation of the children's helplessness brings would move me to help the children where reason by itself had been unable to persuade me.

Indeed, this example not only illustrates how the passions can move us to-wards what reason perceives to be the best option, but also could be expanded to show how "reprogramming" the passions can in fact move us away from harmful behavior that we had earlier been locked into. If, for example, the principal reason why I had been loathe to devote my Saturday afternoons to the dyslexic children was that I have a passion for (say) playing video games and want to spend my spare time on that, then my compassion for the dyslexic children, in moving me to work with them, would in effect take me away from behavior that might be harmful to me.

In sum, then, despite their vast divide in time and philosophical tradition, the sympathy between Descartes's and Mencius's position allows that Mencius's account of extending can be usefully applied to fill the gap in the Cartesian account concerning how one may "train" one's passions to move one to put the community's interests above one's own. The Cartesian position is more complete if we appeal to Mencius to supplement it.[38]

Notes

Editors' Note: This is a revised version of a paper originally published in *The Journal of Chinese Philosophy* 29, no. 2, June 2002.

1. Vance Morgan, *Foundations of Cartesian Ethics* (New Jersey: Humanities Press, 1994), 2.

2. Robert Cumming, "Descartes' Provisional Morality," *Review of Metaphysics* 9 (1955): 207.

3. René Descartes, *The Philosophical Writings of Descartes*, vol. 3, ed. John Cottingham, Robert Stoothoff, and Dugald Murdoch (Cambridge: Cambridge University Press, 1991), 266. In writing this essay, I have also consulted *Oeuvres de Descartes*, vols. 1–12, ed. C. Adam and P. Tannery (Paris: Vrin, 1964–1976).

4. The possibility that these various wholes might have conflicting interests does not seem to have occurred to Descartes.

5. Descartes, *Philosophical Writings*, vol. 3, pp. 257–58.

6. *Ibid.*, p. 261.

7. *Ibid.*, p. 268. For further discussion of this issue, see Martial Gueroult, *Descartes' Philosophy Interpreted According to the Order of Reason*, vol. 2, trans. Roger Ariew (Minneapolis: University of Minnesota Press, 1985), and John Marshall, *Descartes's Moral Theory* (Cornell: Cornell University Press, 1998).

8. Descartes, *Philosophical Writings*, vol. 3, p. 266.

9. *Ibid.*, p. 266.

10. *Ibid.*, p. 273.

11. *Ibid.*, p. 257.

12. *Ibid.*, p. 267.

13. *Ibid.*, p. 264.

14. René Descartes, *The Philosophical Writings of Descartes*, vol. 1, ed. John Cottingham, Robert Stoothoff, and Dugald Murdoch (Cambridge: Cambridge University Press, 1984), 403.

15. René Descartes, *The Philosophical Writings of Descartes*, vol. 2, ed. John Cottingham, Robert Stoothoff, and Dugald Murdoch (Cambridge: Cambridge University Press 1984), 57.

16. John Cottingham, *Philosophy and the Good Life* (Cambridge: Cambridge University Press, 1998), 95.

17. Gueroult, p. 296.

18. Cottingham, *Philosophy and the Good Life*, p. 96.

19. Descartes, *Philosophical Writings*, vol. 1, p. 345.

20. Descartes, *Philosophical Writings*, vol. 1, p. 348.

21. Cottingham also suggests in *Philosophy and the Good Life* that Descartes thinks one can effect changes in passional response through an awareness of the psychophysical bases of one's passions. Once again, it's not obvious that one can be motivated to serve the community through this means.

22. David B. Wong, "Is There a Distinction between Reason and Emotion in Mencius?" *Philosophy East and West* 41, no. 1 (1991): 31–44.

23. David Nivison, *The Ways of Confucianism: Investigations in Chinese Philosophy* (Chicago: Open Court, 1996), 99.

24. See, for example, Antonio Cua, "*Xin* and Moral Failure: Notes on an Aspect of Mencius's Moral Psychology," in *Mencius: Contexts and Interpretations*, ed. Alan Chan (University of Hawaii Press, 2002); Nivison, *The Ways of Confucianism*, 79–119; Kwong-loi Shun, "Moral Reasons in Confucian Ethics," *Journal of Chinese Philosophy* 16 (1989): 317–43; Kwong-loi Shun, *Mencius and Early Chinese Thought* (Stanford: Stanford University Press, 1997), 136–79; Bryan Van Norden, "Kwong-loi Shun on Moral Reasons in Mencius," *Journal of Chinese Philosophy* 18 (1991): 353–70; Bryan Van Norden, "Mengzi and Xunzi: Two Views of Human Agency," *International Philosophical Quarterly* 23, no. 3 (1992): 161–84; Wong, "Is There a Distinction?"

25. Margaret Wilson, "Descartes and the Representationality of Sensation," in *Central Themes in Early Modern Philosophy*, ed. Mark Kulstad and J. A. Cover (Indianapolis: Hackett, 1990), 1–22.

26. Descartes, *Philosophical Writings*, vol. 3, p. 395.

27. See Descartes, *Philosophical Writings*, vol. 3, p. 264.

28. Craig Ihara, "David Wong on Emotions in Mencius," *Philosophy East and West* 41, no. 1 (1991): 45–54. Ihara goes beyond this to maintain that the compassion provides the agent with a reason to act in certain helping ways towards the object. It should also be noted that Wong and Ihara both accept that not all emotions are cognitive in the way that compassion is.

29. Wong, "Is There a Distinction?," p. 32.

30. All quotations from Mencius are taken from *Mencius*, trans. D. C. Lau (Hong Kong: Chinese University Press, 1984).

31. To cite just a few, see Cua, "*Xin*"; Nivison, *The Ways of Confucianism*; and Wong, "Is There a Distinction?"

32. As Shun has noted, the exchange between King Hsuan and Mencius is open to a number of readings, with not enough in the text to favor one reading over the rest. There may be no correct interpretation of the text, only more or less plausible ones (*Mencius and Early Chinese Thought*, 143).

33. Ihara, "David Wong," p. 51.

34. See Nivison, *The Ways of Confucianism*, pp. 97–98; Wong, "Is There a Distinction?," p. 37; and Ihara, "David Wong," p. 52. However, what Nivison subsequently says (p. 99) may suggest that he accepts that extending (*tui*) may also have an affective component.

35. Recent literature discusses whether the king felt any (incipient) compassion for his people prior to his exchange with Mencius, or whether he felt none. The position I have taken (and Ihara's own position as it appears in the article I cite) seems compatible with both positions. But it seems plausible to maintain that the king does (or at least can) have compassion for human beings prior to his exchange with Mencius. This is evinced (as Kwong-loi Shun has pointed out in *Mencius and Early Chinese Thought*, p.

143) by the fact that his compassion for the ox is derived from a comparison between itself and an innocent person about to be executed. That the king does not consciously feel compassion for his own people as he apparently would have for an innocent person being executed may stem, I suggest, from his failure to imaginatively sympathize and recognize at that point that his people are as much innocent sufferers as is a blameless person who is about to be executed.

36. Showing the King that he can come to feel compassion for his people is of course only part of Mencius's reply—the other part, as various commentators have noted, is to ensure that this compassion is not over-ridden by the King's other desires.

37. Descartes himself occasionally uses such apparently utilitarian arguments when deciding how far to go in the service of the community. (See, for example, Descartes, *Philosophical Writings*, vol. 3, p. 266.)

38. An earlier version of this paper was read at the conference on *Self, Family and Community: Aspects of Chinese and Western Ethics* held on 12–13 May 2000 at the National University of Singapore. I would like to thank the participants of the session—in particular, David Chan, Alexandra Serrenti, Bryan Van Norden, and Wong Ka Nar—for their helpful comments on the paper. I would also like to thank Kim-chong Chong for useful discussion of a pre-workshop draft, and John Greenwood for his comments on a revised version of the paper.

A Response to the Mohist Arguments in "Impartial Caring"

4

Bryan W. Van Norden

One of the doctrines that has been characteristic of Confucianism throughout its history is "graded love." The doctrine of graded love states that one should have greater concern for, and has greater ethical obligations toward, those who are bound to one by special relationships, such as those between ruler and minister, father and son, husband and wife, elder and younger brother, and between friends.[1] Kongzi expressed his commitment to the doctrine of graded love in the following famous passage from the *Analects*:

> The Lord of She said to Kongzi, "Among my people there is one we call 'Upright Gong.' When his father stole a sheep, he reported him to the authorities."
>
> Kongzi replied, "Among my people, those we consider 'upright' are different from this: fathers cover up for their sons, and sons cover up for their fathers. This is what it means to be 'upright.' " (13:18)[2]

The Confucian doctrine of graded love seems to capture the common-sense intuitions that many of us have, both in China and in the West. Imagine how you would react if someone told you, in an indignant tone, "People are going hungry tonight in New York, and Bryan isn't doing anything about it!" I think most people would *not* take this to be a particularly serious ethical failing, and would perhaps respond to the statement with the tepid agreement that, Yes, we should *all* do more about the problem of hunger in the U.S. But suppose someone told you, "Bryan's *mother* is going hungry tonight in New York, and he isn't doing anything about it!" If this were true, and if there were no extraordinary explanation for Bryan's behavior, I think most of us would regard it as reflecting a particularly severe ethical flaw in Bryan's character.

Nonetheless, not everyone agrees with the doctrine of graded love. The first philosophical opponent of Confucianism was Mozi, a charismatic and enigmatic figure of the fifth century B.C.E. In opposition to the Confucians, Mozi advocated *jiān ài* 兼愛, a phrase often translated, "universal love," but which I shall render as "impartial caring."[3] The doctrine of impartial caring states that one should have equal concern for, and has equal ethical obligations toward, promoting the well-being of every person, regardless of any special relation a person might have with oneself.

The essay, "Impartial Caring," in which the later followers of Mozi present and defend their master's doctrine, seems to polarize the opinions of interpreters. On the one hand, David Wong, in a thoughtful and insightful essay, dismisses most of the arguments in this essay as "genuinely shallow and unimportant. They are wishes masquerading as arguments. . . ."[4] At the other extreme, Chad Hansen states that the Mohists offer "a nonquestion begging [sic] argument for universal concern," and demonstrate that the Confucian view of partial or graded love is "self-defeating."[5] I agree with parts of both Wong's and Hansen's assessments. Ultimately, I agree with Wong in favoring some version of Confucian graded love over Mohist impartiality. However, like Hansen, I find the Mohist arguments stronger and more intriguing than Wong's quick dismissal suggests. For example, in "Impartial Caring," the Mohists give what is probably the first use of "thought experiments" in Chinese philosophy, and perhaps their first use in the world. Given the intrinsic interest of the Mohist thesis and their arguments for it, it is surprising that, although many works present a quick overview of the arguments in the essay, there are few detailed analyses of it.[6] I hope to partially remedy that lack in this paper.

The Caretaker Argument

One of the key arguments in "Impartial Caring" is the following *gedanken* experiment:

> Suppose one must put on one's armor and helmet and go to war in a vast and open wilderness where life and death are uncertain; or suppose one was sent by one's ruler or high minister to the distant states of Ba, Yue, Qi or Jing and could not be sure of either reaching them or ever returning from one's mission. Under such conditions of uncertainty, to whom would one entrust the well-being of one's parents, wife and children? Would one prefer that they be in the care of an impartial person or would one prefer that they be in the care of a partial person? I believe that under such circumstances, there are no fools in all the world. Even though one may not advocate impartiality, one would certainly want to entrust one's family to the person who is impartial. But this is to condemn impartiality in word but prefer it in deed, with the result that one's actions do not accord with what one says. And so I don't see what reason any person in the world who has heard about impartiality can give for condemning it.[7]

The key question in this passage is "Would one prefer that [one's family] be in the care of an impartial person or would one prefer that they be in the care of a partial person?" The Mohists apparently regard it as blindingly obvious that one would entrust one's family to an *impartial* person, for they do not even bother to explain why this is the best choice. But, in fact, it is far from obvious that the impartial person is the right choice. Suppose that you have gone on a dangerous mission, and have entrusted the care of your family to someone else. Let us call this man "the caretaker." Now consider the following elaboration of the Mohist example. Suppose that, in the community in which you left your family, a famine occurred, leading to widespread starvation. If the caretaker is an impartialist, he will have no reason to promote the health and survival of your family over the health and survival of anyone else. Indeed, if the members of your family are unlikely to survive, the impartialist caretaker may intentionally divert resources *away* from your family to families whose members have a greater chance of survival. I doubt that, if I had entrusted them to an impartialist caretaker in such a situation, the members of my family would say, "Gee, *thanks*, Dad!"

In contrast, if the partialist caretaker is bound to you by a special relationship such as kinship, friendship, et cetera, then he will promote the well-being of your family *over* the well-being of strangers. Thus, in many situations, the Confucian caretaker is a better choice than the impartial caretaker. Even Hansen seems to admit as much: "The Confucian soldier may protect his family *better* by putting them with a relative. Even though they *come after* the original family, they still *come before* starving strangers."[8]

However, if the caretaker acts according to Confucian graded love, he will prefer the well-being of his own closest family members to the well-being of the members of your family. Consequently, if it is a choice between letting your family starve and letting his own family starve, a partialist caretaker will let your family starve. Consequently, one can construct convoluted stories about situations in which one's family is better off with an impartial caretaker. Suppose that the three members of your family and the three members of the caretaker's family are isolated in a cabin, with all the nearby roads snowed in, and suppose there is only enough food to keep three people alive. Since the universalist caretaker is completely impartial, he is as likely to give food to members of your family as he is to give food to members of his own family. So in this situation you are better off with the universalist. However, it is worth pointing out that this is a scenario that is seldom realized. Although I do not think this claim (or its denial) can be proven with mathematical certainty, I would hazard to guess that one's family is better off in most situations with a Confucian caretaker.

So why do the Mohists regard the thought experiment as so obviously favoring the universalist caretaker? The answer can be found in some curious comments that occur in the text immediately prior to the thought experiment:

Suppose there were two people: one who maintains partiality and one who maintains impartiality. And so the person who maintains partiality would say, "How can I possibly regard the well-being of my friends as I do my own well-being? How can I possibly regard the parents of my friends as I do my own parents?" And so when his friends are hungry, the partial person does not feed them. When his friends are cold, he does not clothe them. When his friends are ill, he does not nurture them. And when his friends die, he does not bury them. This is what the partial person says and what he does. But this is not what the impartial person says nor is this how he acts. The impartial person says, "I have heard that in order to be a superior person in the world, one must regard the well-being of one's friends as one regards one's own well-being; one must regard the parents of one's friends as one regards one's own parents. Only in this way can one be a superior person." And so when the impartial person's friends are hungry, he feeds them. When his friends are cold, he clothes them. When his friends are ill, he nurtures them. And when his friends die, he buries them. This is what the impartial person says and what he does. (p. 65)

An aspect of the characterization of the impartialist here is surprising: he is described as regarding the well-being of his *friends* as he regards his own well-being. And the Chinese *yǒu* 友, like the English term "friend," suggests someone with whom one has a special relationship, not shared with people in general. If the Mohist impartialist is someone who is impartial only among the members of the group consisting of his own family and friends, but promotes the well-being of his family and friends over that of strangers, then of course one would choose an impartialist caretaker over a partialist one. But the Mohists are clearly arguing in the essay for impartiality toward humans in general, not toward the members of one's family, or clique, or city, or kingdom. So it seems likely that the Mohists are using the term "friend" in some extended, nonstandard sense. (But they should have alerted us to this fact.) Let us assume, then, that the impartialist is someone who is "friends" with everyone, and cares for everyone else as he cares for himself.

More problematic for the Mohist argument is their characterization of the partialist. It is clear that, characterized in the way that they are, and if *these* are one's only choices, one should choose an impartialist caretaker over a partialist caretaker—because the partialist "caretaker" won't do any caretaking at all! As described in the preceding passage, the partialist will do nothing at all to benefit or assist his friend (and, presumably, nothing for his friend's family). So the addition of this characterization of the partialist saves the Mohist argument from being a simple non sequitur. However, there are now at least two different problems for the Mohist argument.

First, suppose for the moment that the Mohist thought experiment is rationally persuasive. What has it persuaded us of? What the Mohist argument shows is that we have reason to prefer impartialist caretakers for our family. Perhaps we might even be able to generalize the Mohist argument to demonstrate that we should prefer that everyone else in our community be an impartialist. But notice that this does *not* demonstrate to the partialist that he should be an impartialist. The fact (if it is a fact) that the partialist has reason to want *other* individuals or families to be impartial does not show that the partialist has any reason to want *himself* or *his family* to be impartial.

However, Hansen offers a response to this sort of objection, suggesting that a *dào* 道 is intrinsically social rather than individual, so that the question the Mohists (and all other early Chinese thinkers) are concerned with is, "What *dao*-type should society teach to all people?"[9] I am not certain that Hansen is right. However, let us assume (for the sake of the argument) that it is impossible for Chinese thinkers (or at least for Mohists) to entertain the possibility of a *dao* that would instruct me to do one thing myself but to encourage others to do something else. In that case, the only available options are the way of partiality for society as a whole (everyone acting partially) or the way of impartiality for society as a whole (everyone acting impartially). The Mohist argument is still problematic, though. It is true that people who have to entrust their families to the care of others would be much worse off in a society composed entirely of partialists. But it is also true that those who are less crafty, weaker, less aggressive, and generally more in need of the assistance of others would fare worse in a partialist society. Neither of these facts, by itself, demonstrates the conclusion that the Mohists want to demonstrate: that one would be a "fool" to choose to live in a partialist society. All the argument shows is that I should not prefer a partialist society unless I am crafty, strong, aggressive, and unlikely to need the assistance of others.[10]

The second problem with the Mohist argument becomes clear when we ask whom the argument is directed against. We have been assuming so far in our discussion (as Wong, Hansen, and all other interpreters I know of assume) that the critical arguments in "Impartial Caring" are directed against the Confucian position. The difficulty is that partialism, as the Mohists characterize it here, is nothing at all like the Confucian position. Nowhere do any Confucians advocate complete indifference to the well-being of other human beings, and they certainly do not advocate indifference to the suffering of their friends. As Wong observes, "Confucianism has some universalistic tendencies. . . . It holds to a thesis of 'differential [ethical] pull' in such a way that everyone has at least some substantial pull as reflected in the idea that certain things are owed to all."[11] This makes it seem like the Mohists are simply attacking a straw man.

Now the interpretive principle of charity encourages us to look for a different interpretation, if the interpretation we currently have attributes foolishness to the object of our interpretation. The only way to avoid attributing to the Mohists a straw-man argument is to identify someone or some group who (unlike the Confucians) seriously advocated the position the Mohists are attacking. It is possible that the partialists under attack are members of a loose group sometimes described as "self-preservationists." The paradigmatic self-preservationist was Yang Zhu. In characterizing the differences between Yang Zhu and Mozi, Mengzi said, "Yangzi chose egoism. If plucking out one hair from his body would have benefited the whole world, he would not do it. Mozi loved universally. If scraping himself bare from head to heals would benefit the whole world, he would do it" (7A26).[12] Mengzi also claims that, in his era at least, "the doctrines of Yang Zhu and Mo Di fill the world" (3B9). Consequently, Yang Zhu was thought by some people to advocate a view similar to that of the extreme partialist described by the Mohists, and there was a time when the thought of Yang Zhu was a major (perhaps *the* major) intellectual rival to Mohism. In addition, in the next argument of the Mohist essay ("the ruler argument," discussed below), there is a significant phrase attributed to a partialist ruler: "How brief is the span of a person's life upon this earth! It rushes by like a galloping team of horses glimpsed through a crack!" (p. 66). A very close simile is used in the "Robber Zhi" chapter of the *Zhuangzi*, which Angus Graham has argued is Yangist in origin: it says that the passing of a man's life "is as sudden as a thoroughbred steed galloping past a chink in the wall."[13] Furthermore, in the *Liezi* (circa C.E. 300), there is a philosophical dialogue between Yang Zhu, one of Yang Zhu's disciples, and a disciple of Mozi's. Although the *Liezi* as a whole dates from long after the supposed time of this dialogue, Graham thinks the dialogue comes from an earlier Mohist source. This suggests that the Mohists felt a need to respond to Yangist arguments.[14]

There are several problems with an interpretation that identifies the target of the first (and second) Mohist arguments with a Yangist partialist. (1) Yang Zhu lived after the time of Mozi. (2) Although Mengzi accuses him of extreme egoism, more recent scholars read Yang Zhu as having a much more moderate position toward helping others, which might allow for some concern for others. For example, Graham writes that "one has the impression that Chinese thinkers perceive persons as inherently social beings who are more or less selfish rather than as isolated individuals who will be pure egoists unless taught morality."[15] (3) Within "the caretaker argument" itself, the partialist is described as having some concern for his own family.[16] (4) As we shall see, there is an argument later in the essay that assumes the opponents of impartial caring do have a commitment to "filial piety" (*xiào* 孝). This seems to rule out their being narrow egoists.

However, all of these objections can be answered. (1) We do not know when the third version of "Impartial Caring" was composed; it may be a version of that essay, written much later than the time of Mozi himself, as a response to Yang Zhu's ideas specifically. (2) Even if Mengzi misunderstood Yang Zhu's teachings, the fact that he did so shows that this was a misunderstanding they were open to. Perhaps the Mohists made the same interpretive error. (To attribute to them a misunderstanding apparently common in their culture is not a violation of the principle of charity.) (3) A hypothesis that helps to respond to both the second and the third objections is to accept that the Yangists were not pure egoists and did have some concern for those closest to them. If this is true (and if the Mohists knew this) it would explain why the partialists are described as having some concern for close family members. Finally, (4) note that the people concerned with filial piety later in the essay are never explicitly identified as "partialists." It may be that the arguments in the first part of the essay are directed against Yangist partialists, while "the filial piety argument" later in the essay is directed against Confucians.

I am still not certain that the Mohists were thinking of Yangists or quasi-Yangists (rather than Confucians) in their characterization of the partialists. But I do want to suggest it as an intriguing possibility.

Let me review where we have been so far. Our initial examination of the Mohist thought experiment suggested that it was a simple non sequitur. At first glance, a Confucian who is bound to you by friendship seems to generally be a better choice for a caretaker than someone who is completely impartial. But then we noticed that the Mohists provide a description of the partialist in the immediately preceding paragraph of the text. Assuming the Mohist characterizations of the partialist and the impartialists, and assuming that these two are our only choices, the Mohist argument becomes logically valid. However, the partialism thus described seems completely inconsistent with any plausible understanding of Confucianism. That makes it seem like the Mohist argument, although technically valid, is a straw man argument. The only alternative to attributing a straw man argument to the Mohists seems to be identifying the partialist with a Yangist.

However, now we can see two other problems with the Mohist argument. First, if the partialist is a self-preservationist, a Hobbesian might argue that, under certain conditions, a partialist caretaker might be a better choice.[17] Suppose, for example, that you are potentially more dangerous to the caretaker than she is to you, and you have a known willingness to act on your threats. You can then put your family in the care of a partialist, and tell her that, if you return and find that she has not taken good care of your family, you will kill her. As long as the partialist does not know for certain that you are dead, she will have an incentive to take care of your family. Furthermore, she will have a commitment to taking care of your family *over* the families of others, so she is arguably a better choice than an impartialist caretaker. Even if you do die, a Hobbesian will argue that it may be in the interest of a partialist caretaker to go through with her commitment to caring for your family, since she may benefit from acquiring the reputation of one who is reliable in carrying out her agreements. Overall, I am not convinced by the Hobbesian arguments myself. But the Hobbesian alternative does show that there is much more complexity to the choice situation than the Mohists suggest. And this shows that, even if one accepts the premises of the Mohist argument, their conclusion will not follow without additional arguments (which have not been supplied by the Mohists).

The second problem with the Mohist argument is more serious, and has to do with a crucial implicit premise: the Mohists assume that impartiality and partiality (as defined) are the only two alternatives. But this is a false dichotomy.

There are an almost infinite number of theoretical alternatives to impartiality and partiality as defined by the Mohists, and (more importantly) there is at least one prima facie plausible alternative that the Mohists would have been aware of, and should have taken into account: Confucian graded love. A Confucian is almost certainly a better caretaker than an extreme egoist. Furthermore, as we saw above, a strong case can be made that a Confucian is generally preferable to a Mohist impartialist as a caretaker. In other words, the number of "live options" for our choice of a type of caretaker is larger than the Mohists suggest. Our practical choice is actually among an impartial caretaker, a caretaker who is a Yangist, and a Confucian caretaker. And it is not obvious that the impartial caretaker is the best choice. In fact, a plausible case can be made that the Confucian caretaker is the best choice.

I can think of only one way to save the Mohists from this objection. It is possible that the Mohists thought it was only necessary in this section of the essay to show the superiority of Mohist impartialism to Yangist partialism, because they provide an argument later in the essay (the "filial piety argument") that attempts to show that Confucians should become Mohist impartialists. If this is what the Mohists have in mind, the success of the caretaker argument ultimately depends on the success of the filial piety argument (discussed below).

In short, if the partialist in the argument is supposed to be a Confucian, the caretaker argument is attacking a straw man; if the partialist in the caretaker argument is supposed to be a Yangist, then the argument seems to offer a false dichotomy. However, it may be that the caretaker argument is intended only as a response to the Yangists, and that the later filial piety argument is a necessary supplement to it.

The Ruler Argument

In response to the objection that impartiality cannot be used as a standard in selecting a ruler, the Mohists ask us to imagine a partialist and an impartialist ruler: "When his subjects are hungry, the partial ruler does not feed them. When his subjects are cold, he does not clothe them. When his subjects are ill, he does not nurture them. And when his subjects die, he does not bury them" (p. 66). In contrast, the impartial ruler does for his subjects all the things the partial ruler fails to do. The Mohists then ask us to consider the following: "Suppose there were a terrible epidemic in which most of the people suffered bitterly from hunger and cold and many lay dead and unburied in the ditches and gullies. . . . I believe that under such circumstances, there are no fools in all the world. Even though one may not advocate impartiality, one would certainly want to follow the ruler who is impartial" (p. 67).

Once again, we are faced with either a straw man argument or a false dichotomy. Confucians certainly do not hold up as an ideal a ruler who ignores the needs of his subjects. So a Confucian ruler is not like the partialist described in this passage. If, in contrast, the partialist ruler is supposed to be a Yangist, then the Mohists are failing to examine the possible benefits of a Confucian ruler. In fact, the actions the Mohists attribute to the impartialist ruler in this passage are indistinguishable from the actions of a Confucian ruler in the same circumstances, so it is not at all clear why the subjects are better off with an impartialist ruler.

There are some circumstances (not discussed by the Mohists) in which the actions of a Confucian ruler *would* differ from those of a Mohist impartialist ruler, because of the special obligations the Confucian has to his own kin. These special obligations can, in principle, lead to ethical dilemmas. In the early Confucian tradition, these dilemmas are discussed at length by Mengzi. In one case, he is asked,

> "When Sage King Shun was Son of Heaven, and Gao Yao was his Minister of Crime, if 'the Blind Man' [i.e., Shun's father] had murdered someone, what would they have done?"
>
> Mengzi said, "Gao Yao would simply have arrested him!"
>
> "So Shun would not have forbidden it?"
>
> Mengzi said, "How could Shun have forbidden it? Gao Yao had a sanction for his actions."
>
> "So what would Shun have done?"
>
> Mengzi said, "Shun looked at casting aside the whole world like casting aside a worn sandal. He would have secretly carried him on his back and fled, to live along the coast, happy to the end of his days, joyfully forgetting the world." (7A35)

In Mengzi's solution to the ethical dilemma, Shun manages to avoid violating either his obligations as king or his obligations as a son. This is ingenious, but, arguably, Shun's subjects would be better off if Shun were to remain as ruler and simply allow his father to be arrested (and executed).

To my knowledge, the Confucians never directly respond to this objection. (But then again, the Mohists never directly raise it.) I think there is a Confucian response, though. They might acknowledge that, in theory, a purely impartial ruler would be better for his subjects than a Confucian ruler in certain rare cases. However, they might argue that the caring yet impartial Mohist ruler is, at best, extremely rare, because a human who is sufficiently indifferent to the suffering of his own father to allow him to be executed is, as a matter of psychological fact, unlikely to be sufficiently compassionate to be a good ruler. (And if the ideal Mohist ruler is extremely rare, then the Mohist political system is intrinsically unstable in real-world conditions.) As an armchair psychologist, I find this Confucian argument plausible (but it is based on an empirical psychological claim, which should be supported by further evidence).

A Confucian could also point out that there are some circumstances in which subjects would be better off with a partialist king. Suppose there is an international situation in which a particular policy would benefit a larger number of subjects of other states, but at a great cost to the smaller number of subjects in the ruler's own state. Depending on the relative benefits and costs, an impartial ruler would sacrifice the well-being of his own subjects for the greater good, whereas a partialist ruler would protect the interests of his own subjects.

The Historical Precedent Argument

The Mohists next address the concern that practicing impartiality is impossible, like "picking up Mount Tai and carrying it across the" Yangtze or Yellow River (p. 67). The Mohist response is to provide textual evidence from historical sources that impartiality was practiced by the sage kings of former times. If impartiality was in fact successfully practiced by earlier rulers, this is decisive evidence that practicing impartiality is possible. Once again, though, there is a problem with the Mohist argument. The Mohists cite four texts as evidence for their claim. Although the Mohists interpret each of these texts as providing evidence for their brand of impartiality, what is actually written in the first three texts is completely consistent with a Confucian conception of kingship. For example, in the third text, Sage King Tang is quoted as addressing Heaven during a drought, saying, "If those within my domain have committed any offense [which led Heaven to cause this drought], let the responsibility rest with me" (p. 69). The trope of a ruler offering himself as a sacrifice to save others is ancient in China, and is as much a part of the Confucian tradition as the Mohist.[18]

The last text the Mohists cite does provide some evidence that something like Mohist impartiality was regarded as an ideal by earlier rulers. It is an ode, attributed to the time of the Zhou Dynasty, which says (in part), "The King's Way is broad so broad; / without partiality or party" (p. 69). However, I think a Confucian would interpret this as applying only to the king's relationship with his subjects at large. Of course, the Confucian interpretation of this poem may be mistaken, but the ambiguity in the one piece of textual evidence that directly supports the Mohist claim shows that the Mohists have not given us much evidence for the claim that impartiality was practiced historically.

The Filial Piety Argument

This argument is especially intriguing because it seems to take as at least one of its premises the sort of commitment that is definitive of Confucian graded love, but to attempt to argue from this premise to Mohist universalism:

> A filial son who seeks what is beneficial for his parents . . . must want other people to care for and benefit his parents. Given this, how should one act in order to bring about such a state of affairs? Should one first care for and benefit the parents of others, expecting that they in turn will respond by caring for and benefiting one's

own parents? Or should one first dislike and steal from other people's parents, expecting that they in turn will respond by caring for and benefiting one's own parents? (p. 70)

The Mohists appeal to the principle that "anyone who cares for others will receive care from them while anyone who dislikes others will in turn be disliked" (p. 71). On this basis, they conclude, "Clearly one must first care for and benefit the parents of others in order to expect that they in turn will respond by caring for and benefiting one's own parents" (p. 70). Thus, the argument is that, if one is committed (as are Confucians) to filial piety (*xiào* 孝), then one should not "dislike and steal from other people's parents," but rather ought to "care for and benefit the parents of others." Notice that, although the argument is phrased in terms of filial piety, which involves a special commitment to the well-being of one's own parents, it could be generalized to apply to any special commitment: husband to wife, sibling to sibling, parent to child, et cetera. I shall, therefore, treat the argument in its generalized form.

The key premises of this argument strike me as quite plausible. It is not invariantly true that either kindness or callousness toward others is reciprocated. However, we do seem to find that, across a broad range of cultures and circumstances, kindness is often repaid by kindness, and callousness by callousness. Furthermore, most of us are concerned about the well being of our parents (or about other members of our family). Consequently, it seems that we do have good reason, all else being equal, to make friends, and not enemies, of others.

The problem with the argument is that it does not seem to lead to the conclusion the Mohists are using it to establish. Recall that the Mohists are arguing against Confucians and in favor of impartiality. But their argument here, even if successful, does not provide any reason to reject Confucianism, for Confucians certainly do not advocate harming the parents of others. Indeed, Confucians like Mengzi advocate "extending" compassion outward from one's own family to others: "Treat your elders as elders, and extend it to the elders of others; treat your young ones as young ones, and extend it to the young ones of others" (1A7).[19] Furthermore, the Mohist argument does not provide any reason for impartiality: all it shows is that, if one *is* partial to one's family, one should not harm the families of others.

Perhaps the Mohists assume that a policy of Confucian graded love, while not directly commanding us to harm the families of others, will lead to harming others. As a general claim, this is patently false. Most of us do things to benefit our families all the time without needing to harm the families of others. It is true that there are some circumstances in which adherence to graded love will require acting against the interests of other families. Suppose we are on a sinking ship, with one other family and one lifeboat left on board, and there is only room for one family in that lifeboat. In such exigent circumstances, Confucian graded love requires that I attempt to secure the lifeboat for my own family.

However, this example does not show that the Mohist "filial piety argument" provides a reason to be an impartialist. First, the Mohist argument begins from the assumption that we are committed to the well-being of our own parents (or our own family members generally). As long as we are so committed, if we find that we are in a situation like the "life boat scenario" above, we should drop our normal policy of not acting against the interests of others. Second, situations like the "life boat scenario" are likely to be quite rare. It is not clear what practical relevance the small possibility of such situations being realized has.

The Practicability Argument

One common objection that has been raised against certain forms of impartial consequentialism in the West is that complete impartiality is psychologically unobtainable (for most people, at least). Consequently, it does not surprise us that the final Mohist argument in this essay is a counterargument to the objection that "impartial care is too difficult to carry out" (p. 71). This might seem to merely be a repetition of the earlier objection dealt with in the "historical precedent argument." However, the "historical precedent argument" focused on the practicability of impartiality *as a policy for kings to follow* in ruling their subjects. The "practicability argument" here responds to the objection that *most people in society* cannot be made to act in accordance with impartial caring.

The Mohist counterargument is to provide counterexamples to the objection, in the form of successful policies that seem to have required behavioral changes in people at least as drastic as the change to universal love. The examples are a ruler who "was fond of slender waists," and whose subjects, in consequence, "ate no more than one meal a day and became so weak that they could not raise themselves up without the support of a cane nor could they walk without leaning against a wall"; a ruler who "was fond of bravery," and whose soldiers, when so ordered, charged onto burning ships; and a ruler who "was fond of rough and simple attire," so that his subjects "wrapped themselves in sheets of cloth, wore sheepskin jackets, hats of raw silk, and hempen shoes" (p. 71). The Mohists conclude, "Curtailing one's food, charging into flames, and wearing rough and simple attire are among the most difficult things in the world to get people to do, but masses of people did it in order to please their superiors" (p. 72). By comparison, impartial caring is easy to put into effect.[20] The Mohists give a more extensive list later in this section of practices that can modify behavior: superiors delighting in them, encouraging them with rewards and praise, and discouraging alternative practices with penalties and punishments.

We have insufficient historical knowledge to evaluate the Mohist accounts of these rulers and the effectiveness of their programs of behavior modification. However, our own knowledge of human practices suggests that these accounts are plausible, up to a point. For example, the widespread occurrence of eating disorders among women in our own society makes painfully vivid the possibility of a society in which many humans are motivated to become unhealthfully thin. However, what the Mohists intend to show with their examples is something much more extreme. Specifically, the Mohists assume that the structure of human motivations and dispositions is almost infinitely malleable.[21] In other words, humans are like clay that can be radically remolded "within a single generation" (p. 71), so long as rulers provide the appropriate leadership and behavioral incentives. It is tempting to describe this by saying that the Mohists think that human nature is infinitely malleable, but this is somewhat misleading. It is more accurate to say that the Mohists think that there is no human nature.[22]

Not only do the Mohists seem to be suggesting something like this, but they *need* to hold something like this view. For, as I suggested earlier, graded love seems to be the "common sense" view of many of us, not just in the contemporary U.S., but in most societies around the world. Consequently, if there is such a thing as human nature, it seems to be strongly opposed to Mohist impartiality. Now, the Mohists' examples of behavior modification are plausible as examples of practices that were instituted among small portions of the population, or among large segments of the population for short periods of time. However, what the Mohists need to show is that impartial care can be permanently instituted as a practice among a segment of the general population large enough for it to be practically effective. Their examples are insufficiently detailed and (without further documentation) insufficiently convincing to show this. Indeed, the prevalence of graded love in the world and the disastrous failures of social philosophies such as Stalinism and Maoism that have regarded humans as infinitely malleable suggest that there *is* such a thing as human nature, and that we flout it at our peril.[23]

Conclusion

The Mohist essay on "Impartial Caring" is an impressive example of early philosophical argumentation. The essay shows great systematicity in its efforts to argue in favor of impartial caring, to argue against the major alternatives to impartial caring (including, if I am right, both Yangism and Confucianism), and to address every one of the major objections to impartial caring (including the objection that impartial caring cannot be inculcated among the general population). Furthermore, the essay makes use of the classic technique of the thought experiment.

Nonetheless, I believe that the essay ultimately fails to be persuasive. The caretaker thought-experiment offers a false dichotomy unless it relies upon the later *filial piety argument to rule out* Confucian graded love as a choice for a *dao*. And the filial piety argument is a simple non sequitur.

Appendix: Hansen's Interpretation

Hansen regards the Mohist "caretaker argument" as sound, in part because he believes that it is structurally similar to one that Derek Parfit would offer two and a half millennia later, which Hansen takes to demonstrate that Confucian graded love is "directly collectively self-defeating." Parfit says, suppose we have a particular theory of how one should act, call that theory "T," and call the aims that T says one should promote the "T-aims" of that theory. Then, T is *directly collectively self-defeating* when it is certain that, if we all successfully follow T, we will thereby cause the T-given aims *of each* to be worse achieved than they would have been if none of us had successfully followed T.[24]

Theories are self-defeating in situations that are formally like what are called "Prisoner's Dilemmas" in game theory. The classic Prisoner's Dilemma involves only two, purely self-interested agents. However, the choice situation can be generalized to apply to arbitrarily large numbers of either individuals or groups who are concerned only with the well being of themselves or the members of their own group.

Consider the following example. Suppose we have a community of families in which the following conditions hold: the members of each family act according to some T that has as its sole T-aim maximizing their own family's wealth; there are community services (police, public transportation, et cetera) which, if properly funded, would contribute to maintaining and increasing the wealth of each family; it is possible for each family to effectively evade paying its share of the funding for the community services. In this situation, T is directly, collectively self-defeating, because each family in the community knows that, whether the community services end up receiving sufficient funds or not, the family will maximize its own wealth by evading providing its share of the funding for the community services. Parfit takes it to be a serious objection to a theory that it is self-defeating in this sense. For brevity's sake, I shall refer to an argument of this form as "Parfit's argument."

Hansen's analysis of the Mohist arguments raises three distinct questions:

1. Is Parfit's argument directed against T's such as the Confucian doctrine of graded love?

2. Do the Mohists provide a version of Parfit's argument against the Confucian doctrine of graded love (or against any other position)?

3. Does Parfit's argument provide a serious challenge to the Confucian doctrine of graded love?

Hansen's answers to these questions are Yes, Yes, and Yes. However, my own answers are Yes, No, and No.

It seems clear that, although he never mentions Confucianism, Parfit's argument is directed against positions like Confucian graded love. (This is perhaps not surprising, since Parfit is attracted to Buddhist philosophy, and Buddhist and Confucian philosophy are typically seen as conflicting on the issue of universal vs. graded love.) Specifically, Parfit states that what he describes as "Common-Sense Morality" is characterized in large part by "special obligations" to "our children, parents, friends, benefactors, pupils, patients, clients, colleagues," et cetera, and that this morality is directly, collectively self-defeating.[25]

But do the *Mohists* actually use such an argument? Hansen claims to find this argument in the caretaker argument in "Impartial Caring." At first glance, this thought experiment seems to have no similarity at all with Parfit's argument. Parfit's argument applies to situations that are formally similar to Prisoner's Dilemmas. The situation the Mohists describe does not seem to be like a Prisoner's Dilemma at all. More precisely, a theory is self-defeating in Parfit's sense if, were we all to act in accordance with it, it is *certain* that we *each* would do a worse job of achieving what the theory tells us to aim at than if we did not act in accordance with the theory. In contrast, the Mohist caretaker argument shows, at most, that we should prefer a society composed solely of Mohist impartialists to a society composed solely of Yangist partialists *if* we will need to entrust the care of our family to someone. But this does not show that each of us will do a worse job of achieving our goals if we all follow the Yangist *dao*. (I imagine a Yangist would reply to the Mohist argument, "So don't take an official position that will require you to go on dangerous missions of state.")

In order to get closer to Parfit's argument, we need to make two more assumptions. First, assume the Mohists intend the scenario of entrusting one's family to someone else as only an *example* of a large range of cases in which we require the assistance of others. Second, assume it is certain that all of us, regardless of how strong, assertive, et cetera, we are, will have a crucial need to rely upon the assistance of others at some point in our lives. This final assumption implies that it will be impossible for a partialist to attain his T-aims in a society composed of partialists. So if we make all of these assumptions, then the argument seems formally similar to an argument of Parfit's type. Now, I am all in favor of reading arguments charitably, but these are a large number of textually unsupported assumptions to attribute to the Mohists, just to get them to have an argument like Parfit's. Consequently, I find it implausible to attribute to the Mohists a version of Parfit's argument.

As a philosophical historian, I am interested in what the Mohists said. But as a philosopher, I am interested in what the truth is. Consequently, even if the Mohists did not use Parfit's argument, we should examine whether Parfit's argument is a successful refutation of positions like the graded love of Confucianism. I think that it is not successful, for at least two reasons. First, as I have repeatedly stressed, Confucian graded love is not egoism, nor does it advocate concern for one's own family to the exclusion of concern for others. As Parfit himself admits, such concern greatly mitigates the effects of partialism, and makes Prisoner's-Dilemma situations less frequent. However, Parfit also stresses that any version of partialism will occasionally produce Prisoner's-Dilemma situations. This brings me to my second objection. I find quite hokey Parfit's examples of situations that are collectively self-defeating for people who live according to something like Confucian graded love. Consider this example from Parfit:

> Suppose that you and I each have four children, all of whom are in mortal danger. We are strangers, and we cannot communicate. Each could either (1) save one of his own children or (2) save three of the other's children. If I love my children, I may find it impossible to save the lives of three of your children at the cost of letting one of my children die. And the same may be true of you. We will then both do (1) rather than (2). Because we love our children, we save only two of them when we could have saved six.[26]

How often in the history of our species has a situation like this actually occurred? This is not to say that such a situation is impossible. However, I do believe that such situations are extremely rare. And it is not clear to me that it is a serious practical objection to a theory that in certain extremely unusual circumstances it would be self-defeating if everyone adhered to it.

Notes

1. These are sometimes called the "five relations," and are mentioned in *Zhongyong* 20 and in *Mengzi* 3A4 (with "elder and younger" replacing "elder and younger brother" in the latter text).

2. Edward Slingerland, trans., *Readings in Classical Chinese Philosophy*, ed. Philip J. Ivanhoe and Bryan W. Van Norden (New York: Seven Bridges Press, 2000).

3. I here follow Philip J. Ivanhoe's translation of the phrase in Ivanhoe and Van Norden.

4. David Wong, "Universalism versus Love with Distinctions: An Ancient Debate Revived," *Journal of Chinese Philosophy* 16 (1989): 263.

5. Chad Hansen, *A Daoist Theory of Chinese Thought* (New York: Oxford University Press, 1992), 112.

6. E.g., Benjamin Schwartz, *The World of Thought in Ancient China* (Cambridge: Harvard University Press, 1985), 145–51, *passim*; Angus C. Graham, *Disputers of the Tao* (Chicago: Open Court, 1989), 41–43. I deal here only with the third version of the "Impartial Caring" essay. For a general discussion of the textual issues raised by the Mohist synoptic chapters, and a brief summary of the contents of the various versions of each essay, see Scott Lowe, *Mo Tzu's Religious Blueprint for a Chinese Utopia* (Lewiston, NY: Edwin Mellen Press, 1992).

7. All translations from the Mohist writings are from the translation by Philip J. Ivanhoe in Ivanhoe and Van Norden, *Readings*. This quotation is from p. 66.

8. Hansen, *A Daoist Theory*, p. 112. Emphasis in original.

9. *Ibid.*, p. 113.

10. Hansen nonetheless finds the Mohist argument persuasive, for reasons that I discuss in the Appendix to this paper.

11. Wong, "Universalism," p. 253.

12. Translations from the *Mengzi* are by Bryan W. Van Norden in Ivanhoe and Van Norden, *Readings*. References are to the standard sectioning.

13. Graham, *Disputers*, p. 64.

14. *Ibid.*, pp. 60–61.

15. *Ibid.*, p. 61.

16. In the initial description of the partialist, he asks the rhetorical question, "How can I possibly regard the parents of my friends as I do my own parents?" In addition, in the "caretaker thought experiment," the person leaving on the mission is concerned with the well-being of his wife, parents, and children (however, the person leaving on the mission is not explicitly said to be a partialist as the passage defines that term).

17. Although, historically, the Mohists were not aware of Hobbes's philosophy, we can ask, philosophically, whether they would have a response to this objection.

18. For a discussion, see David S. Nivison, " 'Virtue' in Bone and Bronze," in *The Ways of Confucianism* (Chicago: Open Court, 1996), 17–30.

19. That is, treat the elders and young ones of your family as they should be treated, and then extend that treatment to the young ones and elders of other families.

20. My experience in teaching "Impartial Caring" has been that students frequently object that the examples the Mohists give are examples of rulers being cruel to their subjects, rather than examples of impartial caring. This is true, but it is not an objection to the Mohist argument. The Mohists are not *endorsing* the actions of these rulers. They are only using these examples to *demonstrate the possibility* of radically altering the behavior of a population.

21. To my knowledge, the only commentator to have identified this aspect of their thought is David S. Nivison. See his "Weakness of Will in Ancient Chinese Philosophy," p. 83, and "Philosophical Voluntarism in Fourth-Century China," p. 130, both in *The Ways of Confucianism*.

22. Ning Chen suggests that the Mohists believed human nature was evil. (Ning Chen, "The Ideological Background of the Mencian Discussion of Human Nature," in *Mencius: Contexts and Interpretations,* ed. Alan K. L. Chan [Honolulu: University of Hawaii Press, 2002], 17–41.) His challenging argument deserves serious consideration, but it is based largely on a passage in the Mohist dialectical chapters that is extremely difficult to interpret and that may be textually corrupt. The advantage of Nivison's interpretation is that it is based, as we have just seen, on unambiguous statements in a central Mohist text.

23. The received view among anthropologists and Skinnerian behaviorists had long favored something like the Mohist view. However, the empirical evidence for the claim that there is no human nature has recently received extensive criticism. Typical is the view of anthropologist Donald E. Brown who, in a survey of this topic, concluded,

"Whatever the motive may be for resisting the idea that there is a human nature whose features shape culture and society, its intellectual foundations have all but collapsed" (*Human Universals* [New York: McGraw-Hill, 1991], 144).

24. Derek Parfit, *Reasons and Persons* (New York: Oxford University Press, 1984), 55.

25. *Ibid.*, p. 95 and p. 98ff.

26. *Ibid.*, p. 102.

PART II

FRIENDS, AUTHORITY, FAMILY, AND MORAL CULTIVATION

Friendship and Role Morality

5

Dean Cocking and Jeanette Kennett

Introduction

Some advocates of role morality have appealed to the idea that reasons of friendship might compete favorably with conflicting moral reasons, to claim the same kind of moral independence for various other roles, such as certain professional roles.[1] On this kind of view the distinctive features of one's role, say, as a good lawyer or doctor, may guide one against the broader dictates of morality and, like friendship, may license departures from some accepted moral requirements.

We think some of these other roles do share some significant structural features with the friendship case. There are distinctive role-generated obligations and sensitivities across the range of roles in which we might engage. Important agent-relative attachments and loyalties develop in these contexts, such as to one's partner as a police officer or one's patient as a general practitioner, or to one's son, which may on occasion bring us into conflict with some broadly accepted moral requirement. However, the sharing of these structural features with the friendship case, that is, the sharing of distinctive obligations and sensitivities which may involve agent-relative attachments and loyalties, does not suffice to ground the moral independence of these roles. For, we claim, it is not these common structural features that capture the incompatibility, noted by many philosophers, between the claims of friendship and the claims of morality. The morally subversive potential of friendship and the moral departures it will license result primarily from something distinctive about the nature of friendship, and thus from something that is not an important mark of these other roles and relations.

We have argued elsewhere that a distinctive constitutive feature of close friendship is the process of mutual drawing that goes on in it, and that closer analysis of this mutual drawing in friendship, which we outline below, helpfully explains the nature of and potential for conflict between friendship and morality.[2] In this essay we show that this is not the case for other significant personal and professional roles and make further use of the drawing account to provide an account of some significant contrasts between friendship and these other roles and of the relation of each to morality.

Role Morality and Moral Conflicts

It is generally accepted that certain personal and professional roles, such as the parental role or the role of doctor or lawyer, are largely defined by their constitutive goals and that those goals generate substantive rules governing conduct within the role. These conduct-governing rules have guiding regulative force because agency governed in this way is thought to well serve some important moral good. So, for example, if, as it is often claimed, the lawyer's zealous advocacy of her client's interests against the conflicting interests of others provides one of the substantive guiding rules of her conduct as a good lawyer, then it must be because such advocacy ultimately serves an important moral good of the role, such as justice. And argument over whether or not such advocacy really does provide a substantive guiding rule of the good lawyer's conduct will, ultimately, turn on whether it can plausibly be claimed to serve this moral good. If it turned out that certain sorts of advocacy of one's client's interests would, ultimately, be against justice, then in the absence of some other significant moral grounding, it is hard to see how such behavior could provide a substantive guiding rule for one's conduct as a good lawyer. If this is right, then any conflict between the requirements of the role, and what appears to be required of any morally conscientious agent, is properly cast as a conflict *within* morality. One would be licensed to act against some moral value, say, compassion for the victim of a crime, on account of so acting being of service to some conflicting moral good, say, justice. In the context of one's role as a lawyer then, it might be argued that justice properly overrides compassion. And since this is a conflict between moral values it is a conflict that may be understood and accommodated as such by proponents of broad-based or impartialist plural value systems.

Friendship too can provide one with good reasons, on account of one's special relationship with another, to act against competing moral demands. So, for example, close friendship might provide a context where one has good reason to cover for or tell a lie for one's friend or to favor the friend's interests over the weightier interests of others. However, the nature of these good reasons to act for a friend at the expense of a conflicting moral claim are different from the reasons one might have to do so in other familiar social and professional roles. Friendship does not in fact provide a helpful model for understanding these other role-based departures from ordinary moral requirements. To help show this, we will begin by setting out some intuitive differences between the reasons one might have from friendship to act against some moral claim, and the reasons one might have due to one's professional or parental role to so act. We will then use our drawing account to provide some formal analysis of these differences.

Special Relationships and Moral Conflicts

Friendship, parent-child relations, and various professional relations are all significant special relationships with particular others that give rise to particularistic, agent-relative reasons for action that have the potential to conflict with important moral considerations. The contrast we will focus on is between the reasons of this sort one might have from friendship that might direct one to act against morality versus the reasons of this sort one might have as a parent or in a professional relationship that might direct one to act against morality. There are two general kinds of cases we have in mind here.

First, there are cases where, as a result of the bonds of loyalty towards, and altruistic concern for, a particular other, which develop in the context of the relationship, one might be moved to act for that other and against some moral claim. Because one's reason to act against some moral claim might be altruistic, one might well be thought, in both the professional and personal cases, to have some *moral* justification for one's departure from an accepted moral requirement. Thus, such cases might present a conflict *within* morality. Whether one is licensed to act against a moral requirement and for one's friend, child, patient, or client may then depend on the relative weights of the competing moral claims and the special agent-relative moral permissions or exemptions that may plausibly be necessary for the proper fulfillment of one's role.

Second, we think there are cases of friendship where it is on the basis of one's interest in the friend as such, rather than in response to any specifically altruistic, and so plausibly moral, concern to promote the friend's well-being, that one acts against some moral claim or takes part in some morally wrong activity. This kind of case presents a stark contrast between what might be appropriate or permissible for a friend, qua friend, to do, and what might be appropriate or permissible as an occupant of these other personal or professional roles.

Let us start, then, by considering the first kind of case where one acts against some moral claim from loyalty and non-self-centered concern for the well-being of a particular other. Idealized parent-child relations are, like friendships, typically marked by strong bonds of affection, loyalty, and dispositions to promote the interests and well-being of particular others. Similarly, various professional relationships also involve ties of loyalty and professional concern to promote the interests and well-being of particular others. Clearly then, whether one is acting as a friend, a parent, or in some professional capacity, there are many potential situations where one's loyalties and one's concern to promote the interests and well-being of the other would direct one to act against some moral claim. However, despite this structural similarity in how one's special relationships gives rise to agent-relative loyalties and concerns which might conflict with morality, there are important differences between the guiding loyalty and altruistic concern for the other found in friendship and that found in the parental and professional cases.

Loyalty to a friend and concern for her well-being and interests might well direct one to some minor wrongdoing such as telling a lie to cover for her. Similarly, such bonds of loyalty and altruistic concern also feature heavily in parent-child relations and may similarly direct or dispose a parent to tell a lie for her child. Familial and friendship relations, then, appear to share *this* way of being directed by one's relation to the other to act against some moral claims.[3] In one's professional role one might also be moved to act against some moral claim from a particular professional loyalty to act in the interest of another party. So, for example, a doctor or a lawyer might keep client confidentiality against the weightier interests of some third party, and a policeman might cover for his partner in police work. However, we believe that acting from professional loyalty for the sake of a particular other's interest is importantly unlike acting from loyalty and concern for the other's well-being and interests in the friend and parent-child cases. Let us consider these cases first and then return to the comparison between friendship and familial relationships.

When a doctor acts in the interest of her patient, or the lawyer from loyalty to her client, against some ordinarily accepted moral claim, each does so through the prism provided by the governing conception of her professional role. The doctor, for instance, may be guided by her understanding of how a general practitioner promotes the good end of human health to act in the interest of *her* patient and against the legitimate claim of some third party. Patients need to be able to trust their doctors to act in *their* interests rather than in the interests of those who are not their patients, otherwise this good end will be compromised. If patients cannot trust their doctor in this way, they will not seek help when they should or they will not disclose information a doctor needs to make an accurate diagnosis and institute appropriate treatment. Thus, the doctor keeps patient confidentiality, though she knows, for example, that the patient's sexual activity places his partner at risk. Or, in seeking to find a needed hospital bed for her own patient, the doctor does not consider broader resource allocation issues such as whether the bed is more urgently needed by another.[4] And insofar as she is justified in so acting against the legitimate claims of others, this justification must be sourced in the moral good provided by her proper performance of her professional role in this circumstance—here, the good of the agent-relative concern she shows in promoting the interests of her own patients above others, is given by her professional goal of serving and promoting human health as a general practitioner. Of course, a doctor may understandably develop a warm concern for particular long-standing patients that she does not have for patients seen once or twice, and that provides additional impetus to promote those patients' interests. Even so, the expression of this warm particularistic concern for and loyalty to the other is strictly role-governed.

It is not, as it is in the friendship case, that she can have reason to promote the other's interest simply on account of it being her interest. As a doctor she may properly spend some time during the consultation asking after her long-term patient's adult children and chatting about their progress, but she is not given a reason to say, go on a picnic or to the opera with her patient, just because it might be in the interests of the patient, broadly considered, for her to do so. As a friend, on the other hand, one's responses to the perception that something is in the other's interest are not constrained by rules or conventions. One can have reason to go on a picnic or to the opera, or to visit the hospital, or to stay up late talking, just because it is in a friend's interest for one to do so. Of course, one is not always given such a reason, and such reasons need not always win the day (perhaps one hates insects and so simply cannot stand going on picnics). However, that something is in a friend's interest is a commonplace and appropriate reason for one to do that something even where it brings one into conflict with some other moral requirement—say to take part in a collection for charity or keep a promise to one's boss. The reasons the good doctor has to act with respect to her patient's interest—namely, reasons to do with medical health—are far more tightly governed by the guiding concerns appropriate to her role as a doctor. The agent acting within a professional role is guided by a quite narrow and determinate scope of concerns that are constitutive of the proper performance of the role, and it is within the prism provided by this scope that they act, for example, as a lawyer who is loyal to the *legal* interests of her client or the doctor who is loyal to the patient in the promotion of her health.

Parental roles, on the other hand, may involve a loyalty to, and loving concern for, the interest and well-being of the child, which, unlike the professional roles cases and more like the friendship case, is quite global in scope. And so the potential for conflict with other moral considerations seems similarly broad. The parent, like the friend, may neglect some other obligation in a wide range of cases where the child's interests are at stake; for example, he might take the child on a picnic or to the museum rather than attend an important meeting of the Oxfam committee because he sees the child is miserable and in need of attention. However, the way in which the altruistic disposition is expressed in the parent's case is nevertheless much more clearly governed by social and moral imperatives than it is in friendship. It is closer to the professional case than it may first appear. Let us return to the case, flagged earlier, of telling a lie for the other. We have argued elsewhere that it is a commonplace that friends will tell small and sometimes large lies for each other.[5] So I might ring your boss for you and say you are ill when in fact you just need more time to complete a report. It may similarly be in a child's interests for the parent to tell a lie for her and say she is ill, when in fact the child needs a day at home to complete a school assignment. Now sometimes, the parent may, like the friend, act directly out of her loving concern and affection in going against some moral precept or requirement. But the parent will be rightly more concerned than the friend about the example she sets the child in telling a lie or the effect on the child's character of being permitted to evade the consequences of her tardiness. In the end the parent may decide that the lie is justified—perhaps the teacher is too severe in such cases, and the child's confidence will suffer unacceptably from public criticism. However, to count as a good parent, one's actions must substantially be governed by the moral requirements of the role. A good friend may tell such a lie without any all-things-considered moral justification for doing so. Typically friends tell such lies for each other without any moral deliberation at all.

The second kind of contrast case mentioned above further illustrates how immoral actions that might be well within the scope of good and close friendship would, in other contexts, constitute striking examples of role violation. Close friends sometimes act against some moral claim or consideration, not out of any laudable altruistic concern for the friend's welfare—a concern that some advocates of role morality might want to endorse (and some impartialists might claim to have accounted for)—but simply out of their interest in the friend's interests, *qua* friend. Friends are to some extent disposed to place themselves at moral risk in acting with and for each other, and friendship can give rise to reasons that cannot even indirectly be sourced in a moral system, whether construed in an impartialist or role-based way. One illustration of the fact that we do ordinarily think that good and close friendship can, to some extent or in certain ways, be morally subversive is that, in a friendship involving some clear moral bads, we nevertheless have no difficulty in recognizing the uncontroversial goods of friendship, such as the intimate affection, caring, and concern to help one another that exists between friends, and we find nothing odd about such a juxtaposition. Examples of this juxtaposition of good friendship and morally bad action abound in film. In the recent Australian movie *Two Hands*, two street kids display obvious love, loyalty, and protective concern for each other. In the course of expressing that concern they commit theft, assault, and finally murder when one avenges the other's death by obtaining an illegal handgun and shooting several local criminals. Or consider the movie *The Sting*, in which the protagonists engage in an illegal card game and trick the other players out of the winnings. Their actions are hardly morally exemplary, but movie-goers do not typically use this fact to argue that they cannot, after all, be the good and close friends they appear to be.[6] Their immoral actions are seen as perfectly compatible with their being good and close friends and indeed it would appear that their friendship provided them with additional reasons to stick with the plan. But movie-goers are equally unlikely to conclude that because their actions were well within the scope of good friendship they were thereby *morally* justified.

Now consider how we would respond if it were a lawyer suggesting to his client that they set up such a sting. Here it is manifest that the lawyer does not act as a good lawyer in suggesting such a thing to his client or helping him carry it out. He does not act as a lawyer at all, and his use of his position of influence and violation of professional boundaries seem particularly disgraceful. Here, it is true, the lawyer suggests something illegal and not just immoral to his client, but would our judgment be any different if he suggested a visit to a strip club or asked the client to cover for him with his wife? Good friends may ask such things without violating the status of their relationship, but good lawyers never can. Similarly, the parent, if she is to act appropriately within her role, ought not to engage in or encourage morally dubious activities, such as gambling or cruel witticisms, with a child, though she might with a friend. Good parents do not encourage or gloss over their children's minor vices. As a good parent I might be moved to curb a wild or reckless streak in my son that I would celebrate in a friend. Again, consider how commonly parents assess their children's friendships through a prism of protective moral concern that they would not consider applying to other friendships, including their own. So, while I enjoy *my* friend's wild streak, I try to discourage my son's friendship with his reckless sidekick.

Let us now provide some more formal analysis of these contrasts between the ways in which different roles and relations provide reasons to act against some accepted moral requirements, by comparing more closely the nature and governing conditions of friendship with the nature and governing conditions of these other familiar social and professional roles.

Minimally and Maximally Structured Relationships

Laurence Thomas claims that social interaction is "on a continuum with respect to being structured. At one end we have maximally structured social interaction, where the interaction of the parties in question is highly governed by the social roles they occupy; at the other end we have minimally structured social interaction where how the parties interact is not primarily a function of social roles."[7] Thomas claims, and we agree, that close friendship is a paradigmatically minimally structured relationship where the nature of the interaction is not defined by a set of social rules, so the parties to the relationship could agree to all sorts of arrangements without changing the nature of the relationship.[8] As Marilyn Friedman says, "No particular people are assigned by custom or tradition to be a person's friend": friendship "receives far less formal recognition in our rituals and conventions, including legal conventions, than do familial relationships and is maintained by fewer of those formalities."[9] Neither are any formal qualifications required to enter into friendship. Friendship is voluntary, egalitarian, and *open-ended* in a way that these other social and professional relations are not.

This points to a very significant structural difference between friendship and the other relations and roles we have considered. Whereas the parent, like the friend, has strong attachments of love and affection to the other and as a result a highly particularized concern for the other, the parent-child interaction is nevertheless governed to a very high degree by the legal, conventional, social, and moral expectations attached to the parental role. In this respect the parental role is more like some of the professional roles we have considered, such as the doctor's role with regard to her patients, than it is to friendship.

In distinguishing the more structured professional and parental roles from friendship it will be helpful to highlight a distinctive kind of interaction that occurs between close friends and compare this to its counterpart in these other relations and roles. We have argued elsewhere that a process of mutual drawing, involving an interaction of reciprocal direction and interpretation between friends, is a key distinctive and constitutive feature of close friendship. Let us briefly explain what we mean by this.

All accounts of the nature of close friendship agree that such things as mutual affection, trust, loyalty, and the disposition to promote the other's serious interests and well-being are necessary constituents of the relationship. But as we have noted, many of these agent-relative features are also features of other roles, especially familial roles. They do not by themselves provide an account of the kind of engagement with the other that is distinctive of close or companion friendships. In our view, what does provide an important marker of the nature of close friendship is that close friends are especially receptive to being directed and interpreted and so in these ways *drawn* by each other.

Thus, as a close friend of another I am atypically disposed to be directed by her in our shared activities. At her suggestion I play in a card game or try a new cuisine. She comes bushwalking and to the theater with me. I might also be disposed, at her suggestion, to take up more long-term projects that I have previously had no interest in. I might for example, try to acquire a taste for red wine or take up windsurfing because she enjoys those things. My reasons for action where she is concerned do not depend on any contingent similarity of interests, neither are they derivative on other personal, moral, or professional commitments. In the case that my close friend's interests diverge from mine, her interests continue to have action-guiding force for me, since in friendship it is her interests *as such* that are important, not her interests viewed through the prism provided, say, by my moral or professional concerns. I might not necessarily be directed by her interest to, for example, try to acquire a taste for red wine, but it is a commonplace that within friendship something's being the friend's interest can in itself provide me with reason to pursue that something in a way that, for example, my boss's interests do not.

A second significant feature of close friendship is the way in which friends contribute to each other's self-conception. Close friends often recognize and highlight aspects of one another's character; they often accept such interpretations from one another; and their self-conception is often changed and enriched by seeing themselves through their friend's eyes. Through your interpretations of me I may come to see myself as generous, impulsive, clumsy, or funny, and my evaluation of these characteristics is also influenced by your responses. I may become more confident in making witty comments, or less embarrassed and more inclined to make a joke of my clumsiness than formerly.

Close friends, then, have a mutual atypical receptivity to each other's suggestions and interpretations and are provided, through the friendship, with reasons not shared by others. This drawing of each other is a dynamic and ongoing process, which progressively shapes and defines the particular relationship between the two friends and makes it distinct in character from other friendships that they each may have. As Friedman says, "Voluntariness in friendship seems to require, overall, a measure of roughly equal and mutual adaptation, a synergism achieved through the combined and mutually inter-ested adjustments of those who are becoming, or are already friends."[10] Mutual drawing is the way in which this adjustment is achieved. The friends, in so shaping their relationship, and in being shaped by it, are responsive, not to a set of social or conventional norms, which they take to have some governing force over their interactions, but directly to each other. The drawing engaged in within any particular friendship is not therefore directed to the achievement of some formal goal of friendship; often it is not goal directed in any determinate sense. However this mutual receptivity to the other is crucial to the *intimacy* of close friendship and is thus crucial to the value that friendship ordinarily has for us.

The place of direction and interpretation in friendship, as we have outlined it, is in clear contrast to the ways direction and interpretation may feature in other relations and roles. We will now illustrate this contrast and show how this asymmetry between friendship and other relations and roles we might occupy underwrites our claims about the ways in which moral conflicts arising out of the latter should be understood.

In the other personal and professional roles and relations we consider, the nature of the interaction between parties is quite strictly governed by the consti-tutive ends or goals of the role, as is evidenced by the fact that such interaction ceases or loses its point once those goals have been met. So, for example, teach-ers do not insist that students continue to attend class and submit assignments after they have graduated, nor would they feel any obligation to grade work submitted by former students. And though one does not cease altogether to be a parent once one's children have reached maturity and independence, one's role does, appropriately, change.

In these roles, the drawing process is highly limited and specific in scope. It may be part of the doctor's role to provide some direction and interpretation to the patient within the boundaries of the professional consultation. He may, for example, note that the patient seems highly stressed and that this might be contributing to her migraine attacks and suggest to her some techniques for controlling stress. In discussing her stress with her he may increase her self-knowledge and make some contribution to her self-conception, just as a friend might do. His patient is in these circumstances appropriately receptive and responsive to the doctor's direction. He may not, however, comment on her taste in clothes or recommend a sexy perfume to her without violating his role boundaries. It is not merely that the doctor has no special expertise in matters of fashion that makes direction and interpretation here inappropriate (the friend might not have either). It is rather that the subject matter here is altogether irrelevant to the concerns a doctor *qua* doctor might appropriately have toward his patients. Even if, as it happens, one's doctor is something of a fashion expert his advice here is not a relevant aspect of his role as your doctor.

In addition to the limitations on the *scope* of direction and interpretation within professional practice there is also a restriction on who may engage in it. The patient is not free to engage in directing the doctor, even on matters of his health. If she attempts to do so her efforts will likely misfire. Insofar as the doctor is guided by his professional role he will not respond. Insofar as he does respond and takes on her interpretations or follows her direction they have changed the nature of the relationship between them. *Mutual* direction and interpretation is simply not a feature of professional/client relationships. It is certainly no part of any ideal conception of such relationships.

Now consider familial relations. The parent/child relationship contains a great deal of direction and interpretation and unlike the professional case it is not obviously limited in scope. But that does not mean that this relationship is more like friendship in being less structured and conventional. For notice that here too the drawing is overwhelmingly one way. Parents shape their children through their interpretations of them and through determining and directing their activities. Their interpretations of the child are, for the most part, seen by the child as authoritative. The child's capacity to shape her parent's self-interpretations is limited and perhaps fortunately so. We don't want parents to take their child's accusations of meanness or unfairness when they don't get that expensive new toy too seriously. This lack of mutuality, however, imposes particular obligations on the parent to use his influence and inordinate power over the child's self-conception and character in the child's best interests. And this obligation also arises in professional settings, such as medical, counselling, or educational settings, where the direction and interpretation that takes place lacks mutuality.

Notice too that though the drawing the parent engages in is broad in scope, it is properly constrained and guided by what we might think of as the particular goals or ends of parenthood, just as the doctor's drawing of the patient must be guided by the goals of medicine. Insofar as being a parent is a social and moral, and not merely biological, role, one of the constitutive goals of parenting must be to enable one's child to take her place as a morally responsive and responsible member of the community. The good parent aims at promoting and protecting the child's physical, emotional, and moral welfare, and this imposes a tight structure on the way in which direction and interpretation can proceed.

Direction and interpretation in these settings is not, therefore, likely to give rise to reasons that run counter to moral requirements since it is strictly governed by goals that themselves serve important moral ends. And insofar as these roles do generate reasons that might justify acting against a legitimate moral claim, such reasons seem themselves sourced in some conflicting moral goal. This is not the case for close friendship. Direction and interpretation in friendship can give rise to reasons which lie outside of morality and can do so precisely because it is not here constitutively constrained by social or moral convention. Indeed, commitment to one's friend is in tension with being strictly governed by a commitment to moral principles. Friedman says:

> Partiality for a friend involves being motivated by the friend as an individual, by who she is and not by the principled commitments of one's own which her circumstances happen to instantiate. . . . For one's response clearly to reflect a commitment to another person in her particularity, as such, it must be prompted, at least in part, by a readiness to act on her behalf . . . even when one's general moral values and principles do not support such action.[11]

We agree with Friedman that an overriding commitment to abstract moral guidelines may interfere with a commitment to the friend as such. We further believe that it is not the case that friendship can be governed to any great degree by a set of role-specific moral guidelines which mark out appropriate conduct, for these too may interfere with the commitment to the person as such.

Our argument here and elsewhere, then, is that the justifications from friendship for acting against moral claims need not themselves be moral justifications. The challenge that friendship poses is thus to the *overridingness* of morality *per se*. Other role-based conflicts we have considered do not pose this fundamental challenge. Rather, they raise questions regarding the proper interpretation of the *requirements* of one's role, or the proper source of moral *authority* for one's actions. Are role-based moral considerations to be authoritative, or, are impartialist requirements to be decisive in cases of conflict between the two? We have not attempted to give any complete answer to this question. What we seek to show is that the conflict between friendship and morality cannot be defused by a move to role-based morality and that the account we give of such conflicts in the friendship case is not transferable to these other structurally dissimilar roles.

Conclusion

The disposition to take on and respond to a friend's interpretations and to, in concert with the friend, shape and refine one's self-conception is crucial to the intimacy and particularity of friendship. But a clear consequence of being open to and engaging in mutual direction and interpretation in this way is that one exposes oneself to various risks. Indeed it does not seem possible to gain the great benefits of intimacy in friendship without also exposing oneself to various risks. There is risk of the pain of losing the other, of one's openness, vulnerability, and trust being betrayed, and there is also moral danger, which we have focused on: the risk of being led morally astray both out of concern *for* the friend's interests and *by* their interests. Good and true friendship, unlike ideal professional roles or ideal parent-child relations, is, of its nature, distinctively morally subversive and so especially problematic for the project of interpreting conflicts between friendship and some other moral considerations as conflicts only *within*, and not against, morality. As such, friendship, and the ways in which it might license acting against certain moral considerations, does not provide a particularly helpful or accurate model for how we should understand moral conflicts from agency within professional and other familiar social roles.

Notes

1. See James F. Drane, *Becoming a Good Doctor: The Place of Virtue and Character in Medical Ethics* (Kansas City: Sheed & Ward, 1988); Charles Fried, *Medical Experimentation: Personal Integrity and Social Policy* (Amsterdam: North Holland Publishing Company, 1974), 76; and Charles Fried, "The Lawyer as Friend: The Moral Foundations of the Lawyer Client Relationship," *Yale Law Journal* 85 (1976): 1060–89.

2. See Dean Cocking and Jeanette Kennett, "Friendship and the Self," *Ethics* 108 (1998): 502–27, and Dean Cocking and Jeanette Kennett, "Friendship and Moral Danger," *Journal of Philosophy* 97 (2000): 278–96.

3. Here, there will be some cases where we think the altruistic concern shown to promote the interest of either one's friend or one's child provides moral license for overriding the conflicting moral claim. There will be cases where we think it does not over-ride the moral claim for either the friend or the parent. And, in yet other cases, we may find dissimilarities in the judgments we would make of the moral departures directed by friendship and parent-child relations.

4. This is a live issue for doctors who often claim a conflict of interest if they are required to balance their own patient's interests against the need to conserve the health care dollar. They may claim then that though the medical profession and the health system as a whole exists to serve the end of human health, different players in the system have different contributions to make to that good end. Just resource allocation is best secured by administrators and triage staff in hospitals who remain at arm's length from individual patients and so can adopt an impartialist perspective on their relative needs. Treating doctors, on the other hand, should act out of agent-relative concerns for their own patient's interests. Whether this argument works may be debatable. It remains the case, however, that if the doctor is justified in acting out of agent-relative concerns and against some impartial moral concern, his justification comes from the proper requirements of his role as a GP in achieving the goal of health.

5. Cocking and Kennett, "Friendship and Moral Danger."

6. One might claim here that while this might be true, it would be a better friendship were one to have the goods without the bads. However, first, whether or not one also has the bads is importantly a contingent matter of circumstantial luck, and second, the reason for this is that, as we go on to argue in the next section, it is in the nature of friendship that one is atypically disposed to be drawn by the other in ways well beyond one's own antecedent values and interests. Thus, since friendship necessarily involves this dispositional openness to the influence of the other, it is not only an unrealistic view of friendship to think one might have the goods but never the bads, but also an incoherent one. The nature of friendship unavoidably involves the risk that one might get involved in activities or ways of relating that are morally objectionable and so it is to some significant extent a matter of contingent luck whether or not one's friendships turn out this way.

7. Lawrence Thomas, "Friendship and Other Loves," in *Friendship: a Philosophical Reader*, ed. Neera Kapur Badhwar (Ithaca, NY: Cornell University Press 1993), 50.

8. Thomas makes the caveat that such arrangements must not violate any moral precepts, a point with which we disagree. There are of course moral reasons for not violating the precepts, but, as we have argued elsewhere (Cocking and Kennett, "Friendship and Moral Danger"), the bare fact that we violate some moral precept in the course of our friendship does not of itself impinge upon the status of the relationship as being one of close friendship.

9. Marilyn Friedman, *What Are Friends For?* (Ithaca, NY: Cornell University Press, 1993), 208–9.

10. *Ibid.*, p. 211.

11. *Ibid.*, p. 192.

Pluralism and Moral Authority

6

John Kekes

Much has been written about political authority, but moral authority is a neglected topic in contemporary thought. The purpose of this paper is to argue that its neglect is unjustified because moral authority is a reasonable, important, and ubiquitous feature of moral life, even in a pluralistic society. The argument proceeds by discussing authority in general, then focusing on moral authority, then considering the qualifications that make those who possess them into moral authorities, and finally offering a justification for relying on moral authorities by explaining why they are needed in a pluralistic society.

Authority in General

Discussions of authority tend to go wrong from the beginning. They start with considering authority, and then, usually without notice or excuse, switch to the consideration of political authority. This tendency is shown equally by those who regret its loss and wish to shore it up,[1] by those who deny its legitimacy,[2] and by those who want to defend some suitably circumscribed and attenuated version of it.[3] They all assume that authority is a relation in which the authority makes those subject to it conduct themselves as the authority directs. The authority is thus thought to have a power, which it uses to get people to do things that they would not do if it were not for the power the authority has over them. Opinions vary across the political spectrum as to the legitimacy of the power that authorities have and use, but they all respond to the supposed tension succinctly expressed as follows: "The defining mark of the state is authority, the right to rule. The primary obligation of man is autonomy, the refusal to be ruled. . . . Insofar as a man fulfills his obligation to make himself the author of his decisions, he will resist the state's claim to have authority over him."[4] The standard discussion thus begins with a suspicion of authority, and it goes on to consider how far the suspicion is justified.

The trouble with this approach to understanding authority is that it leaves no room for the thought that authorities are individuals, not states or other political units, and that what makes someone an authority is experience and good judgment, rather than power. That this approach got it wrong is made obvious by the fact that the everyday lives of most people are permeated with various relations in which they seek out, willingly follow, and regard themselves as lost without authorities. These attitudes need not be unreasonable, craven, bamboozled, indoctrinated, or intellectually or morally slothful. That this is so becomes obvious if some of the prevalent forms of authority are recognized as more reasonable starting points than the exclusive concentration on political authority. Such forms are the relations between parents and children, teachers and students, physicians and patients, coaches and athletes, lawyers and clients, directors and actors, masters and disciples, established practitioners in a field and beginners, clergymen and the faithful, experienced old friends and inexperienced young ones, management consultants and floundering firms, superiors and subordinates in the army, police, religious orders, and other hierarchical organizations, plumbers and homeowners, judges and juries, mentors and advisees, umpires and competitors, editors and authors, pilots and passengers, and so forth. Given these forms of authority, the idea that reason and morality dictate resistance to them must be seen as perverse. To be sure, authorities may be phoney rather than genuine, and then it would be folly to do as they say. But if an authority truly is one and if people rely on it to help them to do something that they have difficulty with doing on their own, then folly is to fail to do as they say.

The right question to ask therefore is how to tell real from spurious authorities, rather than the politically inspired one of why reasonable people would subject themselves to authorities. The wrong question, however, has dominated discussions of authority: "There has been a remarkable coalescence of opinion around the proposition that authority and authority relations involve some species of 'surrender of judgment' on the part of those who accept, submit or subscribe to the authority of persons or a set of rules or offices."[5]

The attempt to understand authority through the notion of the surrender of judgment is highly misleading. It stresses submission, subordination, and the abandonment of responsibility. It implies that the recognition of authority is demeaning, detrimental to self-respect, and that people with integrity and courage would reject it. And then one should ask how this fits people who recognize the authority of their parents, teachers, older friends, physicians, mentors, or plumbers? The recognition of authorities may be unreasonable, but only if they are unnecessary or unsuccessful. If they are genuine authorities, however, then they respond to the needs of those who turn to them. Their recognition in that case does not merit suspicion. The question is whether those who recognize an authority are in need of it and whether the authority they recognize is genuine. This is why the salient fact about authority relations is whether it is reasonable to recognize the supposed authority as such, and not the fact that those who recognize it have surrendered their judgment. People often turn to authorities precisely because they cannot rely on their judgment: they do not know how to judge some complex situation, they distrust their own judgment, or they feel the need to reconcile the conflicting judgments of other people.

In trying to arrive at a better understanding of the nature of authority, it is necessary to start by distinguishing between a descriptive and a normative approach. The descriptive one is a historical, sociological, or anthropological inquiry about what authorities are recognized in some particular context and what reasons are given in that context for regarding the authorities as such. The normative approach aims to discover whether these reasons are good. The normative approach presupposes the descriptive one, and the two often go together, but they are nevertheless different because they aim to answer different questions.

Continuing then with the discussion of authority in general, but with the qualification that the discussion is normative, not merely descriptive, it is useful to distinguish between *de facto* and *de jure* authorities.[6] A *de facto* authority is one who is actually recognized as an authority in a particular context. *De facto* authorities, however, may or may not have official status. Authorities that have official status are *de jure*. They derive their status from some formal procedure, training, rule, institution, or custom which gives them the right to exercise authority. *De facto* authorities may or may not be *de jure*, and *vice versa*. During his presidency, Bill Clinton had *de jure*, but increasingly less *de facto*, authority, whereas Hillary Clinton, as gossip had it, had *de facto*, but not *de jure* authority.

Both *de facto* and *de jure* authorities may be legitimate or not. *De facto* authorities are legitimate if people have good reasons to recognize them as such. Legitimate *de facto* authorities not only exercise authority, but they also possess the qualifications necessary for it. Similarly, the legitimacy of *de jure* authorities derives not merely from the fact that the method by which the status is conferred has been followed in their case, but also from the additional fact that the method is successful in identifying those who ought to be in a position of authority.

Many legitimate authorities have no official standing because their status is not conferred on them by any formal method. Friends, mentors, teachers, religious, financial, aesthetic, literary, or mechanical advisers may be legitimate *de facto* authorities, without being *de jure* ones. One reason why thinking about authority in political terms leads to misunderstanding is that in politics legitimate authority is *de jure*. If political authority is thought to be the model for all authority, then, if an authority is *de facto* without being *de jure*, the suspicion naturally arises that it is illegitimate. If the suspicion could be allayed only by identifying and justifying the formal method by which the status has been conferred on them, then *de facto* authorities could not be legitimate. The reasonable alternative, however, is not to take political authority as the model and to recognize that the legitimacy of *de facto* and *de jure* authorities is established in different ways.

A further distinction will help to understand better what is involved in an authority being legitimate. The distinction between being *an* authority and being *in* authority.[7] Being *in* authority is being in a position that carries authority with it. Those who are in that position are necessarily *in* authority. The position may be *de jure*, such as that of an elected official, or it may be *de facto*, like that of a mentor. Being *an* authority is to possess qualifications which make the judgments of the authority better than the judgments of other people. But an authority may or may not be in authority, because the comparative excellence of the authority's judgment may lack either *de facto* or *de jure* acknowledgment. A person thus may be an authority and not be recognized as such. The ideal case is when the person who is in authority has that position in virtue of being an authority. In that case, the authority is legitimate because the status and the qualifications required for it coincide.

The ideal case, of course, often fails to obtain. A person may be an authority, but not be in authority; and the person in authority may not be an authority. If the suspicion of authority is based on thinking that the person in authority is not really an authority, then it deserves to be taken seriously. But if there is good reason to think that the two coincide, then suspicion is misplaced and the judgments of the person in authority should be accepted. It must be added, by way of caution, that, even in the ideal case, authority holds only in a particular context and in some particular respect. It is an illegitimate use of authority to exercise it beyond its proper sphere. Once again, however, if the authority is exercised in the appropriate context and respect, then it is legitimate and it ought to be recognized as such.

The nature and legitimacy of different forms of authority vary with the context and the respect in which they are candidates for recognition. Their legitimacy varies because their contexts determine who should recognize them. The legitimate authority of an older friend, a music critic, and a president has different scopes. Authorities are authorities for a specifiable range of people who are their potential subjects. Their nature also varies because the respects in which they are supposed to hold sway are determined by the different qualifications that make people authorities.

In trying to understand the necessary qualifications, it is crucial to bear in mind that the topic is considered normatively, not descriptively. The question is not what qualifications make people recognize an authority as legitimate, but what qualifications make an authority legitimate. The descriptive question is answered if it is explained why people recognize someone as an authority. The normative question is answered if it is explained why people ought to recognize someone as an authority. The attempt to answer the descriptive question must begin with the distinction between three ideal types of authority: traditional, rational-legal, and charismatic.[8] Much has been written about this,[9] but it is irrelevant to the present question, which is the normative one.

When people recognize an authority, they do not so much surrender their judgment, but rather realize that they do not know how to judge or that their judgment is defective, and that the authority's judgment is better than what they could arrive at on their own. As it has been perspicuously put:

> He who accepts authority accepts as a sufficient reason for acting or believing something the fact that he has been so instructed by someone whose claim to do so he acknowledges. . . . It is to act or believe not on the balance of reasons, but rather on the basis of a second-order reason that precisely requires that one disregard the balance of reasons as one sees it. Likewise, to exercise authority is precisely not to have to offer reasons, but to be obeyed or believed because one has a recognized claim to be.[10]

There are countless cases in which it is reasonable to accept authority in this sense and in which it would be unreasonable not to do so. In these cases, people need to form some belief and/or perform some action, but they are confused or uncertain about what the belief or action should be, they realize this about themselves, and they have good reason to follow the direction of someone else. In this manner, a student may accept a teacher's authority about how to understand a difficult work, a patient may accept a physician's authority about what medication to take, a novice may accept an experienced practitioner's authority about when routine operations have become so defective as to require not reform but drastic change, and a young person may accept an older friend's authority about the advisability of turning down a lucrative job offer because it would be corrupting. In all these cases, the authorities have reasons for their judgment. These reasons can be stated, explained, and argued for. They are capable of what has been aptly called "reasoned elaboration."[11] But the people who accept the authority's judgment are not in the position to appreciate the reasons or elaborations. They are confused and uncertain because they lack the qualifications that the authority has. The reasons support the authority's judgment, but their significance, weight, and contestability are not available to the people.

The legitimacy of authority depends on its qualifications. People are reasonable in recognizing authorities if they have good reasons to believe that they possess the necessary qualifications. These reasons, of course, cannot be derived by people from a direct evaluation of the authority's qualifications, since for that they would already have to have the qualifications which they *ex hypothesi* lack. But the reasons can be derived indirectly by considering such matters as the authorities' official status, if they have one, their reputation, the success or failure of their past judgments, and so forth.

This way of thinking about the qualifications that make an authority legitimate is derived from the private realm in which one individual recognizes the authority of another. Not all authority relations, however, are like these. There are also public, especially political, authorities whose qualifications need not involve any particular personal excellence. Their qualifications derive simply from the procedure that is followed in placing them in a position of authority. The reason for having public authorities of this kind is to cope with what has been called the "coordination problem." That problem is to impose order and predictability on the otherwise chaotic actions of people living together in populous societies. Someone has to decide what forms contracts should take, when elections are to be held, what days are holidays, where public buildings should be built, and so on. If public authorities of this sort perform their tasks competently and if their status is conferred on them by the appropriate procedure, then they too are legitimate and it is reasonable to recognize them as such.

In conclusion, it may then be said that authorities in general may or may not be legitimate. Their legitimacy depends on their qualifications. If people lack the qualifications an authority has and if they need to make judgments about beliefs and actions to which the qualifications are relevant, then they are reasonable in accepting the authority's judgment in place of their own. If these conditions are met, there is nothing intellectually or morally questionable in recognizing someone else's authority over oneself. If suspicion of authority is motivated simply by a desire to make sure that a putative authority has the qualifications that make it legitimate, it is a healthy attitude. But if the suspicion is based on the very nature of authority relations, then it is groundless.

The Nature of Moral Authority

If authority is the genus, then moral authority is a species. There has not been much written on the latter.[12] The characteristics of moral authority vary with historical and social contexts, but the discussion will concentrate on moral authority in the context of a pluralistic society. The salient feature of such a society is that there neither is nor is it thought that there ought to be a single generally recognized moral authority in it. At other times and in other kinds of societies, the pope, the king, the party leader, the oracle, the elder, the president, and so forth may have been publicly recognized moral authorities, but times have changed. There still are moral authorities of course, but they are many, not one, and they tend not to be public, but private. Moral authority relations hold between individuals, and even if the authorities happen to have some official status, that is not what gives them authority.

Legitimate moral authorities are *in* authority because they are *an* authority. What makes them so is that they possess the appropriate qualifications. Since pluralistic moral authority relations tend to be private, moral authorities tend to be *de facto*, not *de jure*. The latter requires some formal method to confer the status of authority, but in private relationships there is no such method. One individual may recognize the moral authority of another, but the recognition is a personal matter based on the belief that the authority possesses the relevant qualifications. This belief, of course, may or may not be justified. If it is justified, then the moral authority is legitimate and it is reasonable to recognize it as such.

To understand what moral authorities do, consider an account of one occasion on which Confucius exercises moral authority:

> we read of the Master teaching a return to the purity and sincerity of the ancient ceremonies. He deplores superstition and the mere outward observance of forms. Then Tzu-kung (Zigong), one of the disciples, asks about the monthly ceremony at which the new moon is announced. . . . Would it not be better, he queries, if the practice of sacrificing sheep were done away with? Confucius reproves him gently. He calls him by his familiar name. "Ssu (Si)," he says, "You care for the sheep. I care for the ceremony."[13]

This story reveals several significant features of moral authority. First, Confucius responds to a question that is put to him. He speaks because he was asked. He does not issue a command, impose his will, or tell Zigong what he should do. He rather shows how he, Confucius, thinks about the matter. There is, to be sure, the clear suggestion that Confucius's way of thinking is better than Zigong's, but let that go for the moment. Second, in thinking as he does Confucius mediates between the moral tradition that both he and Zigong recognize as their own and the moral problem that Zigong raises. Confucius then thinks about the problem in the light of the shared tradition in the background. Third, in Confucius's opinion, the tradition is defective because the significance of ancient ceremonies has been lost and they have become empty forms. Zigong's problem arises precisely because of this defect in the tradition. The ceremonies used to mark important occasions in the lives of people who belong to the tradition, but they no longer do that. An important part of their moral identity, therefore, has been lost. They are impoverished in the same way as Christians are who think of Christmas without religious sentiments or as Americans are who think of Fourth of July without patriotic feelings. It may be, of course, that the religiosity and patriotism would be misplaced, but there is no doubt that even if that were so, it would be a serious loss for those in whose lives they used to be significant values. Fourth, the question Zigong is asking is difficult. There is no simple solution to the problem of how to cope with the defects that people recognize in their own moral tradition. Should they reaffirm the old values that are being violated or should they seek to replace them with new values that reflect changing circumstances? Answering that question requires understanding both the moral tradition and the new circumstances, judging the importance of the old values, and weighing whether the possible new values would be adequate substitutes for the old ones. It is not to be expected that most people, kept busy by the demands of their lives, would have the understanding, judgment, and sense of proportion, as well as the inclination, time, and seriousness, to ask and answer these questions. That is why they need a moral authority.

Consider now why and how moral authorities mediate between their moral tradition and some particular problematic case. The chief reason why the mediation of moral authorities is needed is that the knowledge that most people in a moral tradition can be expected to have has become insufficient. As a result, they cannot rely on their moral intuitions. They encounter an increasing number of situations in which the simple connection between a hitherto morally acceptable variable convention and a particular case that clearly falls under it has been broken. The case is there and it is pressing for evaluation and response, but it is unclear how it ought to be seen.

Is the sacrifice of sheep just an act of cruelty? Is it a waste of livestock? Is it a hypocritical show of piety? Is it a stalwart adherence to old values in a changing world? There is no intuitively persuasive answer because the old convention governing the sacrifice is no longer generally observed. So people do not know whether they should evaluate the sacrifice of sheep according to some other convention, or whether they should continue to stick to the old one that is falling into desuetude, or whether they should just do as they please because the case no longer falls under the jurisdiction of any convention. What is happening is that their moral identity has been changing. In a particular area of their lives their intuitions have become unreliable, and they feel uncertain in their moral outlook. Their situation is not unlike that of contemporary Americans with respect to marriage. It is called into question by secularization, countless people living together without marriage, the frequency of divorce, single-parent families, and homosexual unions. It is in just such cases that individuals need moral authorities to help them evaluate the situations they face in the no longer clear light of their moral tradition.

In order to answer the question of how moral authorities provide the needed help, it is important to remember that they offer a judgment, not a command. They do not say: do this, rather than that; they say: if you look at the situation in this way, then it will become clear to you what you should do. Their judgment is not a decision, which they hand down, but an interpretation of a complex situation formed of a particular case, conventions of uncertain relevance, and the moral tradition itself. Do not think of the sheep, says Confucius, think of the ceremony. What really matters, he suggests, is that human lives should be meaningful, not the life expectancy of sheep or the money that it takes. Or, as it might be said in response to current uncertainties about marriage, what matters is that people should form lasting intimate relationships with one another, that they should face the world together, that they should be united by love, appreciation, and delight in each other. To focus on whether they can or cannot have children, whether their relationship is sexual, whether their sexual relationship takes one form or another is to misjudge what is important. The judgments of moral authorities are based on an appreciation of their moral tradition that is deeper than what other people have, and on their ability to see through the complexities that bedevil others.

The Qualifications of a Moral Authority

The judgments of moral authorities are better because they possess qualifications that people who solicit their judgments lack. The first of these qualifications is a thorough familiarity with the conventions of the moral tradition and considerable experience and skill in evaluating particular cases by subsuming them under the appropriate conventions. For the sake of brevity, this may be described as knowledge of the moral tradition. It should be understood, however, that the knowledge is both factual, involving knowledge of the conventions, and practical, having to do with the application of the conventions. It is, moreover, moral knowledge because its subject matter is living a good life, as it is understood in a particular moral tradition. The tradition is assumed to be pluralistic, so the moral knowledge will be of one or few of a large number of morally acceptable conceptions of a good life. The more pluralistic a tradition is, the less likely it is that there will be moral authorities whose knowledge ranges over all the morally acceptable conceptions of a good life in the tradition. Pluralistic moral authority is likely to be confined to specific conceptions, such as those involved in artistic or academic life, business, politics, the training of athletes, criminal justice, scientific research, social work, or news reporting.

This knowledge is not particularly hard to acquire. Experience and continued participation in a way of life are normally sufficient for it. People who possess it know how to distinguish between simple and complex, routine and controversial, banal and surprising cases. They know what it is to treat someone in that context fairly or unfairly, harshly or indulgently, generously or meanly. They know what counts as negligence, scrupulousness, diligence, efficiency, or going beyond the call of duty. They know when they can trust their intuitions and when they have to stop and think. They are in general experienced practitioners who are skilled in applying the vocabulary of their moral tradition to evaluate relevant conduct. Anyone with sufficient motivation, moderate ability, and long enough practice will meet this elementary, but by no means sufficient, requirement of moral authority.

That this kind of knowledge is not sufficient for moral authority becomes obvious once it is seen that its possession is compatible with the rejection of or indifference to the moral tradition. Anthropologists studying the society, hypocrites living in it, and wicked people violating it whenever they can may all be familiar with the conventions and be skilled in mediating between the tradition and complex cases. They may know what the moral tradition prescribes, but they do not accept its prescriptions. They may act according to them, but only because expediency dictates it.

It is necessary therefore to add a second qualification required for being a moral authority: commitment to the moral tradition. People who are committed do not just know what the conventions are and how to apply them in complex situations, they also believe that they ought to live and act according to them, and they endeavor so to live and act. Such people do not merely know what conceptions of life are regarded as good in a moral tradition, they also think that they really are good. This, however, is still insufficient for moral authority because much depends on the manner in which the knowledge and commitment are acquired and acted upon. They may just reflect a rigorous moral education in the course of which people's minds and hearts are so thoroughly influenced as to make it impossible for them to regard any other moral tradition or basic dissension from their own as a live option for themselves. They know of course that other people at other places follow different conventions and have different commitments, but they know it only intellectually. There are cannibals, samurai, shamans, men with harems, and women with bordellos, but what has that got to do with them? They are immersed in their lives, they have no doubts about their moral tradition, what they can spare of their intellect and emotions for moral purposes is fully engaged in it, they see the world from its perspective, and, in so far as they are morally motivated, their motivation has no contrary sources.

It is much easier to sustain this attitude in an absolutistic than in a pluralistic moral tradition. But even in an absolutistic one, the prevailing moral tradition, with its one or few approved conceptions of a good life, is bound to be challenged by the failure of many people to follow the conventions. Evil is an unignorable feature of all moral traditions, and its existence and prevalence raise questions that cry out for an answer. If the countenanced conceptions of life are good, then why do so many people live in violation of them? If they so live, how could it be that they often flourish? And why are good lives so difficult and chancy? Why is it that living decently and reasonably according to the conventions often fails to result in a good life?

To these questions, which will be asked in any moral tradition, others will be added, if the tradition is pluralistic. For if pluralism prevails, competing conceptions of a good life will be spatially and temporarily contiguous, and thus evident in everyone's life. People do not then have to go far afield to see others live in ways that cannot but appear as challenges to their own. It is therefore not only the prevalence of evil, but also moral possibilities other than what they have adopted that will pose questions to most people. Moral authorities ought to be able to give convincing answers to them. If, however, their knowledge and commitment are formed without awareness of such questions, they will lack the means to do so.

It is necessary therefore to add a third qualification to the making of a moral authority: reflectiveness. This is a large topic that cannot be treated fully here.[14] In general, however, reflectiveness may be said to be directed more deeply into the moral tradition and more broadly to compare the moral tradition with other moral traditions. The greater depth and breadth that result enhance the appreciation of the moral tradition, if it is a morally acceptable one, or they lead to its criticism and possible improvement or abandonment, if it has moral defects.

One object of reflectiveness is to understand the moral vision that is meant to be expressed by the conventions of a moral tradition. The vision is of human possibilities and limits and of how best to pursue the first and recognize the second. It is to penetrate to the deepest level of a moral tradition and understand what motivates it. For Christians, it is the imitation of Christ; for Jews, it is the covenant with God; for liberals, it is autonomous life; for utilitarians, it is the happiness of humanity; for Plato, it is the transformation of the self as guided by knowledge of the Good; and so on for each of the major religions and moral philosophies. If the conventions of a moral tradition are seen as the forms in which the underlying vision is given concrete expression, then there will be a principled way of justifying, criticizing, or changing the conventions. For it will then be understood that it is not conformity to the conventions that is of the greatest importance, but the translation of the vision into concrete forms. Conventions are the means by which this is done, and they can be more or less adequate to their purpose.

The conventions may change with times and circumstances, and they may become more or less faithful, practical, or realistic. Having understood the vision, however, there will be a ready way of evaluating actual changes or judging the advisability of future ones. Part of the authoritativeness, attraction, and persuasiveness of moral authorities comes from their possession of greater depth than most people have. Depth creates the ability to cut through the moral complexities caused by changing conventions. It involves judging the adequacy of conventions in the light of the underlying moral vision that they were meant to express. The judgment may not be favorable, and so moral authorities may be critics of the moral *status quo*.

Reflectiveness is directed also toward understanding that the vision of one's own moral tradition is merely one among many. To have the breadth of this kind of understanding is to see that here "there are truths but no truth."[15] It is the essential feature of pluralism that it recognizes that the morally acceptable visions of a good life are many. The fact remains, however, that of the many only one is one's own. One of the most difficult tasks of a moral authority in a pluralistic society is to combine the recognition of the plurality of morally acceptable traditions with allegiance to a particular one. If one knows that there are many truths, why live according to one of them?

The answer is that people's knowledge of the truths of other moral traditions is not like knowledge of their own. Moral traditions other than their own do not provide the perspective for evaluating the lives and conduct of themselves and others, they do not protect their conceptions of a good life, they do not inspire and motivate them, and they do not engage their feelings and imagination, at least not to the same extent as their own. And if two conceptions of a good life derived from two moral traditions were found to be equally attractive, it would still be necessary to opt for one of them, for one person can live and act reasonably only by trying to follow one of two incompatible moral visions. One task of a moral authority therefore is to remind people whose allegiance to a moral tradition is challenged by the possibilities of another that the evaluative dimension of their lives is defined by their own tradition, that its moral vision is theirs too, and that their conception of a good life is intimately connected with the moral tradition whose framework makes living according to that conception possible.

This is not to deny, of course, that people may have reason to exchange their commitment to one morally acceptable tradition for another. The role for moral authority is not to dictate what commitments people should have, but to make vivid to them the moral vision that lies behind the commitments that they have made. The vision may fade; limited energy, lack of emotional agility, and the demands of everyday life often make it hard to concentrate on it; wickedness, weakness, and love of comfort frequently act as countervailing motivational forces; and the inevitable defects of the prevailing conventions further cloud the original vision. People often turn to moral authorities for help when they find themselves beset by such conflicts, doubts, and weakening commitments. The way they can be helped is to remind them of what they already know, but tend to forget under the pressure of their lives and circumstances: the moral vision that provides the rationale for living as they do.

Implicit in this account of reflectiveness is the further qualification that moral authorities must be morally articulate. They can make simple the situations others find complex because they have reflected more deeply and broadly on their moral tradition than those who turn to them for help. But they could not help if their reflectiveness merely enabled them to see clearly what appears to be obscure for others. They must also be able to communicate what they have seen, and to communicate it in a way that would make those who have not seen it see it too. Moral authorities must therefore be teachers, and as teachers they must know how to bring those who want to learn from the point of being lost in complexities to the point where their own efforts will suffice.

The plain statement of the plain truth will rarely accomplish this because what is plain to someone who has reflected sufficiently will not be plain to those who have not. This is why moral authorities in widely different contexts tend to communicate through stories, allegories, parables, myths, and striking images. The imaginative and emotive aura with which they surround the truth is not sugarcoating that will make swallowing it easier, but a method of making its significance apparent. One of the greatest of these literary devices is Plato's allegory of the cave.[16] It is most apposite in the present context because it is not only a classic illustration of how moral authorities can communicate successfully, but also a depiction of the predicament of both moral authorities and those in need of it. Plato writes: "the eyes can become confused in two different ways. . . . It can happen in the transition from light to darkness and also in the transition from darkness to light."[17] Moral authorities must overcome the clouding of their vision as they proceed from light to darkness when they return to the cave; and they must do so in order to help those in the cave to see better as they try to proceed from darkness toward light.

There are, however, two significant differences between Plato's and the present way of thinking about moral authority. The first is that Plato thinks that ultimately there can be only one authoritative moral vision, whereas in fact there are many. The second is that Plato thinks of moral authority in a far more intrusive way than it is warranted to do. For Plato, the vast majority live in darkness, and they must be made to see, otherwise they will not be able to see by themselves. According to the present approach, the darkness is not unrelieved; most people can see, if only obscurely; they may come to realize this about themselves and then ask for help. It is only then that moral authorities should do what they can to show them how their own moral vision can illuminate the obscurities they face.

There is one further qualification that moral authorities must possess in addition to the four already discussed. Its necessity emerges if it is borne in mind that people's recognition of someone else's moral authority is always a matter of trust. It involves the belief that the judgment of the moral authority is better than their own. What is it about moral authorities that would make it reasonable for people to trust their judgment more than they trust their own? The answer cannot just be that the moral authorities possess the necessary knowledge, commitment, qualifications, and not just claim them. Putative moral authorities, after all, can be pretended, phoney, false, or deluded. There must, therefore, be something about the moral authorities themselves that would make it reasonable to trust them. It must not be hidden; it must be readily observable to anyone who cares to look. These requirements are met by the conduct of moral authorities being exemplary in the area of life where their authority holds.

The trust placed in moral authorities is warranted, therefore, by the way they live. They are placed in authority by others because they have shown how to live well according to a particular conception of a good life. Their authority derives from the successful experiments in living that their lives represent. They show to those interested that their conception of a good life is indeed good, that it is possible to live that way and succeed, and so they stand as examples to those who want to live that way. The qualification that the conduct of moral authorities must be exemplary bridges the gap between being a moral authority and being recognized as such. Articulateness alone is insufficient for this because it is unclear whether verbal facility is evidence of knowledge, commitment, and reflectiveness, or merely of rhetorical talent. But if the life and conduct of puta-tive moral authorities are of a piece with the moral vision they articulate, then they demonstrate in the most convincing way possible that they mean what they say, that it is reasonable to trust them, and that they are moral authorities indeed.

It is an implication of this way of understanding moral authorities that they do not set themselves up as such, but rather that they are discovered. They are found to be conspicuous successes at living according to their conception of a good life, and that is why authority is attributed to them. The possession of moral authority, however, is only an unintended by-product of their conduct, not its goal. What primarily matters to them is to live what they regard as a good life. That is and must continue to be the true center of their conduct. If others turn to them for help, then decency and good will prompts them to try to give it. Their ability to help, however, is contingent on their lives remaining exemplary. It would undermine that very ability to use it in a way that would interfere with living as they have been. The exercise of moral authority, therefore, must always be a subordinate activity for those who genuinely possess it.

The point, of course, is not that moral authorities must be self-centered, but rather that they must be centered on living according to their conception of a good life. If it is a reasonable one, it will include concern for the well-bring of others. But the nature of that concern will not be to impart a vision to them or to teach them how to resolve the complexities they face; it will not be didactic or pedagogical. It will be to interact with them in the ways appropriate to the conception of a good life. That there are other people similarly engaged, and that they see their conspicuous success, and therefore recognize them as moral authorities, may often come to those so recognized as a surprising and unsought honor. It may also come as a burden because it may interfere with living the life they want and enjoy. This is probably part of the reason why moral authorities seem often distant and somewhat removed to those who turn to them. In any case, it will perhaps be obvious why genuine moral authorities will not aim to impose their will on others and they are likely to find their status an embarrass-ment of riches.

A further implication of the present account is that moral authorities are not exceptional figures who are hard to find, but familiar people often encountered in everyday life. If the knowledge, commitment, reflectiveness, articulateness, and exemplary conduct were thought of in absolutistic terms approaching per-fection, then moral authorities would indeed be rare. But this is not how they should be regarded. Being a moral authority is a relation that holds between individuals. Moral authorities, therefore, are such for particular persons. Their authority derives from the possession of the qualifications to an extent sufficient to enable them to judge better than others who turn to them for help and who distrust their own judgment about the complexities they face. Moral authority relations thus depend on the respective qualifications of the people who participate in them. Moral authorities may themselves need moral authorities and people who recognize a moral authority may themselves be recognized as moral authorities by others. The essential feature of these relations is that a moral authority is recognized as having better judgment about complex situations than the people who turn to them. And having better judgment depends on and it is demonstrated by the authority's possession of the qualifications to a high enough degree so that they could help those who cannot help themselves. The possession of the qualifications, however, is always a matter of degree, and that is why a person who is a moral authority in one context may be in need of moral authority in another context. The determining factor is whether people possess the qualifications to a sufficient degree to resolve the complexities they face when the variable conventions of their moral tradition do not provide clear guidance.

One last implication of the account of moral authority remains to be made explicit. The possibility of being a recognized moral authority presupposes allegiance to a shared conception of a good life and to a moral tradition upon which living according to that conception depends. A moral authority excels at living in the way those who recognize it want to live. Their shared allegiance provides participants in moral authority relations with an objective standard of evaluation: that set by the conception of a good life. Moral authorities excel because they approximate it more closely than others. That is what makes them authorities, and not that they are charismatic, possess the trappings of status, command a large audience, or speak powerfully.

The Justification of Moral Authority

The preceding account was meant to provide two considerations that jointly require that moral authorities be recognized by all morally acceptable conceptions of a good life. The first concerns the necessity to recognize the possibility of moral authority. This is a logical requirement, and it follows from understanding the nature of good lives and of moral authority.[18] Those who commit themselves to living according to some conception of a good life thereby commit themselves to recognizing that conception as an objective standard with reference to which both their own and the conduct of others who share their commitment could be compared and evaluated. The standard is objective in the sense that how closely lives and conduct approximate it is a factual question whose answer is independent of what anyone thinks, feels, hopes, or fears. The standard is not objective in the sense that any reasonable person would have to accept it. There are many reasonable conceptions of a good life, and people can accept or reject any of them without violating reason or objectivity. What cannot be done without the loss of reason and objectivity is to make a commitment to a particular conception and then refuse to recognize it as a standard of moral evaluation that applies to all those who are similarly committed.

It follows from this that other people's lives and conduct may approximate the standard more closely than the agents' own. Others may have done better than they have done themselves at the most important endeavor of their lives, which is to make them good. If it is accepted further that at least some of those who have done better have done so deservedly, through their own talents and efforts, and not undeservedly, through injustice or luck, then reasonable people will see them as possible moral authorities from whom they may be able to learn how they themselves could do better.

The second consideration is that people's recognition of moral authority is not just an abstract possibility, but a pressing practical need. For, as a matter of moral psychology, no longer of logic, people are often confronted with complexities in trying to live according to their conception of a good life, but they find themselves unable to resolve them. These complexities arise because the conventions of their moral tradition provide inadequate guidance about how they should respond in some particular situation. They recognize that their intuitive responses have become unreliable, but they do not know how to find a reliable response because they are wanting in knowledge, commitment, or reflectiveness. This is the situation in which people feel the need to rely on the judgment of others. If they are reasonable, they will rely on those whose lives and conduct are better than their own and who therefore can be supposed to have to a greater extent the qualifications which they themselves lack. If they receive the help they need because the people to whom they turn have the qualifications to provide it, then it is justified to recognize them as moral authorities, with all that such recognition entails.

This justification is in no way committed to the infallibility of moral authorities. Moral authorities are legitimate if they possess the appropriate qualifications. It is reasonable to recognize them as moral authorities if their qualifications enable them to make more reliable judgments about complex situations than the people for whom they count as authorities. This does not mean that their judgments could not be mistaken; it means only that they are less likely to be mistaken than the judgments of those who lack their qualifications. There are three importantly different ways in which moral authorities may be mistaken.

The first is that they may be insufficiently informed about or attentive to the complex situations they are called upon to judge. These failings may or may not be culpable. They may lack the relevant information because they have been lied to, or because they have not bothered to look. Similarly, their lack of attention may be the result of fatigue caused by the great demands placed on them, or to laziness and indifference. Assume, however, that they do not fail in these ways, that they are informed and attentive.

The second way in which they may fail is that their qualifications are unequal to the task at hand. Their knowledge, commitment, reflectiveness, conduct, articulateness, and the judgments based on them, are, to be sure, better than those of the people who rely on them, but they are not sufficiently better to make their judgments reliable. They judge in good faith, and as well as they can, but that is still not good enough. If they had the qualifications to a greater extent, they could make better judgments, but lacking them, culpably or otherwise, they cannot. But even if their qualifications are adequate and they do not fail on their account, they may still fail for another reason.

The third kind of failure stems from the defects of the moral tradition within which they are recognized as legitimate authorities. Their judgments are good in mediating between the moral vision of their tradition and complex cases, but the tradition is morally defective. They judge well how complexities could be resolved in conformity with the tradition, but they end up making a mistaken moral judgment because in some respects their tradition is morally unacceptable. Confucius may be right that his tradition requires caring about the ceremony and not about the sheep, but he and his tradition may still be wrong to sacrifice sheep.

Suppose, however, that there is no reason to think that some moral authorities are defective in any of these ways, that their lives and conduct are exemplary, and that the judgments they have made seem to be reliable. There are then good reasons to recognize them as moral authorities and to rely on their judgments when the complexities of some situation make people distrust their own.

It needs to be added as a reminder that, although legitimate moral authorities always judge from the point of view of their moral tradition, it is by no means the case that their judgments must always reflect the conventions of their tradition. Moral authorities are bound to be traditional because they bring the fundamental moral vision of their tradition to the judgment of complex situations. But they need not be conventional because they may think that some conventions prevailing in their tradition are defective expressions of the fundamental vision. Their judgments then serve the direct purpose of resolving the complexities they face, as well as the more indirect purpose of criticizing and trying to remedy the defective conventions of their moral tradition.

Notes

1. E.g., Hannah Arendt, "What is Authority?" in *Nomos I: Authority*, ed. Carl J. Friedrich (Cambridge: Harvard University Press, 1958), and Carl J. Friedrich, *Tradition and Authority* (New York: Praeger, 1972).

2. E.g., Robert P. Wolff, *In Defense of Anarchism* (New York: Harper & Row, 1970).

3. E.g., Stanley I. Benn and Richard S. Peters, *Social Principles and the Democratic State* (London: Allen & Unwin, 1959), ch. 14; Richard E. Flathman, *The Practice of Political Authority* (Chicago: University of Chicago Press, 1980); Richard B. Friedman, "On the Concept of Authority in Political Philosophy," in *Concepts in Social and Political Philosophy*, ed. Richard E. Flathman (New York: Macmillan, 1973); and Joseph Raz, *The Morality of Freedom* (Oxford: Clarendon Press, 1986), chs. 2–4.

4. Wolff, *In Defense of Anarchism*, p. 18.

5. Flathman, *The Practice of Political Authority*, p. 90.

6. See Stanley I. Benn, "Authority," in *The Encyclopedia of Philosophy*, vols. 1–8, ed. Paul Edwards (New York: Macmillan, 1967); Steven Lukes, "Power and Authority" and "Perspectives on Authority," both in *Moral Conflicts and Politics* (Oxford: Clarendon Press, 1991); Richard S. Peters, "Authority," *Proceedings of the Aristotelian Society*, supplementary vol. 32 (1958): 207–20; Raz, *The Morality of Freedom*, chs. 2–3.

7. See Lukes, "Power and Authority" and "Perspectives on Authority," and Peters, "Authority."

8. Max Weber, *Economy and Society*, vols. 1–2, ed. and trans. G. Roth and C. Willick (New York: Bedminster, 1968).

9. See Lukes, "Power and Authority" and "Perspectives on Authority."

10. Lukes, "Power and Authority," p. 92.

11. See Friedrich, *Tradition and Authority*.

12. One notable exception is Samuel Fleischacker, *The Ethics of Culture* (Ithaca: Cornell University Press, 1994). The present account is indebted to this work.

13. The account is in Richard Wollheim's "The Sheep and the Ceremony" in *The Mind and Its Depths* (Cambridge: Harvard University Press, 1993), 1. Wollheim's account draws on Confucius, *Analects*. Trans. with exegetical notes by James Legge (New York: Dover, 1971), 3.17. It must be said that the text does not quite support Wollheim's interpretation, but that may be ignored for the present purposes.

14. For a fuller treatment, see John Kekes, *Moral Wisdom and Good Lives* (Ithaca: Cornell University Press, 1995).

15. Peter F. Strawson, "Freedom and Resentment," in *Freedom and Resentment* (London: Methuen, 1974), 29.

16. Plato, *The Republic*, trans. Robin Waterfield (Oxford: Oxford University Press, 1993), 514a–518c.

17. Plato, *The Republic*, 518a.

18. See Peter Winch, "Authority," in *Proceedings of the Aristotelian Society*, supplementary vol. 32 (1958): 221–40.

Love and Respect in the Confucian Family

7

A. T. Nuyen

Sociologists and anthropologists readily agree that the family structure in present-day China and East Asia is no longer traditionally Confucian. However, enough of the Confucian ideals and family virtues remain and the commitment to them is still strong enough to allow us to speak of the Confucian family in the modern context. The recent changes in the family structure have been largely in response to modern political, economic, and technological conditions. Many commentators have characterized the changes that have taken place in the latter half of the twentieth century as revolutionary and have cast doubt on the ability of the Confucian family to survive into the new millennium. The aim of this paper is not to dispute the prediction of demise of the Confucian family. It is rather to pose the question whether the recent changes are to be welcomed or whether the predicted demise is a matter of regret. Some commentators are of the opinion that the observed changes are for the better in view of what they take to be the shortcomings of the Confucian family structure. According to one such commentator, Confucianism in "its traditional format . . . was rigidly authoritarian and bolstered by a social matrix that was essentially totalitarian."[1] There is nothing to be regretted about the demise of a structure in which the "rights of women and children were minimal, and during various historical periods they were essentially nonexistent."[2] Insofar as the "traditional format" of the Confucian family grew out of Confucian teachings, such teachings seem to be indefensible in the modern context.

The focus of this essay is on the conceptual side of the relationship between Confucianism and the family. I shall identify the Confucian doctrines and through them the conceptual elements that are most probably responsible for the alleged authoritarianism in the traditional Confucian family structure. I shall then defend Confucianism against the charge of authoritarianism by closely examining the underlying conceptual elements in their proper philosophical context. Before doing so, I shall review the anthropological data in order to gain a better understanding of the charge against Confucianism.

The Case against the Confucian Family

The picture of the traditional Confucian family painted by many anthropologists on the basis of their empirical data is not an appealing one, not just to the modern mind that subscribes to equality and personal liberty, but also to most of those caught up in that family structure. Numerous social and psychological problems have been attributed to contemporary Asian families' attempt to maintain the Confucian family structure. The victims are said to be not just the children and the wives, but the fathers and the husbands as well. The indictment is so severe that one wonders how the Confucian family has survived for so long and why East Asia does not follow Communist China in denouncing it, along with Confucianism, for its terrible effects on the family, among other things. Indeed, one wonders why, despite the efforts of the Communist regime, traces of the Confucian family structure can still be found in many parts of China itself. What, then, is the case against the Confucian family? How much of it is also against Confucianism?

For Slote, the traditional Confucian family format reinforces the "hierarchical social structure" designed to entrench the authority of those in power, that of the husband and the father in the family context.[3] Slote supports his claim that the "father was the ultimate disciplinarian" with an example reported to him by a Vietnamese informant showing "an elderly father ordering his fifty-year-old son to lie on the floor, arms outstretched, and beating him with a switch."[4] In applying disciplinary actions, the Confucian father is "forced [to withhold] affection"[5] and suffers the resulting emotional consequences. On the basis of his observations, Slote concludes that the "men were frequently abusive and demeaning toward their wives, diminishing the women's spirit and the vitality and spontaneity of the relationship."[6] The effect on the child is equally appalling: "[it] was to reduce the child . . . to impotence—helpless, frustrated, furious, and floundering."[7] Thus, father/husband, wife, child, all suffer the terrible effects of the Confucian family: "Each pays a price. The result is that the burden of proper conduct weighs heavily upon everyone."[8] There is worse to come, if that is possible. Wives frequently entertain "incestuous fantasies" toward their sons to compensate for "the affection that is not forthcoming from their husbands"[9]; the struggle for power within the family results in "[s]ibling rivalry and sibling envy"[10]; the enforcement of authoritarian domination results in "fear, dependency, and hostility" within the family.[11] On hostility, Slote reports that on "a number of occasions where I have seen it expressed, it has taken the form of what I can only describe as murderous rage."[12]

The "terrible effects" of the Confucian family structure on family members are similarly reported by anthropological field workers in non-Chinese communities such as the Japanese, the Korean, and to a lesser extent, the Vietnamese communities. In the case of Japan, for instance, De Vos claims that there is "no doubt that Confucianism was used politically and socially as a conservative ideology concerning the state, the economic system, and gender relationships."[13] Lebra observes that as a result of the adoption of Confucianism in Japan, "[m]an is placed above woman, just as the heaven is above the earth, and the head above the body," an "asymmetry involving female inferiority, subordination, and vulnerability."[14] In the case of Korea, Yim claims that the "moral axiom . . . [of] . . . filial piety" has resulted in *"a sense of guilt"* in family members who "cannot fulfil their moral responsibilities," and in *"the suppression of hostile feelings* toward parents."[15] The Korean psychiatrist Bou-Yong Rhi points out that there are psychiatric data linking incidents of mental illness in many Korean communities to conflicts within the Confucian family structure. He writes: "I would suggest that the frustrations experienced among Korean women after marriage into a traditional patriarchal family still play an important role in the production of conversion symptoms [of hysterical disorders]."[16] Rhi also quotes another psychiatrist who attributes incidents of homosexuality and incest in Korean families in America to "the strict early separation between roles for boys and girls in the Confucian tradition," to "the culturally sanctioned relationship among same-sex siblings in hierarchical terms," and so on.[17]

To be sure, the negative effects of the traditional Confucian family structure are not uniform. However, those communities that escape the worst excesses are those that manage to loosen the Confucian stricture with their own home-grown traditions or those that are forced by economic and other circumstances to modify the "traditional format." At least, this is the impression one gets from social scientists who are critical of the Confucian family. According to Young, "the Vietnamese have preserved a resolute individualism [and] have insisted upon a compromise on power within the family, blending patrilineal authority with matriarchy."[18] Those Vietnamese families that manage to temper Confucian orthodoxy with home-grown traits are more likely to escape the negative effects observed elsewhere, albeit at the cost to an individual of an inner conflict between "orthodoxy and opposition to orthodoxy."[19] In the case of Singapore, Kuo reports that the "Chinese family, which still draws fundamental values of Confucian ethics from various sources, has to adapt to the reality of a new urban-industrial state."[20] The necessity to adapt arises because "industrialization and urbanization are incompatible with the maintenance of Confucian family traditions."[21] By adapting well, the Singaporean Chinese manage to avoid many of the negative effects mentioned above. Indeed, Kuo expresses the hope that a "new synthesis . . . will emerge [in Singapore] representing a fusion of tradition and modernity."[22]

Confucianism and the Confucian Family

The anthropological data surveyed above appear to be damning. It is not within the scope of this essay to dispute, or even discuss, the nature of the anthropological findings. What is of interest is whether the case against the Confucian family *as it exists historically* is also the case against Confucianism itself, against Confucian ethics and Confucian philosophy generally. Some social critics are prepared to accept that the two cases are separate, and are reluctant to conflate them. Indeed, the psychiatrist Bou-Yong Rhi cited earlier is critical of those of his colleagues who tend to conflate the two. His own view is that it is "apparent . . . that some dysfunctional aspects of Confucian family life are the results of distortions or misperceptions and the undue rigidification of potentially more flexible interactions actually accepted within Confucian thought."[23] By contrast, many other social scientists take for granted the causal link between Confucianism and the family structure that has historically evolved. For them, the case against the latter is the case against the former. For instance, Slote is in no doubt that the authoritarianism found in the Confucian family originates from Confucianism itself: "Confucianism was based on authoritarianism, and filial piety was the principal instrument through which it was established and maintained."[24] Hsu tells us that during "the Chinese Renaissance of 1919 led by Hu Shih, Chinese intellectuals attacked filial piety and Confucianism,"[25] clearly blaming Confucianism for the lack of progress in China and for the inferiority of China vis-à-vis the West. For them, the Confucian family was merely the symptom of the disease, the disease being Confucianism itself. For Cho, since filial piety "was upheld as the ultimate value in Confucianism, at least in Koreanized Confucianism,"[26] anything negative about the Confucian family (in Korea) can be attributed to Confucianism. Indeed, the methodology that Cho adopts to study "male dominance" in Korea consists in "the analysis of Confucian philosophy, values, and norms."[27]

Critics of Confucianism and its manifestation in the family structure typically point to Confucian writings on the doctrine of the Three Bonds, on filial piety and on the virtue of *li* (propriety). The idea of filial piety is embedded in the so-called Three Bonds doctrine. The first textual appearance of this doctrine is in the *Hanfeizi* in the chapter called "Zhong-xiao" ("Loyalty and Filial Piety"). The often-quoted passage is the following: "The minister serves the king, the son serves the father, and the wife serves the husband. If the three are followed, the world will be in peace; if the three are violated, the world will be in chaos." The common interpretation of the doctrine of the Three Bonds is that it seeks to establish the authority of the king over his minister, of the father over his son and of the husband over his wife. Relevant to the family structure is what the doctrine seems to say about the father-son and the husband-wife relationships. Clearly, a strict application of the Three Bonds doctrine requires the son to yield to the authority of the father and the wife to yield to that of the husband. It is understandable that many critics have cited this doctrine as the source of authoritarianism in the Confucian family, and for some, it is as well the source of totalitarianism, domination, and oppression.

Other writings on filial piety have also been commonly cited. Even if we dismiss the notorious *Twenty-Four Examples of Filial Piety (Ershisi xiao)* as non-canonical, there is enough in the canonical works to serve as grist for the critics' mill. In the *Analects*, filial piety is often referred to as a key virtue. A favorite of critics is *Analects* 1.11: "Confucius said, 'When a man's father is alive, look at the bent of his will. When his father is dead, look at his conduct. If for three years [of mourning] he does not change from the way of his father, he may be called filial."[28] Other often-quoted passages include *Analects* 2.5 ("Meng Yizi asked about filial piety. Confucius said: 'Never disobey'")[29] and *Analects* 2.7 ("Confucius said, 'Filial piety nowadays means to be able to support one's parents. But we support even dogs and horses. If there is no feeling of reverence, wherein lies the difference?'").[30] From passages such as these, critics draw conclusions such as: "The most salient feature of filial piety is the subordination of the will and welfare of each individual to the will and welfare of his or her real classificatory parents,"[31] and "Filial Piety is quintessentially described as the subordination of a son to his father."[32]

For many critics, filial piety and for that matter, the Three Bonds doctrine, are rooted in the Confucian notion of *li* (propriety). The respect, reverence, obedience, loyalty, and so forth that must be shown by the wife toward her husband and by the son toward his father are aspects of *li. Analects* 2.5 is often cited in partial support of this claim. Thus, "Confucius said, 'When parents are alive, serve them according to the rules of propriety. When they die, bury them according to the rules of propriety and sacrifice to them according to the rules of propriety.'"[33] As one critic sees it, *li* was "a core concept for Confucius [and] was demanded of all."[34] This rather uncontroversial claim is followed by the claim that *li* "defined the correct, stylized behaviour which was attached to social roles and forestalled the idiosyncrasies of individual expression."[35] It is by *li* that society is ordered "into a hierarchy of superior and subordinate roles."[36] The implication is that it is by *li* that the family is likewise ordered, with wives and children occupying subordinate roles. This is how *li* ultimately gives rise to authoritarianism and totalitarianism in the family. Furthermore, insofar as respect, reverence, and obedience are incompatible with love and compassion, the strict observance of *li* leads to "stylized behavior" which is correct but heartless, proper but cold, in accordance with rituals but uncaring.

The Roles of Love and Respect: A Defense of Confucianism

Conceptually, the Confucian notion of *li* seems to be the main source of the trouble. My defense of Confucianism consists largely of a reading of *li* as it functions in the context of the family. I shall borrow from Kant's account of the dynamics between love and respect and argue that *li* functions, or at least is meant to function, as a counterpoise to other forces that naturally exist in the family context. Before doing so, however, it is worth reassessing the textual evidence in support of the charge of authoritarianism.

It is interesting to note that the Three Bonds doctrine was nowhere discussed by Confucius and major Confucianists, such as Mencius. Dong Zhongshu discussed it in his writings, but he was a minor philosopher who managed to play a large role in politicizing Confucianism. The *Hanfeizi* in which the Three Bonds doctrine made its first appearance is a text of the Legalist school. The doctrine came to be regarded as part of Confucianism only through the politicization of Confucianism during the Han dynasty and subsequently. As Tu Wei-ming sees it, "the Han ideologists, like the Legalists, were mainly concerned about the functional utility of the Three Bonds as mechanism of symbolic control for the primary purpose of social stability."[37] Indeed, "the politicized Confucian implementation of the Three Bonds is much more demanding than their legalist origin and nature may suggest."[38] Given this history, it is not unreasonable to suggest that the Three Bonds doctrine is not canonically Confucian. Those critics who cite the doctrine to support the charge of authoritarianism against Confucianism have largely failed to make the distinction between philosophical Confucianism and politicized Confucianism. The only thing that bears any resemblance to the Three Bonds doctrine in canonical Confucian writings is the notion of the Five Relationships found in the *Mencius*. But as Tu has pointed out, the "ethics of the Three Bonds as an integral part of [the] politicized Confucian mechanism of symbolic control is a far cry from the Mencian idea of the Five Relationships."[39]

The statement of the Five Relationships occurs at *Mencius* BK.III PT.I 4.8: "the sage *Shun* . . . appointed Hsieh (Xie) to be the Minister of Instruction, to teach the relations of humanity—how, between father and son, there should be affection; between sovereign and minister, righteousness; between husband and wife, attention to their separate functions; between old and young, a proper order; and between friends, fidelity."[40] It is interesting to note that righteousness governs only the relationship between the sovereign and the minister. The family relationships of father and son and husband and wife are governed respectively by affection, or love, and separateness, or distinction. For Mencius, then, "the proper relationship between [father and son] is mutual affection rather than one-way obedience."[41] There is also mutuality in the husband-wife relationship. The "underlying spirit" in the governing principle of attention to separate functions "is not dominance but division of labour."[42] It is no wonder that critics ignore the *Mencius* when it comes to textual support for the charges of authoritarianism, totalitarianism, and domination.

Turning to filial piety, the talk of reverence and obedience in the canonical texts is never far from the talk of love and affection. In the passage in the *Analects* (1.6) where it is stated that "(y)oung men should be filial," it is also stated that they "should love all extensively."[43] In the *Mencius,* filial piety is always discussed in relation to affection and mutuality. Thus, at *Mencius* BK.IV. PT.I 28.2, it is said that the effect of "great filial piety" was that "all fathers and sons in the kingdom were established *in their respective duties.*"[44] In the preceding section (BK.IV PT.1 27.1), it is said that the "richest fruit of benevolence is . . . the service of one's parents."[45] The same thing can be said about the main text on filial piety, the *Hsiao Ching (Xiao Jing)*. Thus, it is stated in chapter V that the "connecting link between serving one's father and serving one's mother is love."[46] In chapter XV, we find that the Master denies that "filiality consists in simply obeying a father."[47] Indeed, the filial son must "reason" with his father and "must never fail to warn his father against [moral wrong]."[48]

A somewhat different picture seems to have emerged. However, if what I have said is a defense of anything, it is at best a defense of the authors of the texts cited and by no means a defense of Confucianism itself. If the critics mentioned above are in danger of failing to distinguish between philosophical Confucianism and politicized Confucianism, then one who focuses too narrowly on the canonical texts runs the risk of failing to distinguish between the philosophy of Confucius (and of Mencius and so on) and Confucian philosophy, or Confucianism generally. Thus, it may be insisted that despite what Confucius, Mencius, and other key Confucianists actually said, Confucianism has to be taken as a blend of what was said and the interpretations of what was said, not to mention the applications in daily life of the actual teachings and their interpretations. It may be insisted that whatever flexibility there is in the writings of Confucius, Mencius, and so forth, it has dissipated in the blend that is Confucianism. Accepting this, one commentator, Tu Wei-ming,[49] remains optimistic and argues that precisely because Confucianism is a blend of various strands of thoughts and practices, there is room for each individual to respond creatively to his or her circumstances. Tu argues that the Confucian stricture should not be seen as a limiting factor but rather as an opportunity for self-cultivation. The Confucian blend is "laden with fruitful ambiguities"[50] to allow each individual to explore avenues for self-creation. In particular, the father-son relationship, despite the emphasis on filial piety, "provides a context and an instrumentality for self-cultivation,"[51] not just for the son but for the father as well.

There is something to be said for Tu's defense of Confucianism. One is here reminded of Kant's implicit defense, in the *Doctrine of Virtue,* of his rather rigoristic ethics. Kant claims that ethics has to be supplemented with casuistry. The ultimately wise person is a casuist who can cleverly and imaginatively apply the strict moral rules. As I have argued elsewhere,[52] while one may not lie to the would-be murder at the door who wants to know where his victim is hiding, one may, within the Kantian framework, employ the casuistic trick of stamping one's foot on the doorstep and saying "He is not *here.*" However, this is an admission that the ethics itself is rigoristic and that an unimaginative application of it must still be accepted no matter how regrettable the consequences may be. The same thing can be said about Tu's defense of Confucianism. It is an admission that Confucianism is authoritarian and restrictive *in theory.* While opportunities exist to respond creatively to its strict demands, there are no theoretical grounds to criticize the noncreative response manifested in the historical development of the Confucian family. I believe we can do better.

There is no doubt that when we shift from the actual teachings to their interpretations and applications, there is a shift toward a more or less exclusive adherence to *li* as far as the family structure is concerned. At the extreme, what we can have, and perhaps did have at some historical point, is a social system, and within it a family structure, dominated by the concern for *li*. We do not get very far by claiming that this extreme form, or what some critics call the "traditional format," is no longer Confucian in any sense, for then we will be forced to draw the line between what is Confucian and what is not. It is better to come up with a reading of *li* such that an exclusive and inflexible adherence to *li* in any doctrine or any practice is theoretically indefensible. As a preliminary step, we can remind ourselves that what is distinctive about Confucianism is the idea of harmony (which becomes the idea of social stability and order in a rigid application). There has to be harmony not just in the world without but also in the mind within, or in our conceptual systems. Given that this is so, there has to be a reason for any emphasis on any conceptual element. If there is an emphasis on *li* in the family context then there has to be a good reason for it. Conceding that there is such an emphasis in Confucianism, we need to find out what the reason might be. I shall try to show that once we have understood the reason, the charge of authoritarianism can be avoided in the very theory that governs historically observed practices. We will then have a theoretical case against the excesses unearthed by anthropological findings to add to the criticisms already voiced by social scientists, but it will be a case against politicized Confucianism which is not at all a case against Confucianism itself.

The social and emotional manifestations of *li* are typically respect and reverence. The virtue of *li* may be usefully compared with *ren* (humanity) the social and emotional manifestations of which are typically love, affection, and benevolence. From the psychological point of view, *li* and *ren* tend to pull in different directions. This is so because respect tends to inhibit love and love tends to dull respect. Yet, both love and respect, together with their cognate feelings such as affection and benevolence on the one hand and reverence and deference on the other, are necessary in human relationships, and living well requires a proper balance between the two. Kant's view on love and respect is particularly instructive. In the *Doctrine of Virtue*, Kant compares the forces of love and respect with the forces of attraction and repulsion in the physical world as described in Newtonian mechanics. The attractive force in nature causes physical bodies to gravitate toward each other while the force of repulsion keeps them apart. In the natural world, the two forces cooperate and as a result, planetary and other systems are formed without heavenly bodies colliding into each other or flying off in all different directions. Likewise in the human world, the centripetal force of love operates to bring us together while the centrifugal force of respect operates to insert a distance between us. Kant writes:

> The principle of <u>mutual love</u> admonishes men constantly to *come nearer* to each other; that of <u>respect</u> which they owe each other, to keep themselves at a *distance* from one another. And should one of these great moral forces fail, "then nothingness (immo-

rality), with gaping throat, would drink the whole kingdom of (moral) beings like a drop of water" (if I may use Haller's words, but in a different connection).[53]

Love and respect, then, are the "*attraction* and *repulsion* [which] bind together rational beings (on earth)."[54] While these two "can be considered separately . . . and can also exist separately," they are "always joined together in a duty, only in such a way that now one duty and now the other is the subject's principle, with the other joined to it as an accessory."[55] For Kant, "*love* and *respect* are the feelings that accompany the practice of . . . duties [to others]."[56] I have suggested that the same feelings of love and respect (and their respective cognate feelings) accompany the practices of *ren* and *li*. Since love brings us together and respect separates us, the practice of *ren* has the attracting function and that of *li* the distancing function. They are both necessary for the human world. Extending the Kantian analogy with Newtonian physics, we may say that both practices must be in balance for there to be order and harmony in the human world, just as the forces of attraction and repulsion have to be in balance for there to be a physical world as we know it. Too much *ren* will draw people too close to each other to the point where we merge into an undistinguishable mass of humanity, where the individual lacks a personal space for growth and development, where everyone can pry into everyone else's affairs without proper respect. By contrast, too much *li* will put great emotional distances between us, distances that no rites and ceremonies can make up. *Ren* and *li*, love and respect, have to harmonize properly. Without harmony, without proper balance, the human world will be either a congealed mass of nothingness or a brittle aggregation of beings without deep and meaningful relationships, a nothingness of a different kind. Either way, "nothingness, with gaping throat, would drink the whole kingdom of beings like a drop of water," to use Kant's use of Haller's words.

My invocation of Kant is not arbitrary. Confucius and Confucianists themselves frequently invoke the model of cosmological harmony in discussing human affairs. Indeed, as I have shown elsewhere,[57] the human world is understood in Confucian writings as being continuous with the non-human world, and the human way is continuous with the way of Heaven, both being different manifestations of the Way, the *dao*. Thus, in the book of *Chung Yung* or *Zhong Yong*, it is said that the laws of the human society "form the same system with the laws by which the seasons succeed each other and the sun and the moon appear with the alternations of day and night."[58] Furthermore, nature possesses a mechanism of checks and balances to keep the natural opposing forces in balance. One force would act as a balance, a counterpoise, to compensate for the effect of an opposing force. Days compensate for nights; winter balances out summer; water keeps fire in check; predators are in turn preys. Each must stand in a position of due measure and degree with its opposite. The right balance is *zhong yong*. Speaking of the opposing emotional forces, the book of *Zhong Yong* states: "When [the] passions [e.g. love, respect, grief, joy] awaken and each and all attain due measure and degree, that is *harmony*, or the moral order (*he*)."[59] Thus, insofar as love and respect pull in different directions, they must be maintained in "due measure and degree" for there to be a proper "moral order."

In the family context, it is natural to assume that there is an abundance of love and affection. Between the father and his children, love and affection are natural feelings originating from human biology. Between husband and wife, love and affection come either from a romantic attraction or from the sexual union of the two. It is natural to assume that there is already a great deal of *ren* in the family context. Without something that acts as a counterpoise, the naturally existing *ren* could well become dominant, enough to turn a family into a congealed mass in which members are not separable from each other in any meaningful way. Drawn too close to each other, family members become too "familiar" with each other. This would not be so bad if family members melded into an organic whole and responded and reacted to the outside as a unified whole. The trouble is that there are inevitably enough individual differences left to give rise to conflicts, the kind of conflicts that cannot be resolved without someone's authority being respected, without someone's directives being obeyed, that is, without respect and reverence. The Western saying "Familiarity breeds contempt" is particularly apt here. As Confucius himself admitted, "When it comes to the practice of humanity, one should not defer even to his teacher" (*Analects* 15:35).[60] Herein lies the danger of familiarity: Too much "humanity" leading to a lack of deference, which could in turn lead to contempt. The contempt bred by familiarity, by too much love and affection, or too much "humanity," can only be avoided by an injection of some element that has the effect of maintaining a respectful distance between family members. The affection to the teacher has to be balanced by respect for there to be learning. In the family, there has to be an emphasis on respect and reverence to counteract the effect of natural love and affection. There has to be an emphasis on *li* to serve as a counterpoise to the naturally occurring *ren*. Given the Confucian emphasis on harmony, on the balance of opposing forces in the world, including the human world, it is to be expected that there is an emphasis on *li* in the family context. There ought to be an emphasis on *li*, there ought to be an emphasis on respect and reverence, and for a good reason. That reason is to be found in the doctrine of *Zhong Yong*.

If I am right, the strict adherence to *li* in politicized Confucianism is a mistake, at least as far as the family is concerned. To interpret filial piety as purely a demand for respect, reverence, and obedience is to misunderstand the dynamics between love and respect. While love and respect, *ren* and *li*, can "exist separately" and so can be "considered separately," to borrow Kant's words, they are "always joined together" in a dynamic harmony. "Now one and now the other," again to borrow Kant's words, may be "the subject's principle," or principal emphasis, but one must always remember that "the other is joined to it as an accessory." We may make *li* a principle but should never lose sight of *ren*. As Confucius himself said, "If a man is not humane (*ren*), what has he to do with ceremonies (*li*)?" (*Analects* 3:3).⁶¹ Insofar as the doctrine of the Three Bonds is Confucian, its emphasis on *li* has to be understood in terms of the dynamics between love and respect, between *ren* and *li*, as I have explained. Adherence to *li* at the expense of *ren* is decidedly not *zhong yong* and thus un-Confucian. While it is often a difficult matter to draw the line between what is Confucian and what is not, we can certainly say that the sole emphasis on respect, reverence, and obedience in the so-called Confucian family is not Confucian.

The traditional, or historical, Confucian family may well be authoritarian and totalitarian. However, it does not follow that the Confucianism that underlies the traditional structure is *ipso facto* authoritarian and totalitarian. It is true that Confucianism emphasizes *li* in the family context, but only as a counterpoise to the love and affection that naturally exist in the family. Critics of the authoritarian structure are right in predicting its demise. In such structure, the force of love and affection that attracts one to another is either missing or has clearly failed, and so we can expect, with Kant, that "nothingness, with gaping throat, would drink the whole kingdom of beings like a drop of water." However, the family structure that allows for a proper balance between respect and reverence on the one hand and love and affection on the other, for a harmony of *li* and *ren*, is more than likely to weather the storm of modernity. The death notice of the Confucian family issued by many of its critics will prove to be premature if by "the Confucian family" we mean a structure that respects the dynamics between love and respect. Casting our eyes beyond the family structure, it can be seen that, just as *li* is emphasized to counterbalance the naturally occurring *ren* in the family, where there is a tendency for humans to drift apart, Confucianism calls for an emphasis on *ren* as a counterbalancing force, as a practice that reduces the distances between us. Pessimists who see the modern society disintegrating and who see in that disintegration the breaking up of the traditional family structure should call for a return to Confucianism rather than castigating it. For, given the Confucian emphasis on the harmony of opposing forces, the general Confucian structure is the most likely one to survive into the new millennium.

Notes

1. Walter H. Slote, "Psychocultural Dynamics within the Confucian Family," in *Confucianism and the Family*, ed. Walter H. Slote and George A. De Vos (Albany: State University of New York Press, 1998), 37.

2. *Ibid.*, p. 38.

3. *Ibid.*, p. 39.

4. *Ibid.*, p. 41.

5. *Ibid.*

6. *Ibid.*, p. 42.

7. *Ibid.*, p. 43.

8. *Ibid.*, p. 44.

9. *Ibid.*, pp. 44–45.

10. *Ibid.*, p. 45.

11. *Ibid.*, p. 46.

12. *Ibid.*, p. 47.

13. George A. De Vos, "A Japanese Legacy of Confucian Thought," in *Confucianism and the Family*, ed. Slote and De Vos, p. 110.

14. Takie Sugiyama Lebra, "Confucian Gender Role and Personal Fulfillment for Japanese Women," in *Confucianism and the Family*, ed. Slote and De Vos, p. 211.

15. Dawnhee Yim, "Psychocultural Features of Ancestor Worship in Modern Korean Society," in *Confucianism and the Family*, ed. Slote and De Vos, p. 165, emphasis original.

16. Bou-Yong Rhi, "Mental Illness in Its Confucian Context," in *Confucianism and the Family*, ed. Slote and De Vos, p. 286.

17. *Ibid.*, p. 287.

18. Stephen B. Young, "The Orthodox Chinese Confucian Social Paradigm versus Vietnamese Individualism," in *Confucianism and the Family*, ed. Slote and De Vos, p. 147.

19. *Ibid.*, p. 159.

20. Eddie C. Kuo, "Confucianism and the Chinese Family in Singapore: Continuities and Changes," in *Confucianism and the Family*, ed. Slote and De Vos, p. 237.

21. *Ibid.*, p. 244.

22. *Ibid.*, p. 246.

23. Rhi, "Mental Illness," p. 289.

24. Slote, "Psychocultural Dynamics," p. 46.

25. Francis L. K. Hsu, "Confucianism in Comparative Context," in *Confucianism and the Family*, ed. Slote and DeVos, p. 61.

26. Haejoang Cho, "Male Dominance and Mother Power: The Two Sides of Confucian Patriarchy in Korea," in *Confucianism and the Family*, ed. Slote and De Vos, p. 193.

27. *Ibid.*, p. 191.

28. Wing-Tsit Chan, *A Source Book in Chinese Philosophy* (Princeton, New Jersey: Princeton University Press, 1963), p. 61.

29. *Ibid.*, p. 23.

30. *Ibid.*

31. David K. Jordan, "Filial Piety in Taiwanese Popular Thought," in *Confucianism and the Family*, ed. Slote and De Vos, p. 268.

32. *Ibid.*, p. 269.

33. Chan, *A Source Book*, p. 23.

34. Young, "The Orthodox Chinese Confucian Social Paradigm," p. 139.

35. *Ibid.*

36. *Ibid*, p. 138.

37. Tu Wei-ming, "Probing the 'Three Bonds' and 'Five Relationships' in Confucian Humanism," in *Confucianism and the Family*, ed. Slote and De Vos, p. 122.

38. *Ibid.*, p. 123.

39. *Ibid.*, p. 124.

40. James Legge, ed. and trans., *The Works of Mencius* (New York: Dover, 1970), 251–52.

41. Tu, "Probing the 'Three Bonds,'" p. 125.

42. *Ibid.*

43. Chan, *A Source Book*, p. 20.

44. Legge, *The Works of Mencius,* p. 315, emphasis original.

45. *Ibid.*, p. 313.

46. Mary Lelia Makra, trans., *The Hsiao Ching* (New York: St. John's University Press, 1961), 11.

47. *Ibid.*, p. 33.

48. *Ibid.*

49. Tu Wei-ming, *Confucian Thought*: *Selfhood as Creative Transformation* (Albany: State University of New York Press, 1985).

50. *Ibid.*, p. 115.

51. *Ibid.*, p. 127.

52. A. T. Nuyen, "Lying and Deceiving," *International Journal of Applied Philosophy*, vol. 13 (1999).

53. Immanuel Kant, *The Doctrine of Virtue*, trans. Mary J. Gregor (New York, Evanston and London: Harper and Row, 1964), 116, emphases original.

54. *Ibid.*, emphases original.

55. *Ibid.*, p. 115.

56. *Ibid.*

57. A. T. Nuyen, "Chung Yung and the Greek Conception of Justice," *Journal of Chinese Philosophy* 26 (1999).

58. Lin Yu-tang, *The Wisdom of Confucius* (New York: The Modern Library, 1938), 130.

59. *Ibid.*, p. 105.

60. Chan, *A Source Book*, p. 44.

61. *Ibid.*, p. 24.

Confucian Moral Cultivation: Some Parallels with Musical Training

Karyn Lai

A significant theme in the Confucian classics, including Confucius's *Analects*, the *Xunzi*,[1] the *Book of Rites*,[2] the *Book of Music*,[3] the *Book of Poetry*, and the *Book of Filial Piety*,[4] is the connection between morality and music. In these texts, it is held that music is causally related to moral cultivation: music has influential power through its harmonizing [*he*] effects, both in the moral cultivation of the Confucian gentleman (*junzi*) and on the common people:

> Ceremonies and music should not for a moment be neglected by any one. When one has mastered completely [the principles of] music, and regulates his heart and mind accordingly, the natural, correct, gentle and honest heart is easily developed, and with development of the heart comes joy. (*Book of Rites* XVII.iii.23)

> In music the sages found pleasure, and [saw that] it could be used to make the hearts of the people good. Because of the deep influence which it exerts on a man, and the change which it produces in manners and customs, the ancient kings appointed it as one of the subjects of instruction (*Book of* Rites XVII.ii.7)[5]

These early Confucian texts allude to the complimentary roles of music and *li* (norms of social intercourse), particularly in the education of the Confucian gentleman. In later Confucianism (around the Han Dynasty), discussions about music involved its place within cosmological ideas: in particular, correlations and resonances between music, Heaven and Earth, the five elements, and the prevailing sociopolitical order were discussed. Within the Confucian tradition, these ideas are articulated in Xunzi's works, the *Book of Music*, and in the works of Dong Zhongshu, notably, the *Chunqiu Fanlu*.[6]

This essay compares particular aspects of moral cultivation and musical training. It moves away from the theme that music is an instrument of moral education[7] to examine some parallels between the two projects. The point of the comparison is to allude to various aspects of the musical training process to illuminate the process of self-cultivation in Confucian thought.[8] Parallels in music and morality are significant especially when we consider the depth of expression and mood in both moral and musical performance. Siu-Chi Huang, who examines music in early Confucian thought, makes a note regarding the *content* of musical sounds:

> Confucius and his early followers recognised the existence of some quality or value in music itself which apparently is capable of arousing the listener's feelings and emotions. . . . According to the Confucian theory . . . the intrinsic value of musical art belongs not only to a sensuous medium or "surface," that is, the tone of music, but to its mood and association, that is, the content of musical sounds.[9]

Another aspect of Confucian moral practice which lends further credence to this comparison rests in the Confucian concept *li*. The Confucian notion of *li* retains, from ancient Chinese thought and practice, a sense of ritual action embedded in tradition and culture. David Hall and Roger Ames, scholars of Confucian thought, allude to the parallels between music and ritual practice: "Like a body of literature or a corpus of music, these rituals continue through time as a repository of the ethical and aesthetic insights of those who have gone before."[10] In this connection, some aspects of the two practices and forms are discussed in this essay. This includes examination of how, for example, the beginning musician learns to perform a given piece and needs to acquire technical skills through constant and ongoing practice. The accomplished musician, by contrast, seeks not merely to reproduce a piece in a technically perfect manner but also to perform in an expressively rich style; indeed, he is expected to perform according to *his* interpretation of the piece.

The view of self-cultivation in the *Analects* has important parallels: the initial stages of self-cultivation are portrayed as arduous in terms of the required compliance with Confucian norms. At the beginning of the self-cultivation process, the learner acts within a fairly circumscribed context, and there is little room for flexibility. In contrast to those at this stage of self-cultivation, the *junzi*, not unlike the accomplished performer of music, is expected to draw upon his own resources in his deliberations, at times even improvising on existing norms (*Analects* 9.3).

In the first section, I explore, broadly, the Confucian project of self-cultivation. In the following sections, I discuss the different dynamics of application in different stages of self-cultivation. In view of that, the progression of the argument in these sections may be seen in terms of developmental stages. However, the features discussed in each section are indicative rather than prescriptive marks of the respective stages. The aim of the essay is to offer a fresh, Confucian-inspired approach to moral development, which places the learner in a given socio-cultural context, and which takes into account the skills and moral sensitivity required for moral practice within that context. In addition, this essay will demonstrate that a developmental interpretation of the Confucian concept *li* explains away many apparent inconsistencies among its many uses in the *Analects*. Finally, I will argue that the Confucian approach to self-cultivation embodies an aesthetic, performative aspect.

Confucian Moral Practice and Performance

In Confucian thought, moral action and behavior are inseparable, both onto-logically and epistemologically, from the notion of a cultivated life. The *Analects* does not offer simply a code of appropriate conduct but, rather, proposes a view of human flourishing underscored by a philosophy of relatedness. On this view, the cultivation of the individual *qua* person-in-relation includes both the development of a *perspective* that sees oneself as situated within a particular historical, cultural, and social context, as well as the nurturing of the self, in its relations with others, within that context.

The context within which relationships are forged is of primary importance in Confucian thought. This is reflected in the priority given to familial relation-ships, notably to the concept of filial piety, *xiao*: the family context provides the primary locus within which one's first relationships are formed. The dynamics of relating to others, including processes of negotiating, balancing obligations, moral deliberation, and fostering affective ties, are first practiced in this con-text.

What emerges from this view of the self is a picture of morality couched in concrete and developmental terms, rather than in terms of abstract principles or isolated behaviors or actions. The moral development of the individual, which includes the cultivation of meaningful and harmonious relationships, is necessarily situated within the individual's social and cultural environment. In the deepest Confucian sense, a cultivated life can only be realized within one's social environment.

This does not mean, however, that the harmonizing (*he*) of relationships is a primary concern, nor that the individual becomes a mere automaton within a society driven by status quo. The first view, that Confucian ethics consists primarily in harmonizing relationships, could be based in superficial observa-tions of Chinese cultural norms coupled with cursory readings of the Confucian texts. According to such a view, the *Analects* would appear in a negative light, combining elements of rigidity, hierarchical power, and nepotism that, at best, support a system for maintaining social harmony.

In contrast, however, passage 1.12 of the *Analects* makes it clear that while harmony is a desirable outcome of actions guided by *li*, it is not an end-in-it-self. Rather, the passage seems to suggest that harmony is a matter of style and hence of aesthetic value. Furthermore, harmony is only a by-product of actions carried out according to *li*:

> Master You said: "Achieving harmony (*he*) is the most valuable function of observ-ing ritual propriety. In the ways of the Former Kings, this achievement of harmony

made them elegant, and was a guiding standard in all things large and small. But when things are not going well, to realise harmony just for its own sake without regulating the situation through observing ritual propriety will not work."[11]

Tu Wei-ming, a Confucian scholar, emphasizes that, from the Confucian point of view, the perception that harmony is a primary concern is mistaken:

> The self as the center of relationships has always been the focus of Confucian learning. One's ability to harmonize human relations does indeed indicate one's self-cultivation, but the priority is clearly set. Self-cultivation is a precondition for harmonizing human relations; if human relations are superficially harmonized without the necessary ingredients of self-cultivation, it is practically unworkable and teleologically misdirected.[12]

The rejection of harmony as the end of Confucian society was already an issue for the early Confucians; the aim of self-cultivation is *not* mere social acceptance. In *Analects* 13:24, there is a qualification regarding what it means to be liked and disliked:

> Tzu-kung asked, "'All in the village like him.' What do you think of that?"
> The Master said, "That is not enough."
> "'All in the village dislike him.' What do you think of that?"
> The Master said, "That is not enough either. 'Those in his village who are good like him and those who are bad dislike him.' That would be better."[13]

An examination of the Confucian gentleman paradigm, the *junzi*, demonstrates the independence of the paradigmatic individual of the demands and norms of popular culture. The *junzi* seeks what is within himself while the small man, by contrast, seeks that in others (*Analects* 15.21; see also 15.22). In the description of Confucius's own developmental path in *Analects* 2.4, the stages of progress involve the cultivation of inner resources quite independent of the then contemporary norms. In this sense, the Confucian project may be seen to involve a gradual and appropriate detachment from some conventional expectations. The detachment suggested here does not refer to detachment from other people, nor does it refer to detachment from one's social and cultural environment; both these are alien to Confucian philosophy.

Rather, the term 'detachment' used here points to the *junzi* as an independent assessor of required and right action in particular situations. In *Analects* 13.23, the point is made that seeking harmony in relating to others is a different enterprise from seeking to be *like* those others: "The *chun tzu* (*junzi*) seeks to be harmonious but does not attempt to be similar (*tong*). The small man, by contrast, seeks to be similar and is not harmonious." The emphasis on the subtle differences between harmony and similarity is important: in the pursuit of harmony, a tendency to work towards similarity, and hence towards conformity, is an easy slip to make. The reduction of conflict between individuals would be a distinctly easier process if people shared similar views and goals. However, the slide to similarity in one's pursuit of harmony is an inappropriate price to pay. In his personal experience, Confucius is reported to have rejected compromise, holding out instead for a proper appreciation of himself[14]:

> Tzu-kung said, "If you had a piece of beautiful jade here, would you put it away safely in a box or would you try to sell it for a good price?"
>
> The Master said, "Of course I would sell it. All I am waiting for is the right offer." (*Analects* 9.13; tr. Lau)

The preceding discussion prompts us towards a view of Confucian self-cultivation that seeks to strike a balance between the self and the demands of social relationships. There is little doubt in the *Analects* that the self is at least in part constituted by its relationships and by the way it participates in relationships. There is a striking and appealing acknowledgment in Confucian thought that a person is not an isolated entity but is indeed partly molded by interaction with particular others in particular contexts. The dynamics of the Confucian process of self-cultivation based on this model of personhood are discussed in the following sections.

The Beginner: *Li* as Technique

A beginner in any field is akin to a clean slate: information is absorbed and, where applicable, attempts are made to apply the new knowledge. Especially in the early stages of the process, the beginner might be expected to make enquiries regarding, but not to question, the received information. In cases where the learning process involves the acquisition of skills, the dynamics of knowing-how are involved.[15] In contrast to knowing-that—for instance, in the mere propounding of propositions—Gilbert Ryle argues that:

(a) knowing-how involves the actualization or exercise of knowledge;

(b) knowing-how involves performance which is "in some way governed by principles, rules, canons, standards or criteria . . . his observance of rules, principles, etc., must . . . be realised in his performance of his tasks. . . . He *must* play judiciously; he *may* also propound judgments"[16]; and

(c) the acquisition of know-how might in some cases involve the use of manuals. However, the instructions in these manuals, some of which might include principles extracted from their applications by people who know-how, are not in themselves applications of know-how. Rather, they are imperatives of pedagogical value only for the novice.

Confucian self-cultivation is an acquisition of know-how: "[t]he artisan, in any of the hundred crafts, masters his trade by staying in his workshop; the gentleman perfects his way through learning" (*Analects* 19.7; tr. Lau). The *Analects* views the beginning stage of self-cultivation as a phase in which the primacy of practice is emphasized. In this connection, there is a sense of conservative traditionalism, often presented in terms of Confucius's stress on adopting norms from an earlier, feudal period of the *Zhou* dynasty (1112–249 B.C.E.) (see *Analects* 7.1 and 7.5). Chapters in the *Analects* that articulate this theme give the impression that individuals in the Confucian community find themselves in a constrained, controlled environment, under the instruction of one's superiors or mentors, with little room for divergence of views from one's superiors. However, I contend that this conception of *li* as primarily technical and inflexible is applicable only in the case of the beginner in the self-cultivation process.

Drawing on Ryle's characterization of "knowing-how" alluded to earlier, we see that the acquisition of know-how in its initial stages might involve a manual of imperatives of pedagogical value for the novice. We could take Book 10 of the *Analects*, which presents Confucius as an antiquated figure, fastidious about details of comportment and context, as a manual of this kind, albeit a rather outdated one.

It should be noted that an earlier, pre-Confucian usage of the term *li* was in reference to the ethico-spiritual conduct of the sage kings in ritual sacrifice. In a well-learned ritual—one in which participants have had much practice—the coordination of movements and gestures, both overt and subtle, is polished such that the ritual seems to be carried out with ease.

The proper understanding of the meaning and context of a ritual, as well as one's efficient participation in the ritual, comes only after much practice.[17] Hence, as indicated in the *Book of Odes*—and as discussed by Confucius in *Analects* 1.15—the process of learning *li*, and of practicing it, involves much *constant* work:

> Like bone cut, like horn polished,
> Like jade carved, like stone ground (tr. Lau)

The skill required to carve a piece of jade is acquired only through continuous and rigorous practice. There are two aspects relevant to the emphasis on practice: chronologically, practice is a precondition of the mastery of the skill; ontologically, the manifestation of the skill is possible only through its practical expression.[18] It is quite clear that the technicalities of *li* were important to Confucius because they are what the beginner first learns. With reference to some of the considerations that have been raised so far, it would not be too farfetched to suggest that passages in the *Analects* such as 12.1 ("To regulate oneself with commitment to *li* [*kezi fuli*], is *ren*.")[19] embody a belief in the effectiveness of behaviorist internalizations of codes and norms, at least in the beginning stages of self-cultivation.

The Confucian theory of *zhengming* is significant in this discussion. Often translated as the 'rectification of names', *zhengming* is perhaps better translated as 'regulation according to names'. This doctrine, broadly speaking, refers to the view that specific requirements and/or obligations arise within the context of relating to others, with the requirements varying according to one's position within particular relationships. According to the view of *zhengming*, "Individuals have to live *appropriately* according to the titles and names, indicating their ranks and statuses within relationships, by which they are referred to. These terms prescribe how values upholding the various roles are to be realized within the fundamental reality of the lived human world."[20] In this sense, *zhengming* has a regulative function.

It is sufficient for the purposes of this paper to note that Confucius accords *zhengming* chronological priority in ordering the country (*Analects* 13.3). Furthermore, there was fairly firm insistence that the requirements of the various relationships be kept to (see *Analects* 13.20; 6.27; 8.18; 4.6 and 2.7). One might say that these requirements are encapsulated in *li*, appropriate actions and gestures in particular contexts. The beginner has to learn which actions and gestures are appropriate in which contexts. This learning is, in the first instance, technical.

In comparison, the beginner in music first learns to play strictly according to the printed music, or seeks to reproduce what she hears. The beginner has no capacity or skill for improvisation. Confucius's allusion to music in Analects 3.23 is instructive at this juncture: "The Master talked to the Grand Music Master of Lu about music, and said: 'Much can be realized with music if one begins by playing in unison, and then goes on to improvise with purity of tone and distinctness and flow, thereby bringing all to completion.'" There are a few important themes in this passage; one of them is a reference to specific stages of progression, leading to completion [*cheng*: also meaning success]. Playing in unison, in the early stages, suggests a moderated, careful approach to the process.

It is important at this point to draw a comparison between playing in unison in musical training and the exercise of filial piety in Confucian thought. There are at least two significant factors which arise from the comparison. First, because the family is the first context for moral training, filial piety occupies a central position in Confucian thought. Antonio Cua, discussing Confucian ethics, emphasizes the family context as the initial and primary locus of ethical practice: "the acquisition of these virtues presupposes a locus in which these particular, dependent virtues are exercised. Thus among dependent virtues, filiality and fraternity are considered primary, for the family is the natural home and foundation for the extension of *jen*—affection."[21]

The second and related point is that the attitude in the *Analects* towards filial piety—as analogous to playing in unison—is conservative and seems rather inflexible. Part of the reason for this would be that the beginner is neither in a position to challenge, nor to improvise. The position in the *Analects* regarding the priority of filial piety is obvious, but in some cases, would appear extreme. In *Analects* 4.18, one may remonstrate only gently, and disagreements are masked by a respectful demeanour towards parents. In *Analects* 13.18, loyalty to one's family members overrides truth telling.

The priority accorded to filial piety marks out the primacy of the family context in moral training. Presumably, if one has received training within a familial context, one is then ready to improvise outside of that context without always having to play in unison.[22] In the *Analects*, there is a sense that rote learning and imitative practice of *li* constitutes only an initial stage of moral cultivation. In other words, training in *li* is necessary though insufficient for moral cultivation. Antonio Cua sees training in *li*, as opposed to the acquisition of *ren*, as rule-following. He describes self-cultivation from the point of view of the *junzi* as having two aspects: "[The *junzi* has] an indispensable, educational role, not only in providing models for competence in *li* or rule-following, but also in inculcating *jen*-attitude or ethical concern and reasonableness in rule-application."[23] Cua's distinction between *li* and *ren* is a useful one. However, as Cua himself is aware, from the point of view of self-cultivation, the connection between *li* and *ren* should not be seen as dichotomous. The *junzi*'s life encompasses both aspects. Here, suffice it to say that it is not merely in the acquisition of *li*, norms of appropriate behavior, that the concept of *cultivation* achieves its full significance; the Confucian notion of learning involves the development of one's "inner" resources as well—these include moral sensitivity to different situations as well as to other individuals. The following section discusses the next developmental phase through articulating the connection between *li* and the cultivation of the expressive self.

The Developing Learner: Expressions of Humanity

A music student, in playing a piece of music, must first get the notes correct before she is competent and feels comfortable to express herself through her performance of that particular piece. There is a chronological priority of first acquiring technical skill and, later, of expressing oneself through the music. While technical perfection is a *necessary* element of a good performance it is itself not *sufficient* to constitute good performance; a musical performance that strives only to be technically perfect would be lacking.

The connection between technical skill and expression in music performances is analogous in some key respects to the connection between two central Confucian concepts, *ren* and *li*. For example, there are significant similarities between technical skill and *li*, on the one hand, and between expressivity and *ren*, on the other.

Two passages draw an analogy between *li* and music, and their connection with *ren*:

> The Master said, "What has a person who is not authoritative (*ren*) got to do with observing ritual propriety (*li*)? What has a person who is not authoritative got to do with the playing of music (*yue*)?" (*Analects* 3.3)

> The Master said, "In referring time and again to observing ritual propriety, how could I just be talking about gifts of jade and silk? And in referring time and again to making music, how could I just be talking about bells and drums?" (*Analects* 17.11)

Analects 3.3 draws a connection between *ren* and *li* on the one hand, and *ren* and music, on the other. The implication in this chapter is that *ren* is the basis for both *li* acts and musical performances. In *Analects* 17.11, while *ren* has not specifically been identified as the basis of *li* and music, Confucius poses a rhetorical question which dismisses mere external compliance to convention. There is a strong sense that perfunctory behavior in the case of both *li* and music is to be rejected.

In this context, the concept *ren*, and how it is associated with *li*, needs to be examined. *Ren* is often viewed as the psychological and motivational basis of *li* acts. The depth of the connection between *ren* and *li* is substantiated in a number of passages in the *Analects* (2.8; 3.3; 3.12; 3.26; 17.17; 17.21; 19.14). Confucius emphasizes the importance of having the appropriate disposition in the performance of *li*. In almost all of these passages, Confucius points to the futility of mechanically and thoughtlessly going through the motions associated with particular rituals in specific contexts. In *Analects* 3.26, which sums up the tone of these passages, Confucius remarks, "What could I see in a person who in holding a position of influence is not tolerant, who in observing ritual propriety is not respectful, and who in overseeing the mourning rites does not grieve?" An anecdote about meeting the requirements of the mourning period (for one's parents) further demonstrates the connection between *ren* and *li* in the *Analects*. In 17.21, Confucius is consulted by Zaiwo who, after a year of engagement in mourning practice, is reluctant to fulfill the required three years. Confucius's response is to release Zaiwo of his obligation. This is to be understood in the context that Zaiwo does not seem to be appropriately sorrowful at the loss of his parents. However, after Zaiwo's departure, Confucius traces his unwillingness to fulfil the requirements of mourning to his lack of *ren* (*buren*).

In the light of passages such as 17.21, it seems that *ren* is more fundamental than *li* because *li* is often construed in terms of "external" behavior and contrasted with *ren*, often thought of as "inner" disposition. Hence, Confucius in Zaiwo's case dismisses the need for behavior and practice associated with mourning given that Zaiwo lacks the appropriate inner disposition.

According to such an interpretation, *li* is at times understood to be merely behavioristic and incidental to the cultivation of the self. For instance, in "The Creative Tension Between *Jen* and *Li*," Tu Wei-ming views *ren* as a concept of "personal morality," which functions "as an inner morality . . . not caused by the mechanism of *li* from outside. It is a higher-order concept which gives meaning to *li*."[24] On this view, one would see *li* as a vehicle for the expression of *ren*, just as one might view technical expertise in music as merely instrumental for the performer's expression. According to Tu's definition, there seems to be a dichotomy between "inner" and "outer," as well as a hierarchy: *ren* is a higher-order concept.

Tu's articulation of the connection between *ren* and *li* could be misinterpreted: the idea that *ren* is *personal* morality could give the impression that there is some dichotomy between the inner and the outer, corresponding to a dichotomy between the personal and the impersonal, or between the individual and the social. However, such dichotomies are problematic as they are alien to the Confucian concept of self. To construe *li* as "outer" and *ren* as "inner" is inappropriate because there is an unacceptable fragmentation between the two concepts. Hence, in a later article, Tu moves beyond such dichotomization, arguing for the inseparability of *ren* and *li*: "although *jen*, especially when used as a comprehensive virtue, gives meaning to *li*, *jen* without the manifestation of *li* is also inconceivable."[25]

Shun Kwong-Loi, a Confucian scholar, takes the discussion further.[26] He characterizes *li* and *ren* as inseparable, and as necessary and sufficient for each other. Shun rejects interpretations of *ren* as more fundamental than *li* (that *li* have only an instrumental role), as well as those interpretations of *li* as more fundamental than *ren* (that *li* define *ren*). Shun argues that each of these interpretations is reliant only on selected readings of the *Analects*. His strategy is to draw together passages from the *Analects* which refer to the connection between *ren* and *li*. In this regard, Shun contends that neither *ren* nor *li* is merely instrumental to the other. He uses an example, that of getting married, to illustrate his thesis.[27] In this example, we are to imagine a community in which the only way to get married is through the performance of certain motions appropriate to the ceremony. In this context, the performance of these motions, and getting married, are not separate occurrences. Furthermore, they are not reducible to the other.

Shun's view of *ren* and *li* is not merely about the relative priority of the concepts. It also addresses their interconnectedness. To say that *ren* and *li* are necessary and sufficient for each other is to make the point that each *li*-act should be imbued with *ren*. Taking the argument back to the issue of successful musical performance, it is clear that the expression of musicality and sentiment, on the one hand, and technical excellence, on the other, are mutually interdependent. The novice musician develops the skill of expressing herself through her technical abilities. With regard to effective self-cultivation in Confucian thought, the process involves *both* the nurturing of a virtuous character *and* the expression of that character in interaction with others. This means that the development of the self necessarily takes place within the context of the community. The next section continues the discussion of the connection between *ren* and *li* from the point of view of the embedded self.

Culture, Tradition, and Cultivation: *Li* and *Ren* in Context

The conceptualization of *li* and *ren* as necessary and sufficient for each other is important in the conceptualization of the Confucian project. Henry Skaja presents Confucian self-cultivation as a socialization process:

> In his effort to establish the future of civilized culture, Confucius creatively selected, used, and transformed the traditional behavioral norms of conduct (*li*) which were still of educational value. He thereby *transformed* and *generalized* the meaning of *li* from mere "rite" or "ritual sacrifice" to the necessary educative and self-reflective socialization process, itself, whereby man becomes humanized, i.e. socialized.[28]

However, there needs to be some caution here; Skaja's use of the term socialization could be misleading: while it appears that for Skaja the term refers rather broadly to a person's cultivation, which includes self-reflection, he could be understood, more narrowly, to be characterizing Confucianism in terms of an indoctrination process. However, this latter reading is a rather extreme and drastic interpretation of the Confucian project.[29] Typically, the socialization process would consist in the introduction and induction of the learner to existing norms and values. But, surely, this does not fully constitute Confucian self-cultivation as described thus far. It appears then, that socialization is a necessary *though not sufficient* part of one's initial induction into society.

We can think of socialization within the self-cultivation process as a background against which self-cultivation takes on its full meaning.[30] Antonio Cua describes the significance of this background—*wen*—in Confucian thought as a context for moral action:

> [In Confucian ethics and traditional Chinese culture,] [t]he characteristic concern with the *form* of proper behavior is still present. However, the form stressed is not just a matter of fitting into an established social structure or set of distinctions, nor is it a matter or methodic procedure that facilitates the satisfaction of the agent's desires and wishes, rather, it involves the elegant form (*wen*) for the expression of ethical character.[31]

According to Cua's analysis, *wen* is not merely indoctrination or induction. Cua includes in his interpretation of *wen* a sense of aesthetic refinement which may also be applied to moral action. The Chinese character *wen* signifies 'character script', with a broader connotation of language, education, and learning; it is commonly translated into English as 'culture', though *wen* includes a sense of tradition as well.

In two instances in the *Analects*, Confucius and Zigong, his disciple, are responding to their contemporaries who are keen to shrug off the significance of *wen*:

> The Master said, "When one's basic disposition (*zhi*) overwhelms refinement (*wen*), the person is boorish; when refinement overwhelms one's basic disposition, the person is an officious scribe. It is only when one's basic disposition and refinement are in appropriate balance that you have the exemplary person (*junzi*)." (*Analects* 6.18)

> Ji Zicheng inquired "[*Junzi*] are determined by nothing other than the quality of their basic disposition (*zhi*); what need do they have of further refinement (*wen*)?"
>   Zigong replied, ". . . refinement is no different from one's basic disposition; one's basic disposition is no different from refinement. The skin of the tiger or leopard, shorn of its hair, is no different from the dog or sheep." (*Analects* 12.8)

In both passages, there is an emphatic reminder that cultivation is at least as important as innate virtue (whether that refers to a disposition or a capacity).[32] There is another important implication in these two passages, and that is that in regard to practical aspects of self-cultivation, there should be no dichotomy between basic character (*zhi*) and its cultivated expression (*wen*), even if theoretical distinctions may be made between innate and acquired behaviors.[33]

According to my interpretation, self-cultivation *is* the process whereby what is innate and what is acquired are finely proportioned and harmoniously balanced (*binbin* in *Analects* 6.18).[34] Additionally, if basic character and cultivated expression are "no different" from each other, the message we get from these passages is that self-cultivation is meaningful and possible only *within* its social environment.[35] The lived context of human interaction is of fundamental significance in Confucian thought. It follows then that the cultivation of *ren* and *li* needs to take place against the background of *wen*. In *Analects* 6.27 and 12.15, "the Master said, 'Learn broadly of *wen*, discipline this learning through observing *li*, and moreover, in so doing, remain on course without straying from it.'" Here, it seems that *wen* encompasses norms in general, such as decorum, comportment, traditional customs, and other culturally-specific norms including etiquette. *Li*, on the other hand, connotes acting in ways that are morally and perhaps even religiously acceptable.[36]

The distinction between *li* and *wen* is a fundamental one if *li* is not to be reduced to the dictates of the status quo. Importantly, if both *li* and *wen* signify subscription to existing cultural and traditional norms, and if *wen* is guided by *li*, then the essential moral content that is provided by *li* must be distinguished from mere status quo. It is worth noting that Confucius emphasizes that, while it might be a simple task to *acculturate* oneself (*wen*), it is a much more difficult task to *cultivate* oneself [to become a *junzi*] (*Analects* 7.33). Roger Ames and Henry Rosemont, Jr.[37] provide an animated translation of the passage: "The Master said, 'In the niceties of culture, I am perhaps like other people. But as far as personally succeeding in living the life of the *junzi*, I have accomplished little.'" Here, it is clear that the ends of *wen* and moral cultivation are different. To avoid circularity, the connection between the two might be characterized in terms of interdependence: one can only cultivate oneself if one is familiar with existing cultural and traditional norms and customs. However, acting strictly according to normative prescriptions and ideals within a particular tradition is insufficient for self-cultivation. As demonstrated in an earlier section, the Confucian *junzi* is in many ways detached from popular opinion and popular valuations. To express it in a Confucian manner, cultivation of the self, which includes the cultivation of meaningful relationships with other people, requires more than an awareness of one's historical and socio-cultural setting and of the norms that operate within that setting.

In view of the Confucian concept of the interconnected self, the practice of *li within the socio-cultural context* is a prerequisite for the cultivation of the self. In practical terms, this means that in order for one to fully engage with others within a particular social and cultural setting, one needs first to understand existing social, cultural, and moral norms operative within that framework. In this connection, it could be said that one of Confucius's great insights lies in the acknowledgment of the influential forces of tradition and culture in shaping moral norms (see *Analects* 15.10).[38] The idea of an environment within which self-cultivation takes place highlights the notion of *li* as being rooted in tradition. In other words, *li* are intelligible only within the context of (inherited) tradition. As Fingarette points out, "[*li*] rest primarily on the inheritance by each age of a vast body of conventional language and practices from the preceding age."[39]

From a slightly different angle, if we are to understand the Confucian paradigmatic man, the *junzi*, as an "embodiment of a cultural life style"[40] then the cultivation of the self *must* involve an appreciation of that cultivated self by others within the community. In probing further into questions about the constitutive elements of culture and tradition, an allusion to musical performance will shed light on the complexity of self-cultivation.

Imagine a performance of Beethoven's *Moonlight Sonata*. The pianist, if she is a virtuoso musician, engages the audience *in her performance*. In turn, a learned audience, in appreciating a performance of the piece, becomes engaged with, and engrossed in *the performance of* the music.[41] In this scenario, the music provides a medium whereby the pianist and her audience communicate. Inasmuch as the pianist is an initiator (in her playing of the music), she yet relies

on the responses of her audience. A restless and distracted audience is one that
has failed to engage with the performance. Whether the cause of the restlessness
rests on the part of the performer or on the audience itself is, needless to say, an
important issue. The restlessness is a symptom that the intended communication (through the performance) has failed.

It would hardly be surprising to speculate that such restlessness in the audience might severely affect the performer and her performance; feedback on her
performances is crucial for the performer. Indeed, without it, the pianist cannot
advance very far in further developing her technique. She may rely on her own
intuitions to develop her skills, but a performance without critical feedback
from a learned audience is hardly worthwhile. For it appears that if there is a
complete lack of response to the pianist's self-expression, it is almost as if the
pianist herself has been ignored in her performance.

Obviously, a crucial part of the performance by the pianist, and the response
from the audience, lies in their sharing of a cultural-historical background.
Furthermore, in order that communication occur between performer and audience, both are presumed to have background knowledge of the musical work
(eg., the kind of work it is and the composer's style and intentions in writing
a particular piece).

This background knowledge may be taken as a parallel to the inherited
tradition, or *wen*, in Confucian self-cultivation. Any informed evaluation of a
person's actions must take place against this background of shared knowledge.
In comparison with moral practice, an evaluation of a particular moral act
needs take into account both the circumstances of the situation, as well as
the accepted norms which are part of a community's socio-cultural heritage.
Antonio Cua comments on the use of moral notions within a community:

> In general we may regard vindication in discourse as a piece of argumentation that
> occurs in a practical context characterized in terms of the presence of moral rules
> or notions. What is taken as a moral rule depends on the sort of activity deemed
> important by the participants as in some way indispensable to a common way of life
> embedded in a culture and a *form of life*. The moral audience is a particular audience
> within a cultural setting. . . . The use of moral notions is thus tied to a common
> background in which they are regarded by the agents as in some fashion a definitive
> expression of a communal way of life. The particular contexts of the uses of moral
> notions may be regarded as a partial articulation of the aspects of the background
> shared by both the speaker and his audience. [42]

With regard to musical performances, critical comments such as "a sensitive performance of Beethoven's *Moonlight Sonata*," "a poor interpretation of
the second movement," "she is a celebrated performer of Beethoven's piano
sonatas," or "he is a renowned performer of Mozart's but not of Beethoven's
piano works," have significant and deep meaning only for those who under-

stand the performance in the context of the continuing tradition of the musical works.

In much the same way, the practice of *li* requires a shared, communal context. Within this context, each *li*-act is an event which allows for self-expression; the self is a communal self. It is in this sense that the boundaries between self and community become blurred: commentators have often noted that the Confucian view of self veers sharply from the atomistic model of self. Herbert Fingarette expresses succinctly parallels between the evaluation of *li*-acts and of musical performances and discusses their necessary contextualization:

> Acts that are *li* . . . are subtle and intelligent acts exhibiting more or less sensitivity to context, more or less integrity in performance. . . . We distinguish sensitive and intelligent musical performances from dull and unperceptive ones; and we detect in the performance confidence and integrity, or perhaps hesitation, conflict, "faking," "sentimentalizing." We detect all this *in* the performance; we do not have to look into the psyche or personality of the performer. It is all "there," public.[43]

Fingarette's articulation of the logistics of a performance is significant because it transcends a dichotomy between the "personal" and the "public" in a performance. This understanding of a performance is particularly applicable in the practice of *li* within the Confucian society because there is no assumed dichotomy between *ren* and *li* or between one's feelings for others and its cultivated expression.

Hence, while one has to be careful not to reduce self-cultivation to socialization, one should not, on the other hand, neglect the role of inherited tradition.[44] *Analects* 19.22, which remarks on Confucius's attainment in self-cultivation, makes the point that self-cultivation necessarily takes place within a particular context:

> Gongsun Chao of Wei asked Zigong, "With whom did Confucius study?"
>
> Zigong replied, "The way of Kings Wen and Wu has not collapsed utterly—it lives in the people. Those of superior character have grasped the greater part, while those of lesser quality have grasped a bit of it. Everyone has something of Wen and Wu's way in them. Who then does the Master not learn from? Again, how could there be a single constant teacher for him?"

With regard to the expression of the self within one's cultural and traditional context, it should not be overlooked that there is an aesthetic element in the practice and performance of *li*-acts. *Li*, as a vehicle for self-expression, is to be understood within the context of the "harmony and beauty of social forms."[45] Self-cultivation may be understood as a creative, aesthetic process. For the person advanced in the self-cultivation process, *li*-acts may be seen as *performances by and expressions of the cultivated self*. Here, we are keen to avoid a more trivial reading of the idea of performance as mere outward show. A performance is an event through which the musician expresses and reveals herself. She demonstrates not only her technical capabilities with regard to the musical instrument, but also, and more importantly, she expresses the depth of her feelings and knowledge about the musical work. It is not through technical excellence alone, but through her expression of self *in her technical excellence*, that she engages with her audience. Indeed, it could not be further from the truth to suggest that there are two distinct parts to a musical performance, the outward show and some other inscrutable, mystical "inner" feelings of the performer. The performance *is* the expression of the performing self, and conversely, the accomplished musician can only express herself through performance. Hence, *li* appear to have a civilizing function in one's self-expression: *li*-acts *are* refined and cultivated acts. Furthermore, it is *only* through the practice and performance of *li* in the initial stages of self-cultivation that one gradually learns to become a person of *ren*. Returning to the earlier discussion of Gilbert Ryle's description of the "know-how" type of knowledge, it can be seen that performance is an essential aspect of know-how: "(b) knowing-how involves performance which is 'in some way governed by principles, rules, canons, standards or criteria. . . . His observance of rules, principles, etc., must . . . be realised in his performance of his tasks.'"[46] It does not take much to imagine that Ryle could be speaking about the practice of *li* in relation to *ren*. In other words, in cases of the know-how type of knowledge, the only measure of competence is through performance. As Ryle points out, the performer demonstrates his competence not through the recitation of formulae or theorems, but through his ability to perform well. In his actions, the competent performer "*must* play judiciously; he *may* also propound judgments."[47]

A point that needs to be clarified at this stage is that the connection between *ren* and *li* is not a circular one. To say that *ren* is necessary for *li*, and vice-versa, is not to claim that the two terms are identical. Fingarette describes the non-circular yet interdependent connection between *ren* and *li*: "*Li* also refers to the particular act in its status as exemplification of invariant norm; *jen* refers to the act as expressive of an orientation of the person, as expressing his commitment to act as prescribed by *li*."[48] To further elaborate on Fingarette's argument, we might view *ren* and *li* as aspects of the self-cultivation process. In other words, for the beginner in self-cultivation, it is mandatory that one be introduced to existing *li*-practices. The beginner's practice of *li*-acts would typically be formalistic and rule-bound. As a person progresses in her self-cultivation, one would see her *li*-acts as expressions of the self rather than as evidence of her conformity to existing norms. Indeed, a person in the advanced stages of self-cultivation might see the need to veer from existing norms of *li* in particular situations. She has the resources for improvisation because she has grasped not only the basic operative principles but has also acquired an orientation and skills of deliberation applicable in a range of situations.

The discussion of the self-cultivation process so far is incomplete: some of the most important and interesting questions regarding the definition of the self by others and by the community and the limits to individual freedom need to be addressed. From a Confucian point of view, answers to these questions will begin with an assessment of the extents to which modification of *li* or, more generally, abeyance from the norm, is expected to occur. The following section examines the process of self-cultivation as an ongoing, dynamic, and responsive process built upon the interdependence of the self and others in the community.

Playing in Harmony: Realizing the Self

From the Confucian perspective, human persons cannot be decontextualized because they are interdependent with others in their community, continually responding to others and receiving responses from others. It follows that one should be watchful in avoiding dichotomization between self and society. Indeed, the depth of the Confucian concept *ren*—sometimes translated as 'humanity'—lies *between* self and society. We note that in the *Analects*, the highest accolade—well beyond the achievements of *Yao* and *Shun*, revered Confucian sages—goes to one who, in cultivating himself, enriches the lives of other persons (6.30).

The self that is constantly developing is an embedded self within a particular socio-cultural tradition. It is continually acting on its environment and, in turn, being acted on by it. Responsiveness of one person to another is particularly important in an environment where persons are viewed as interdependent. One cannot realize oneself except within one's socio-cultural environment.

At this point, a key question that will emerge is, how is responsiveness understood in practical terms? In other words, what kinds of skills and resources are required for responding to other persons within a Confucian environment? To answer this complex question, an analogy from musical performance is instructive: while Beethoven's *Moonlight Sonata* is a set piece composed two hundred years ago, each performance of it will differ. For instance, some pianists might prefer a slightly quicker tempo for the second movement, some others might have a more forceful third movement, and so forth. Indeed, thoughtfulness *about* the structure and performance of the piece, set against its historical background, is a crucial feature of an intelligent performance.

The personal aspect in every performance is emphasized particularly in works which require improvisation. When a musician improvises on a piece of music, there are several important considerations. These include the nature of the piece, its general mood, structure, length and tempo, and where the improvised section sits within the whole work. It is in the light of such considerations that a true virtuoso performance stands out. An improvised section consisting of a mere technical display, which sits uneasily with the rest of the musical work, does not reflect well on the performer as a musician. For a musician, improvisation is a true opportunity for creativity.[49]

Drawing on this model of improvisation, it is interesting to note the striking similarities in the modification of *li*-acts in Confucian thought. Modification of a particular existing *li*-practice would involve parallel considerations. For instance, in his deliberations on the use of the hemp or silk cap, Confucius takes into account, among other factors, what is traditional and what is contemporary (ie., the general mood and context surrounding that particular *li*-practice):

> The Master said, "The use of a hemp cap is prescribed in the observance of ritual propriety (*li*). Nowadays, that a silk cap is used instead is a matter of frugality. I would follow accepted practice on this. A subject kowtowing on entering the hall is prescribed in the observance of ritual propriety (*li*). Nowadays that one kowtows only after ascending the hall is a matter of hubris. Although it goes contrary to accepted practice, I still kowtow on entering the hall." (*Analects* 9.3)

I want to emphasize that it is not a case of "anything goes" whether *li* should be modified. *Analects* 9.3 is careful to spell out the *context* and *content* of Confucius's deliberations to modify *li* in particular situations.[50] Confucius reflects on the rationale for the existing practice and on the various weights given to different factors. In this case, the economical aspect of using silk overrides the significance of the material used to make the cap. In contrast, we see in the same passage that Confucius is unwilling to modify the traditional *li*-practice of bowing below the hall because he deems the then current practice (of bowing above the hall) to be based on arrogance and presumptuousness.

A practical issue that needs to be addressed at this point is, to what extent is this example indicative of a deliberative Confucian life? Is Confucian moral deliberation different from other kinds of moral deliberation? Is the modern Confucian *junzi* constantly modifying existing norms *in order to live a Confucian life*? More generally, what are the limits of modification and how frequently is it expected to occur? The answer to these questions will reveal in part what the ideal Confucian society is like in terms of its structures and institutions that promote or discourage such modifications of existing norms and practices. It should be noted at the outset that improvisation of existing *li* was not a skill or ability every person had; *Analects* 8.9 makes it quite clear that the common people (*min*) did not have these skills or such capacities.

But what is this capacity that only the *junzi* are meant to have, which presumably guides their deliberations? What is it that makes the *junzi* better able to handle situations where there are different and at times conflicting demands, expectations, and obligations that pull in different directions? Here, we may note that the *junzi*, in contrast to the small man (*xiaoren*), is characterized as being at ease (*tai*) (*Analects* 13.26). One can easily imagine, with the help of

Ryle's discussion of knowing-how, that a person generally lacking deliberative skills to balance demands and negotiate relationships would be anxious in a range of situations.

Shun Kwong-Loi discusses the themes of modification of *li*, change, and tradition in Confucian philosophy.[51] The discussion points to a tendency in Confucianism towards conservatism with regard to modifying existing *li*-practices. It seems that the extent of conservatism within the *Analects* depends largely on emphasis: those who construe Confucius's project primarily in terms of the cultivation of *ren* (see *Analects* Book 4, passages 1 to 6) are more likely to perceive creativity and liberalism as features of the *Analects*. On the other hand, if the *Analects* is understood as a treatise on *li*, then it would most likely be seen as conservative (see, for example, *Analects* 2.5).[52] Returning to Shun's analysis, however, it is worth noting that he attempts to maintain both the possibility for revising existing norms, and a sense of conservative, backward pull. His analysis is consistent with the view presented in this paper, which aims to preserve a sense of conservatism present in some of the applications of *li* in the *Analects*.

The question that then arises, particularly in a philosophy which is often seen as emphasising tradition, is what element prevents the self from being "swallowed up" by the norms and dictates of the community? It appears that this element would be especially important within a philosophical framework that does not hold the autonomy of individuals as a fundamental ideal or value. In the context of Confucian philosophy, what is to prevent *li* from collapsing into a system of social control and indoctrination? For example, if a particular existing *li*-practice requires what is morally unreasonable (eg., substantive discrimination against women), what kinds of resources might be available to individuals to refuse to subscribe to that particular *li*-practice? Tu describes an instance of this in China's history:

> The so-called "doctrine of *li*" (*li-chiao*), which was under such violent criticism during the May 4th period, especially by literary writers like Lu Hsün, is a good example [of *li* degenerating into social coercion incapable of conscious improvement and liable to destroy any true human feelings]. . . . During the Ming-Ch'ing period, quite a number of widows committed suicide hoping to show that their acts were in conformity with the *li* of chastity. In view of such stupidity, Lu Hsün was quite justified in calling this type of *li* "eating man" (*ch'ih-jen*).[53]

Tu's solution to the problem of *li* disintegrating into mere social conformity is expressed in terms of *ren*, whereby *ren* provides substantive moral content to *li*. However, as most scholars would agree, the concept *ren*—as revealed in its character script—relates more to human relatedness than it does to a sense of rightness or morality, or to "personal" morality. Precisely because of this reason, many scholars are resistant to the idea that *ren* might be satisfactorily be equated with, or translated as, 'moral', 'morality', or 'virtue', because to do so would amount to a reductionistic rendition of *ren*.

Furthermore, in the example of widows committing suicide (*li*) in order to demonstrate their chastity, it is not immediately clear that an analysis according to the conduct of human relationships or of the well-being of the human condition (*ren*) will result in a critical rejection of that *li*-practice. Indeed, an application of reasoning according to *ren* may well proceed this way:

> According to the norms of human relatedness (*ren*), a wife 'belongs' to her husband; where a married woman excels is in her capacity as a wife. As a consequence of his death, she would find life meaningless. This is because she is forever devoted to him, even in death. Hence, widows may as well end their lives not merely in view of their chastity but also of their devotion to their deceased husbands.[54]

To rearticulate the problem of using *ren* to fill the gap in the *li*-problem: if *ren* is a notion distinctive of human-heartedness expressed only in human relationships, and if *ren* is the only resource available to effect a redress of *li*-practice, then any significance or vestige of individual expression will not merely be embedded in the dictates of community but, ultimately, fully subject to them. This would be particularly true in a philosophical framework that emphasizes the communal over the individual.

It seems, then, that a concept other than *ren* is required to do the work in the problem described by Tu. This concept needs to be somewhat independent of *ren*, *li*, and *wen* in order to provide an independent and objective basis for a proper evaluation of existing *li*-practices.

It may be the case that the concept *yi* serves this function. A number of Confucian scholars agree that the operative concept in deliberations regarding the modification of *li* is *yi*, often translated 'right', 'rightness', or 'moral'.[55] *Analects* 15.18 suggests that *yi* is the moral standard put into practice through *li*:

> The Master said, "The gentleman has morality [*yi*] as his basic stuff [*zhi*] and by observing the rites [*li*] puts it into practice, by being modest gives it expression, and by being trustworthy in word brings it to completion. Such is a gentleman indeed!" (D. C. Lau trans.)

> The Master said, "The superior man *in everything* considers righteousness [*yi*] to be essential [*zhi*]. He performs it according to the rules of propriety [*li*]. He brings it forth in humility. He completes it with sincerity. This is indeed a superior man." (*Analects* 15.17 in Legge trans.)

What Lau has translated as 'basic stuff' and Legge as 'essential' is the term *zhi*, meaning basic disposition. This is the same term that is contrasted with *wen* in *Analects* 6.18, as I discussed previously. If *zhi*, as contrasted with *wen* (culture and refinement), may be interpreted to mean a basic or innate disposition, then it seems that Confucius is saying here that *yi* is innate rather than acquired.

It appears that most commentators on the Confucian tradition have interpreted *yi* in terms of its moral content. For example, Legge's use of the term 'righteousness' signifies a certain dispositional state of the moral agent. In a similar way, Lau's interpretation of *yi* as 'morality' or 'rightness' specifies the moral content of the concept. Lau takes care to explain that *yi*, explained in terms of rightness, derives essentially from the character of actions, rather than from the moral agent's disposition and motives. This is where Lau would differ from Legge. For Lau, rightness would depend on circumstances of particular situations. Although Lau doesn't say it explicitly, he does seem to suggest that it is a matter of "fit" whether actions are right in the context of particular circumstances. In that regard, *yi* may also be interpreted as duty: one has a duty to do what is right in a particular kind of situation.

The idea of fit or appropriateness of particular actions comes through best in *Analects* 4.10, where the *junzi* is described as having no prior biases; he measures or evaluates his actions according to what is appropriate in particular circumstances. On this understanding of *yi*, it emerges that the kind of deliberator referred to in *Analects* 9.3 is one who has the skill or capacity to make judgments regarding appropriateness.[56]

The notion of appropriateness is especially important in the framework of a tradition that emphasizes practice and application rather than abstract universals. We need to see the application of *yi* as non-arbitrary or not ultimately reliant on circumstances. It is pointed out in no uncertain terms in the *Analects* that deliberating in view of *yi* is to be contrasted with utility- or outcome-driven considerations. More specifically, *yi* is cast as moral guidance, sharply contrasted with profit (*li*) (see *Analects* 4.16, 14.12).

A creative reading of *yi* has been proposed by Hall and Ames, who see *yi* not essentially in terms of moral content, but of process:

> The primary reference of *yi* is to the organic process comprised by the harmony of action and circumstance. . . . The sort of world required by our analysis of *yi*, however, cannot be characterized primarily by the sort of harmony achieved by the imposition of antecedently existing patterns upon events, for *yi* acts involve the deriving or bestowing of meaning in such a way as to realize novel patterns uniquely suited to each concrete circumstance.[57]

Hall and Ames's interpretation of *yi* is substantiated by many references to classical Confucian texts such as the *Mengzi*, the *Xunzi*, and *Chunqiu Fanlu*.[58] According to Hall and Ames, their interpretation of *yi* is significant in that it overcomes the rigidity of more conservative renditions of the relation between *li* and *yi*. In particular, they argue against interpretations that impose on *yi* a basic sense of normativity or that construe *yi* in terms of principle. It seems that their fundamental objection to both moves rests on a strong conviction that *yi*, construed either as norm or principle, would be external to, and hence imposed on, individual persons.[59]

In light of the preceding discussion, a plausible account of *yi* would capture a sense of moral rectitude somewhat separate from indoctrination or social conditioning. The assertion in Analects 15.18 that *yi* is one's basic disposition (*zhi*) as contrasted with *wen* invokes a notion of *yi* as suggesting an innate moral sensitivity. On this account, *yi* would play a role in the modification of *li* through the application of moral intuition to the various *li*-practices. It would also allow one to judge whether these practices might be contradictory to or inconsistent with one's innate sense of right.

While the idea of an innate moral intuition is difficult to justify within contemporary moral philosophy, the concept did play a role in the historical and intellectual context of Confucian thought. For instance, the Mencian interpretation of Confucius's thought captures this idea of an innate morality, often understood by interpreters in terms of the innate goodness of human nature. For Mencius, both *ren* and *yi*, together with *li* and *zhi* (wisdom), are the four "beginnings" human beings are born with—an analogy Mencius draws with the four limbs (*Mencius* 2A:6.6). It is also significant that for Mencius, *ren* is innate—one of the four beginnings—and, when cultivated, develops into a feeling of compassion (*ceyin*), while *yi* is the beginning that, when cultivated, develops into a sense of shame and revulsion (*xiue*) (*Mencius* 2A:6.5). The Mencian conception of *ren* encompasses a sense of sympathy for others based on human relatedness, while the conception of *yi* revolves around a personal system of regulation based on shame and revulsion. These aspects of *ren* and *yi* are not inconsistent with the distinction made earlier between *ren* and *yi*, that *ren* applies more appropriately to human relatedness while *yi* applies to moral sensitivity.

Returning to Tu's example of particular *li*-practices that threaten human well-being, it would not be unreasonable to suggest that persuading or requiring a widow to commit suicide in order to prove her chastity is morally counterintuitive. Hence, within Confucian moral reasoning, the concept *yi*, referring to moral intuition, is a resource which provides grounds for challenging existing *li*-practices where necessary. In other words, this interpretation of *yi* helps to establish that *li*-practices are not to be understood as fundamental and overriding.

If *li*-practices do not have ultimate priority in determining morality, it follows that there are reasons that run deeper, that justify *li*. In other words, *li* are not practiced as ends-in-themselves. It would be reasonable then to presume that, if there were morally-cultivated persons, these persons would understand the underlying bases and the functions of *li*.[60] Shun repudiates the idea of *li* as rule-following and also implies the functionality of *li*, rather than its ultimacy: "even when a rule of *li* should be observed, one should observe the rule only because it is appropriate or right to do."[61]

Based on the discussion so far, one could construct a tripartite relation between *li*, *ren*, and *yi*. *Yi* is that innate moral sensitivity to what is right. Within relational contexts, this innate moral sensitivity is at times brought to bear on *li* (acceptable patterns of behavior) and *ren* (the proper sentiments toward particular persons, which serve as the necessary motivational force of *li*-acts). *Ren* applies most appropriately within the arena of human relatedness: in its general form, it is manifest as a concern for the human condition; in its more specific instances, it is manifest as a concern for particular others. It could be said that *yi* provides moral content for this concern for others, or for human sympathy in general. Arising out of concern for others, *li*-practices, rooted in tradition and existing norms, are "humanized" through their necessary connection with *ren*. In some cases, the appropriateness of particular *li*-practices or *li*-acts may be evaluated according to *yi*.

The account described so far presents Confucian moral cultivation in a fairly positive light. However, interpreting *yi* as innate moral intuition is less contemporary or modern than Hall and Ames's understanding of *yi* as appropriateness at the crossroads of action and circumstance. The view upheld in this essay accords a greater role to *li* and to tradition, as compared with Hall and Ames's view. This is not to say that Hall and Ames do not pay heed to the role of tradition in shaping a person.[62] However, it is clear that creativity, on the one hand, and deference to tradition, on the other, are inversely proportional factors in self-cultivation.

It is relevant here to note that a critic of Confucian thought, Michael Martin—who has a strong preference for a liberal, Kantian conception of self—proposes the model of a composer, rather than that of a performer, as analogy for creative self-development.[63] According to Martin, while the performer is still confined within the predetermined path of the musical score, the Kantian will only be satisfied with the model of a composer because "the Kantian will want to know who creates the *tao*; even more, the Kantian will want to create it himself, autonomously, and with suitable justification."[64]

Martin moves on to anticipate that "many Confucians will simply ignore this Kantian conception of the self and press ahead with a rival conception of their own."[65] This may be true, but perhaps not without reason: Martin's rather brief account of what is available to the Kantian in terms of creativity seems rather more an ideal than normative or descriptive. It would seem, not merely from a Confucian point of view, but drawing from empirical evidence, that the depth of tradition and other normative forces that shape one's thinking cannot be as easily ignored as if one were to wipe a slate clean. Indeed, there are many aspects of Confucian thinking about human persons and community that realistically reflect how human lives are shaped.

The account of expressive moral action described in this paper allows for each unique personality to have its own play. However, within Confucian thought, such creativity is meaningful only within a particular context, for the Confucian community is not merely a sum-total of individuals and their actions. Within the Confucian framework, the view that persons are intrinsically related calls for a recognition that every action will impact on other persons and, ultimately, on the socio-cultural environment. Fingarette describes the relation between a musical work and particular performances of that work as expressing an inter-dependence of self and community:

> There are legitimate personal aspects of the musical performance, aspects that are irreducible and valuable. . . . Yet, although style and interpretation may be unique to the performer, that is, personal, it remains basic that the true artist's style *serves* the work; the personal interpretation is a genuine interpretation *of* the work . . . the musical concept cannot resolve unambiguously *every* aspect of the concrete reality to be actualized. . . . And so the performer, the one who makes *actual*, cannot be denied the office of creating a reality that is denser and richer than any concept, and that therefore is necessarily personal in important ways—even though the personal only serves and enhances the governing and pervading concept, which is nonpersonal.[66]

Fingarette's analysis of the performance of a musical work brings out several important aspects of the performer's involvement with the musical work, and the place of her contribution in the continuing development of that work. Fingarette uses this example to illustrate some of the dynamics in play within the Confucian community. His thesis captures the subtle aspects of a person's place and involvement within the context of the continuing inherited tradition. There is a sense of the delicate tension between expressing the self, sometimes in creative and novel ways, and acting meaningfully within the limits of existing norms and standards. Within Confucian philosophy, only within frameworks that allow for a healthy interplay of both these elements can the self meaningfully be realized within the community.

In a deep Confucian sense, the realization of the self occurs only when others in an individual's circles of involvement have been enriched. Drawing on Fingarette's analogy, the musical performance and the work are intimately intertwined: individual performances enrich the continuing tradition of the work, and the work is actualized only if it is performed. In the case of *li* in self-cultivation, we see the relevance of the analogy in the way in which individual *li*-acts serve the person as well as the community: the continuing tradition is enacted in and through the *li*-acts of individuals, which in turn sustain and enrich the community and its traditions.

Conclusion: Playing in Concert

A key operative concept in the Confucian community is responsiveness: in a flourishing community, an effective leader works in a mutually responsive mode with the people. That the common people *respond* to the leader is a prerequisite of a flourishing community, one that seeks to approach the teleological *dao*.[67] In *Analects* 19.12, Confucius notes that the influence of the leader and the response of the people to the leader are paramount in the ideal Confucian society:

> Ji Kangzi asked Confucius about governing effectively, saying, "What if I kill those who have abandoned the way to attract those who are on it?"
>
> "If you govern effectively," Confucius replied, "what need is there for killing? If you want to be truly adept, the people will also be adept. The excellence of the *junzi* is the wind, while that of the petty person is the grass. As the wind blows, the grass is sure to bend."[68]

From this, it is clear that the Confucian ideal of political leadership moves beyond discussions of political coercion and lack of freedom. Individuals in a community—in particular, the cultivated Confucian *junzi*—who engage in appropriate and meaningful *li*-practices enrich the life of the community. Confucius makes the point in *Analects* 4.1: "In taking up one's residence, it is the presence of *ren* (-persons) that is the greatest attraction. How can anyone be called wise who, in having the choice, does not seek to dwell among *ren* (-persons)?"

The notion of people within a community who participate in its moral life and enrich each other is a theme of profound significance in Confucian thought. This idea evokes the picture of musicians playing in concert where every member of the ensemble has an important role to play, and a good performance is assessed not merely with reference to the technical competence of each of the players, but also to how well the musicians play together. Confucius uses the analogy of music to demonstrate the participatory nature of the ideal Confucian society: in such a community, the players no longer play in unison (as they might during the training period), but in harmony (*Analects* 3.23). In other words, each person plays a different tune; the players sound good *together*, although they perform *different* notes.[69]

In discussing aspects of musical practice and performance, this essay highlights several important themes in moral cultivation and self-realization that need to be adequately addressed in contemporary moral philosophy.

First, we need to be wary of moral philosophies which tend to overemphasize distinctions between self and society. The effects of a false dichotomy drawn between self and society seep into many areas of moral philosophy, resulting in misunderstandings and misrepresentations of morality. For instance, the view that self-cultivation is primarily a personal pursuit that benefits only the individual is problematic because it artificially sets the individual apart from her webs of interdependence. The cleaner the distinction between self and society, the more it will be the case that relationships fall through the cracks and are not accounted for. In discussing some parallels between moral and musical performance, I have argued that the audience's response to a performance plays a central role in the performer's advancement. In other words, if a musical performance was accounted for either solely in terms of the performer or the audience, key aspects of the performance, such as the communication of the performer's feelings via the music and the audience's appreciation of the performance, would be lost. Moral philosophy needs to avoid creating irreconcilable dichotomies between self and society because issues relating to the connectedness of persons would be left unaccounted for. In this regard, it is worth noting that the notion of responsiveness in the moral practices of a community is particularly significant in, though not restricted to, a social philosophy that emphasizes relatedness of persons. Indeed, the concepts of interrelatedness and interdependence between self and community should be among the fundamental features of a moral theory.

The embeddedness of morality in existing modes of life is the second important theme of this essay. An account of moral development needs to be realistic and to give full play to circumstantial factors and other contingent matters in moral life. In this regard, we may draw parallels between moral life and the appreciation and assessment of musical performances against their historical and cultural backgrounds. The analogy highlights the situatedness of morality: morality is not a phenomenon that runs independently of all other aspects of human life. Rather, the significance of culture and tradition to moral theory and practice needs to be dealt with adequately in moral philosophy. From a practical point of view, aspects of culture and tradition associated with one's moral practice are at least as important as the need for self-cultivation. Failure to deal with the embeddedness of morality within existing socio-cultural frameworks could have negative consequences in practical terms, such as the creation of a false separation of moral pursuits from other aspects of one's life.

Thirdly, the emphasis in this paper is on the *process* of self-cultivation, rather than on its content alone. An advantage of a process-oriented approach to moral cultivation is that it takes into account the dynamics and structures of the various developmental phases. In this regard, allowance is made for different emphases within the different phases. It needs to be mentioned at this point that a developmental approach to self-cultivation accounts for many of the apparent inconsistencies in the application of the concept *li* in the *Analects*. Scholars have noted that there is a range of meanings of *li* in the *Analects*, some of which are more formalistic and rigid, and others which are more flexible; these accounts are not inconsistent if we consider discussions of *li* in the *Analects* in the context of developmental phases. We can also draw a parallel with musical training. For the beginner, technical competence is paramount, while a mature musician focuses upon expressivity in performance. We must recognize different levels of competence and their corresponding measures of appropriateness, at different developmental phases. Drawing inspiration from a Confucian perspective, a process-oriented approach, as contrasted with a content-based one, allows for an organismic view of the community. Within such a framework, morality is understood as a living phenomenon, deeply intertwined with the sphere of personal and social relations, and vibrant and dynamic as existing cultures and traditions evolve.

Notes

1. Xunzi (298?–238? B.C.E.), the author of the text, belonged to the Confucian school. See *Hsun Tzu: Basic Writings*, trans. Burton Watson (New York: Columbia University Press, 1963).

2. James Legge, trans., "The *Li Ki*," in *The Sacred Books of the East*, vols. 27 and 28 (Oxford: Clarendon Press, 1885). The *Book of Rites* consists of various records compiled by members of the Confucian school during the Han Dynasty (202 B.C.E.–220 C.E.).

3. The *Book of Music* (*Yueh Chi*), is a chapter in the *Book of Rites* (chapter 17). The *Book of Music* contains many ideas similar to those articulated in the *Xunzi* text.

4. James Legge, trans., "The *Hsiao Ching*," in *The Sacred Books of the East*, vol. 3 (Oxford: Clarendon Press, 1879).

5. Both cited in Siu-Chi Huang, "Musical Art in Early Confucian Philosophy," *Philosophy East and West* 13 (1963).

6. See James Legge, trans., *The Chinese Classics*, 5 vols. (Hong Kong: Hong Kong University Press, 1960; reprinted from the 1893–1895 Oxford University Press editions), vol. 5: *Chunqiu Fanlu* (Spring and Autumn Annals) and *Zuozhuan* (Commentary on the Spring and Autumn Annals).

7. There is some existing literature on this topic, notably, Huang, "Musical Art"; Kathleen Higgins, "Music in Confucian and Neo-Confucian Philosophy," *International Philosophical Quarterly* 20 (1980); Kenneth DeWoskin, *A Song for One or Two: Music and the Concept of Art in Early China* (Ann Arbor: Center for Chinese Studies, University of Michigan, 1982); and Kongyang Jiang, "Aesthetics of the "Musical Records," in *Contemporary Chinese Aesthetics*, ed. Zhu Liyuan and Gene Blocker (New York: Peter Lang, 1995).

8. With this in mind, two points regarding the use of examples in this paper should be noted. First, the examples from music are illustrative only; there is no intention to suggest, unless explicitly stated, that the dynamics and features of the two processes are the same. Secondly, the choice of examples from particular musical traditions is indicative only of the author's lack of knowledge regarding theoretical aspects of the range of musical traditions. Readers may feel that there are some other musical traditions which could better exemplify some of the points made in this paper. However, that should not weaken the aims of this paper, which is to explore the idea of self-cultivation

in Confucian philosophy. Most of the examples of music referred to in this paper are taken from eighteenth- to nineteenth-century European musical forms. The focus on harmony (as opposed to dissonance, say) in music of this period may shed light on ideas of proportion and balance in Confucian self-cultivation. However, it would be simplistic to hold that the concepts of harmony in Confucian self-cultivation and those in eighteenth- and nineteenth-century European music are similar.

9. Huang, "Musical Art," p. 57.

10. David Hall and Roger Ames, *Thinking Through Confucius* (Albany: State University of New York Press, 1987), 88.

11. Roger Ames and Henry Rosemont, Jr., *The Analects of Confucius: A Philosophical Translation* (NY: Ballantine Books, 1998), 74. All the quotations in this paper from the *Analects* are from this translation, unless otherwise stated.

12. Tu Wei-ming, *Confucian Thought: Selfhood as Creative Transformation* (Albany: State University of New York Press, 1985), 55–56.

13. D. C. Lau, trans., *Confucius: The Analects* (Harmondsworth: Penguin, 1979).

14. See also *Analects* 18.4.

15. Gilbert Ryle makes a distinction between what he terms "knowing-how" and "knowing-that" in "Knowing How and Knowing That," *Proceedings of the Aristotelian Society* 46 (1946): 1–16. In his article, Ryle argues against the prevailing doctrine, which holds "(1) that Intelligence is a special faculty, the exercise of which are those specific internal acts which are called acts of thinking . . . and (2) that practical activities merit their titles "intelligent," "clever," and the rest only because they are accompanied by some such internal acts of considering propositions" (p. 1). Ryle transcends the theory-practice gap and contends that, (1) knowledge-how cannot be defined in terms of knowledge-that; and (2) knowledge-how is a concept logically prior to the concept of knowledge-that (pp. 4–5).

16. *Ibid.*, pp. 8–9.

17. The idea of *li* could be understood in a range of ways; Antonio Cua, a Confucian scholar, discusses the "increasing extension" of *li* in "*Li* and Moral Justification: A Study in the *Li Chi*," in *Philosophy East and West* 33, no. 1 (1983). By this, he refers to the "evolution of *li*," in other words, the history of *li* usage. The "extension of *li*" in this paper is examined not from a historical perspective, but from a developmental one: the practice of *li* over the course of personal cultivation.

18. See Antonio Cua, "The Conceptual Framework of Confucian Ethical Thought," *Journal of Chinese Philosophy* 23 (1996). In pp. 153–54, Cua discusses the dynamics of Confucian ethics and emphasizes its focus on the practical and concrete.

The comparison between learning *li* and learning a craft is an interesting one, though subtle differences should be noted. I am indebted to Nicholas Gier ("The Dancing Ru: A Confucian Aesthetics of Virtue," paper presented at the Australasian Association of Asian and Comparative Philosophy Conference, University of Melbourne, July 1999) for the suggestion that there is an interesting comparison between learning a virtue, and learning a skill. Drawing on Aristotle's distinction between *praxis* (acting) and *poeisis* (making) in the *Nicomachean Ethics*, Gier points out that in the case of the latter, a potter produces a pot that is separate from herself, while in the case of the former, bravery produces a brave action, not a separate product. Whether Aristotle's distinction between *praxis* and *poeisis* is applicable in discussing *li* and music would depend on whether *li* is construed as virtue in the Aristotelian sense. This discussion is beyond the scope of this paper.

19. My translation. Tu Wei-ming provides a rather positive account of this passage in the *Analects*. See Tu's "Creative Tension Between *Jen* and *Li*," in his book *Confucian Thought: Selfhood as Creative Transformation* (Albany: State University of New York Press, 1985), 5–16. See also Fung Yu-Lan's analysis of this passage. Fung emphasizes the notion of the social self in Confucian thought. According to Fung, this passage points to the use of *li* to stipulate *ren*. See Fung Yu-Lan, *New History of Chinese Philosophy* (*Zhongguo zhexueshi xinbian*), vol. 1 (P.R. China: People's Press [Renmin Dabanshe], 1980), 136.

20. Karyn Lai, "Confucian Moral Thinking," *Philosophy East and West* 45, no. 2 (1995): 252.

21. Cua, "Conceptual Framework," p. 161.

22. There is a tendency in some interpretations of Confucius's attitudes to sacrifice and mourning to overemphasize his inflexibility in these areas. However, that Confucius might appear inflexible on such matters arises from a narrow interpretation of these practices. The misunderstanding lies in overemphasizing the *moral* aspect of sacrifice and mourning practices. A more plausible interpretation is to see the apparent inflexibility not in the *morality* of the practices, but in the *ontological* status of these practices: they are important not because they affirm belief in gods or spirits, but because they comprise an initial stage in self-cultivation whereby the participant begins to experience emotions in and through the practice. This point is made by Antonio Cua in "*Li* and Moral Justification."

23. Antonio Cua, "Conceptual Framework," p. 157. In *Analects* 15.36, one is not expected always to acquiesce to one's teacher: "[w]hen faced with the opportunity to practise *jen* do not give precedence even to your teacher" (tr. Lau). In the arena of public service, the tone is even more relaxed as Confucius seems at times to make light of those who accord preponderance to *li*: "You will be looked upon as obsequious by others if you observe every detail of *li* in serving your lord." (*Analects* 3.18, tr. Lau. See also *Analects* 14.22).

24. Tu, "Creative Tension," p. 9.

25. Tu Wei-ming, "*Li* as Process of Humanisation," *Philosophy East and West* 22, no. 2 (1972): 188.

26. Shun Kwong-Loi, "*Jen* and *Li* in the Analects," *Philosophy East and West* 43, no. 3 (1993).

27. *Ibid.*, p. 466.

28. Henry Skaja, "*Li* (Ceremonial) as a Primal Concept in Confucian Spiritual-Humanism," *Chinese Culture* 25, no. 1 (1984): 62–63.

29. Tu Wei-ming discusses this issue extensively in his "*Li* as Process of Humanisation." See also the discussion in section one of this paper.

30. Antonio Cua explores the idea of self-cultivation through evoking the notions of "form of life," "way of life," and "style of life" as part of a selective cartography of moral experience. He writes, "The notion of the form of life focuses on the consensual background of the moral tradition, which renders intelligible the uses of moral concepts. The notion of a way of life focuses on the coherence and convergent ways of behavior as congruent with a set of formulable rules of conduct; while the notion of the style of life draws attention to the diverse qualitative significance of the way of life for individual agents." (Antonio Cua, "Reflections on Moral Theory and Understanding Moral Traditions," *Interpreting Across Boundaries*, ed. G. Larson and E. Deutsch [Princeton, N. J.: Princeton University Press, 1988], 283–84.)

31. Antonio Cua, "Conceptual Framework," p. 166.

32. James Legge's translation of *wen* as 'ornamental accomplishments' and of *zhi* as 'substantial qualities' is questionable because it introduces an unnecessary dimension of contrast between the two terms; the opposition between 'ornamental' and 'substantial' is one of the dichotomies the *Analects* tries to transcend. Legge's characterization is exactly what the two passages refute: one is as important as the other, and both are crucial for self-cultivation; *wen* is not merely ornamental. See his commentary on *Analects* 12.8 in *The Four Books* (Hong Kong: Culture Book Company), 285.

33. In these two passages, there is a sense that the *Analects* is striving to move away from the then contemporary norm of hereditary nobility. Confucius and Zigong are portrayed as challenging such claims; the bone of contention is between hereditary nobility and what may be described as meritocracy, with strong moral overtones. In the latter passage, Ji Zicheng's remarks are interesting: he presents as an official, a gentleman with social and political status, caught within this debate. Ji appears unwilling to acknowledge that he may have to exert some effort in maintaining his status bestowed by hereditary means.

34. Within the Confucian tradition, Mencius is noted for his insistence that civilization and culture mark the difference between humans (*ren*) and other animals (*shou*). See, for instance, *Book of Mencius*, 3B. 9.

35. See, for example, Lauren Pfister, "Considerations for the Contemporary Revitalization of Confucianism: Meditations on *Te* in the *Analects*," *Journal of Chinese Philosophy* 13 (1986). Pfister argues that there is little distinction between moral activity and social expression: "There must be a concern for the concrete expression of morally appropriate behavior and a creative intuition which preserves one's moral activity as a harmonized whole and extends it into the world of social relationships. The concreteness of its expression is displayed in its production of 'memorable sayings' (14.4) and service (12.21); its preservation is manifested in those who love it (9.18, 15.13) and 'hold on' to it (19.2); its extension is accomplished through its cultivation (7.3) and exaltation or accumulation (12.10)" (p. 241).

36. Regarding the religious dimension of *li*, it is clear that the term was originally used in reference to religious rites. According to Fingarette in his book bearing the provocative title *Confucius: The Secular as Sacred* (New York: Harper and Row, 1972), Confucius transformed and extended that sense of *li* to the social, secular context whereby

the secular and mudane begins to take on spiritual significance. Interpreting Fingarette's analysis of Confucius's innovations in political and ethical terms, it could be argued that a significant innovation of Confucius was to extend the possibility of self-cultivation to all men. This extension meant that education and, more generally, self-cultivation was no longer the special prerogative of those with noble lineage. Carried on to greater depths by both Mencius and Xunzi, this Confucian meritocracy was, in effect, an affirmation of humanistic and democratic principles which upheld that the avenues for achieving human excellence, as well as the ideal itself, was available for all.

37. Ames and Rosemont, *The Analects*, p. 118.

38. Some mention should be made of the notion of *jiao*, normally translated 'teach' (v), 'teaching' (n), or 'philosophy'. In Confucius's times, the Chinese term for philosophy, *zhexue*, was not in use. Rather the term *jiao* was commonly used to describe a body of teachings, a tradition, or a religion. The left radical in *jiao* is the term *xiao*, meaning filiality. Hence, there would have been a significant deference to authority or tradition, or more generally, received wisdom from the sages of the past, in the ancient Chinese schools of thought. It is quite clear that, in Confucius's case, aspects of *Zhou* culture were deemed authoritative.

39. Fingarette, *Confucius*, p. 69. See also Benjamin Schwartz's discussion of the significance of tradition in Confucian thought, in *The World of Thought in Ancient China* (Cambridge: Harvard University Press, 1985), the "Confucius" chapter.

40. Antonio Cua, "The Concept of Paradigmatic Individuals in the Ethics of Confucius," *Inquiry* 14 (1971): 4.

41. In Confucian terms, intelligent responses are the result of learning and experience. As stated in the *Book of Music*, i.7, "it is only the *junzi* who can really know music." Legge's translation.

42. Antonio Cua, "Reasonable Action and Confucian Argumentation," *Journal of Chinese Philosophy* 1 (1973): 62–63.

43. Fingarette, *Confucius*, p. 53.

44. It is worth noting that in the *Book of Music* there is a rejection of the then contemporary styles and forms of music that are not anchored in tradition. III.8 reads: "But now, in the new music, (the performers) advance and retire without any regular order; the music is corrupt to excess; there is no end to its vileness." From "The *LiKi* (Book of Rites)," in *The Sacred Books of China*, trans. James Legge (Delhi: Motilal Banarsidass, 1855), *YoKi (Book of Music)* part 4, book 17, p. 117.

45. Fingarette, *Confucius*, p. 16.

46. Gilbert Ryle, discussed in section 2.

47. *Ibid.*

48. Fingarette, *Confucius*, p. 42.

49. To illustrate this point, improvisation in jazz music provides clear examples.

50. Regarding the use of principles, we might draw on Ryle's characterization of knowing-how. Here, Ryle notes that the person who knows-how is able to work with principles extracted from their applications.

51. See Shun, "*Jen* and *Li* in the *Analects*," pp. 468–72. Shun's discussion of *ren*

and *li*, which attempts to place equal emphasis on the roles of the two concepts, allows for modifications to *li*, though these would be rooted in *ren*-considerations (that *ren* is necessary for *li*), and vice-versa.

52. See, for instance, Michael Martin's understanding of Confucian philosophy, which takes *li* as central. Refer to Martin's article, "Ritual Action (*Li*) in Confucius and Hsun Tzu, " *Australasian Journal of Philosophy* 73, no. 1 (1995).

53. Tu, "Creative Tension," p. 13.

54. Note that this reasoning is even more likely if *Analects* 12.1 is appealed to for support.

55. See, for example, D. C. Lau's translation of the *Analects* and his discussion of the concept in the introductory chapter to his translation. See also Legge's translation of the *Analects*. Legge translates *yi* as 'righteousness'.

56. This conception of *yi* is held by a number of Confucian scholars including Lau (*Confucius: The Analects*, pp. 37–39; 47–50), Antonio Cua ("Confucian Vision and Human Community," *Journal of Chinese Philosophy* 11[1984]: 230 ff); and Kwong-Loi Shun ("*Jen* and *Li* in the *Analects*," p. 472 ff).

57. David Hall and Roger Ames, "Getting It Right: On Saving Confucius from the Confucians," *Philosophy East and West* 36, no. 1 (1984): 16–18.

58. Hall and Ames, *Thinking Through Confucius*, pp. 91 ff.

59. While many scholars are sympathetic to Hall and Ames's attempt to establish that Confucian philosophy affords opportunity for change, development, or redress, some have voiced concerns that the references to *yi* in the *Analects* are too few and too vague to fully substantiate the kind of postmodern interpretation proposed. See, for example, Michael Martin's review of Hall and Ames's book, *Thinking Through Confucius*, in the *Journal of Chinese Philosophy* 17 (1990): 495–503, esp. p. 500 f. There is also follow up of this discussion in Hall and Ames, "Against the Greying of Confucius: Responses to Gregor Paul and Michael Martin," *Journal of Chinese Philosophy* 18 (1991): 333–47, and Martin's "A Rejoinder to Hall and Ames," *ibid.*, pp. 489–93.

60. See Cua, "Conceptual Framework," p. 164. On pp. 162–63 of his article, Cua discusses the idea that *li* represent an *enlightened* tradition.

61. Shun, "*Jen* and *Li* in the *Analects*," p. 474.

62. See their comments in Hall and Ames, *Thinking Through Confucius*, esp. pp. 105 ff.

63. Martin, "Ritual Action," p. 18.

64. *Ibid.*

65. *Ibid.*

66. Herbert Fingarette, "The Problem of the Self in the Analects," *Philosophy East and West* 29, no. 2 (1979): 137.

67. The *Analects* holds a particularistic, rather than universal, view of the concept *dao*. In contrast to the Daoist ideal of *dao* as a permanent, transcendent, and universal order, *dao* in the *Analects* varies in its application. Hence, there are various *dao* including:

—the *dao* of Heaven (*tiandao*): 5.13;
—the *dao* of the *junzi*: 5.16; 14.28; 19.7; 19.12;

—Confucius's *dao*: 4.15; 6.12;
—the *dao* of the prevailing human condition: 5.2; 5.7; 5.21; 6.24; 12.23;
14.1; 14.3; 14.36; 15.25; 15.32; 16.2; 18.6; 18.7;19.2.

It is with regard to this last conception of *dao* that one gets a sense of *telos*. It could be said that the *dao* of (improving) the prevailing human condition is that which the community (ideally) works towards. In this regard, two passages are particularly enlightening. 15.29 reads: "It is the human being who furnishes *dao* with value and meaning; simply abiding by the *dao* does not render human life meaningful or worthwhile" (my translation). In 16.2, Confucius describes the *dao* of the flourishing community: "When the *dao* prevails in the world, *li*, music, and punitive campaigns are initiated by the emperor" (tr. Ames and Rosemont).

68. See also *Analects* 2.19; 2.20; 8.2; 9.14; 12.17; 12.18; 13.1; 13.2; 13.6; 13.13; 14.41; 14.42.

69. Crispin Sartwell discusses the image of society as a musical ensemble in "Confucius and Country Music," *Philosophy East and West* 43 (1993): 243.

PART III

IDENTITY: INDIVIDUAL AND SOCIAL

Personal Identity and Family Commitment

Alan Montefiore

In what sense—if any—is my membership of "my" family and my position within it a part of my own identity? And if it is, do I have to accept that that aspect of my identity carries with it certain inescapable obligations or responsibilities, incumbent upon me simply by virtue of the place that I occupy within the family structure and, in that sense, of who and what I am? To what degree, if any, might I be free to determine my own identity in these respects? In what follows I shall take these as quite general questions. If the answers to them turn out to suggest some sort of conceptual cultural relativism, the next step would no doubt be to take a fairly close comparative look at some relevantly different cultures (taking such account as we may of the problems involved in finding a way of characterizing them that was as neutral as possible between them). To attempt to do this here would be to go well beyond the limits of the present essay; in any case many of the other essays in this volume do in effect explore these very issues. In this essay, however, my main aim will be rather to try and show something of the complexity of the network of conceptual problems that bear upon such answers as one may attempt to these questions.

We may start by noting that there are a number of important contexts in which use of the term 'identity' tends to run over into uses of such other adjacent terms as, most notably, 'self' and 'person'; often, indeed, they are combined as in the expressions 'self-identity' and 'personal identity'. It would take us too far off track to enter into a full discussion of these other terms here.[1] Suffice it to say that the term 'self' bears a primarily reflexive reference, while 'person' has come, over the latter stages of its history, to refer very often to the human subject as the locus of responsible agency or the bearer of values. One may think in this context of John Locke's famous distinction between the identity of a man and that of a person; 'person', he says, is "a forensic term"[2]—that is to say that to treat someone as a person is to treat him or her as accountable, as someone to whom one may properly impute responsibility; or of Kant's insistence that persons are to be treated as ends in themselves and never simply as means; or, again, of the revealing title of Carl Rogers's famous book *On Becoming a Person*.[3] As to the term 'self', let me just quote from a recent article by Professor Theodore R. Sarbin entitled "The Poetics of Identity"[4]:

In some contexts, 'self' and 'identity' are treated as synonyms; in other contexts identity is subsumed under self. Karl Scheibe[5] has made a convincing case for treating the two terms as coordinates in a four-fold table in which the presence or absence of self is combined with the presence or absence of identity, indicating their separate conceptual status. The usefulness of this distinction is illustrated by a classroom exercise. I distributed blank sheets of paper at the top of which was typed a brief excerpt from a story:

"There was a momentary lull in the conversation. He was looking out the window. He turned round quickly. 'You want to know who I am', he said. He took a deep breath and almost inaudibly muttered, 'yes, who am I?'"

On half the sheets 'what' was substituted for 'who'. The instructions to the students were simply to write one or two paragraphs to continue the story. Analysis . . . showed clearly that the 'who' question pulled for social categories such as roles, statuses, occupations, placement in social structures and so on. Responses to the 'what am I?' question almost never made use of social categories: instead they were focused on cosmological categories, such as membership in the human species, a body occupying space, a temple for the spirit, organized bits of protoplasm, body and soul, and so on. Consistent with Scheibe's formulation, the answers to 'what am I?' might be summarized as 'self', reflecting the fact of being; the answers to 'who am I?' might be summarized as 'identity', reflecting the fact of being-in-place.

It is important to emphasize that one's identity is a construction that arises in dialogue.[6]

One may be unsure how closely Sarbin's way of recording his distinctions fits the facts of normal common usage, but, considerations of prevalent idiom apart, the distinctions themselves are worth noting. (Here as elsewhere, normal common usage in fact shows itself to be shifting and always less than one hundred percent consistent with itself.) It is also worth noting that of the items that he lists as contributing to his students' understanding of 'identity', it makes sense to suppose that people may have some varying degree of choice with respect to their names, occupations, and at any rate certain roles, and even, over time, with respect to their placement in social structures. The question of the part played in the establishment of an identity by the role that a person may occupy is of crucial concern in the present context, and we shall return to it a little later on. Meanwhile, let it also be noted that in many contexts the term 'identity' itself has taken on a powerful value-connotation in its own right. Nowhere is this more clearly apparent than in Charles Taylor's account in his *Sources of the Self*:

To know who I am is a species of knowing where I stand. My identity is defined by the commitments and identifications which provide the frame or horizon within which I can try to determine from case to case what is good or valuable, or what ought to be done, or what I endorse or oppose.[7]

None of the factors contributing to Sarbin's students' understanding of 'self', on the contrary, would seem to be open to any degree of self-determination or choice: membership in the human species, a body occupying space, and so on. Though I have no reason to suppose that it was present in the students' understanding of the matter, it is worth noting that this latter reference (to a "body occupying space") bears a significant relationship to the basically reflexive self-referential sense of the term 'self'. Indeed, according to an argument that I shall try to sketch out a little later on, it is a condition of membership in the universe of language and reflective thought in general that we should be able to identify ourselves, as well as our interlocutors, as standing in whatever the positions of speech we actually stand in at any given moment; and it is precisely our spatiotemporal embodiment that provides the necessary principle of recognizable self-continuity over time. At this point, one might say, self and (numerically identifiable) identity come together; and given that their doing so constitutes a necessary condition of entry into a universe of discourse, one clearly has no choice in the matter of whether this should be so or not.

Numerical identity, indeed, that is to say one's identity as the particular individual that one is, as a particular passport-holder, for instance, or as one appears and will one day reappear in the Register of Births and Deaths, is not something that anyone would normally think of as being subject to their own power of choice. One's individual self-identity has to be taken as fixed from the moment of one's birth to the particular parents to whom one is born; its continuity is traced out by one's spatiotemporal (i.e., bodily) passage through life. Our question is rather whether such aspects of a person's identity as may be determined through his or her occupancy of a particular family role and are, as such, bound up with some particular cluster of claims and responsibilities, may be equally resistant to any preferential choice that the person concerned might wish to exercise in the matter.

When I first went to Singapore in the course of my army service as long ago as 1947, I was attached to what was then known as a Civil Labour Control Team, of which there were at that time two on Singapore Island. We were known as CLTC(J)—why "J" or what it may have stood for I have no idea—and we lived in a small compound in what were the as-yet-unbuilt-over grounds of the General Hospital in Kampong Bahru. In my off-duty time in the evenings, I used to wander off down New Bridge Road—having first changed into civilian clothes—and to stroll among the swarms of local people, themselves for the most part also just wandering about among the miscellany of the street traders' stalls, some of them occasionally buying something—a durian, for instance, smelling strongly of decay, a piece of cloth, a pair of tennis shoes, or some patent medicine guaranteed to defeat any possible mishap that might befall them. I used to enjoy myself by pretending at first not to understand anything of what people were saying around me—the ubiquitous small boys cheerfully alerting all and sundry to the fact that a "red-haired devil" was approaching—and then

by suddenly pointing out in the distinctly uncertain Hokkien Chinese that the
Army had taught me back in London that my hair was in fact of very nearly
the same color as theirs. Their first reaction was very naturally one of surprise
at such an incongruous and unexpected intervention, followed invariably by a
stream of what was always the same set of questions. Where did I come from?
How old was I? What was my family? Was I married? Did I have any children?
Any elder or younger brothers or sisters? Where had I learnt Chinese? (Or, more
usually and rather oddly, seeing that I spoke neither Cantonese nor Hakka, had
I learnt it in Hong Kong?)

Neither of the two small English-Hokkien dictionaries that I then possessed
(and that are still in my possession) provided an entry either for the noun
'identity' or even for the verb 'identify'. Yet, it is fair to say, in asking these sorts
of questions, they were seeking to place me on some recognizable map, to
determine for all immediately relevant purposes what sort of person I was—in
other words, to identify me in terms of those descriptive categories or classes of
which my membership might characterize me in terms recognizable to them.

In asking such questions of me, they were not, of course, concerned with
my identity as the particular and self-same individual that I was as distinct from
all other individuals of possibly the same general 'sort' or description. That
is not to say that the question might not have arisen, if, for example, finding
themselves faced on a number of successive occasions with a young 'devil' with
allegedly red hair and speaking indifferent Hokkien, they had wanted to check
whether or not it was the same one or possibly another with apparently the same
relevant characteristics. In that sense of 'personal identity' what is at stake is the
continuing numerical sameness of the one individual over time and throughout
whatever other changes the passage of time may bring to him or to her. In fact,
of course, a very large part of the philosophical literature on personal identity
has been devoted to the nest of problems involved in determining the criteria for
the numerical identity of persons. Locke, for instance, notoriously looked to the
continuity of memory to provide the crucial criterion, taking in effect the view
that when memory failed, while one might be left with the same man, woman,
or child *qua* human animal as it were, the person as such, he or she who might
properly be held responsible for his or her own actions, must be reckoned to
have undergone a transformation. However, the difficulties to which this view
gives rise have been demonstrated often and convincingly enough—indeed,
Locke himself was clearly aware of a number of them—and there would today
be a large measure of agreement that some reference to the body (or at the very
least to some aspect thereof) and to the spatiotemporal coordinates that define
its path through life, must figure as a necessary element in any set of criteria for
establishing the identity of a uniquely individual person.

It is, however, that other sense of 'personal identity', the sense that has come
to play a major role across such a wide range of contemporary thinking, with
which we are concerned here. It has to be admitted that this sense is generally

more important than precise; it may be, indeed, that its effective importance derives in part from its very imprecision. The French philosopher Clément Rosset, for example, in referring to what he takes to be a commonsense distinction between a social and a personal identity, suggests as alternative terms for the latter "the intimate identity of the self, or psychological identity, or again real identity"; and then adds "for my part I have always regarded this distinction as very doubtful. More exactly I have always thought one's social identity to be one's only real identity, and the other, one's alleged personal identity, to be a complete illusion."[8] Illusion or not, the concept has become a familiar one well beyond the bounds of philosophy; and whatever the relation may be between the personal and the social, the term 'identity' must owe much of its subsequent impact on so many contemporary forms of discourse to the psychoanalyst Erik Erikson.

So far as I know, Erikson first made serious use of the term in his paper "Ego Development and Historical Change," published over fifty years ago.[9] Probably his most useful account of what lay behind his use of it there and elsewhere is to be found, however, in a slightly later and more accessible paper called "The Problem of Ego Identity."[10] In this paper Erikson explains himself as follows:

> First a word about the term 'identity'. As far as I know Freud used it only once in a more than incidental way . . . when he tried to formulate his link to the Jewish people [and] spoke of an 'inner identity', which was less based on race or religion than on a common readiness to live in opposition and on a common freedom from prejudices which narrow the intellect. Here the term 'identity' points to an individual's link with the unique values, fostered by a unique history, of his people. . . . It is this identity of something in the individual's core with an essential aspect of a group's inner coherence which is under consideration here; for the young individual must learn to be most himself where he means most to others—those others, to be sure, who have come to mean most to him. The term 'identity' expresses such a mutual relation in that it connotes both a persistent sameness within oneself (self-sameness) and a persistent sharing of some kind of essential character with others. . . .
>
> At one time, [the term 'identity'] will appear to refer to a conscious sense of individual identity; at another to an unconscious striving for a continuity of personal character; at a third, as a criterion for the silent doings of ego synthesis; and, finally, as a maintenance of an inner solidarity with a group's ideals and identity. . . .

This passage points to many of the themes and forces, often highly charged, that find expression in the diverse discourses of identity today. Moreover, Erikson's way of explaining his use of the term displays clearly enough the difficulty, even the impossibility, of making any very neat and sharp distinction between a personal and a social identity, whether conceptually or in terms of psychological formation. Clément Rosset puts the point this way: "[it is a] philosophical truth . . . that apart from the signs and actions of which I am the source and by which I am recognizable as being who I am, there is nothing further that belongs to me or is characteristic of me. Thus it is as if my personal identity were some sort of ghostly person, haunting my real (social) person and lurking round me, often nearby but never palpable or within my grasp. . . ."[11] Here, however, Rosset goes well beyond Erikson, who is very far from seeking to present personal identity as a "complete illusion"; on the contrary, for Erikson "the term 'identity' . . . connotes both a persistent sameness within oneself (self-sameness) and a persistent sharing of some kind of essential character with others. . . ." One may presume that the "sameness within oneself" to which he refers is to be understood, as he says, *both* as a (sometimes) "conscious sense of individual identity" *and* as "a continuity of personal character," and this latter must indeed be understood, as Rosset puts it, in terms of "the signs and actions of which I am the source and by which I am recognizable as being who I am. . . ." But while some dispositional characteristics may be just that and nothing more—that is to say, nothing but a tendency to behave in certain typical ways in a certain range of typical situations without there being any determinate underlying structure or condition of which this tendency might be explicable as an outcome—this is evidently not true of all dispositions. To say that glass, for instance, is brittle is to say that it will tend to break under a certain wide variety of conditions of stress; but this tendency may, of course, be explained by reference to its molecular structure. Both Rosset and Hume, on whose testimony he calls more than once, are doubtless right when they say that there is and indeed can be no such experience as an introspective glimpse of some sort of pure, persistent self. But, to push my no doubt rather wobbly analogy just a little further, there is (and, for creatures such as us, can be) no such experience as a direct glimpse of the persistently underlying molecular structure of glass. In neither case does it necessarily follow that there is no persisting underlying structure or condition. And indeed, to put the matter in what must still be thought to be somewhat speculative physicalist terms, it is not unreasonable to suppose that a given individual's "continuity of personal character" might be whatever it is in virtue of a similarly continuing overall configuration of his or her particular brain. (How that configuration had come to be what it might be, would, of course, be another as yet only in principle answerable question.)

Be all this as it may, we must surely accept that, whatever we may mean exactly by talking of personal identity, such an identity cannot be without all sorts of social entanglements. This is, no doubt, one of the central lessons of psychoanalysis. So too, if a little less obviously perhaps, is the fact that the ability both to reflect on and to commune freely with oneself about oneself is intricately bound up with the ability to communicate with others—and, psychologically speaking, with those whom Erikson called one's "most significant others." The intellectual credentials of psychoanalysis are, notoriously, fiercely controversial. However, there are also good and by now widely accepted philosophical reasons why the ability to speak meaningfully to or with oneself, about oneself or indeed about anything else, is essentially bound up with the ability to speak to and to be understood by others. These reasons are by now familiar enough to philosophers—including, indeed, philosophers to whom they may still appear less than wholly convincing. It may nevertheless be worthwhile to remind ourselves briefly of them here.

The reasons to which I refer are those which are most commonly thought of as lying at the heart of Wittgenstein's so-called 'anti–private language argument'. In brief outline they may be understood as follows. When anyone, and in particular a newcomer to the institution of language, makes a sound, or produces some other physical gesture such as a mark on paper or a movement of the hand, this can only count or function as a symbol—that is, as a bearer of meaning—insofar as there is a distinction between its use in ways that are appropriate and those that are, or would be, inappropriate to the context. Otherwise it would make no difference that one should utter any one sound, make any one mark or gesture, rather than any other; and whatever sounds, marks, or gestures that one did happen to utter or to make, would remain nothing more than mere physical occurrences. However, the reference to any such distinction will in turn remain empty unless there is, at least in principle, some way in which the inappropriateness of the use of a sound, mark, or gesture can be brought effectively to one's attention by something that might hold one up and give one pause to reflect that, in producing, say, the sound that one had produced, one might have got something wrong. If there was nothing at all to be encountered that might serve as a check—in both senses of that usefully ambiguous English word, that is *both* as something that might serve as an obstacle, something that might hold one up and prevent whatever move one happened to make from going through unimpeded simply on the strength of one's making it *and* serve thus as a form of verification, then one would be merely a maker of sounds, marks, and gestures, none of them either appropriate or inappropriate, but simply devoid of any (differential) meaning. But what in principle might serve as such a check? Not, as some have thought, one's own memory; for apparent memory on its own cannot, evidently enough, serve as a check upon itself. So what other possible basis could there be for distinguishing between a genuine memory belief, referring to something at least relatively independent of what one might currently have in mind, and a mere arbitrary production of some new content of consciousness? Not any feature of the silent or at any rate non-language-using world around us, for whatever sound, mark, or gesture we may produce when confronted with the nonspeaking world, it will not answer us back to indicate that we may have got something wrong. The only possible check that the would-be producer of a sound or mark as a symbol, that is as a bearer of meaning, might encounter would be that of the incomprehension or expressed dissent of another speaker of the same language. Of course, it remains true that the first speaker must still rely on his or her own memory to recognize or to interpret whatever series of sounds or marks his interlocutor may have produced as being itself a bearer of meaning; and this in turn presupposes his ability to recognize his interlocutor as a speaker, occupying now the first position of speech, where previously he was still in the second or perhaps even in the third. Of course, too, the check provided by the second speaker can never function as a guaranteed infallible arbiter of meaning; after all, the second speaker's memory may turn out to be at fault rather than that of the first speaker. But this is but one of the many areas of human life and discourse in which it would be utterly mistaken to look for guaranteed infallibility. A check is simply something that holds one up, not a mark of guaranteed certainty; and it is provided here through the interplay of the two parameters, that of apparent memory and that of the relatively independent fact with which one is confronted.

This argument stands, no doubt, in need of further detailed elaboration. But if it, or one very like it, is sound—and, certainly, it seems to me that, in one version or another, it is to be regarded as at least a very powerful argument, it must follow that any one person's ability to structure even his or her own silent thoughts according to conceptually ordered rules, *including any thoughts that he or she might have about his or her own personal or self-identity*, must be inextricably tied in with the recognizable possibility of encountering other speakers of the same language, other users of the same conceptual structures, other members of the same linguistic community or society. (In practice, as we know, children who somehow grow up without contact with other speakers, though they may in rare circumstances survive, do not develop their potential capacities for speech.)[12]

There is a further characteristically Wittgensteinian-flavored argument of which it is relevant to take note. This centers on the impossibility of pointing in any successfully identifying way at an individual of any sort whatsoever, persons—including one's own person—no less than any other, unless one is also in a position to say something about the individual in question, to describe her or him in at least some minimally characterizing way. Indeed, it is impossible definitively to establish the physical act of, say, stretching out one's finger and aligning it in a given direction as being an act of pointing unless one is able to indicate in some less merely physical, more discursive way which feature, or which kind of feature, of the surrounding environment it is to which one is seeking to point. In other words, there can be no way of establishing or rejecting the continuing identity of a person (or anything else) through one moment of time to another unless one can say at least something—*in a language which one shares with other members of one's speech community*—about what kind of individual (item) it is that one wishes to speak. If all this is basically correct, then, it means that, in order to be able to refer in any meaningfully discursive way to oneself, one must of necessity stand in a set of more or less complex relations with such other members of one's community as might be capable in principle of understanding and themselves using the same range of terms as one might be using oneself.

There is yet another quite general consideration that should be noted once again before we arrive at last at the question of family commitment. At the 'logically' most fundamental level, persons, as we here understand the term, are, as we have seen, the initiating producers (or authors) and receivers of speech. Locke, as we have noted, was already emphatic that the notion of a person is bound up with that of responsibility for the actions—and not only the speech acts—of which the person concerned is the author. Indeed, to establish personal identity in any given case is typically to establish responsibility for the performance or the failure to perform some relevant action. The continuity that we have to establish in the maintenance or restoration of personal identity is that of an agent among other agents. This is why any major break in the continuity of the story of a person's life is almost bound to raise questions and create discomfort and uncertainties about the nature and even reality of his or her identity and attendant responsibilities, whether for past acts of commission or omission or in relation to present and future commitments.

Individual persons are, then, as such accountable for those of the actions or failures to act that may reasonably be deemed to be or to have been under their voluntary control. But there is, of course, another important way in which individuals may find themselves entangled in various putative obligations and responsibilities by virtue of the very way in which they may find themselves identified as the persons whom they are. This may come about when their personal identity is seen as being inseparably linked with some role in which they may find themselves, either by virtue of their own choice or by virtue of their socially apparently indisputably recognizable position.

At this point something needs to be said about the notion of a role. I use the term here, in what I take to be the common way of most social scientists, as a tool of analysis, meaning roughly "a cluster of socially sanctioned claims either upon other persons or upon society in general."[13] I do not use it by way of any presumed contrast between the 'true' and the artificial, between 'role-playing' and that which is 'authentic'; in this latter contrast a role becomes, as it were, a mask, behind which the 'real person' hides. (We may remember that the term 'person' itself has as one of its points of origin the 'persona' or mask adopted by an actor in a drama). On the contrary, I take it that the idea of an 'authentic self' being somehow able to opt out of all recognizable patterns of social behavior by some heroic act of will is in general a mere fantasy; for different societies generate their own specific forms or patterns for what is still the recognizable role of 'drop-out', 'renouncer', social rebel, or hermit. Indeed, it is rather those who find themselves suddenly uprooted and in a strange land, or in a society whose rules have so changed that they no longer recognize them, where they have thus no role recognizable to themselves or to anyone else, who may tend to become so disorientated as to feel that they have lost all personal identity—and with it, indeed, any claim to recognizable authenticity.

To what extent do (or should) I see my own personal responsibilities, for example, as being bound up with those of the roles in which I find myself or which, so to speak, I inhabit? It would seem that if I freely accept a given role, I do have a *prima facie* responsibility or commitment, as the author of the action by which I accept it, to take on the responsibilities of the role as such. This, indeed, holds irrespectively of whether or not I 'identify myself' with the role in question; for I 'myself' undertook to respect the obligations attendant upon it when I agreed to take it on. The closest analogy would seem to be with the responsibilities that one assumes when one makes any general sort of promise; the fact that one does not and cannot at that moment know in any detail just what that promise might commit one to does not absolve one from such responsibilities as might turn out to be involved in it in the light of unfolding experience—though in cases of borderline uncertainty the question of just where that line is to be drawn may be quite reasonably debatable. I am, for example, President of the Wiener Library at the present time. But I do not identify 'myself' with that role—nor, I feel pretty confident, would most other people regard it as forming any part of my 'intimate' or 'real' identity—partly, perhaps, because, although I take it seriously enough, it is, for better or for worse, relatively peripheral to my life as I conceive it, but mainly because it is a role into which I entered voluntarily and from which I could at any moment voluntarily withdraw and be recognized as having so withdrawn.

There is, however, a whole range of other types of role, entrance into or exit from which, or both, are for different reasons far from being such a matter of generally acceptable personal voluntary decision, and with which, therefore, my very identity as being the person who I am may more easily be seen as tied up. Once ordained, for example, it takes more than an act of individual decision to disengage from the role of orthodox Catholic priest. Family roles are in a way even more complicated, for while, as general clusters of claims and obligations, they may, of course, vary from one society to another, they are tied—both logically and sociologically, as it were—to the more strictly invariant and individuating facts of one's position within a network of individual blood and contractual relationships. For instance, as eldest son of my father and as my grandfather's grandson—I take the autobiographical case for ready ease of example—I find myself occupying a certain role within a family structure, a role that to some variably important degree may be seen to interact with that which my family has been taken and may still be taken to occupy within the wider Anglo-Jewish society and beyond. That different people and different sections of these societies may at different times hold very different views as to the exact nature of these roles and the responsibilities that go with them goes without saying. But my own freedom of maneuver in relation to them, while not entirely nonexistent, is strikingly more limited than in the case of the presidency of the

Wiener Library. Nowhere is it possible to resign from one's factually given position within the family of one's birth; and in the great majority of societies it is extremely difficult to make a clean break by resignation from the roles that such facts normally entail; though many may have tried their utmost to do so, even their most determined attempts are likely, sooner or later, to confront the most intractable social—not to mention psychological—resistances. There are few if any societies in which the modern individualist ethic has been pushed so far as to lead to abandonment of that basic category of mutual and self-identification by reference to placement on a family map. Indeed, the individuating or particularizing aspects of such references appear, if not on one's actual identity card or passport, then certainly on such basic documents as certificates of birth or death. And while I may indeed protest that it is nothing to do with myself as the person that I take myself to be that I happen to be my father's son, I am unlikely to be able wholly to disengage myself from the role and responsibilities associated with that position or from 'the cluster of socially sanctioned claims' that others in my family or society may make upon me in virtue of my identity as so determined.

My role position within a given family, tribal or national structure, or history is, then, one in which I find myself willy nilly; I may try to turn my back on it, but it is not a position from which it is easy simply to resign. The quite general question, then, is one of the degree of free play that individuals have to distance themselves from any given role that they may be taken to inhabit or may have chosen to assume; the particular question here is what degree of free play may be available with respect to family roles. Most fundamentally, the degree of free play available to individuals with respect to any role that they may be taken by themselves or by others to inhabit or to have assumed must depend on what concepts are available to them to think of themselves as distinct from that role. Clearly, this is always going to be easier, at any rate conceptually if not necessarily psychologically easier, in cases where both entrance to and exit from the role is manifestly within the individual's own voluntary power. For in order simply to think about this eventuality, one depends on the availability of concepts necessary to identifying the individual in question independently of the role that he or she may be about to occupy or to leave or may already have left. It is clear that in situations of mobility between different social or institutional roles, some relatively independent form of identification will be needed to keep referential track of those who do or who might move from one role to another; and where the general forms of social life give rise to such a need, the language will surely evolve in such a way as to meet it. However, in both these cases, individuals who had either moved in or out of one open role or another, or who had simply changed some of their role occupations for others, might still be identified not by way of any strictly individually identifying expression, but by reference to some other given role, one from which they seemingly could not in principle escape.

It will no doubt be objected that the mere fact of being the blood descendant of a given progenitor cannot logically necessitate one's imprisonment in any particular family role, that it cannot as a matter of logic follow from the mere physical facts of one's genetic origins that one's consequent relationships have to be set within any particular structure of values or of obligations. If in the general understanding of my community the term 'eldest son' refers not only to a biological relationship, but always at the same time to a certain cluster of socially sanctioned claims and obligations, I might, for example, reply that 'in myself' I am straightforwardly and factually identifiable as the biologically determined outcome of an encounter between a sperm and an egg deriving from certain specific human sources. And are not the basic facts and needs of human existence such that the language of any society whatsoever must contain devices enabling its speakers to identify and to keep track of individual items, including individual human beings, in ways that make it possible to distinguish the continuity or repetition of a function or role from the succession or multiplicity of its individual instantiations, just as it may be necessary at times to distinguish individuals from the multiplicity of roles or functions that they may at one time or another happen to occupy?

Here we find ourselves having to encroach on the territory of the long-standing controversies concerning the nature of the distinction and consequent relations between what are generally known as value judgments and statements of fact. It is a conceptual truth that individuals can only envisage the possibility of taking their own evaluative stands in relation to their contexts of origin (or, if it comes to that, to those of their current insertion) insofar as they have learnt to operate with appropriate evaluative concepts—that is to say, concepts that obey (or incorporate) some version of the principle that has found one of its most famous (if not most strictly accurate) expressions in the slogan *No 'Ought' from an 'Is'*. To hold otherwise is to accept that there may be facts—facts of one's birth, facts of one's nationality, facts concerning the nature of the groups to which one belongs as a matter of descriptive classification, *facts concerning one's very identity in virtue of the roles in which one finds oneself and from which one cannot escape*, facts from which certain normative judgements, whether of value, obligation or duty, follow as a matter of 'natural' entailment. In general, of course, a recognition of this general principle is not so much a matter of explicit doctrine as a presupposition written deep into the conceptual bases of much contemporary language and thought—the so-called discourses of modernity.[14]

This assumption of 'the autonomy of values' is equally a necessary, and probably also indeed a sufficient, condition of being able to conceive of groups as consisting in nothing more than the set of complex relations holding between the distinct and in principle autonomous individuals who happen to comprise them. For if, on the contrary, values could in theory be unrenounceably determined by facts, the individual members of a group might in principle be so marked by their de facto membership of it as to continue to belong to its network of collective obligations and responsibilities simply by virtue of the fact of their membership roles and identities, whatever their own purely personal preferences in the matter might be.

It has often been remarked, of course, that this principle of "no 'ought' from an 'is'"—whatever the imprecisions of its various formulations might be—is of strikingly individualist import. Facts confront individuals as fundamentally resistant to their preferences or powers of choice. (In the initial language-learning stage, indeed, they have to come to terms with the facts concerning the generally accepted conventions governing the meanings and forces of symbols within their own particular language community.) If, therefore, it were possible validly to derive value judgments from statements of fact, individuals would be similarly constrained in their recognition of values and obligations. If, on the other hand, whatever the facts that they find themselves constrained to recognize, they are left necessarily free to determine their own evaluative attitudes towards them, then, and then only, are they ineluctably free, in whatever factual situation they may find themselves, to determine their own values and, with them, their own identity insofar as this is conceived in role-normative or evaluative terms.

Once again, this crucial point may be illustrated by returning to the anti–private language argument. For present purposes let me take it for granted that, in some version or another, this argument can be successfully made out. If, then, to learn a language is to take upon oneself the basic public commitments of the rules governing the use of its vocabulary and the formation of its concepts, it is clear that these are interpersonal normative commitments that have to be discovered, learnt, recognized, and respected in the context of the facts of the ways in which already existing members of one's language community use the materials (sounds, marks, etc.) that constitute the vehicles of whatever language is in question. Once one has learnt a language, there will, no doubt, always be a certain degree of free play for creative innovation—but only on the basis of what has been already learnt and accepted. Given the intimate dependence of the capacity for self-identification (as, indeed, for the identification of anyone or anything else), on the terms and nature of the language through which this capacity is acquired, this interplay between a necessary respect for rules as given and the room that such rules may allow for their creative revision or extension may well be taken to represent a roughly parallel interplay between what has to be taken as given and what is open for creative self-redefinition in respect of one's identity itself.

It is here that we encounter the limits of the principle of *No 'Ought' from an 'Is'* and, thus, those of individual evaluative autonomy. While it may be true that individuals who have the necessary concepts of autonomy can never be constrained by the particular facts of their situation to any particular value judgment signifying their approval or disapproval of them, it is also true that, *so long as they are unprepared, or perhaps even unable, to risk exclusion from the realm of intelligible communication*, they cannot hope meaningfully to dissociate themselves from all the values of their speech community at once. This means that my own understanding of the terms through which I may identify myself cannot be rendered wholly independent of the ways in which I may be identified by everybody else. Where, for instance, there is and can be no dispute as to whether I was in fact born and brought up as, for example, a (non-Orthodox) Jew, or as the eldest son or daughter of a traditional Chinese family, the views that others may have, above all those others who were also so born and brought up, as to the relevance of these facts to my "core" identity and to my consequent commitments, are bound to form part of that horizon within which, as Charles Taylor put it, I have "to take my stand."[15] This is not to say that I have necessarily to accept their views. Their weight will depend *inter alia* on the general circumstances in which both they and I may find ourselves at the time, on my own self-confidence and resolution and on whatever may be (or may be thought to be) the further implications of my being identified in one way rather than another. But it would not be plausible for me to maintain that they need have in principle no weight or relevance at all. The contrast between the situation of the German Jew at, say, the beginning of this century and that in which his grandchildren would have found themselves in 1939 provides a sobering example of the way in which the weight that has sometimes inescapably to be accorded to what others regard as my identity may be judged to shift with changes in circumstance—even if the weight which they are accorded in any particular case falls short of being universally decisive.

In fact, the very versatility and persuasive power of the language (or languages) of identity surely owes much to the way in which it manages to reflect so many deep, but also deeply conflicting, pulls and constraints. On the one hand there are the pulls towards individual autonomy and everything that goes (conceptually) with it; but on the other hand, there are in the end always the limiting constraints of the rules of reciprocal intelligibility and recognizability in the eyes of significant others—as well, of course, as the practical pressures of a given situation. It seems to me that no amount of argument can succeed, in our present discursive situation at any rate, in finally settling such questions, be they of theory or of practice, in favor of confining our thinking about identity and membership within the limits of either the pulls or the constraints. In the end each case must come down to some essentially contestable matter of judgment and an always challengeable decision as to where to take one's stand. This is itself, of course, a basically autonomist, liberal individualist conclusion to come to. But how, if the whole drift of my arguments is approximately correct, could it be otherwise? Always acknowledging, of course, the historically and personally variable limits within which any such decision must always admit itself to be constrained.

In any language there must be ways of evolving an Autonomy of Values principle, at least in some form or another and within the sort of limits that I have just indicated. That this possibility must always exist is illustrated by the fact that this is a development that has actually taken place within languages (as aspects of forms of life) that previously allowed for no natural gap between what we might nowadays call evaluative and non-evaluative (or descriptive) expressions. But in some languages and in some forms of life this will be more difficult, more artificial than in others. I suspect that the more detailed and specific the terms of kinship in a language, the more tightly blood relationships and role clusters will be bound together; however, this is but an untested suspicion that would clearly stand in need of much checking out.

To return, however, to the objection that "the mere fact of being the blood descendant of a given progenitor cannot logically necessitate one's imprisonment in any particular family role." To anyone accustomed to operating within the assumptions—linguistic, conceptual and, in a broad sense of the term, logical—of the principle of *No 'Ought' from an 'Is'*, the objection will seem so obviously valid as to need no further arguing. Assumptions of this sort can become so transparent as to disappear, so to speak, into the very fabric of the language in which one thinks. Moreover, there have been a number of well-known attempts to show that evaluative and/or normative expressions are of such a logically different order from descriptive or definitional statements that the impossibility of any valid derivation of the one from the other can be exhibited as, in effect, a theorem of logic.[16] But once the move is made from treating value judgments as, in Hare's phrase, a "class of sentences"[17] with a special meaning-content to treating them as speech acts carrying a particular sort of force, the whole basis for treating the distinction between value and fact as a matter of universally valid logic is seriously undermined. Sentences may be held to entail other sentences, but acts, being events of a certain type, may not plausibly be said to entail other acts. So now other sorts of questions need to be asked—questions concerning the existence of any sharp boundary distinction between matters of meaning and matters of force; questions concerning what is involved in learning and mastering a language; whether an understanding of the forces conventionally associated with particular uses of the language is part of any adequate understanding of the language as such. For instance, it may form part of the standard, proper understanding of a given language (and the form of life of which it makes a part) that "F is the biological sire of S" strictly implies that S is his son, and that "S is his son" carries as part of its standard meaning/force that S has certain obligations towards his father and/or *vice versa*, *whether they like it or not*, simply by virtue of their meaningfully undeniable identities as sire (or father) and son. Of course, it remains the case that if S is sufficiently disenchanted with this situation—and, crucially, if he is conceptually gifted enough—he may in principle be able to learn, or perhaps even to evolve for himself, a language within which these relationships of meaning and force do not hold; and within which it therefore becomes possible to express a dissenting value judgement to the effect that to be the biological descendant of a given F does not necessarily mean that one has any commitments towards him. But he cannot reasonably expect that those with whom he has hitherto shared a common language will be willing or even able to follow the shifts that he has made. In which case, so far as his speech and effective social community is concerned he will continue to have his obligations as a son—as an elder son or a younger son, as the case may be, if their language makes it normally impossible to escape articulating such a distinction—so far as others are concerned. And as I have already argued, questions of even personal identity must in the end be regarded as being in essential part matters of identification as the individual whom one is within a (speech) community of one's fellows.

It would be a mistake to conclude from all this that I have somehow been arguing that individuals will typically find all the materials necessary to the construction of their identities simply from those made available to them by their own natural languages, whether native or subsequently acquired. It is, for one thing, a matter of ultimately somewhat arbitrary decision as to where exactly one should situate the boundaries, both synchronic and diachronic, between one natural language and another. But quite apart from this consideration, it is, of course, the case that people more typically build their identities out of far more local affective commitments to and identifications with communities and even places, which may be separated hardly at all by language; and, equally, that both the subjective and publicly recognized identities of those who share a common language may have very little else in common at all. Rather, only those whose language (or linguistic culture) provides them with the conceptual resources necessary to formulate what we may call, however tendentiously, a quite general distinction between value and fact will be able to see the establishment of their own identity as a choice genuinely open to them.

Nor have I been arguing for a certain form of relativism, one which would make the degree of individuals' freedom to determine their personal identity relative to the speech community of which they were members. Such a relativism would be open to all the familiar objections to the incoherence of any attempt to affirm a thesis of absolute relativism. From where I, for instance, stand, both linguistically and conceptually, nobody is committed merely by the facts of his or her blood position in a given family to any particular obligations towards it. I simply observe that I cannot expect everyone, whatever the nature of their own linguistic and conceptual community, to acknowledge my position as being logically incontrovertible. From where they stand I may indeed be thus family-committed. And if this sounds as if I was thereby committing myself to the contradiction of saying that a son may be both committed and yet not committed to certain obligations vis-à-vis his father, then I have to acknowledge myself as being subject to a different sort of commitment, namely one to finding a noncontradictory way of formulating this seemingly contradictory statement of what I take to be the case.

The answer to this challenge would seem to lie in the following direction. One form of discursive life may have come to evolve a set of terms such that what is recognizable within it as an evaluative or normative judgment of the facts of any given situation can be shown always to rest in the last instance on the self-committing choice of the individual responsible for making the judgment. Another—possibly earlier?—form of discourse may—as yet?—simply lack any way of making the necessary overall distinction between fact and value. There is, it seems to me, no sense to the idea that one of these two forms of discourse might be shown to be simply mistaken and the other certified as correct. At most it should be possible to show how, from the Autonomist or individualist position it is possible to render the other one intelligible in the sense of being able to give a coherent explanation of how it works; while the reverse can not be the case. This is because in order to render the Autonomist position intelligible, one would have to make intelligible the crucial distinctions between value and fact, in which case one will already have transformed one's own discourse into that of the Autonomist. So one might perhaps argue that the superiority of this discourse is shown by its ability to make space within itself for an intelligible account of the other, which, for its part, is unable to respond in kind.

From the discourse of Autonomy, however, there can be no deliberate going back. (Which is not to say that distinctions may not simply be lost again with the long passage of time and social change.) There are those who, like Alasdair MacIntyre in his *After Virtue*,[18] while fully recognizing the individualist implications of the evaluative discourse of their own time, nevertheless still hanker after the more firmly communitarian discourses of evaluation out of which it has evolved and which have now been left behind. But, however paradoxical it may seem, it is a constraint of the discourse of individual evaluative choice that one cannot simply choose one's way out of it again. For in attempting to make such a choice, one would in effect be reaffirming once again the primacy of deliberate individual choice, and in so doing demonstrably relying on the availability of the concepts necessary to its formulation. There is more than one sense in which the modern world may find itself condemned to be free.

I have, then, no one clear answer to the questions with which I started. Charles Taylor, for example, would not be alone in holding that it is part of the modern conception of the self that individuals are seen to be in essential principle free to determine their own identities. Since, clearly enough, the facts of my position within the family into which I am born are in no way open to determination by me, and since, furthermore, I am free to determine even my position within my family by marriage only at certain key moments and even then to a culturally variable extent, for those who think of personal identity as primarily a matter of self-determining self-identification the degree to which my family position should be understood to form any part of my own self-identity must be largely, if not entirely, a matter for me to determine myself. But, while

Taylor's characterization of the spirit and conceptual commitments of modern individualism may well be faithful enough, he would no doubt agree—it is indeed the other side of his thesis—that it can make no claim whatsoever to universal validity.

It is, of course, entirely possible to hold that my family position must be regarded as an indissociable aspect of my personal identity while still maintaining that this in itself implies strictly nothing about any family responsibilities or commitments that may or may not be held to be incumbent upon me. But on this matter too I have likewise no one clear answer to give. All will depend on whether or not my family position is understood as constituting not only an aspect of my own identity, but also and *ipso facto* a certain role, a role from whose attendant responsibilities I can not simply free myself by my own sovereign will.[19] And whether one understands all these matters in one way or the other will depend on the concepts available to one in one's language and, more generally, in the culture within which one's very ability to identify oneself or anyone or anything else will have been formed. And on *this* matter, one has to conclude, one has indeed very little, if any, choice at all. At least, if we can understand how and why all this is so, we shall to that degree have made some genuine progress.

Notes

1. Amélie Rorty provides a useful recall of the main outlines of the evolution of the term 'person' in her very helpful introduction to her *The Identities of Persons* (Berkeley: University of California Press, 1976).

2. John Locke, *An Essay Concerning Human Understanding*, Book II, ch. XXVII.

3. Carl Rogers, *On Becoming a Person: A Therapist's View of Psychotherapy* (London: Constable, 1967).

4. Theodore R. Sarbin, "The Poetics of Identity," *Theory and Psychology* 7, no. 1 (1997): 67–82.

5. Sarbin is referring to Karl Scheibe's *Self Studies: The Psychology of Self and Identity* (Westport, CT: Praeger, 1995).

6. For the ideas expressed in the last sentence of this passage, Sarbin credits Harré and Gillet's *The Discursive Mind* (London: Sage, 1994) and Shotter and Gergen's *Texts of Identity* (London: Sage, 1989).

7. Charles Taylor, *Sources of the Self* (Cambridge, Mass.: Harvard University Press, 1989), 27.

8. Clément Rosset, *Loin de moi: étude sur l'identité* (Paris: Les Editions de Minuit, 1999), 10–11. (The translation is mine.)

9. Erik Erikson, "Ego Development and Historical Change," in *The Psychoanalytic Study of the Child*, vol. 2 (New York: International Universities Press, 1946), 359–96.

10. Erik Erikson, "The Problem of Ego Identity," *Journal of the American Psycho-*

analytic Association 4 (1956): 56–121: it is now most easily to be found in a small paperback called *Identity and the Life Cycle*, which includes, indeed, both these papers together with a third intermediate one, "Growth and Crises of the Healthy Personality," itself first published in 1950. *Identity and the Life Cycle* was first published as a Norton (New York and London) paperback in 1980 and reissued in 1994.

11. *Ibid.*, p. 28.

12. I do not wish to suggest that children, or indeed many of the higher animals, who lack the powers, or at any rate the full powers, of language, must necessarily, therefore, be regarded as incapable of anything that might reasonably be called 'thought' in any sense of that term; no serious argument can be made to turn simply on legislating for some restrictive definition, whether explicit or merely implicit, of the verb ' to think' and its cognates. (Some animals may even possess some rudimentary capacity, not only for elementary conceptualization, but even for self-reference; recent experiments with certain of the higher apes and mirrors, for example, seem to suggest that they can at any rate distinguish between themselves and their own mirror images.) Nor do I want to suggest that even quite sophisticated forms of thought may not be conducted 'non-linguistically', that is, without being accompanied by words and sentences or being cast in propositional form. Artists, for example, may think very hard about what they are about when confronted by their canvasses without doing anything remotely like talking to themselves; and vervet monkeys, so it is said, both give and respond appropriately to different alarm signals warning them of the differently threatening presence of eagles, snakes, or leopards. It must, however, be extremely doubtful whether anyone can be accounted capable of second-order reflection or of the kind of structured thinking that may be ordered in the form of arguments open both to checking and criticism without recourse to language and its conceptualizing formulations.

13. See Michael Banton, *Roles* (London: Tavistock Publications Ltd., 1965), 2. See also Dorothy Emmet, *Rules, Roles and Relations* (London: Macmillan, 1996).

14. Moreover, for those for whom this is indeed a presupposition of their evaluative vocabulary, it functions not only as a necessary condition of their own evaluative autonomy, but also, like it or not, as a sufficient one; as Richard Hare for one has often insisted, for them there is in the end no escape from personal evaluative responsibility.

15. Taylor, *Sources of the Self*, p. 27.

16. One may think, for example, of Karl Popper and his in its time influential paper "What Logic can do for Philosophy?", Aristotelian Society, Supplementary vol. 22 (1948); or again of R. M. Hare and his analysis of value judgments in terms of sentences that entail imperatives first set out in his *The Language of Morals* (Oxford: Oxford University Press, 1952), see in particular pages 168–69; this analysis was reaffirmed, with certain important nuances, in his subsequent *Freedom and Reason* (Oxford: Oxford University Press, 1962) and *Moral Thinking* (Oxford: Oxford University Press, 1982).

17. Hare, *The Language of Morals*, p. 169.

18. Alasdair MacIntyre, *After Virtue* (London: Duckworth, 1981).

19. It must be recognized that on the non-Autonomous (as opposed to the Autonomous) view of matters my own will is and cannot be sovereign in such contexts.

Individualism and Collectivism in Moral and Social Thought

John D. Greenwood

Western moral and social theories are often characterized (or caricatured) by reference to their distinctive emphasis on individualism and personal autonomy. In contrast, Chinese moral and social theories are often represented as attaching far greater significance to collective social units, such as family, community, or state. There is, no doubt, some historical truth and philosophical merit in this common characterization. However, it also seriously distorts our understanding of the relation between individual and social forms of being that underlie *any* moral or social system.

When Western and Chinese moral and social systems are characterized in terms of their supposedly contrasting commitments to individualism and collectivism, Western moral and social systems are also generally contrasted with other non-Western systems, such as African and Indian moral and social systems.[1] However, the individualistic culprit is often not Western moral and social systems *per se*, but the moral and social systems of elite and college educated Western males. This is despite the fact that only a very few of them (less than 20 percent) reach Kohlberg's final developmental stage, with its concept of individual autonomy and abstract principles of justice.[2] According to Gilligan, fewer women (East or West) reach this stage, because women have a different moral vision, based upon caring relations embedded within social communities.[3] Some have noted the close parallels between Gilligan's female vision and non-Western systems of morality,[4] and prima facie, at least, Gilligan's morality of care seems not far distant from the venerable Chinese tradition of emphasizing "concern for others" embedded within a system of social relations.[5]

Some see these avowed parallels as providing further support for the original contrast. Others see them as grounds for intellectual suspicion of the basis of the supposed contrast. After all, don't Western males (even college educated ones) care about their mothers and sisters (and brothers and colleagues) too? I admit to being one of those of a more skeptical bent. In the following remarks I try to cast some doubt upon these familiar contrasts, and sketch a rather different perspective on the fundamentally individual and collective dimensions of any moral or social system.

I

Let me begin by stating what I hope will be obvious. Human beings have recognized themselves as distinct individuals, as distinct physical and psychological beings, with individual hopes, fears, goals, and memories, in just about every civilized society of which we have records. As Durkheim's disciple Marcel Mauss put it: "Let me merely say that it is plain, particularly to us, that there has never existed a human being who has not been aware, not only of his body, but also at the same time of his individuality, both spiritual and physical."[6]

Consider the following extracts from a Chinese poem from around the second quarter of the first millennium B.C.E., in which a woman regrets her marriage to a social inferior:[7]

> Man of the people! How you kept me laughing,
> Hemp-cloth in your arms, came to barter for silk.
> But skeins of silk were not what you were after.
> —You were there with schemes to make me come to you.
>
> And so—I went with you. Across the Chyi River,
> To the mounds of Duenn, we went together.
>
> When leaves drop off the mulberry tree,
> They lie brown and discoloured.
> In three years with you,
> I have eaten poor food.
>
> Three years a wife!
> Effort no effort,
> Getting up early, late to bed,
> No day for myself.
> —It is finished now.
> My brothers ignore me
> With biting laughter.
> I think in silence. Sad for myself.
> I came to you to grow old with you.
> We grew older. You made me resent you.
>
> Chyi at least has its shorelines,
> Marshes at its edges.
> —When my hair was still up, as a girl's is,
> How we talked, how we laughed our contentment,

Vowed good faith so intently,
Not thinking it might be altered,
The change that was not to be thought of,
This change that has happened.

Book of Odes, Ode 58

The poem is easy to understand, I believe, because the conception of a distinct physical and psychological individual with a history and biography is universally shared. It is the common conceptual coinage of all literate ages and cultures. This conception of the individual as a distinct physical and psychological being is itself a major historical and cultural achievement: a conceptual achievement of socialized individuals with shared languages, cultures, and histories. Yet although the basic conception of individuals as discrete physical and psychological beings is universal, the contents of any particular conception of individuality are a product of culture and history: the product of distributed "social representations"[8] of individuality shared by members of some social collectivity in some particular time and place.

II

All conceptions of individuality are shared social representations, whether they be Western or non-Western, male or female, Northern or Southern, European or Middle Eastern, or suchlike. In this respect all conceptions of individuality are fundamentally *collective* in nature: they are products of culture and history that are sustained by culture and history. Yet these fundamentally social or collective conceptions of individuality (and of morality and society) vary cross-culturally and transhistorically with respect to their contents. Different cultures (and the same cultures at different historical periods) differentially value the individual in relation to the social group or collectivity.

Thus some cultures (and historical periods) value individuality in the form of nonconformity with social rules and norms; others treat this form of individuality as indicative of personality disorder. Some cultures (and historical periods) privilege individual rights and welfare over the rights and welfare of social collectives; others privilege the social collective over the individual, subordinating individual rights and welfare to the rights and welfare of the social collective, be it family, tribe, clan, or nation. The classic defense of the Western conception of moral individualism is Mill's *On Liberty*; recent defenses by some Asian governments of their actions that place the interests of the social collective over the interests of individuals appear to epitomize the collectivist viewpoint.[9]

However, the basic difference is not merely or even essentially a matter of conformity, rights, or legitimate degrees of social interference. For differences in the contents of social representations of individuality represent fundamental differences with respect to our psychological being. Different cultural and historical conceptions of individuality not only have different contents, but engage networks of social conventions and principles governing the behavior, and the thought and emotion, of individuals who conceive of themselves in terms of such (social) representations of individuality. One determines one's individuality, or one's identity, if you like, by reference to these conventions and principles—by one's success or failure in living up to them.

This appears to be another universal aspect of social representations of individuality. Individuals determine their individuality (or identity) by reference to social conventions and principles, which determine, given one's actions or failures to act, whether one is noble or ignoble, honorable or dishonorable, good or bad, and so forth. These conventions and principles determine, for example, what *counts* as being a good mother or father, good citizen, good Christian or Muslim, good knight or ruler, from one culture and historical period to another. Among these many differences, which concern matters of reputation in relation to other members of a social collectivity, some conceptions take the individual and others the collective as their focus. That is, the actions of individuals in any social collective may be regulated and evaluated by reference to their impact upon the individual *or* the collective.

Western moral and social systems in the liberal-democratic and laissez-faire tradition of Mill and Bentham represent one example of an *individualist* conception of individuality. Individuals tend to be evaluated according to how well or badly they manage their self-interest: pride and shame are oriented to the success and failure of individuals in promoting their personal goals and projects. Other moral and social systems represent the collectivist extreme. In Inuit and Maori culture, for example, actions are orientated toward the interests of the whole collective, and the emotions of pride or shame are experienced by all members, according to the success or failure of the actions of individuals in relation to the goals of the social collective. Thus all take pride in the success of individual warriors, and all are ashamed by their failure. According to the Maori custom of *muru*, a man may be punished (*via* institutional plunder) for accidental injury to himself. Since his accident damages the collective (he can no longer usefully contribute to collective activities), the collective is entitled to reparation.[10]

Of course, these are extremes. Maori myths also extol the individual virtues (such as bravery, oratory, and leadership), and forms of collective focus similar to the Maori can be found in the West, in athletic teams and combat groups. This is important to stress, because couched in these terms, it is in fact doubtful if the common contrast between East and West in terms of collectivism versus individualism can be sustained.

III

The Chinese tradition is fairly ambiguous, because it is culturally and historically diverse. The existential angst and isolation of the poet Qu Yuan [11] (circa 3rd–4th century B.C.E.), for example, is more akin to Hamlet than the Maori. Yang Zhu's (circa 4th century B.C.E.) denunciation of social institutions, as forms of imprisonment that constrain individual expression, is probably about as far away from a collectivist conception of individuality as one can get. The position of Confucius himself is unclear, and largely dependent upon whether one conceives of the virtue of "concern for others" as an expression of individuality or subordination of it. Certainly Confucius's familiar claim that one has a duty to protect errant family members from the offices of the state puts him some distance from the collectivist extreme.

It appears that the only really unambiguous Chinese collectivist vision of individuality is to be found in the revolutionary communism of Ai Shiqi:

> We have revolutionary thoughts and actions. We exert ourselves to serve the great people. This is the main side of our character, and an aspect of the path of development of the distant future. But we also contain dregs of the thought of petty-bourgeois individualism, and even the dregs of the consciousness of the other exploiting classes. We often make calculations for our own private profit, which prevents us from serving the people with whole heart and whole will. This is the reverse side of our character, the rotten side that must be smashed.[12]

This collectivist conception was itself presaged in the Chinese tradition by a radical conception of individuality that involved the rejection of *all* social conventions and principles (other than those of friendship grounded in equality), as represented by the work of the nineteenth-century theorist Tan Sitong, for example: "We must break through the net of conventional scholarship. . . . Then we must break through the net of having rules. Then we must break through the net of moral norms. Then through the net of [believing in] Heaven. Then though the net of the world's religions."[13] Tan Sitong's rejection of conventional social norms (including moral norms) had the peculiar consequence of effectively eliminating individuality as a value, promoting instead a "borderless" society of homogeneous individuals: "In the Government of the world, there should be an All-Under-Heaven but no nation-state. . . . Since everyone is free, no one should be the citizen of any particular state. If there are no states, then boundaries will dissolve, wars cease, suspicions end, distinctions between self and others vanish, and equality appear."[14]

While Tan Sitong's position was effectively anarchistic, Kang Youwei[15] moved towards revolutionary communism by maintaining that governments should take steps to ensure uniformity, for example, by abolishing families (which were held to encourage small-scale collective selfishness). Interestingly enough, the ultimate philosophical justification for this decidedly non-Confucian position was unambiguously and unashamedly utilitarian: to "reduce men's pain and to increase their pleasure." [16]

IV

The traditional characterization of Western moral and social systems as individualistic also tends to ignore the variety and complexity of that tradition. The familiar egoistical and laissez-faire conception of individuality promoted by Bentham and Mill is a relatively recent and contested position. In medieval thought, for example, the term "individual" meant "inseparable," and was generally employed to individuate "a member of some group, kind, or species."[17] Persons were defined *as* individuals by reference to the groups of which they were members: their very identity as "units" was determined by their group memberships. Thus individuals were conceived as *intrinsically* related to the groups of which they were members: [18] "to describe an individual was to give an example of the group of which he was a member, and so to offer a particular description of that group and of the relationships within it."[19]

Partly as a result of the Renaissance and Reformation, and the rise of capitalism, the concept of the individual came to be divorced from its original connection with social community.[20] In the tradition of social thought from Hobbes, Locke, and Smith to Bentham and Mill, individuals came to be treated in isolation and abstraction from social community—as "self-contained" individuals. The liberal political tradition that developed from this conception emphasized the "bare" individual as bearer of absolute personal rights, as the parallel tradition of laissez-faire economics emphasized the purely egoistical rational agent.

Yet the original medieval conception of moral individuality as embedded in social community was also maintained, and continued to play a significant role in Western moral and social thought. It was developed in particular by Rousseau and Hegel, and by idealists such as Bosanquet[21] and Green.[22] It was precisely this conception of moral individualism as embedded in social community that William McDougall, for example, embraced in *The Group Mind*.[23] According to this conception, a person's moral worth and individuality is grounded within social community, rather than independently of it, or as opposed to it. Where others saw sociality as a threat to individuality, McDougall, like Dewey,[24] Cooley,[25] Baldwin,[26] and Mead,[27] saw it as the very *source* and *medium* of individuality, and commended:"The vital relation between the life of the individual and the life of community, which alone gives the individual worth and significance, because it alone gives him the power of full moral development; the dependence of the individual, for all his rights and for all his liberty, on his membership of the community."[28]

McDougall traced this conception of the "vital relation between the life of the individual and the life of community" to the Greek city-state, contrasting it with the utilitarian and laissez-faire conception of Bentham and Mill, in which the individual is ideally conceived in terms of his or her independence from external social influence and interference. According to McDougall (quoting Barker[29]), the virtue of the community based conception of individuality was that:

> it could satisfy the new needs of social progress, because it refused to worship a supposed individual liberty which was proving destructive of the real liberty of the vast majority, and preferred to emphasize the moral well-being and betterment of the whole community, and to conceive of each of its members as attaining his own betterment and well-being in and through the community.[30]

This Western vision of community based individuality promoted the notion that social groupings would eventually become so inclusive that the final pinnacle of civilization would be forms of individuality grounded in humanity itself. Such an idealized development was generally conceived as the natural product of a historical evolution from primitive or primary groups (such as families and tribes) through nation-states to world-government.[31] Significantly, this was also precisely the sort of vision expounded by later Chinese theorists such as Tan Sitong and Kang Youwei.

V

To sum up, all societies appear to have collectively-grounded representations of individuality, which differ in their collective conceptions of individuality and norms associated with it. Some take the collective, and others take the individual, as the normative object of an individual's moral projects. These sorts of differences do not appear to be distinctively Western as opposed to Chinese (or opposed to non-Western in general). No doubt one could explore the relative degrees of emphasis on the individual and the collective in different cultures and historical periods, but that is a question for the cultural historian. My aim has simply been to cast doubt upon the traditional contrast between Western and Chinese traditions.

Yet that is not quite the end of it. For one may ask, reflexively, why is there supposed to be such a problem with the Western individualist tradition that stresses individual autonomy and self-interest? It is surely because it is presumed that a moral system that promotes autonomy and self-interest will not give sufficient attention to the rights and welfare of others. The Chinese tradition, in supposed contrast, is held to be "other-directed."[32]

Now Western utilitarian and deontological moral systems do provide philosophical justifications for including the rights and welfare of others in the moral equation, although they often have a problem providing a psychologically compelling motivation for caring about others beyond one's own immediate "primary group" structure of friends and family. Yet conceptions of individuality that locate the social collective as the object of moral focus have the same problem, or at least a version of the same problem. For the question arises as to *which* population of individuals should form the proper focus of an individual's moral project: his or her family, community (religious, professional, or neighborhood), or state or nation? Significantly, Confucian and more recent feminist "care" ethics tend to advocate a graduated system of obligations to others according to their social distance, beginning with immediate family and friends, but diminishing as one relates to colleagues, fellow citizens, and strangers.[33]

The guiding metaethical assumption that moral systems ought to promote general altruism or concern for others suggests that individuals ought to take the whole of humanity as the object of their moral concern, and indeed this appears to be the rationale of those who complain about the ethnocentrism or natiocentrism of contemporary conceptions of the moral universe.[34] This type of complaint may be illustrated via reflection on the Singaporean national mantra that encourages Singaporeans to place nation before community, and community before family. This is fine for nation building, of course, but why stop at nations (especially smallish ones) when it comes to morality? Yet there is some real point to the implied restriction.

It is commonly assumed that the best (if not the only) way to encourage and promote general altruism or concern for others is to get people to see themselves as members of one giant collective: as members of one family, one university, one nation, one world, and so forth. Yet this is not logically necessary, and doubtfully very efficient from a psychological point of view. Herbert Hyman (1942), the American social psychologist who explored the multifarious ways in which human individuality is comparatively oriented to the norms and principles of social groups, which he designated as "reference groups," noted that very few Americans identified American society as their reference group. Most Americans cited smaller local groups such as family, neighbors, colleagues, gangs, unions, and the like. Few appeared to feel bound to concern themselves with others because they saw themselves as members of one society, because few saw themselves essentially as members of society. Analogously, a recent poll of younger Singaporeans found them to be primarily orientated to immediate family, friends, and classmates rather than communities, ethnic groups, or nation.[35]

This sounds like a problem, but it's not the real problem. For a universal collective conception of individuality and morality may just as easily endorse an autonomous and egoistic conception of individuality and morality as any nationally or socially restricted conception. Conversely, a social group as restricted as a family or a local church congregation may take the whole of humanity as its object of moral concern (while recognizing the practical limitations on what it can do for them). What matters in the end for any person is what his or her psychologically potent social group prescribes as its object of moral concern, and the only way to promote the expansion of that object beyond the confines of the membership of any social group is *to work for its expansion from within that social group*. This suggests that if you want to promote universal concern and fellowship, don't aim for the world brother- and sisterhood or the society of nations. Aim rather to persuade your families, friends, colleagues, co-religionists, and co-politicals to extend the boundaries of their moral concern. There does not appear to be any other way, East or West.

Notes

1. D. Allen, *Culture and Self: Philosophical and Religious Perspectives, East and West* (Boulder, Co.: Westview, 1977).

2. L. Kohlberg, *Essays on Moral Development* (San Francisco: Harper and Row, 1981).

3. C. Gilligan, *In a Different Voice* (Cambridge: Harvard University Press, 1982).

4. S. Harding, "The Curious Coincidence of Feminine and African Moralities: Challenges for Feminist Theory," in *Women and Moral Theory*, ed. E. F. Kittay and D. T. Myers (Totowa, N.J.: Rowman & Littlefield, 1987).

5. The parallels between Confucian ethics and feminist ethics of care are explored in *The Sage and the Second Sex*, ed. C. Li (Chicago: Open Court, 2000).

6. M. Mauss (1938), "A Category of the Human Mind: The Notion of Person; the Notion of Self," in *The Category of the Person: Anthropology, Philosophy, History*, ed. M. Carrithers, S. Collins, and S. Lukes, trans. D. W. Walls (Cambridge: Cambridge University Press, 1985), 3.

7. B. Karlgren, *The Book of Odes* (Stockholm: Museum of Far Eastern Antiquities, 1950), trans. and quoted in M. Elvin, "Between the Earth and Heaven: Conceptions of the Self in China," in *The Category of the Person*, ed. Carrithers, Collins, and Lukes, 157.

8. S. Moscovici, "The Phenomenon of Social Representations," in *Social Representations*, ed. R. Farr and S. Moscovici (Cambridge: Cambridge University Press, 1984).

9. Although it may be doubted if such positions are always shared by the folk subjects of such positions. For example, the laissez-faire individualism of Herbert Spencer (1870–1872) that entailed the rejection of "poor relief" was probably not very popular with the poor of his day, and the collectivist positions of governments are not always shared by those individuals whose individual rights are denied by them.

10. J. Smith, "Self and Experience in Maori Culture," in *Indigenous Psychologies*, ed. P. Heelas and A. Lock (London: Academic Press, 1981).

11. I shall substitute *hanyu pinyin* in place of other systems of romanization found in the references.

12. Ay Sychyi, *Dah Jong Jershyue* [*The Philosophy of the Masses*] (N. p. Shinhwa, 1949), 125–26, cited in Elvin, "Between the Earth and Heaven," 185.

13. T'arn Ssu-t'ung, "Renshyue," in *Tarn Syhtorng Chyuan Jyi* [The Complete Works of T'arn Ssu-t'ung.] (Beijing: Sanlian, 1954), 3, cited in Elvin, "Between the Earth and Heaven," p. 174.

14. T'arn, "Renshyue," p. 76, cited in Elvin, "Between the Earth and Heaven," p. 175.

15. K'ang Yu-wei (1935), *Dahtorng Shu* [*The Book of the Great Uniformity*] (Beijing: Guujyi, 1956). See Elvin, "Between the Earth and Heaven," pp. 178–81.

16. It might be objected that this is to focus too narrowly on recent theorists, to the neglect of the earlier classical Chinese tradition. However, the point of discussing such theorists is to illustrate that the Chinese tradition is not historically continuous, and those who wish to develop contrastive positions based upon cultural differences must also acknowledge historical differences. Moreover, as argued in the following section, the Western "individualist" position, with which the Chinese position is frequently contrasted, is itself a relatively recent cultural phenomenon.

17. R. Williams, *The Long Revolution* (New York: Columbia University Press, 1961).

18. The concept of the individual developed originally in the context of medieval debates about the nature of the Holy Trinity, where the individual natures of the Father, Son and Holy Ghost were treated as determined by their relation to an indivisible whole (C. Morris, *The Discovery of the Individual, 1050–1200* [New York: Harper & Row, 1972]).

19. Morris, *Discovery of the Individual*, p. 91.

20. J. O. Lyons, *The Invention of the Self* (Carbondale: Southern Illinois University Press, 1978) and Morris, *Discovery of the Individual*.

21. B. Bosanquet, *Philosophical Theory of the State* (New York: Macmillan, 1899).

22. T. H. Green, "Lectures on the Principles of Political Obligation," in *Collected Works*, vol. 2 (London: Longmans, Green, 1900).

23. W. McDougall, *The Group Mind* (New York: Putnam, 1920).

24. J. Dewey, *The Public and Its Problems* (New York: Henry Holt and Company, Inc., 1927).

25. C. H. Cooley, *Human Nature and the Social Order* (New York: Charles Scribner's Sons, 1902).

26. J. M. Baldwin, *The Individual and Society* (Boston: The Gorham Press, 1911).

27. G. H. Mead, *Mind, Self and Society: From the Standpoint of A Social Behaviorist*, ed. C. W. Morris (Chicago: University of Chicago Press, 1934).

28. McDougall, *The Group Mind*, p. 17.

29. E. Barker, *Political Thought in England from Herbert Spencer to the Present Day* (London: Home University Library, 1915), 11.

30. McDougall, *The Group Mind*, p. 17.

31. W. Wundt, *Elements of Folk Psychology: Outlines of a Psychological History of the Development of Mankind*, trans. Edward Leroy Schaub (New York: Macmillan, 1916) and McDougall, *The Group Mind*.

32. F. I. K. Hsu, *Americans and Chinese: Passage to Differences*, 3rd ed. (Honolulu: University of Hawaii Press, 1983) and Y. Yu, "Intellectual Breakthroughs in the Tang-Sung Transition," in *The Power of Culture*, ed. W. J. Peterson, A. H. Plaks, and Y. Y. Yu (Hong Kong: The Chinese University Press, 1991).

33. C. Li, "The Confucian Concept of *Jen* and the Feminist Ethics of Care: A Comparative Study," in *The Sage and the Second Sex*, ed. Li.

34. P. Singer, "Famine, Affluence and Morality," in *Doing and Being: Selected Readings in Moral Philosophy*, ed. J. G. Haber (Toronto: Macmillan, 1993).

35. W. C. Chang, L. Lee, and S. Koh, "The Concept of Self in a Modern Chinese Context," paper presented at 50th Anniversary of the Korean Psychological Association, Seoul, South Korea, 1996.

PART IV

Rights and Civil Society

Regulating the Family

11

Margaret M. Coady and C. A. J. Coady

In his article "The Clash of Civilizations," later to develop into his famous book of the same name, Samuel Huntington argued that "the people of different civilizations have different views on the relations between God and man, the individual and the group, the citizen and the state, parents and children, husband and wife, as well as different views of the relative importance of rights and responsibilities, liberty and authority, equality and hierarchy."[1]

There are several interesting aspects of Huntington's dramatic claim that are pertinent to our concerns in this essay. The first is the fact that Huntington's restriction of difference on these matters to differences *between* civilizations obscures the fact that there are equally striking differences *within* civilizations about the matters that he seeks to contrast; indeed these differences often mirror the very ones that he puts in opposition between civilizations to such alarming effect. In the case of the contrasts individual/group, citizen/state, parent/child, husband/wife, for instance, what Huntington somewhat breezily refers to as "Western civilization" exhibits a striking array of conflicting positions. On the citizen/state, it includes Plato's elitist states and Mill's liberal individualism; on the family, both with regard to its internal structure and its external relations to the state, the picture is equally conflictual as we can see from the clash between Plato's plan to discard the family in the interests of social unity and Aristotle's defense of the affective ties fostered by the family, not to mention the debates about the family generated by the rise of Marxism. An influential defense of the "integrity" of the family is that of Goldstein, Freud, and Solnit who argue that "the child's need for safety within the confines of the family must be met by law through its recognition of family privacy as the barrier to state intrusion upon parental autonomy in child rearing. These rights—parental autonomy, a child's right to autonomous parents, and privacy—are essential ingredients of 'family integrity.'"[2] By contrast, many recent writers see problems in a family's having a right to privacy,[3] claiming that such privacy cloaks and rationalizes many injustices and harms in families. All these differences, and many more, are to be found, and found as influential, within the one civilization, and we think it certain that similar variety exists in the other civilizations announced by Huntington, for instance, the disputes about the requirements of filial piety as against public benevolence so vigorously pursued by Confucians and the followers of Mo Tzu.[4]

There is a second striking puzzle raised by Huntington's thesis. This concerns the status of families, and particularly the role of children in them, and it will serve to focus many of our concerns in this paper. The second puzzle is posed by the broad acceptance accorded to the *United Nations Convention on the Rights of the Child* which has become the most widely ratified human rights treaty in history.[5] The *Convention on the Rights of the Child* contains many of the elements—rights, authority, relations between parents and children—about which, it is claimed, cultures differ so fundamentally. This is not only puzzling for Huntington's thesis but for much that has been written about different cultural attitudes towards rights. Most notably in the political field, there were the claims of Lee Kuan Yew (Senior Minister, Singapore) and Mahathir Mohamad (Prime Minister, Malaysia) that human rights as understood in the West were a product of Western individualism, and were not compatible with the collectivist spirit of Asian cultures. Despite understandable criticisms of the politically self-serving nature of their claims, Lee Kuan Yew and Mahathir Mohamad were not alone in their views, but were echoing a strong theme which had existed for some time in sociological thought,[6] and which became an influential paradigm in cross-cultural studies of business management, of education, and of families in the 1990s.

Claims that in Chinese societies the family is the fundamental unit of society and that within the family the preservation of the family unit and its authority structures are more important than the good of the individual members[7] further compound this sort of skepticism about rights. Even in countries where rights are frequently, some say too frequently,[8] appealed to, such as the U.S., there are many who argue that the family is not the appropriate arena for the claiming of rights. The argument is that rights discourse belongs in the field of business and contract, whereas love and care belong to family relationships. Families are places where members forget about their own rights in order altruistically to look after the good of the other members. This is the argument which has been used by several writers[9] to argue against nonfamilial childcare. More will be said later about the claimed opposition between rights discourse and care discourse. For the moment we shall merely note how these restrictions on the scope of rights are not only problematic for the applicability of the discourse of rights within the family and between the family and the state, but also for the complex question of the international regulation of children's rights.

Protective Rights for Children

The question could be simplified by seeing children's rights as very different from adult rights, that is, as being solely rights to protection. This is the way they were seen in the earlier attempts by international bodies to provide universal rights for children. In 1924, the League of Nations adopted a *Declaration of the Rights of the Child* which was aimed at providing for all children the basic necessities of life. When the League of Nations was dissolved, the Temporary Social Commission of the United Nations began work on a new *Declaration of the Rights of the Child*. Even more than the earlier document, the new *Declaration*, adopted without abstention by the United Nations in 1959, stressed the need of the child for protection. The child is "immature" and it is this very fact which gives her the right to "special protection." Apart from the right to a name and nationality, to adequate nutrition, to medical attention, housing, and recreation, all included in the earlier declaration, the new declaration included protection against neglect, a ban on employment of the young child in any work which would interfere with the child's health or development, and special treatment and education for the physically, mentally, or socially disabled child. The "best interests of the child" was to be the guiding principle.

As far as rights to protection are concerned, the argument about cultural difference would seem to have minimal hold. Few from any culture would disagree about children needing protection from possible harms. However there are still arguments about what constitutes harm. Is clitoridectomy harmful? When is the use of certain traditional medical practices harmful to children? Is children's involvement in the workforce really harmful, or can they actually benefit from the experience? Many of these debates can be partly resolved empirically, especially in cases where the harm to the child is grievous. However in cases of less grave harm there remain questions both of the interpretation of harm and of the tradeoff between the minor harm and cultural identity. There is also the issue, particularly in cases of the employment of children, of the relation between human rights and economic necessity. The questions of tradeoffs between different values, of the relation between human rights and economic necessity, and of the interpretation of harm require and have received philosophical consideration, and we will not further address them directly here.

Some concessions do need to be made to the protectionists. The concept of childhood that lies behind the protective statements of children's rights stresses the vulnerability of the child and the consequent need for protection. There is of course a truth in this view of childhood, since there are a variety of ways in which children are more vulnerable than most adults, ranging from physical weakness (especially in the early years), to lack of experience and of an associated capacity for foresight and mature judgment. Unlike women as a group, there is no doubt that children, or at least young children, are often in need of protection. Compared with the rest of the animal kingdom, they are among the least able to look out for themselves at birth, and require at a minimum some years of care. No doubt adults and groups of adults require protection as a result of contingencies like war or famine, but children require it more constitutionally. Of course, this "constitutionality" does not imply permanence; unlike other dominated groups, children's need of protection is temporary. Their ultimate remedy, as Onora O'Neill argues, is "to grow up."[10] Nonetheless, prior to this happy release, they remain vulnerable and a sense of their various vulnerabilities lies behind the opposition to two of the most serious forms of exploitation of children, namely sexual and military, and it is no accident that they often go together. The widespread use of child soldiers is one of the great scandals of our world today, and it is often accompanied by other forms of abuse such as prostitution.

This is a matter which needs more attention; suffice to say here that vulnerability and the need for protection are real, but not the whole truth. Indeed a view of children as merely beings needing protection can have pernicious effects, feeding both the adult's desire for power and the child's feeling of passivity and incompetence. Feminist writers and others have pointed out the dangers of protectionism. In personal as well as political relationships protection is often of more benefit to the protector than to the protected. The history of the treatment of women in English law makes this particularly clear. Blackstone defended the extensive limitations on women's rights under English law in the eighteenth century by explaining that "for the most part (they were) intended for her protection. So great a favourite is the female sex of the laws of England."[11] On a slightly different tack, O'Neill's point about "growing up" is misused if it is taken (as she herself takes it) as a reason for delaying recognition that even quite young children have, as we shall later argue, some kind of autonomy rights.

Autonomy: A New Direction

These issues of protection are also the concern of the UN *Convention on the Rights of the Child* which came into force in 1990, but the most notable difference between earlier statements of children's rights and the current *Convention* is the incorporation of freedom or autonomy rights for children. These autonomy rights include freedom of expression, freedom of thought, conscience, and religion, freedom of association and peaceful assembly, and the right to privacy. In each of these cases the right is qualified. As with adults, freedom of expression can be restricted when its exercise can threaten the rights of others. While the child has the right to freedom of thought, conscience and religion, the rights of the parents or legal guardians to give guidance in such matters is recognized. And it is only "arbitrary" interference with the child's privacy which is interdicted.

While protection of the child remains a major focus, as in the earlier declarations, there is more acknowledgment of children as competent decision-makers on matters which concern their future. For example, in addition to clauses declaring the child's right to freedom of expression, freedom of association and freedom of thought, conscience and religion, there is a clause asserting the child's right to be heard in all judicial and administrative proceedings affecting the child (Article 12(2)).

Another novel aspect of the *Convention* is the detailed attention it gives to the family. On the one hand, it recognizes the importance of the family, while on the other it represents a move away from previous international law where the family was treated as inviolate to a situation where there are limits to the kinds of decision which can be made by parents with regard to their children.[12] The *Preamble to the Convention* proclaims the family as "the fundamental group of society and the natural environment for the growth and well being of all its members and particularly children," and declares that the family should be given the "protection and assistance" to carry out its responsibilities. In addition, the *Convention*, in recognizing children's right to freedom of thought, conscience, and religion, calls on the state's parties to respect "the rights and duties of the parents and, when applicable, legal guardians, to provide direction to the child in the exercise of his or her right in a manner consistent with the evolving capacities of the child" (Article 14).

However, while giving greater recognition to families, the provisions of the *Convention* also put restrictions on the way in which families carry out their role. If the child is competent to exercise the right to freedom of thought, conscience, and religion, then the family must allow the child to exercise this. In addition, recognition of the importance of the family does not mean that parents can abuse their children. Article 9, though generally supporting the nonseparation of child from parents, does envisage situations where a child may be separated from the parents but only when "competent authorities subject to judicial review" deem it to be in the child's best interest.

Some writers[13] in attempting to persuade their representatives to ratify the *Convention* have played down the revolutionary nature of the *Convention*. It is true that the *Preamble to the Convention* reaffirms that the family "is the fundamental group of society." However, Van Bueren notes that it has more radical implications in that it recognizes the child as an individual who may have interests different from or even opposed to its family.[14] These novel aspects of the *Convention* have raised vociferous objections to it by authors like Hafen,[15] Maley,[16] and some members of the Joint Standing Committee on Treaties,[17] in both Australia, which ratified the *Convention* in 1989, and the U.S., which is one of only two nations (the other is Somalia) that has not yet ratified it. Hafen, for example, specifically argues that giving autonomy rights to children will set them against their families.[18] Interestingly, the dominant arguments of the opponents to the *Convention* in both these countries, neither of which is strongly influenced by Confucian thought, expressed opposition to the freedom or autonomy rights and warned of the effect these could have on relations in the family.

This essay canvasses the view that there is a sense of autonomy which can be applied to children and which is not incompatible with their membership of a community, or more likely many communities, including their families. This autonomy is something which needs to be recognized both in relations between the family and the state as well as within the family itself. It is a sense of autonomy which is a plausible rendition of the aims of the *Convention*, and which, in addition, seems consistent with certain interpretations of Confucian views on the child in the family.

We mentioned at the outset classical philosophical debates about the relations between the family and the state. One issue that naturally arises from such debates is the need for a delicate balance here between any autonomy for the family and the rights of the individual members of the family. There is no pattern for good parenting. Parenting involves both knowledge and judgment about competing values. Bringing up children is an inescapably moral activity and can be impeded if the parent feels that state bureaucrats or other interfering groups are constantly evaluating current performance or dictating future performance. The most effective interventions from outside the family are usually in the form of provision of facilities and access to education and information, but more radical interventions will be needed when members of the family are being harmed or are likely to be harmed. In this way the state could be seen as some kind of super-parent.[19]

An added complication, however, occurs with the *Convention*. For here, it seems, is intervention by something like a superstate, namely the United Nations. A couple of points need to be made on this matter. The first is that most of the provisions in the *Convention* are directed towards protecting the child's rights against states' actions or omissions rather than towards regulating the activities of individual families. On the other hand the *Convention* does seek to establish some ways in which parents must act. For example, while it recognizes the family as the basic group of society and insists that states must protect and support this unit, it does prescribe broad parameters to the kind of upbringing which is acceptable, namely one which respects the evolving capacities of the child, which develops the "child's personality, talents and mental and physical abilities to their fullest potential" (Article 29), which leads the child to respect human rights and fundamental freedoms and which prepares the child for "responsible life in a free society, in the spirit of understanding, peace, tolerance, equality of sexes, and friendship among all peoples, ethnic, national and religious groups and persons of indigenous origin" (Article 29). Parents, as well as the state, need to respect and protect the rights stated in the *Convention*. How any breaches by parents will be dealt with depends on the way the *Convention* has been incorporated into the domestic law of each member state. In general, however, the *Convention* is directed towards governmental policies, and not at individual families. The United Nations' main method of monitoring compliance is through requiring each signatory to make periodic reports to the Committee on the Rights of the Child set up by the *Convention*.

Against this background we address two related issues: (1) the role of rights in a community, and (2) an account of the kinds of autonomy which children, including young children, may be said to have.

The Role of Rights in a Community

Many of the opponents of autonomy rights for children echo the view that groups, who are bound together by affection, do not need to consider justice and rights. If people really love one another, why do they need to talk about justice, contracts, agreements, and rights? Communitarian critiques of the supposed unencumbered nature of liberalism have provided useful ammunition in this respect to the opponents of the *Convention*. However, the debate about the nature of the relation between rights and community has a much longer history than the recent debate between often caricatured versions of liberalism and communitarianism. Marx sneered at human rights which are the freedoms of a "monad isolated and withdrawn into himself." He goes on to say that "none of these so-called human rights . . . goes beyond the egoistic man, . . . withdrawn into his private interests and his private will, separated from the community."[20] As far as the family is concerned Hegel could be seen to be making a similar point in his attack on Kant's view of marriage as a contract, when he urges an emphasis on love and trust instead of contract.[21]

The general argument is that there is no need of justice within the family because of a unity of interests held by the members of the family. Okin points out that this is the same argument which, claiming that women's interests were identical to their husbands', deprived women of political and property rights for so long. She also points out that in fact few if any families live up to the ideal of affective relationship.[22] Her argument certainly casts doubt upon the idea that if families are in some ideal sense "communities of love" then rights discourse has no place for their members. But the position of women does not provide an exact analogy for that of children, as we have already granted, so there remains the question of how significant the rights discourse can be for children. Okin's appeal to the empirical realities of family life to show the deficiencies of the idealized picture of family relationships can, however, be readily applied to the place of children within families with increasing recognition of the degree of physical, cultural, and sexual abuse in families.

Recognizing these empirical facts may be one reason why many contemporary writers are prepared to see some form of individual rights as appropriate in families. However even those who concede this are cautious. Joseph Chan, for example, states: "I am sympathetic to this view that rights do not play an important role in virtuous relationships. I agree that in a healthy, close relationship parties should best ignore rights and focus on mutual caring and love. But what if the relationship turns sour?"[23] Chan sees rights in affective relationships as a regrettable necessity. Waldron, in an article entitled "When Justice Replaces Affection: The Need for Rights," sees the necessity for a structure of rights in marriage, but only as a fallback apparatus, a structure to be appealed to if the loving relationship fails. In these circumstances justice replaces affection.[24]

However, there are arguments against this narrow view of rights, the view that the nature of rights necessarily distances the rightholder from affective ties. This view tends to be shared both by critics and defenders of rights. Both tend to see rights as claims we are making *against* others. It is partly because of this view of rights that they are seen as divisive, and those who want to be able to exercise their rights but are being denied the chance are seen as strident protesters. But in fact most of us, most of the time, exercise our rights without having to make claims, and certainly without being strident. Our rights to freedom of association, freedom of expression, even freedom of religion are rarely denied especially to the relatively well off in democratic societies. Perhaps the emphasis on "rights *talk*," on the discourse of rights, may have led to a distorted picture of rights as necessarily being claims *against* others and therefore as divisive. We *talk* about rights mainly when we, or others with whom we sympathize, do not have them; most of the time we just exercise them quietly and enjoy them. The stridency, the angry demand for rights, arises when people feel (rightly or wrongly) that they are being denied rights which they should have. But it is also true that those who are deprived of care and affection just as naturally often want these, and, given the chance, may vociferously and even stridently ask for them if they have the strength and courage to do so.

A second related point is that rights can exist even when they are not acted on. I have a right to freedom of association, but I may choose not to exercise it. Nevertheless the knowledge that I could exercise that right may provide me with a sense of security and dignity even when I choose to remain aloof from community. People who do not choose to exercise their civil right to vote, may nonetheless see that right as a mark of dignity and inclusion, so that they would react indignantly to any attempt to remove it.

Far from being destructive of community, rights can help build communities. We often feel a common bond in exercising and enjoying rights. Critics of rights may claim they are destructive of community and solidarity but the joint exercise of rights is often creative and restorative of community. Think of groups that have asserted and exercised their rights against tyrants. This will divide them off from the tyrants, but that may well be no bad thing. Finally, a very frequent assertion of rights is by those who already have the rights but who are claiming them on behalf of others who have been denied them. This is the very opposite of the strident self-assertion so often said to be inherent in rights-talk. Indeed it is a remarkable distortion of the function of rights discourse to see it as wholly restricted to the claiming of rights on behalf of oneself. Organizations such as Amnesty International and Human Rights Watch are defined by a concern for the rights of others, and indeed those who advocate the rights of children and who author such legal instruments as the UN *Convention on the Rights of the Child* are predominantly adults concerned for other people's rights, namely children's.

Children's Autonomy

The assumption is often made that the ideas of atomistic individualism, independence, separateness, self-determination, and autonomy are interchangeable or at least always conceptually connected. But autonomy is clearly not necessarily the same as the individualism described by William Galston when he says: "To individualism corresponds the liberal virtue of independence—the disposition to care for, and take responsibility for, oneself and to avoid becoming needlessly dependent on others."[25] A lot depends, of course, on the interpretation of the word "needlessly" in this assertion. If the emphasis is on economic independence, children certainly are not in a position to be independent in this sense, particularly in countries which do not allow child labour. And none of us can be cognitively independent of each other with respect to theoretical and conceptual resources, nor even informational capital. Clearly, a sensible notion of autonomy, for adults or children, cannot be encumbered with too rigid an understanding of independence or self-determination. But blurring the distinctions between these concepts, and not revealing the contexts in which they are used, leaves the way open for glib *reductio* arguments against the idea of giving children rights. Kay Hymowitz, speaking of the U.S., engages in just such a *reductio* in her attack on the idea that children should have more autonomy: "Kids are rational, autonomous creatures. We should tell them from their earliest days, 'We will give you information; you do with it as you see fit. You are a free and self-determining individual—ready or not.'"[26] She refers also to the "chilly independence" of current childhood, again assuming a necessary relation between autonomy and lack of an affective relationship. Hafen and Hafen too in the very title "Abandoning Children to Their Autonomy" see an opposition between children having autonomy rights and their being cared for.[27]

Apart from these views of autonomy construed in terms of isolated individuals, there are other inadequate models of autonomy which have been influential in child development and educational theory. Lawrence Kohlberg was an important figure in the study of moral development in the last decades of the twentieth century.[28] There are two aspects of Kohlberg's work, one in which he talks about how schools can be made just communities, where he emphasizes the role of the community, the other where he traces moral development through six stages, with the highest stage being similar to Kantian achievement of the capacity for universalizable second-order reflection on one's first-order preferences. Interestingly it is this second aspect of Kohlberg's work which has been more influential whereas his discussion of the just community is rarely referred to. The common picture of Kohlberg's theory of moral development is a very individualist one of the child gradually and quite late in childhood moving from egocentrism towards autonomy as its cognitive skills develop. It is the image of the child as an isolated thinker working its way to moral maturity through its developing cognitive powers.

Until recently most interpreters of Piaget's[29] work in child development also presented the child, for much of its childhood, as dominated by authority, either submitting to it, or rebelling against adult authority and risking punishment. However, this is a very restricted view of childhood, and underestimates even very young children. Empirical evidence presents a more complex picture. Smetana conducted a study of three- and four-year-olds who showed concern about obeying adults who were asking them to harm another person.[30] An even more interesting experiment was conducted by Turiel. This showed that not only did very young children distinguish between transgressions of social conventions and transgressions of moral rules, but that by the age of forty-two months young children indicated their belief that moral transgressions would be wrong even if an adult did not see them, or there was not a rule proclaimed against them. Furthermore this belief did not seem to depend on parental input since the same study showed that parents were just as insistent on social conventions being adhered to as they were insistent that their children should obey moral rules.[31] Neither of these studies presents a picture of the child bound by authority to either accept it or rebel against it; rather the children in these studies seem to be actively constructing a moral viewpoint. The child here is a person with its own moral life.[32] Some recent interpretations of Piaget by writers such as Davidson and Youniss reject the individualist interpretation of Piaget, arguing that Piaget's view was not that the child achieved autonomy through development of its powers of logical thought, but through testing its views and attitudes via reciprocal relationships.[33]

Prior to these reinterpretations the usual image of the relation of the child to its culture was of a child passively receiving the cultural deposit from its parents and later from its teachers. However, a preferable metaphor of the child in relation to the adult bearers of the culture to which it is being introduced is that of a conversation in which the child is a participant.[34] While the terms of the conversation are controlled by others, nevertheless the child has a voice. This metaphor fits with the empirical evidence cited above, which showed very young children constructing a viewpoint separate from their parents; and it captures the idea connected with this, that children are at once both individuals and part of a community. The child establishes its identity through being involved in an active manner in the discourses, social structures, and practices of its world. And this involvement commences at a very early age. Another advantage of the conversation metaphor is that it allows for the evolving nature of cultures rather than suggesting that cultures are static. It conveys a view of autonomy which is not the Kantian exercise of the capacity for universalisable second-order reflection on one's first-order preferences, but is that of an individual human being actively constructing its identity.

Will Kymlicka writes of humans' essential interest in "leading our lives from the inside," and he explains the importance of the traditional liberal virtues of education, freedom of expression, freedom of the press, and artistic freedom in terms of their being important in allowing us to live our lives from the inside, examining our beliefs "in the light of whatever information and examples and arguments our culture can provide," judging what is valuable "in the only way we can judge such things — i.e. by exploring the different aspects of our collective cultural heritage."[35] The same rationale could be given for the recognition in the *Convention* that children have these same rights. Very young children are in fact, as we saw, making judgments about what is valuable. This judgment is not the simple acceptance of authority. To this extent they are already autonomous beings in the sense of already constructing their individuality. Their right to the resources which make this feasible is what is recognized in the autonomy rights in the *Convention*. It could be argued, against Kymlicka's claim, that there are many examples of people denied human rights who nevertheless are able to "live their lives from the inside," who have established a coherent identity, and that therefore there is no need to give children these rights. But we may concede the premise and deny the implication. The fact that human ingenuity and courage can occasionally rise to some limited forms of autonomy in circumstances that are extremely inauspicious for it does nothing to support the conclusion that we have no obligations to provide the normal conditions for autonomy to flourish, especially for the very young. We would not want to treat an imprisoned slave as a paradigm of an autonomous person, even if an exceptional slave were able, in extreme adversity, to create a sort of shadow of autonomy — retreating perhaps to silent self-expression in his soul or living by private rituals beyond the comprehension of his jailers. We do not want to rule out the possibility that a child in a very authoritarian, even oppressive, family may have the resources to develop some kinds of autonomy, but what is at issue are the normal or optimal conditions for cultivation of autonomy. The criticism here is somewhat like the claim that people do not need political conditions that allow or foster freedom of expression because (look!) some great creative writing is done in totalitarian regimes.

If leading their lives from the inside, or exercising autonomy in our sense, is what even very young children are attempting to do, it is not appropriate, as O'Neill and others assert, to tell children that the remedy for their lack of rights is simply to "grow up." Some writers have noted that children need to have practice in making decisions, and therefore they should be treated not as creatures with autonomy, but as with "the capacity for autonomy," and allowed to determine certain restricted areas of their lives.[36] Though age and maturity need to be taken into account, as the *Convention* states, children in making judgments of value are not just "practicing." One problem with suggestions that children should wait for their rights or just practice for their exercise, is raised by the case of a child with a terminal illness. Has this child any autonomy rights? "Waiting for adulthood" is ruled out. Yet the child does make decisions when facing death, and she needs support from a community. But she also needs the powers that come from a nurtured autonomy. While this is a special case, there is no reason to believe that a child facing death has a right to freedom of speech, to be heard, and so on which is totally denied other children of similar age when they face less dramatic life contingencies.

How Compatible Is This View with That of Confucius?

It is a very interesting question how this account of the autonomy of the child within the family meshes with various styles of Asian thought. This is a question that can only be answered seriously by detailed examination of the different styles of thought to be found in this very diverse region, and any such project is beyond both the scope of this paper and our scholarly capacities. One such style that would clearly repay investigation in the light of this question is that of Confucianism, varied as that tradition itself is. Again, we cannot begin such an investigation here, for the reasons given, but although neither of us are experts on Confucius, we shall venture a suggestion about the direction in which such an investigation might proceed in the case of Confucius's own ideas. Here, as nonexperts, we are very dependent on what we judge to be knowledgeable and sensitive secondary sources. One of these which is very pertinent to our concerns here is Joel Kupperman's discussion of "Tradition and Community in the Formation of Self" in his book *Learning from Asian Philosophy*. Kupperman compares Aristotle's and Confucius's views on moral psychology. From this it emerges that Confucius views the moral development of persons as intimately connected with tradition as mediated through their parents. He does not however see this as static transmission, but very much on a model that has distinct similarities to the conversational paradigm we have been advocating. As Kupperman interprets the Confucian outlook on teaching (which is itself closely related to moral development) the learner plays a significantly responsive role: "It (teaching) must present only, as it were, a corner of the subject, leaving the student to complete the rest (cf. V.8, 109; VII.8, 124)."[37] He adds: "If the goal is to develop really good people, his teaching strategy makes a great deal of sense, in that it engages the student and forces the student to be active rather than passive. We have already seen that passive absorption of an ethics does not guarantee reliable goodness, and it is plausible that only someone who comes of himself or herself to certain conclusions is likely to internalize them properly." [38]

Kupperman's account touches on several controversial issues of exegesis and interpretation of Confucius's thought. It is often noted that there are very powerful elements of submission and obedience to parental authority in the Confucian emphasis on filial piety. In this connection, the famous passage in the Analects (IV.18) is often cited. Here, Confucius seems to say that if gentle persuasion cannot move your parents from wrong-doing you must refrain from persisting and adopt a stance of reverent obedience. Joseph Chan has argued that the passage need not be interpreted in this way, and that, in any event, the primary Confucian emphasis on *ren* is sufficient to show that filial piety must be subordinated to *ren* so that if such passages are treated as recommending total obedience then Confucius is at odds with his own best instincts.[39] It would be presumptuous for us to engage further with these contentious matters, but it seems that there is at least room for the thesis that our account of the child's autonomy (and its relevance to the UN *Convention*) is compatible with some plausible understandings of Confucius. This accommodation may not please our old friend Sam Huntington, but this need not be regarded as detracting from its merits.

Notes

1. Samuel Huntington, "The Clash of Civilizations?," *Foreign Affairs* 72 (Summer 1993): 25.

2. Joseph Goldstein, Anna Freud, and Albert J. Solnit, *Before the Best Interests of the Child* (New York: The Free Press, 1979), 9.

3. David Archard, *Children: Rights and Childhood* (London: Routledge, 1993) and Frances Olsen, "Children's Rights: Some Feminist Approaches to the United Nations Convention on the Rights of the Child," in *Children, Rights and the Law, ed.* Philip Alston, Stephen Parker, and John Seymour (Oxford: Clarendon Press, 1992).

4. See Burton Watson, *Mo Tzu: Basic Writings* (New York: Columbia University Press, 1963).

5. Susan Kilbourne, "The Wayward Americans—Why the USA Has Not Ratified the UN Convention on the Rights of the Child," *Child and Family Law Quarterly* 10, no. 3 (1998): 243.

6 T. Parsons and E. Shils, *Toward a General Theory of Action* (Cambridge, Mass.: Harvard University Press, 1951) and G. Hofstede, *Culture's Consequences: International Differences in Work-Related Values* (Beverly Hills, Calif.: Sage Press, 1980).

7. H. Chan and R. P. L. Lee, "Hong Kong Families: At the Cross-Roads of Modernism and Traditionalism," *Journal of Comparative Family Studies* 26 (1995): 83–99.

8. Mary Ann Glendon, *Rights Talk* (New York: The Free Press, 1991).

9. *Ibid.*, p. 129; Kay S. Hymowitz, *Ready or Not* (New York: The Free Press, 1999), 70; Jean Bethke Elshtain, *Public Man, Private Woman: Women in Social and Political Thought* (Princeton, N.J.: Princeton University Press, 1981).

10. Onora O'Neill, "Children's Rights and Children's Lives," in *Children, Rights and the Law*, ed. P. Alston, S. Parker, and J. Seymour (Oxford: Clarendon Press, 1992).

11. William Blackstone, *Commentaries on the Laws of England*, I (1765), 445.

12. Geraldine Van Bueren, *The International Law on the Rights of the Child* (Dordrecht: Martinus Nijhoff, 1995), 137–38.

13. Kilbourne, "The Wayward Americans."

14. Van Bueren, *International Law*, p. 46.

15. Bruce Hafen, *Transcript of Evidence to Joint Standing Committees on Treaties Inquiry*

into the Status of the United Nations Convention on the Rights of the Child, 9 May 1997, Commonwealth of Australia, 1997.

16. Barry Maley, *Children's Right*, Policy Monograph 43 (Sydney: Centre for Independent Studies, 1999).

17. Joint Standing Committees on Treaties, *Inquiry into the Status of the United Nations Convention on the Rights of the Child* (17th Report Commonwealth of Australia, 1998).

18. Hafen, *Transcript*.

19. Kenneth Kipnis, "Introduction," in *Kindred Matters*, ed. Diana Tietjens Meyers, Kenneth Kipnis, and Cornelius F. Murphy Jr. (Ithaca: Cornell University Press, 1993), 5.

20. Karl Marx, in *Marx: Early Political Writings*, ed. and trans. Joseph O'Malley with Richard A. Davis (Cambridge: Cambridge University Press, 1994.), 44–46.

21. G. W. F. Hegel, *Philosophy of Right*, trans. T. M. Knox (New York: Oxford University Press, 1967), 58.

22. Susan Moller Okin, *Justice, Gender and the Family* (New York: Basic Books, 1989).

23. Joseph A. Chan, "A Confucian Perspective on Human Rights for Contemporary China," in *The East Asian Challenge for Human Rights*, ed. Joanne R. Bauer and Daniel A. Bell (Cambridge: Cambridge University Press, 1999).

24. Jeremy Waldron, "When Justice Replaces Affection: The Need for Rights," in *Liberal Rights: Collected Papers 1981–1991* (Cambridge: Cambridge University Press, 1993).

25. William Galston, *Liberal Purposes: Goods, Virtues and Duties in the Liberal State* (Cambridge: Cambridge University Press, 1991).

26. Hymowitz, *Ready or Not*, p. 218.

27. Bruce C. Hafen and Jonathan O. Hafen, "Abandoning Children to Their Autonomy: The United Nations Convention on the Rights of the Child," in *Harvard International Law Journal* 37, no. 2 (1996).

28. L. Kohlberg, *Essays on Moral Development* (San Francisco: Harper and Row, 1981).

29. J. Piaget, *The Language and Thought of the Child*, trans. M. Worden (New York: Harcourt, Brace and World, 1926).

30. J. G. Smetana, "Preschool Children's Conceptions of Moral and Social Rules," *Child Development* 52 (1981): 1333–36.

31. Elliott Turiel, *The Development of Social Knowledge: Morality and Convention* (New York: Cambridge University Press, 1983).

32. Hymowitz sneers at much of the work done recently on the inner life of very young children. She interprets it as part of a misguided attempt to show that very young children are "geniuses," and therefore not in need of cultural input. The point we are making is not about exceptional cognitive skills of young children, but simply about their normal active search for identity.

33. P. Davidson and J. Youniss, "Which Comes First, Morality or Identity?" in *Handbook of Moral Behavior and Development Theory*, vol. I, ed. W. Kurtines and J. Gewirtz (Hillsdale, N.J.: Lawrence Erlbaum Associates, 1991).

34. A similar metaphor is used by Michael Oakeshott to describe the process of education, though the present writers do not necessarily endorse the implications of Oakeshott's use.

35. Will Kymlicka, *Liberalism, Community and Culture* (New York: Oxford University Press, 1989), 13.

36. For example, Jeffrey Blustein, *Parents and Children: The Ethics of the Family* (New York: Oxford University Press, 1982), 133.

37. Kupperman is referring here to the numbered passages in the *Analects*.

38. Joel J. Kupperman, *Learning from Asian Philosophy* (New York: Oxford University Press, 1999), 42.

39. Chan, "A Confucian Perspective," pp. 222–25.

Can There Be a Confucian Civil Society?

12

Sor-hoon Tan

Civil society has become one of those "motherhood-and-apple pie" causes that politicians everywhere love to espouse.[1] In Singapore, the government's recent call on Singaporeans to develop civil society has provoked some lively discussions in the media and other public forums. Interest in civil societies has been gathering strength in various parts of Asia for the last two decades.

In this essay I shall examine whether and how the concept of civil society can be applied in Confucian contexts. I shall argue that the ideal Confucian socio-political order could accommodate a Confucian civil society. In the process, not only do we engage in a reinterpretation of Confucianism, we shall also reconstruct the concept of civil society. I shall conclude by suggesting one area in which Confucianism could contribute something significant to cross-cultural civil society discourses.

The Quest for Chinese Civil Society

As early as the 1980s, Chinese scholars as well as Western Sinologists began using the civil society concept. Roger des Forges traces the antecedents of three models of civil society to the Zhou dynasty, the Spring and Autumn Warring States period, and the Han dynasty. William Rowe, Mary Rankin, David Strand, and others identify social and group autonomy in various forms of associational life—guilds, surname and neighborhood associations, religious groupings, deity cults, secret societies, professional associations, chambers of commerce, cultural groups, social and political movements and so on—existing from late imperial China to today.[2]

However, these studies often end with reservations about comparing Chinese associational life and local group politics with Western civil societies. At most they talk about "proto," "embryonic," or "nascent" civil societies. Heath Chamberlain argues that, even then, these efforts conflated "civil society" with "society"—social activism, in the form of asserting local elite control that reinforced parochial outlooks and traditional social relations, "may have hindered more than enhanced any real movement toward civil society." Frederic Wakeman and Philip Huang find attempts to discern even incipient public spheres and civil societies in China "poignant" but quite futile. Research like David Wank's analysis of the relation between private businesses and political change in the last two decades, casts serious doubts on the applicability of the popular East European view of civil society to China.[3]

Is Chinese Civil Society Confucian?

Even if there can be a civil society in China, would it be Confucian? Liu Zhi-guang and Wang Suli are not alone in seeing the creation of a civil society as antithetical to China's tradition, especially Confucian thought. Even the feature common to many Western definitions of civil society, its location between family and state, may be problematic given the Confucian tendency to view all relations in familial terms. Wang and Liu argue that the Confucian tradition does not acknowledge the abstract concept of society separate from individual existence. Its influence leaves China with a 'mass society' that does not recognize the idea of 'a free person' (*ziyoumin* 自由民) whose civil entitlements are protected by legal checks upon the exercise of power.[4] Does China have to choose between civil society and its Confucian heritage? Or is it possible to build civil society in a Confucian polity, a civil society desirable on Confucian terms?

Chinese scholar, Deng Zhenglai, who does not reject the use of the concept itself in studying China, criticizes the tendency among writers to assume the universal validity of Western models of civil society and neglect the cultural specifics of each country.[5] Why should an elusive idea of European origin become a universal model? To Tu Wei-ming, recent events may have opened up an ever-extending space for "civil society, . . . but the concept of civil society which presupposes not only a substantial middle class but also a full-fledged public sphere directly challenging the authority of the political center is not applicable to the Chinese situation today." Is civil society no more than "a nostalgic myth that Westerners live by and still seek to impose on others"?[6] The applicability of the concept of civil society has been questioned in the contexts of East Asia and post-communist eastern and central Europe. Some writers foresee the "withering of civil society," while others doubt its very existence in the West. The usefulness of the concept in both theory and practice has been questioned. Many sociologists and political scientists prefer to treat civil society as an "ideal type" which is at best partially realized, in different ways in different societies.[7]

We should be cautious about using the concept of civil society in the Confucian context, but we need not reject it completely. Borrowing and modifying the Western concept for a different cultural context, if done appropriately, could prove productive not only for those interested in whether and how to build a Confucian democracy, but also for those who seek in civil society a solution for the erosion of public life in Western liberal democracies. I suggest an approach that eschews a universalism that underestimates the importance of cultural differences while avoiding a relativism that renders it pointless, if not impossible, for members of different cultures to engage one another in intellectual discourses and to learn from one another. The search for an account of Confucian civil society should take place in cross-cultural conversations in which Western conceptions of civil society facilitate interpretations and modifications of Confucianism to meet modern demands, in which the encounter with the Confucian world contributes to reassessments of Western responses to the challenges of modernity.

Why Confucian Civil Society?

Historically, the meaning of civil society has gone through enormous variation. Today, civil society remains an essentially contested concept in Western discourse. Western scholars themselves have been engaged in continuous reconstructions of this concept throughout its history. Participation of other cultures in this exercise is increasingly important in the current climate when we are beginning to talk of "global civil society"; otherwise, globalization becomes nothing more than a mask for imperialism.[8]

Vagueness and confusion litter discussions of civil society. In Singapore, for example, people talked about threats to civil society posed by rude drivers and by people who queued overnight and brawled over soft toys sold at fastfood outlets. A sociologist pointed out that if the Singapore government is serious about strengthening civil society, it must get rid of laws that are hostile to associational activities.[9] Are people talking about the same civil society? Is the economy, including huge corporations with the government as a major shareholder, part of civil society? What about political parties? Or voluntary organizations receiving government subsidies? There is no unanimous view among promoters of civil society, nor among its critics, be they scholars or journalists, politicians or citizens. The concept is polysemic and serves different purposes on different occasions.

In attempting to elucidate the concept of a Confucian civil society, I shall start by tentatively locating civil society between family and state, and focus on the link between civil society and democracy. We have to recognize from the start that boundaries between family and nonfamily associations, between social organizations and state organizations, are much more fluid in the Confucian context, compared with certain Western sociological views. The interactive dynamics within relational networks play more important roles in social change than confrontations of clearly delineated groups. Instead of "defining" civil society by drawing clear boundaries, we need to pay more attention to how civil society relations function.

Urging Confucian societies to establish Western-style institutions is not the best democratization strategy, especially when Western scholars are considering seriously the possibility that their societies "may well be in a political context now in which *institutional redesign* of various aspects of the political (and economic) system is necessary to strengthen new sorts of civil sociality." Several writers emphasize the importance of social movements and relational networks (*guanxi* 關係), which are quite different from Western institutions, for building civil society in China. A more flexible strategy is needed to nurture democracy before democratic practices could be institutionalized in forms most suitable to Confucian cultures.[10]

Its promoters often suggest that civil society is a condition of a healthy and enduring democracy. It is the means by which "government by the people" becomes possible as it provides those outside political office access to power and decision-making at the top. When the concept of civil society was revived in the eighties, the successful development of a civil society was considered the key in challenging authoritarian states and establishing democratic regimes. Events in Central and Eastern Europe have been cited as attesting to the necessity of civil society to liberal democracy. Keith Tester notes, "for many, the relationship of civil society with democratic forces, aspirations and institutions is completely and utterly self-evident."[11]

In a recent work offering a Confucian communitarian perspective on human rights, Wm. Theodore de Bary argues that past efforts by Confucians "to strengthen community life and build consensual fiduciary institutions," had they succeeded, might have contributed to a Confucian version of a civil society, understood as an infrastructure of countervailing institutions independent of the state, and providing greater access to power and decision-making at the top. In de Bary's view, the question of civil society is not a side issue but a crucial one in arguing the compatibility of contemporary Confucianism and liberal democracy. Without a civil society, any acquiescence to human rights and claim to democracy would count for little in practical terms.[12]

More than the formal institutions, successful democratization requires a regeneration of communities that would rebuild social identities and a sense of social responsibility. Those who focused only on the institutional forms are more likely to agree with Bronislaw Geremek, who argues that civil society has been inadequate for building a democratic order after the collapse of authoritarian power in Eastern Europe. Jean François Bayart also argues that the link between democracy and civil society is problematic in the African context. Gordon White goes so far as to suggest that "civil society in its current form [diverse, fragmented and potentially anarchic] may be an obstacle rather than an impetus to democratization" in China. Most Chinese writers see civil society as a necessary but not sufficient condition for democracy. Wang Shaoguang points out that emergent civil societies, especially Chinese civil society, are ridden with conflicts and inequalities that can lead to various outcomes, of which democracy is only one. He Baogang has analyzed the "dual roles" of semi-civil society in China, which can act both positively or negatively in a democratization process.[13]

A civil society that would contribute to democratization will not include just any kind of intermediate associations. What are the features that make intermediate associations instruments of democratization? Is it the separation of individual from society, and the exaltation of individual freedom? Is it the distinction between private and public, the insistence on protecting the private realm from state interference, or the emphasis on debating issues of common concern and cooperative decision-making in the public sphere as a realm independent from the state? Is it the capacity to resist and challenge the power of the state? To reconstruct a concept of Confucian civil society, I shall focus on the relation between state and civil society by examining the relation between individual and society, and the relation between private and public.

The Individual and Society

Some writers identify two main trends in civil society theories. In the classical liberal tradition, civil society is seen as the benign self-regulating sphere of individual rights and liberties whose integrity needs to be jealously guarded against the incursions of a domineering state. An opposing trend, usually associated with various socialist traditions, traces its inspiration to Hegel and Marx and sees civil society as an antisocial "war of all against all," economically necessary, but internally contradictory. According to Adam Seligman, both traditions presuppose the Western concept of the "autonomous agentic individual." Neera Chandhoke observes, "Civil society is essentially a concept which belongs to the tradition of political modernity founded on individualism and defense of human rights."[14]

Many scholars have pointed out how problematic the Western conception of the autonomous individual is for Confucianism. Even the most prominent exponent of "the liberal tradition in China" recognizes that Confucianism precludes any radical isolation of the individual; de Bary prefers to talk of Confucian personalism, which "expresses the worth and dignity of the person, not as a raw, 'rugged' individual, but as a self shaped and formed in the context of a given cultural tradition, its own community and its natural environment to reach full personhood."[15] A person is individual in being distinguishable physically and, stemming from this, in various other ways from other people. Her existence is, however, inextricably bound up with the existence of others. Any "thick" description of who she is brings into play her relations with others. A person's worth is more than the worth of her participation in any one relationship. Her worth can even be more than the combined worth of all her relationships—such "additional" worth is however not *separate*, but emerges from the positive interaction of her various relationships.

Confucian communitarianism should not prevent us from recognizing the kind of oppressions Western liberal individualism has been fighting, which show us the pitfalls of inappropriately exalting communities or authorities. We should resist the attempts to foist on Confucianism a stifling holism in which "the destiny of individuals is a function of their relation to the whole and its purposes."[16] Confucian "organic relations" among individuals forming communities do not subordinate individuals to some mystical "whole" and its purpose. The problem in authoritarian or totalitarian polities is not one of "the whole" oppressing individual members, but one of some groups or individuals oppressing other individuals and groups in the name of the whole.

The resistance of Confucianism to certain Western forms of individualism need not prevent Confucian societies from developing civil societies. Today, the increasing popularity of the concept among Western communitarians shows that though individualism favors free association, which is the basis of civil society, if it undermines association, individualism becomes detrimental to civil societies, including Western ones. Only free persons can associate freely, but they may be disinclined to associate, or do so very badly, if they are too individualistic. Communitarians contend that community has been as important as individuality in Western civil society traditions. The individual-society relation should be mutually enhancing rather than parasitic or antagonistic in a civil society, whether Confucian or western.[17]

Private and Public

The value of the individual and the right to privacy are closely linked in Western thinking. Salvador Giner describes civil society as "the abode of privacy in a world which has been divided into two realms: the public and the private." Hegel identifies civil society as the sphere "where everyone's individual private interest meets everyone else's." The bourgeois public sphere identified by Jürgen Habermas evolved "in such a way that it remained itself part of the private realm." In one version of liberal theory, civil society, as the realm of the rights-bearing individual, of the particular, is considered private and contrasted with the state, considered public. In some theories, this private realm is closely associated with the free market. To Benjamin Barber, "the most commonplace understanding of civil society conceives of it as a synonym for the private market sector."[18] Emergence of civil societies has been linked to economic liberalization of markets in postcommunist Europe as well as in China.

Jiang Qing, arguing that building a civil society in China cannot be a matter of indiscriminate imitation of the West, focuses on the "private" market economy aspects of Western civil societies when he suggests that Confucianism has rich resources to offer in alleviating some of their problems. The Marxist critique of liberal civil society, which also reduces civil society to its bourgeois economic features of capitalist exploitation, is relevant in China's context as the most common mandarin translation of "civil society" is *shimin shehui* (市民社會), which was first used to translate *bürgerliche Gesellschaft* in Marx's *Eigh-*

teenth Brumaire.[19] Such reductivist approaches overlook contemporary Western criticisms of capitalism for undermining civil societies. Many who invoke civil society define it to exclude the economy, associate it with the public instead of the private, and contrast rather than identify the public with state control. It is not exclusive association with either public or private that distinguishes civil society; it is the manner in which the two are related.

In discussions of Chinese civil society, "public sphere" and "civil society" have often been linked without sufficient attention to their differences and the relationship between them. To de Bary, what brings Song and Ming dynasties' private academies (*shuyuan* 書院) close to civil society is their role as public forums. But some have questioned if the "public sphere" is even speakable in mandarin. Wang Hui, Leo Ou-fan Lee, and Michael Fischer have explored how a different moral conception of human organization shapes slippages in mandarin translations of terms like "public," "public sphere" and "civil society." The early sense of *gong* (usually used to translate "public") had a sense of "the sum total of the harmonized self-interests of all members of a community," and could refer to the imperial bureaucratic state, what is common or shared, or the altruistic. Though both William Rowe and Mary Rankin notice some overlap between the Chinese notion of *gong* and the Western concept of "public," Rankin also acknowledges differences in "specific manifestations" of the broad category of public spheres.[20]

Overlooking the subtle differences in conceptions of "private" and "public," "*gong*" 公 and "*si*" 私, can give rise to misleading comparisons of different societies. The different senses of public and private, even within Western contexts, are to a significant extent culturally dependent. Less pejorative uses of *si* (usually used to translate "private") refer to areas that are of concern only to a limited group relative to a larger one—in this sense the private realm is associated more frequently with the family than the individual. While the private also used to be associated with the family rather than the individual in Western societies, the private in modern Western societies has come to be identified with the individual. In Confucian societies like China, the lines between private and public are often drawn differently and are more fluid, or by some Western standards, they may not be drawn at all.[21]

In liberal democratic politics, conceptions of the good are ultimately matters of private choice. Writers overeager to discover a democratic strand in the Confucian tradition have sometimes misunderstood Huang Zongxi's (黃宗羲 1610–1695) remark that the greatest evil in the world is the ruler (the kind that existed after the legendary Three Dynasties of Xia, Shang and Zhou), since without him, the people would each have achieved his or her private gains, as advocating the satisfaction of individual private wants as the end of politics or even government.[22] This is not so, as Huang's ideal government is modeled on the legendary ruler who was accorded an exalted position because he came forward to take care of what affects the public (*gongli gonghai* 公利公害) when everyone else is only concerned with what affects himself or herself.[23] In the Confucian tradition, *si* 私, translated as "private," is often synonymous with selfishness, whereas Western modernity endows the private with moral value and capitalism further exalts the satisfaction of given private desires. It is not surprising most Confucians view the Western emphasis on individuals' rights, and some forms of interest group politics that it is associated with, as a kind of selfishness.

What is in one's interest is not simply what one wants, but the two concepts are closely related. Brian Barry gives an approximate characterization of "what is in one's interest" as "what increases one's opportunities to get what one wants," among a list of the differences between the two concepts. In a civil society dominated by competitive, self-centered groups, it is often difficult to engage in reasonable deliberation about the public interest, "those interests which people have in common as members of the public."[24] Instead, the results of political bargaining we see, in the United States, for example, often benefit no more than certain powerful groups in the country. Ideally, its liberal democratic government maintains a level playing field, accommodating as many groups as possible, regardless of their purposes (unless harm to others can be clearly proved). If the results are not optimal, it at least minimizes the risk of tyranny social and governmental.

In a Confucian polity, what is needed politically is not simply an umpire to ensure fair competition among competing selfish individuals or groups. For Confucians, creating a good society, and not just providing the procedural conditions for its creation by individuals, is a chief part of the function of good government. This need not lead us into authoritarianism if we insist that the validity of any common good that guides public policy depends on the people participating actively in its definition. The role of government in creating a good society should be to lead, not to indoctrinate or coerce. However, distinguishing between indoctrination and acceptable forms of influencing people, education being the chief example, is fraught with difficulties, which I cannot take up in this essay.

In contrast to a Western tendency to dichotomize social life into public and private, *gong* and *si* in Confucian thinking are not simple dichotomies, but form a complementary polarity.[25] What is private in one context may be public in another. Moreover, we should not overgeneralize the Western tendency to dichotomize private and public. Some Western thinkers have criticized the classical formulation of the problem. Claus Offe and Richard Sennett, following Habermas, contend that under the pressures of economic and other crises, contemporary capitalist societies have already been forced to give up this once crucial distinction.[26] Even if such oppositions are still constitutive of existence of civil society in the modern Western world, they have gone through many variations. This is not a problem that could find any final solution, but requires continuous efforts at grappling with ever-changing situations.

The tendency to talk in terms of dualistic oppositions may mislead people into thinking that the Western idea of civil society necessarily implies a dualistic worldview, and thereby concluding that it would not fit into a Confucian framework. Actually, a dualistic approach would be self-defeating for civil society. Reification of distinctions which arose from contingent and concrete problems into opposing ontological categories and metaphysical principles makes it impossible to solve the problems through a reconstitution of the situation, and a reconstruction of the relations among the various components to achieve a new synthesis. Viewed dualistically as ontological and metaphysical, separations cannot be bridged, oppositions cannot be resolved. The very attempt to resolve oppositions or tensions assumes either an underlying commonality or the possibility of constructing such a commonality.

One could, however, go too far in the direction of holism. If the assumption of commonality is uncritical and obscures those contingent tensions and oppositions that people do live with everyday, then not only can one not solve the problem, one cannot even see the problem. Whatever the impression the more general cosmological pronouncements of Confucians through the ages might have given us, their writings on social and political issues show a keen awareness of those tensions that lie at the center of the problem of civil society. This awareness is accompanied by a conviction that they can be resolved as harmony is possible and should be the ultimate end of social and political endeavors. Harmony is not homogeneity, it not only encompasses differences, but could also include a dynamic tension.

Civil Society and State

At one time, perhaps as late as the middle of the eighteenth century, civil society was synonymous with political society. But this term for a peaceful political order governed by law came to be used to refer to a realm of life institutionally separated from territorial state institutions. Its dominant meaning in Western discourse and the political events of the 1980s accompanying its conceptual revival emphasize the independence of civil society and its opposition to the state.[27]

In eastern and central Europe, the revival of civil societies was in resistance to totalitarian states. In the United States, the revival of the idea is associated with the crisis of the welfare state and a resulting call "to empower people" through mediating structures, "those institutions that stand between the private world of individuals and the large impersonal structures of modern society." In identifying this "mediating structures project" as a project in strengthening civil society, Michael Novak defines civil society "over against the state."[28] The state is seen as at best a necessary evil; interference by the state in the lives of individuals and the activities of voluntary social groups should always be limited to preventing harm to others.

The state versus society/civil society opposition is salient in critiques of Confucian political culture like Lucian Pye's. Even Gordon White, who at least acknowledges that the Westerner's "usual expectations about the political consequences of an intermediate associational sphere may be wrong or only partly right when applied to China," sees the "dynamic of civil society" in China in terms of "an increasingly generalized contestation between state and society."[29] Such views cast doubt on the usefulness of the civil society concept for Confucian societies, since a radical state–civil society antagonism is incompatible with Confucianism.

State-Society Interpenetration and Countervailing Functions

The economic, financial, social and regulatory relations between so-called "private" organizations and the state authorities are often too close and ramified to justify a comparison with the western ideal of "independent" organizations. John Flower and Pamela Leonard argue that state and society in China form a "seamless fabric of moral interaction." Investigating an NGO development project in rural Sichuan, they find

> a "messy" layer of interaction, where cooptation is a mutual process of negotiation, where market reforms and commoditisation are seen as spurring an "uncivil" unraveling of the social fabric: where gift exchanges and their burden of obligation and expectation extend vertically to involve the "state" as well as horizontally to embrace "society"; and where native categories draw state and society together in the pursuit of encompassing moral equilibrium.[30]

What Flower and Leonard call the "flexible interpenetration" of state and society has deep Confucian roots. In a study of private academies in the seventeenth and eighteenth centuries, Thomas Lee argues that within the Confucian ideal, there is no room for a civil society antagonistic to the state; the traditional assertion of moral independence by Confucian scholars did not extend to a bid for institutional independence; and Confucians in China achieved something resembling a civil society before the eighteenth century only when their "philosophy of unity" broke down.[31]

Contrary to Lee's view, the belief in socio-political harmony notwithstanding, it is possible for the Confucian ideal to accommodate civil society without "the philosophy of unity" breaking down. The vagueness of the very idea of harmony in the tradition allows great flexibility in interpretation. As Confucius recommended that one should "harmonize without being the same (he er bu tong 和而不同)," disagreement and competition do not detract from harmony. The tradition of remonstration (jian 諫) and opposition (zheng 爭) could be understood as countervailing functions. Even removal of those currently in power, if they do not discharge their responsibilities properly, could find sanction in the tradition. While never glorifying radical opposition and destructive conflict, Confucianism can accommodate countervailing forces in its ideal.

Confucian emphasis on a responsibility to speak up against bad government contributes to the argument for a Confucian civil society. But criticisms of bad government should not be left to individual efforts; and efforts should not focus only on awakening the rulers' conscience. Starting from the Western emphasis on a constitutional political order and the rule of law as the framework for civil society, de Bary focuses on the fact that Confucianism has always had a place for both laws and rites, and argues that, with the repeated failures of relying too much on moral persuasion, later Confucians, especially Huang Zongxi, began to focus more attention on laws and countervailing institutions, like private academies and community compacts (*xiangyue* 鄉約), for a more balanced approach to the relationship between state power and autonomy of local communities, if not of individual persons.[32]

According to de Bary, Huang's "Confucian constitutionalism" is a significant step towards a civil society in explicitly recommending *institutionalized* (as opposed to merely moral) limits to the rulers' power. Whatever earlier Confucians might have felt about institutional independence from the court, it could be argued that Huang believed that institutional independence, embodied in the appointment of qualified Confucians as directors of educational institutions through "public discussion in the districts and prefectures" and not by the court, was crucial to the ability of these institutions to fulfill the Confucian purpose of contributing to the welfare of the people.

While advocating independence, Huang sees his Confucian school as a complement, and sometimes an alternative, to the court; it is not necessarily in opposition to the court. Huang is not drawing a hitherto nonexisting battle line between state and society. His is more an argument for redistribution of power among the already existing Confucian institutions (the throne, the court, various imperial authorities, and schools), which improves state-society interpenetration by increasing Confucians' participation in government. Heath Chamberlain notes that in China, "The intellectual's vision of civil society, in other words, is not so much '*counter*structure' as it is '*alternate* structure'—a way of organizing and staffing the state apparatus differently, rather than challenging it altogether."[33] For Confucians, opposition becomes necessary and justified only when those in power do not live up to the Confucian ideal. Or, as Mencius puts it, "When the ruler treats ministers as mud and weeds, they will treat him as an enemy."[34] Destructive conflict is symptomatic of dysfunctional polities. The ideal, in the midst of such conflicts, is not to escalate or perpetuate the division between state and civil society but to achieve harmony.

The Educative Role of Civil Society
and Faith in People

Western thinkers, notably John Dewey, have propagated the idea that educational institutions are the nurseries of democracy. This not only has resonance with Huang's view of the role of schools in government, but the two traditions seem to have merged in the rural reconstruction movement in twentieth-century China, which attempted to modernize China through educational reforms in the villages. The reformers "saw the village schools as embryonic forms of democratic institutions which resembled and could stand in for organizations characteristic of Western civil society." Some of the reformers were inspired by Western ideas, especially John Dewey's philosophy, while Liang Shuming, who spearheaded the movement, was a Confucian.[35] This emphasis on the role of educational institutions in democracy does not posit nor focus on a necessary opposition of civil society to the state. Instead, it is more concerned with how people must be prepared, whether by the people themselves or by the government, for effective political participation.

One reason for not giving too much weight to the "institutional independence" of Huang's ideal private academies when it comes to advancing the cause of civil society and democracy is its persisting elitism. The election of directors of schools by "public discussion" is meant to involve not everybody affected, but only those with a Confucian education. This could be extended into an argument for democratic participation when put together with the Confucian commitment to universal education. But this conditionality of participation is not compatible with Western democratic theory. In a Western democracy, all—even the illiterate or people having little to no understanding of the issues at stake—are entitled to participate; they are not kept away from the polls during election time.[36] Huang's ideal academies are in a better position than the court to understand the people and their needs; they do not *represent* the people in a democratic sense. The educated Confucians continue to see themselves as being a "ruling elite" in relation to the people. If there is representation of the people, it is the "trustee" model and not the "agent" model of representation. Huang is still advocating government for the people without government by the people.[37]

In the Confucian tradition, scholar-officials, literati, and those who had benefited from a Confucian education but held no official posts, have played a critical role in legitimating the state. This legitimating role could become a countervailing force. As Qian Mu saw it, it was "the literati, not as a class of gentry landlords but as the interpreters and transmitters of culture, who had prevented China's autocracy from achieving total authority over the Chinese people." But Confucian scholars and institutions like private academies do not attempt to curb despotic power as members of Western-type civil society. Even today, the modern inheritors of that role, the Chinese intellectuals, seldom cooperate with the people in organizations that directly challenge the state. As David Kelly and He Baogang argue, they collaborate with communist party reformists to liberalize state and society prior to any maturity of civil society. "Chinese intellectuals bear only a pale resemblance to their Polish, Czech, and Hungarian peers who were so successful in promoting what they saw as civil society against the state."[38]

Though some observers take the enthusiastic support of workers and entrepreneurs for the 1989 Democracy movement as an indication of a more vigorous civil society, others note, "the movement as a whole was bedeviled by the intellectual's reluctance to foster closer relations with other social groups." Stig Thogersen observes that even in the rural reconstruction movement, wherein the villagers were the focus, the reformers seemed to have lacked respect for the villagers and often behaved towards them as paternalistically as imperial bureaucrats. While Deng Zhenglai argues that some civil society theorists in China today use the concept to question and criticize both neo-authoritarian and pro-democracy theorists' over-emphasis on the role of the state and the intellectual elite in China's development, more would agree with Thomas Metzger that, even when Chinese intellectuals use the concept of civil society, what they have in mind is very different from the Western model. In Metger's view, the Western model is committed to a bottom-up politics in which highly fallible common people govern, while the Chinese remain committed to a top-down Confucian model of politics in which the most accomplished (ethically and in other ways) should rule.[39]

If the idea of civil society lacks legitimacy in China's cultural tradition, it is mostly because Chinese intellectuals lack faith in ordinary people. By focusing on the tireless devotion of Confucius to education of all, without class distinction, and the Confucian optimism regarding the perfectibility of human beings, we could interpret Confucianism to accommodate more faith in people.[40] Philosophically, Confucianism is committed to neither a completely top-down nor a completely bottom-up politics; its ideal is much more flexible, allowing for a pragmatic mixture of both. Still, it is undeniable that historically China has been plagued by top-down politics. There remains among the educated elite an impatience with the less educated, whose cultural level is perceived as an impediment to progress. But it is precisely these people who make up civil society. From the perspective of its link to democracy, civil society is the avenue through which relatively powerless, even ignorant or ineffectual individuals may become more powerful, more knowledgeable and more effectual through cooperative inquiry and action.

This understanding of civil society precludes an elitist order, though it could accommodate a Confucian deference to authority that distinguishes ethical excellence from political power. The educated may be more suited to leadership, but they alone do not make up civil society *in toto*. One should resist being naïve about the goodness of the masses—studies about popular attitudes and behavior in China, for example, show that much about the Chinese people has to change if civil society is to flourish.[41] Nevertheless, unless Confucianism could accommodate a greater faith in ordinary people than hitherto demonstrated by the educated in China and other East Asian societies, articulating and realizing a Confucian civil society will remain problematic.

Interdependence:
Complementing rather than Confronting

Acknowledging that faith in people is required for Confucian civil society is not to side with the people, or civil society, against the state. What is crucial to civil society is independence, not opposition to the state. Independence has to do with how much say a group has over its role and its relations with other groups. Instead of absolute independence, which requires radical separation, Confucianism understands independence in a relational context as interdependence. Unless a group allows others some say as well, its independence becomes dominance, relegating others to dependence.

Thomas Gold and Michael Frolic speculate that the best chance for civil society in China might lie within the corporatist system itself. In a Confucian civil society, the lines between state and society are unlikely to be as clearly drawn as in Western countries. To most writers such "symbiosis" of society and state means the absence or at least weakness of civil society. But the location of power within the Confucian state-society continuum is fluid and negotiated within specific circumstances. State corporatism could become societal corporatism. Instead of incorporation of intermediate organizations for state purposes, we could have incorporation of state organizations for civil society purposes. In between there could be both types of organizations cooperating where there are overlaps of interests, or maintaining a synergistic tension where neither completely dominates. Absolute separation from and opposition to the state are not necessary to people having a greater say in public policy outcomes. Relations of interdependence, unlike *dependent* relations, do not imply control by any one party; they involve indeterminacy in the resolution of conflicts and the possibilities of mutual benefits—they are cooperative rather than subordinate.[42]

Many undesirable aspects of current state-society relationships should be changed if China is to become more democratic. Nevertheless, it is a procrustean exercise trying to force Confucian societies into Western molds. Interdependence does not necessarily mean that social organizations are "underdeveloped," that civil society is absent or weak, that the state is authoritarian. Rather, it is characteristic of a world in which organizations, as well as individuals, are inherently relational in their identity and functioning. In the Confucian worldview, individuals, families, intermediate organizations, and state form nested and overlapping networks in which cooperation and competition, mutual enhancement as well as tension, are always present together.

Studies show that most Chinese neither conceived of nor wanted a neat separation of society from state. Instead, they incorporated the state into their own moral order. They are not alone in this thinking. A recent letter to the Singapore *Straits Times* newspaper argues against blindly adopting a liberal notion of civil society pitting society against state. [43] For many Singaporeans, the role of civil society is to complement, not confront, the government. Both the reality and the aspirations of East Asian societies resist wasteful and destructively confrontational politics. The relation between the state and civil society in an ideal Confucian polity will always be too close for comfort to those who believe that civil society and state must be fundamentally antagonistic.

If the concept of civil society is to be theoretically and practically useful in Confucian contexts, the fundamentally antagonistic state–civil society relation needs reconstructing. Deng Zhenglai argues that the two main western traditions are too one-sided in their treatment of the state–civil society relationship—the Lockean-liberal tradition privileges civil society while the Hegelian-socialist tradition privileges the state. There is a need to modify the Lockean model of civil society to allow for a "mutually enhancing" relationship between state and civil society in applying the concept to Chinese society. On a practical level, NGOs' projects, for example, often reflect a development discourse on distribution, individual rights, "empowerment," predicated on an opposition between state and society that does not always make the best sense nor achieve the best results in some parts of the world. [44] Those who argue for the possibility of Confucian civil society must take into account the Confucian view of society as forming a continuum with, rather than being necessarily in opposition to, the state.

Such a reconstruction may also be long overdue in Western societies. Habermas suggests that the separation of state and civil society, the former basis of bourgeois public spheres, is now outdated due to "a progressive 'societization' of the state simultaneously with an increasing 'state-ification' of society." Timothy Brook points out that state and society are densely interactive realms everywhere, including Western societies. According to Kai Nielsen, even Antonio Gramsci treats state and civil society as methodological (analytical) distinctions used for theoretical purposes, and recognizes that in the real world, their boundaries are blurred; they flow into each other and are not separable. Charles Taylor argues that in addition to a Lockean strand in Western civil society thinking, stressing separation of society and state, there is another strand indebted to Montesquieu, which emphasizes interdependence. Michael Walzer points out that "the state can never be what it appears to be in liberal theory, a mere framework for civil society. [45]

John Keane's definition of civil society postulates a relative, rather than absolute, separation and opposition between civil society and the state. Keane understands democracy as a special type of political system in which both civil society and state institutions are necessary—they are "separate but contiguous, distinct but interdependent."[46] Democracy is at risk when civil society overwhelms the state, as it is when the state overwhelms civil society. A democracy cannot flourish if the state is in total control of civil society or vice versa; what is needed is a relation of mutual influence wherein each is capable of taking the lead when appropriate.

A civil society that recognizes its interdependence with the state fits better with Confucian democracy. The effective use of the concept of civil society in contemporary Confucian discourse requires, and contributes to, the reconstruction and imaginative transformation of civil society conceptually and politically. There may not be perfect agreement on the exact mix of separation, opposition, and interdependence, or on how different forms of interaction should work; but the door is open for a meaningful conversation.[47] All could contribute something to the debate on how to resolve the tension between separation and interdependence, between support and cooperation on the one hand, and competition and resistance on the other. The critical issue is what kind of sociopolitical arrangements would best facilitate popular participation in matters that affect different publics in a society. Each society must find its own resolutions in specific circumstances. No single answer will work for everybody and every occasion; but all can learn from one another's successes and failures.

Civil Society as Fiduciary Community

Some might think that the concept of Confucian civil society articulated here not only does not fit any empirical entity, but even as an ideal, it is unrealistic or as obsolete as the eighteenth-century model of civil society which based its reconciliation of opposites (individuals and society, private and public) on universal solidarity through moral affections and natural sympathy that expresses individuals' social-embeddedness. Critics might point out that a more accurate depiction of the world is captured in the prisoner's dilemma, wherein at one level people share a common goal (to escape), which will be realized if they trust one another and act on that trust. But if there is insufficient trust, their interests, which were originally convergent, becomes conflicting. Moreover, there is a built-in bias against trust: in less than ideal situations, misplaced trust has a heavy penalty: it is better to be the betrayer than the betrayed.

Adam Seligman's *Idea of Civil Society* recognizes the problem of trust as central to the Western civil society problematic. His pessimistic prognosis for civil society arises from his misgivings about the low level of trust in modern Western society. Piotr Sztompka suggests that the contemporary discourse of Polish civil society has been ineffective in its solidarizing and legitimating tasks because it has failed to gain the trust required for those tasks. Richard Rose argues that the legacy of mistrust is a serious obstacle in the democratization of postcommunist countries. To Robert Putnam and Francis Fukuyama, trust is a kind of social capital that helps democratic institutions, including those of civil society, function more effectively. Many others would agree with Rose that "trust is a necessary condition for both civil society and democracy."[48]

In Singapore, some have asked why the government does not get rid of laws that inhibit freedom of association if it is serious about promoting civil society. As one social worker is reported to say, "How can civil society ever become vibrant if existing laws made it illegal for five people to get together without a permit."[49] The government's response is that people should work within the existing legal framework. The problem of trust lies at the center of this exchange. The government is unwilling to change the laws because it does not trust everybody to act responsibly—it is afraid that unscrupulous individuals and groups will take advantage of any legal provisions promoting civil society to create social disorder. The people want the state to change legislations first because they do not trust the government's profession of greater openness—they are afraid that criticisms and protests could be suppressed at high personal costs to the participants as existing laws provide little protection for individuals and groups.[50] Added to that is distrust of their fellow citizens—they are afraid that few would back them up in a contest with the state, or even respond to their efforts positively.

Before we talk about trust between the government and the governed, we need to examine the problem at a more micro-interpersonal level. Having a legal framework of individuals' rights may not ensure a flourishing civil society. It is a mistake to believe that if a society "becomes more 'litigious', it becomes more civil." In the United States, a litigious "rights-based" society *par excellence*, people are lamenting the decline of civil society and calling for its revival through rebuilding trust.[51] Legal frameworks of rights, which give political and social substance to the idea of civil society, can also undermine its foundations in the idea of a shared realm of solidarity. The general tendency to rely too much on the government and its legislative powers to solve social problems, and on the courts to resolve social conflicts, replaces interpersonal trust with trust in the legal system. It is symptomatic of distrust of one's fellow citizens, a distrust that bodes ill for civil society. Ultimately, the trustworthiness of a system depends on the trustworthiness of those who operate it; over-reliance on the legal system ironically undermines the very basis of its trustworthiness.

Litigation is fundamentally adversarial; it is based on, and engenders, distrust. Some suggest that, in the United States, it is because people no longer trust each other that they place their trust in the vague and conversation-stifling language of "rights" instead. Tactics adopted both in the courtrooms and in politics undermine people's inclination and ability to trust fellow citizens as well as public officials. In this political order structured by a legal framework of rights, where the autonomous individual remains its fundamental component, trust often has only an ephemeral basis in an equal humanity with so little reality in actual social interactions that it cannot support any social solidarity that would affirm both community and individuality.[52] The overly individual-istic and legalistic liberal view of civil society, instead of being the norm that everyone interested in fostering democracy should adopt, is in truth inadequate for solving the problem.

Confucianism could make valuable contributions in reconstituting the problem of civil society to focus on the problem of trust. Tu Wei-ming argues that Confucianism could contribute to the core values that can sustain a "global fiduciary community." In arguing that Song and Ming neo-Confucians almost achieved a civil society, de Bary cites their efforts to "build consensual *fiduciary* institutions." His account of community compacts brings out the importance of trust in the Confucian socio-political vision. The compacts were not *legal* or even informal contractual instruments. They were edifying proclamations aimed at eliciting consensus regarding matters of common interest and coop-eration in promoting social order. The consensus, and the resulting constraint on subsequent behavior, is only possible because interpersonal interactions according to Confucian teachings establish trust in a community—a trust that would be further increased by the compact.[53]

Building Trust through Ritual Practice (*Li* 禮)

A Confucian civil society is a society in which ritual practice (*li* 禮) fosters and nourishes the growth of trust, so that individuals both compete and cooperate in voluntary associations united by common interests, and groups thus formed cooperate and compete in peaceful interaction with one another, and with the state. As Tu noted in *Centrality and Commonality*, Confucian rites are occasions to rehearse symbolically the attitudes various individuals should adopt toward one another. As such, they clarify and reinforce social order and play a key role in the building of a fiduciary community.[54] Much work still has to be done to show how ritual practice could be a more generalized tool for building trust today. It is certainly not a matter of reviving wholesale the rituals of yesteryear, which in old China became so reified in some cases that they stifled social vibrancy and individual creativity.

Flexibility and creativity must be integrated with stability in the ritual prac-tice of a Confucian civil society. Such ritual practice must be understood in a wider sense than previously. Herbert Fingarette has noted that even though external forms vary from culture to culture, and generation to generation, there remains a vast area of human experience wherein interaction is ritual: promises, commitments, excuses, pleas, compliments, pacts. In its broadest sense, ritual practice, as a generic kind of social action, is neither archaic nor exclusively Confucian. Robert Neville has applied Confucian concept of *li* to Boston so-ciety.[55] The Confucian notion of *li* has sometimes been translated as "civility," an idea closely associated with civil society in the West. Stephen Carter, who sees civility as the "manners, morals and the etiquette of democracy," links it to generosity and trust. Edward Shils describes a civil society as "a society of civility in the conduct of the members of society toward each other." As good manners and courtesy toward political opponents as well as toward political allies, civility benefits political activity. "They make opposition less rancorous; they make opponents less irreconcilable."[56]

A comparison of the Western concept of civility and Confucian *li*, and how they operate to nurture trust, is likely to prove edifying for civil society theorists both East and West.[57] Confucian ritual practices are cooperative activities in which all understand what each should do and everybody does his/her part so that all act together harmoniously. The shared meanings as well as frequent practice could result in seamless cooperation that embodies harmony. In acquiring shared meanings embodied in ritual practice through a process of education and socialization, participants acquire certain ways of feeling and thinking. They also acquire self-discipline and a disposition for harmony, which comes from appreciating the value of harmony that they have experienced. The sensitivity and understanding toward other participants engendered in achieving harmony in ritual practice would favor other tasks in which cooperation is required. Ritual practice, designed to achieve harmony in recurrent occasions of daily living, creates the training environment for achieving harmony in more problematic arenas of life.

In conflict situations, predisposition toward a harmonious resolution and avoidance of an adversarial stance can have significant impact on the outcome. Polite and nonconfrontational postures, facilitated by ritual acts understood by all, even in situations of serious conflicts of interests, are not always simply hypocrisy; they are in fact powerful means of increasing the chances of an outcome acceptable to everybody. A harmonious outcome is never easy to achieve since it requires participants to be genuinely disposed toward a harmonious outcome, as well as equipped with the necessary self-discipline, sensitivity, and understanding toward people and events. As an embodiment of shared meanings, ritual practice guides action so that better coordination can be achieved with less effort than would be possible if one has to search anew for appropriate ways of interacting in every situation. It gives us greater confidence in the predictability of others' performance. In a society where ritual practice reigns, it is easier to trust one's fellow citizens. If one trusts one's fellow citizens, it is easier to participate in social action. It is easier to build a vibrant civil society.

Conclusion

This essay began with a reconstruction of the concept of Confucian civil society by tentatively locating civil society between family and state, and focusing on its link with democracy. I then examined how individual persons in Confucian civil society should recognize their inherent sociality and relate to each other in ways that promote social purposes without suppressing individual freedom and creativity. In such a civil society, the private and public are not radically separated realms; they form a complementary polarity whose boundaries shift according to circumstances. Confucian civil society is a reconciliation of private and public, wherein the public should not be equated with state control; neither should the private be equated with the selfish. Confucian civil society cannot be fundamentally antagonistic to the state, and boundaries between organizations are fluid. Their interdependent relationship allows indeterminacy in who decides what happens. It allows situations wherein a good government could effectively represent the people, as well as those in which intermediate organizations could work for the people.

Having articulated some key features of a Confucian civil society, I asked whether such a concept could be part of a realistic socio-political ideal. It is not possible to provide a full answer to this question. But a positive response would, at the very least, require an adequate approach to the building of trust among people who would form civil society; this is also an area in which Confucianism could contribute to a cross-cultural civil society discourse. While the problem could not be explored in full here, the last part of the essay indicates the direction the search for a Confucian account of trust could take.

Notes

1. John Keane, *Civil Society: Old Images, New Visions* (Stanford, Calif.: Stanford University Press, 1998), 2–4, ch. 3.

2. Roger V. des Forges, "States, Societies and Civil Societies," in *Civil Society in China*, ed. Timothy Brook and Michael Frolic (London: M.E. Sharpe, 1997); David Strand, *"Civil Society" and "Public Sphere" in China: A Perspective on Popular Movements in Beijing, 1919/1989* (Asian/Pacific Studies Institute, Duke University, 1990); Mary Rankin, "Some Observations on a Chinese Public Sphere," *Modern China* 19, no. 2 (1993): 158–82; Susan Mann, *Local Merchants and the Chinese Bureaucracy 1750–1950* (Stanford, Calif.: Stanford University Press, 1987); Mayfair Mei-hui Yang, "Between State and Society: The Construction of Corporateness in a Chinese Socialist Factory," *Australian Journal of Chinese Affairs* 22 (1989): 31–60; William T. Rowe, "The Public Sphere in Modern China," *Modern China* 16, no. 3 (1990): 309–29; David Kelly and He Baogang, "Emergent Civil Society and the Intellectuals in China," in *The Development of Civil Society in Communist Systems*, ed. Robert Miller (Sydney, Australia: Allen & Unwin, 1992), 24; Thomas Gold, "Bases for Civil Society in Reform China," in *Reconstructing Twentieth Century China*, ed. Kjeld Erik Brodsgaard and David Strand (Oxford: Clarendon Press, 1998).

3. Heath B. Chamberlain, "On the Search for Civil Society in China," *Modern China* 19, no. 2 (1993), 204; Frederick Wakeman, Jr., "The Civil Society and Public Sphere Debate: Western Reflections on Chinese Political Culture," *Modern China* 19,

no. 2 (1993): 133; Philip Huang, "The Paradigmatic Crisis in Chinese Studies: Paradoxes in Social and Economic History," *Modern China* 17, no. 3 (1991): 321; David L. Wank, "Civil Society in Communist China? Private Business and Political Alliance, 1989," in *Civil Society: Theory, History and Comparison*, ed. John A. Hall (Cambridge: Polity Press, 1995).

4. Liu Zhiguang 劉志光 and Wang Suli 王素莉, "Moving from 'Mass Society' to 'Civil Society' 從群眾社會走向公民社會," *Xinhua Wenzhai* 新華文摘 11, no. 119 (1988): 9–11. This is a majority opinion among both Chinese writers and Western Sinologists writing about civil society. Deng Zhenglai, *Research and Reflection* 研究與反思 (Shenyang: Liaoning University Press, 1998), 105. Apart from de Bary, who argues for a nonauthoritarian view of Confucianism, an earlier exception is Jiang Qing 蔣慶, "Confucian Culture: Its Abundant Resources for Building Chinese Civil Society 儒家文化: 建構中國式市民社會的深厚資源," *Chinese Social Sciences Quarterly* 中國社會科學季刊 3 (1993): 170–75.

5. Deng, *Research and Reflection*, pp. 102–5, 136–40.

6. Tu Wei-ming, ed., *China in Transformation* (Cambridge, Mass.: Harvard University Press, 1994), xviii; Kenneth Dean, "Ritual and Space: Civil Society or Popular Religion," in Brook and Frolic, *Civil Society in China*, p. 192.

7. Salvador Giner, "Civil Society and its Future," in Hall, *Civil Society*; Adam Seligman, "Between Public and Private: Towards a Sociology of Civil Society," in *Democratic Civility*, ed. Robert W. Hefner (New Brunswick, N.J.: Transaction, 1998), 81; *The Idea of Civil Society* (New York: Free Press, 1992), 168–69; Keith Tester, *Civil Society* (New York: Routledge, 1992), chs. 6 and 7; Fang Zhaohui 方朝暉, "The Two Traditions of Civil Society and Their Modern Convergence 市民社會的兩個傳統及其在現代的匯合," *Social Sciences in China* 中國社會科學 5 (1994): 82–102; Jeffrey Alexander, ed., *Real Civil Societies* (London: Sage, 1998).

8. Jean L. Cohen, "Civil Society," in *Routledge Encyclopedia of Philosophy*, vol. 2, general editor Edward Craig (New York: Routledge, 1998), 371; des Forges, "States," p. 94; Michael Walzer, ed., *Toward a Global Civil Society* (Providence: Berghahn Books, 1995); Michael G. Schechter, ed., *The Revival of Civil Society: Global and Comparative Perspectives* (New York: St. Martin's, 1999).

9. Yeong An Seang, "Re-tests and Better Driver Instruction May Be Cures," *Straits Times*, 24 Mar. 2000; Alan John, "Hello Kitty, Then, Goodbye, Golden Arches," *Straits Times*, 19 Jan. 2000; Nirmala Purushotam, "Speaking Out of the Ordinary," *Straits Times*, 20 Feb. 2000.

10. Jean L. Cohen, "American Civil Society Talk," in *Civil Society, Democracy and Civic Renewal*, ed. Robert K. Fullinwider (Lanham: Rowman and Littlefield, 1999), 77. Mayfair Yang Mei-hui, *Gifts, Favors, and Banquets: The Art of Social Relationships in China* (Ithaca: Cornell University Press, 1994), ch. 8; Robert P. Weller, "Horizontal Ties and Civil Institutions in Chinese Societies," in Hefner, *Democratic Civility*; Gordon White, "Prospects for Civil Society in China: A Case Study of Xiaoshan City," *Australian Journal of Chinese Affairs* 29, no. 1 (1993): 82; Chris Hann and Elizabeth Dunn, *Civil Society: Challenging Western Models* (New York: Routledge, 1996), 14, 20.

11. Richard Rose, *Towards a Civil Economy*, Studies in Public Policy, no. 200 (Glasgow: University of Strathclyde Center for the Study of Public Policy, 1992), 3; Larry Diamond, "Toward Democratic Consolidation," in *The Global Resurgence of Democracy*, ed. Larry Diamond and Marc Plattner (Baltimore: Johns Hopkins University Press, 1996), 230–34. Keane, *Civil Society*, p. 19; Tester, *Civil Society*, p. 128.

12. William Theodore de Bary, *Asian Values and Human Rights* (Cambridge: Harvard University Press, 1998), 15–16.

13. Bronislaw Geremek, "Civil Society, Then and Now," in Diamond and Plattner, *Global Resurgence*, p. 247; Jean François Bayart, "Civil Society in Africa," in *Political Domination in Africa:Reflections on the Limits of Power*, ed. Patrick Chabal (Cambridge: Cambridge University Press, 1986), 118; White, "Prospects for Civil Society in China," p. 221; Wang Shaoguang 王绍光, "Some Reflections on 'Civil Society'," *Twenty-First Century* 二十一世纪 8 (1991): 113; He Baogang, *The Dual Roles of Semi-Civil Society in Chinese Democracy* (Brighton: Institute of Development Studies, 1993).

14. Seligman, *The Idea of Civil Society*, p. 5 and "Animadversions upon Civil Society and Civic Virtue in the Last Decade of the Twentieth Century," in Hall, *Civil Society*, p. 215; Neera Chandhoke, *State and Civil Society* (New Delhi: Sage, 1995), p. 26.

15. de Bary, *Asian Values*, p. 25.

16. Donald J. Munro, ed., *Individualism and Holism* (Ann Arbor: Center for Chinese Studies, University of Michigan, 1985), 17. See also Ann Kent, *Between Freedom and Subsistence: China and Human Rights* (Hong Kong: Oxford University Press, 1993), 30–31; de Bary, Tu Wei-ming, and Irene Bloom have separately defended Confucianism as valuing the individual in its own way.

17. John Varty, "Civil Society as Community of Citizens: Adam Ferguson's Alternative to Liberalism," in *Communitarianism and Citizenship*, ed. Emilios A. Christodoulidis (Aldershot: Ashgate, 1998) and contributions by Amitai Etzioni, Jean Bethke Elstain, William Galston, Terry Pinkard, Philip Seznick and Otto Karlscheuer in the section, "The Communitarian Approach," in Walzer, *Toward a Global Civil Society*, pp. 77–145. For an argument of how excessive individualism leads to atomization of society and destruction of public spaces, so that civil society declines and authoritarian solutions to the resulting disorder appear attractive, in the context of globalization, see Ralf Dahrendorf, "A Precarious Balance: Economic Opportunity, Civil Society and Political Liberty," in *The Essential Communitarian Reader*, ed. Amitai Etzioni (Lanham: Rowman and Littlefield, 1998); Adam Ferguson, *An Essay on the History of Civil Society*, ed. Fania Oz-Salzberger, first published 1782 (New York: Cambridge University Press, 1995), 95.

18. Giner, "Civil Society," p. 305; G. W. F. Hegel, *Philosophy of Right*, trans. T. M. Knox (Oxford: Oxford University Press, 1942), 289; Jürgen Habermas, *The Structural Transformation of the Public Sphere*, trans. Thomas Burger (Cambridge, Mass.: MIT Press, 1989), 142; Benjamin Barber, "Clansmen, Consumers, and Citizens: Three Takes on Civil Society," in Fullinwider, *Civil Society, Democracy and Renewal*, p. 12.

19. Qing, "Confucian Culture"; Broadsgaard and Strand, *Reconstructing Twentieth Century China*, p. 10. See also Fang, "The Two Traditions," for an analysis of the difference of the German concept of *bürgerliche Gesellschaft* from the Latin root of "civil

society" and the philosophical implications of their convergence in the modern period. Other translations of "civil society" include *gongmin shehui* (公民社會), *minjian shehui* (民間社會) and *wenming shehui* (文明社會). How the phrase is translated raises many controversial issues regarding the understanding of the concept.

20. Craig Calhoun, "Civil Society and the Public Sphere," *Public Culture* 5 (1993): 267–69; de Bary, *Asian Values*, p. 106; Wang Hui, Leo Ou-fan Lee with Michael Fischer, "Is the Public Sphere Unspeakable in Chinese? Can Public Spaces (*gonggong kongjian* 公共空間) Lead to Public Spheres," *Public Culture* 6 (1994): 597–605. Kelly and He, "Emergent Civil Society," p. 25; Rowe, "The Public Sphere," pp. 309–19; Rankin, "Some Observations."

21. Pamela Leonard and John Flower, "Community Values and State Cooptation: Civil Society in the Sichuan Countryside," in Hann and Dunn, *Civil Society*; William T. Rowe, *Hankow: Conflict and Community in a Chinese City, 1796-1895* (Stanford: Stanford University Press, 1989), 6.

22. Gui Xingyuan 桂興沅 and Ji Xueyuan 季學原, *A Guided Reading of Mingyi Daifang Lu* 明夷待訪錄導讀 (Chengdu: Bashu Book Co., 1992), 31.

23. Huang Zongxi 黃宗羲, *Waiting for the Dawn* 明夷待訪錄 (Beijing: Zhonghua, 1981), 1–2.

24. Brian Barry, *Political Argument* (Hertfordshire, UK: Harvester Wheatsheaf/Simon & Schuster, 1990), 176–90.

25. de Bary, *Asian Values*, pp. 27–29, 33.

26. Stanley I. Benn, and Gerald F. Gaus, eds., *Public and Private in Social Life* (New York: St Martin's, 1983); Habermas, *The Structural Transformation*, p. 142; Claus Offe, *Contradictions of the Welfare State* (Cambridge: MIT, 1984), 37; Richard Sennett, *The Fall of Public Man* (New York: Knopf, 1977); Seligman, *The Idea of Civil Society*, p. 25.

27. John Locke, *Two Treatises of Government*, ed. Peter Laslett (Cambridge: Cambridge University Press, 1988), Book II, ch. 7; Andrew Arato, "Civil Society Against the State: Poland 1980-81," *Telos* 47 (1981); Cohen, "Civil Society," p. 369; Deng, *Research and Reflection*, pp. 125–26, argues that this is also true of the use of "civil society" in Taiwan.

28. Peter L. Berger and Richard John Neuhaus, *To Empower People: From State to Civil Society*, twentieth Anniversary edition, ed. Michael Novak (Washington: AEI Press, 1996), 138, 148.

29. Lucian Pye, *Asian Power and Politics: The Cultural Dimensions of Authority* (Cambridge: Belknap Press, 1985); Gordon White, "Civil Society in Post-Mao China," in *The Individual and the State in China*, ed. Brian Hook (Oxford: Oxford University Press, 1996), 219.

30. Leonard and Flower, "Community Values," pp. 215, 218. See also Philip Huang, "'Public Sphere'/'Civil Society' in China? The Third Realm between State and Civil Society," *Modern China* 19, no. 2 (1993): 216–40; Dorothy J. Solinger, *China's Transients and the State: A Form of Civil Society* (Hong Kong: Chinese University of Hong Kong, 1991); Christopher Earle Nevitt, "Private Business Association in China: Evidence of Civil Society or Local State Power," *The China Journal* 36 (1996): 25–43.

31. Thomas H. C. Lee, "Academies: Official Sponsorship and Suppression," in *Imperial Rulership and Cultural Change in Traditional China*, ed. Frederick Brandauer and Chun-chieh Huang (Seattle: University of Washington Press, 1994).

32. de Bary, *AsianValues*, pp. 33, 109–17.

33. Chamberlain, "Civil Society in China," p. 203.

34. *Mencius* 8.3/41/2. Translation based on D. C. Lau, trans., *Mencius* (Hong Kong: Chinese University Press, 1984), 159.

35. John Dewey, "Democracy and Education," in *John Dewey, the Middle Works*, vol. 9, ed. Jo Ann Boydston (Carbondale and Edwardsville, IL: Southern Illinois University Press, 1980). Neera Chandhoke also noted the "pedagogic character of civil society" in educating individuals in the skills and values of collective action (Chandhoke, *State and Civil Society*, pp. 34, 247). Stig Thogersen, "Reconstructing Society: Liang Shuming and the Rural Reconstruction Movement in Shandong," in Brodsgaard and Strand, *Reconstructing Twentieth Century China*, p. 147; Liang Shuming, *The Gist of Rural Construction* (鄉村建設大意), *Complete Works*, I, pp. 599–720 (Jinan: Shandong People's Press, 1989); *Theory of Rural Construction* (鄉村建設理論) and *Reply to Criticisms of Rural Construction* (答鄉村建設批判), *Complete Works*, II: 141–658 (Jinan: Shandong People's Press, 1990). Several of the activists in the rural reconstruction in Zouping were students of Tao Xingzhi 陶行知, who was Dewey's student.

36. Western liberals like J. S. Mill have also worried about this; but while liberals focus on protecting the educated (and other) minority from the tyranny of an uneducated majority, Confucians adopt a paternalistic stand toward the latter.

37. de Bary acknowledges this in his remarks about "public opinion" in schools not referring to the people or popular opinion as a whole (*AsianValues*, p. 105).

38. Jerry Dennerline, *Qian Mu and the World of the Seven Mansions* (New Haven: Yale University Press, 1988), 54. Kelly and He, "Emergent Civil Society," pp. 33–38; Brook and Frolic, *Civil Society in China*, p. 7. See also See also Andrew George Walder, "The Political Sociology of the Beijing Upheaval of 1989," *Problems of Communism* 38 (1989); Timothy Cheek, "From Priests to Professionals: Intellectuals and the State under the CCP," and Elizabeth Perry, "Casting a Chinese 'Democracy' Movement: The Roles of Students, Workers and Entrepreneurs," in *Popular Protests and Political Culture in Modern China: Learning from 1989*, ed. Jeffrey Wasserstrom and Elizabeth Perry (Boulder: Westview, 1992), 124, 158.

39. Elizabeth Perry and Ellen Fuller, "China's Long March to Democracy," *World Policy Journal* 8, no. 4 (1991): 668–71; Thogersen, "Reconstructing Society," p. 159; Deng, *Research and Reflection*, pp. 121–22; Thomas A. Metzger, "The Western Concept of the Civil Society in the Context of Chinese History," *Hoover Essays*, no. 21 (1998). See also Liang, *Rural Construction*, pp. 657, 698–99, 710.

40. *Analects* 7.2/14/24; 7.34/17/25; 13.9/34/24; 13.29/36/28; 15.39/44/26; 4.6/7/18. *Mencius* 3.6/18/4–12; 5.1/25/3; 12.2/62/9. For more detailed arguments, see chapter 3 in Sor-hoon Tan, *Confucian Democracy* (Albany: State University of New York Press, 2003).

41. Chamberlain, "Civil Society in China," p. 210.

42. Gold, "Civil Society in Reform China," p. 182; Michael Frolic, "State-Led Civil Society," in Brook and Frolic, *Civil Society in China*. On the role of the state in the growth of civil society, see also Zhu Ying 朱英, "Qing Dynasty New Merchants and Civil Society 清代新型商人與民間社會," in *Twenty-first Century* 二十一世紀 3 (1990): 37–44. For distinction between state and society corporatism, see Anita Chan, "Revolution or Corporatism? Workers and Trade Unions in Post-Mao China," *Australian Journal of Chinese Affairs* 29 (January, 1993): 31–61. Positive complementarity is discernible even in sociological studies that tend to emphasize the down side of state-society symbiosis. White, "Prospects for Civil Society in China," pp. 78–85.

43. Leonard and Flower, "Community Values," p. 216; Heng, Swee Hai Michael, "We Can Create an Alternative Model of Civil Society," *Straits Times, Forum Page*, 8 Mar. 2000.

44. Deng, *Research and Reflection*, pp. 130–36, and "Civil Society and the State: Theoretical Separation and Two Kinds of Structure 市民社會與國家: 學理上的分野 與兩種架構," in *State and Civil Society* 國家與市民社會, ed. Deng Zhenglai and Jeffrey Alexander (Beijing: Central Compilation and Translation Press, 1999); Leonard and Flower, "Community Values," p. 204.

45. Habermas, *The Structural Transformation*, p. 142; Timothy Brook and J. Michael Frolic, "The Ambiguous Challenge of Civil Society," in Brook and Frolic, *Civil Society in China*, p. 12; Kai Nielsen, "Reconceptualizing Civil Society for Now: Some Somewhat Gramscian Turnings," in Walzer, *Toward a Global Civil Society*, p. 43; Antonio Gramsci, *Selections from the Prison Notebooks of Antonio Gramsci*, ed. and trans. Quintin Hoare and Geoffrey Nowell Smith (New York: International Publishers, 1971), 159–60; Solinger, *China's Transients*; Charles Taylor, "Modes of Civil Society," *Political Culture* 3, no. 1 (1990): 95–118; Michael Walzer, "The Civil Society Argument," in *Dimensions of Radical Democracy*, ed. Chantal Mouffe (New York: Verso, 1992), 104–5.

46. John Keane, *Democracy and Civil Society* (London: Verso, 1988), p. 14, and Keane, *Civil Society*, p. 8.

47. Keane himself (*Civil Society*, pp. 51–52) is explicit about the fluidity of the concept, and insists that maintaining this fluidity is crucial to its functioning.

48. Seligman, *The Idea of Civil Society*, p. 57; Piotr Sztompka, "Mistrusting Civility: Predicament of a Post Communist Society," in Alexander, *Real Civil Societies*; Richard Rose, "Post Communism and the Problem of Trust," in Diamond and Plattner, *Global Resurgence*, p. 251; Robert Putnam, *Making Democracy Work: Civic Traditions in Modern Italy* (Princeton: Princeton University Press, 1993); Francis Fukuyama, *Trust: The Social Virtues and the Creation of Prosperity* (New York: Free Press, 1995).

49. Chua Mui Hoong, "S21, An Uphill Effort," *Straits Times*, 4 Aug., 1999.

50. It is not surprising that most the essays in a recent book on state-society relations in Singapore raise the issue of mistrust. Gillian Koh and Ooi Giok Ling, eds., *State-Society Relations in Singapore* (Singapore: Oxford University Press, 2000).

51. Chamberlain, "Civil Society in China," p. 210. Albeit that by "litigious," Chamberlain does not mean more quarrelsome, but more willing to take quarrels to courts and accept the latter's judgment. Robert Putnam, "Bowling Alone: America's Declining Social Capital," Diamond and Plattner, *Global Resurgence*.

52. Stephen L. Carter, *Civility: Manners, Morals and the Etiquette of Democracy* (New York: Basic Books, 1998), 67, 121, 286; Mary Ann Glendon, *Rights Talk: The Impoverishment of Political Discourse* (New York: Free Press, 1991) ; Seligman, *The Idea of Civil Society*, p. 155.

53. Tu Wei-ming, "Core Values and the Possibility of A Global Fiduciary Community," in *Restructuring for World Peace*, ed. Katherine and Majid Tehranian (Cresskill: Hampton Press, 1992); de Bary, *Asian Values*, pp. 13, 58–89.

54. Tu Wei-ming, *Centrality and Commonality* (Albany: State University of New York Press, 1989), 48.

55. Herbert Fingarette, *Confucius: The Secular as Sacred* (New York: Harper & Row, 1972), 9–14; Robert Cummings Neville, "Confucianism as a World Philosophy," *Journal of Chinese Philosophy* 21 (1994): 15–21.

56. Carter, *Civility*, p. 62; Edward Shils, "The Virtue of Civil Society," *Government and Opposition* 26, no. 1 (1991): 5, 13.

57. William Rowe has also touched on the potential of such a comparison. William T. Rowe, "The Problem of 'Civil Society' in Late Imperial China," *Modern China* 19, no. 2 (1993): 152.

Minority Rights: A Confucian Critique of Kymlicka's Theory of Nonassimilation

13

Baogang He

Introduction

In developing his systematic liberal theory of minority rights, Will Kymlicka forcefully argues that democratic institutions should include minority rights, in particular, the right of national minorities not to be assimilated into a larger community. His theory justifies and defends the institutionalization of internal boundaries between communities within a nation-state, and fundamentally challenges the Confucian approach to the minority question.

In this essay I will examine Kymlicka's theory against the backdrop of the experience of East Asia and focus on the question of assimilation and its philosophical basis.[1] I will articulate one Confucian response to Kymlicka's theory, that is, the rejection of his idea of nonassimilation.[2]

Western liberal theories of minority rights have quickly penetrated Asian studies,[3] and Kymlicka himself has raised the issue of whether his theory can be extended to handle ethnic problems in Africa and Asia.[4] In particular, the question of whether such a liberal approach can be applied to address the minority problem in East Asia should be investigated seriously because the domination of one ethnicity in many communities, the hidden agenda of assimilation undertaken by governments, and the strong sense of pragmatism in interethnic relations have taken place there.

My goal is to engage in a cultural dialogue, which is currently absent but urgently needed, between liberalism and Confucianism through a comparative study of each underlying political philosophy. In other words, assuming the equal status of the two theories, I will question the basic assumption of Kymlicka's liberal theory of minority rights from the perspective of Confucianism; on the other hand, I will also challenge the basic presupposition of Confucianism and some of the assumptions and practices of Confucian communitarianism from the viewpoint of Kymlicka's liberal theory of minority rights.[5] This kind of cross-cultural engagement is useful in producing some positive intellectual outcomes that will help bring into contact different political ideas in different geographic areas and clear away past philosophies and ideas that have gotten in the way of thinking usefully about what can be done to settle the minority question.

This essay begins with a review of the main ideas of Kymlicka's theory and then focuses on the differences between Kymlicka and Confucianism on the issue of assimilation versus nonassimilation. I will question Kymlicka's normative theory by comparing Confucianism and liberalism with regard to rights in general, and minority rights in particular. In the final section I will discuss one of the key theoretical issues underlying both doctrines: individualism versus communitarianism.

1. Kymlicka's Liberal Theory of Minority Rights

Minority issues pose problems for all political rulers. The problems include achieving assimilation and harmony between the majority and minorities; preventing conflicts between the majority and minorities (or among minorities); maintaining stability and order in the context of a diversity of races and ethnicities; and promoting the coexistence of plural ethnic identities and national identities.

The issue of minority rights troubled liberalism throughout the nineteenth century. On the one hand, both English and continental liberals recognized the right to the autonomy of historically discrete cultures. For example, there was widespread progressive European support for the likes of Garibaldi, Kossuth, and numerous Polish independence fighters. On the other hand, liberal cosmopolitanism required that historical communities be assimilated into the broader progressive world cultures. German liberal nationalists had little time for the separatist claims of Hungarian or Polish minorities; and the Welsh, Irish, and Scots were supposed to assimilate into a broader British culture.

Today, aboriginal and ethnic indigenous communities do not normally share the values and aspirations of the larger society. Historically, the Europeans occupied the land of native peoples, and reached various historical agreements in granting them special status. Should liberal society continue to grant these peoples special status, and recognize their right not to be assimilated by the larger community?

Two approaches within the liberal tradition[6] offer different answers to this question. A classical liberal approach to minority issues can be summarized as follows. First, it aims to indirectly protect cultural minorities by guaranteeing basic civil and political rights to all individuals, regardless of race, ethnicity, and group membership. A "color-blind" constitution will remove all legislation differentiating people in terms of their race or ethnicity. Second, it separates the state and ethnic identity, and the state plays a neutral role. Third, people are free to choose and express their ethnic identities in private life. Fourth, no minority rights need be attributed to members of specific ethnic minorities, because liberalism as a moral ontology recognizes each individual as having equal rights and entitlements, and allows no room for the idea of collective rights. Lastly, classical liberalism is primarily concerned with the stability and unity of the nation-state. In short, classical liberalism and traditional human rights theory exclude minority rights.

This classical approach fails to recognize historically-embedded communities and the rights of these communities not to be assimilated into the larger community. Dissatisfied with the inadequacy of classical liberal theory, Kymlicka offers a neoliberal approach to minority issues. The neoliberal approach can be summarized as: Recognition, Rights, and Resources. The theory is primarily concerned with justice towards minorities and aims to supplement traditional human rights principles with a theory of minority rights. As Kymlicka argues, "A comprehensive theory of justice in a multicultural state will include both universal rights, assigned to individuals regardless of group membership, and certain group-differentiated rights or 'special status' for minority cultures."[7] The neoliberal approach also attempts to explain how minority rights coexist with human rights, and how minority rights should be limited by principles of individual liberty, democracy, and social justice. There are two limits to minority rights—no internal violation of human rights and no external exploitation of other groups.

Kymlicka makes a distinction between cultural and political communities.[8] The political community grants citizenship to individuals who exercise the rights and responsibilities entailed in the framework of liberal justice. The cultural community provides individuals with cultural membership; they share a culture, language, and history.[9] In the modern nation-state system, a single political community could include various coexisting cultural communities. This leads to a further distinction between "multinational" states (where cultural diversity arises from the incorporation of previously self-governing, territorially concentrated cultures into a large state) and "polyethnic" states (where cultural diversity arises from individual and familial immigration).[10]

Kymlicka also distinguishes between national minorities and ethnic groups. National minorities are those that were previously self-governing, territorially concentrated cultures; they now demand various forms of autonomy or self-government so as to maintain themselves as distinct societies alongside the majority culture. Ethnic groups are composed of individual or familial immigrants who wish to integrate into the larger society. While national minorities have the right of self-government and even the right to refuse to be assimilated, immigrant groups do not have the right of self-government and should be encouraged to assimilate.[11]

Kymlicka introduces a typology of minority rights or collective rights.[12] Self-government rights refer to the delegation of powers to national minorities.

For example, under the federal division of powers in Canada, the province of Quebec has extensive jurisdiction over issues that are crucial to the survival of the French culture, including control over education, language, culture, and immigration policies. Another example is the Native Canadian reservation system inside the existing Canadian state in which Native Canadian peoples have been acquiring increased control over health, education, family law, policing, criminal justice, and resource development.[13]

Polyethnic rights include financial support (for example, state funding for ethnic associations, magazines, and festivals) and legal protection for certain practices associated with particular ethnic or religious groups. For example, in order to wear their turbans, Sikh men in Canada have sought exemption from motorcycle helmet laws and from the official dress codes of police forces.[14]

Special representation rights guarantee seats for Native Canadians, Quebecois, or other ethnic or national groups within the central institutions of the larger state. For example, a certain number of seats in the Canadian legislature are reserved for the guaranteed representation of women, ethnic minorities, official language minorities, and Aboriginals.[15]

Kymlicka puts forward three arguments for group-differentiated rights. The first centers on the value of cultural membership. He argues for the primary good of cultural membership, pointing out that "the individuals who are an unquestionable part of the liberal moral ontology are viewed as individual members of a particular cultural community, for whom cultural membership is an important good."[16] The intrinsic value of cultural diversity lies in the context of choice that the cultural structure provides; individual choice is dependent on the presence of a societal culture, defined by language and history.[17]

The second argument concerns equality for minority cultures. It is unjust for a disadvantaged group to compete with the dominant group on unequal terms. Kymlicka claims that "the members of minority cultural communities may face particular kinds of disadvantages whose rectification requires and justifies the provision of minority rights."[18]

The third argument for minority rights is the history-based argument. In defense of group-differentiated rights for minorities, Kymlicka argues that these rights are the result of historical agreements, such as the treaty rights of indigenous peoples.[19] For example, Quebecois leaders agreed to join Canada on the condition that jurisdiction over language and education be guaranteed to the provinces, not the federal government. Honoring such agreements entails respecting the self-determination of the minorities involved, as well as ensuring that citizens have trust in the actions of government.[20]

A classic liberal would disagree with these arguments and suggest that minority rights are incompatible with individual rights. For example, reservation systems restrict mobility, property, and voting rights. The classic liberal would argue further that the primary good of cultural membership undermines the principle of equal liberty, for minority rights make an exception to the liberal commitment to equality and universalism. There is inconsistency between a "color-blind" constitution and special arrangements for minorities. Finally, a classic liberal would argue that much as Kymlicka intends to save liberalism, his attempt has failed since his theory undermines individualism, blurs the distinction between private and public lives, and undermines the effectiveness of a modern state.

Classic liberals may charge Kymlicka with the view that minority rights institutionalize contingent factors and the privileged position of top groups in a cultural community. Human beings are "accidentally" born within a particular community. An institutionalized cultural community goes against the equality principle which aims to reduce the impact of "accidents" on individual life.

Against these charges, Kymlicka emphasizes the fairness of protecting the cultural life of minorities so as to reject the argument that the reservation system violates fundamental rights. He says:

> It doesn't seem fair for the Indian and Inuit population to be deprived of their cultural community just because a few whites wish to exercise their mobility rights fully throughout the country. If aboriginal peoples can preserve their cultural life by extending residency requirements for non-aboriginal people, or restricting the alienability of the land-base, doesn't that seem a fair and reasonable request?[21]

More importantly, Kymlicka's notion of justice stresses differences.[22] To achieve justice one must recognize complexity and differences. His notion of justice recognizes heterogeneity and the differences of status of historical communities.

Taking his argument about the compatibility of minority rights and liberalism further, Kymlicka claims that a liberal theory of minority rights is not only consistent with the principles of liberal equality, but also required by them.[23] This is because individuals, as ontological agents, are members of cultural communities and because a just concern with disadvantaged communities requires and justifies the provision of minority rights.[24] Aboriginal groups are outbid for resources, and outvoted, for example, in the use of their own language. This inequality generates legitimate claims which can only be met through certain forms of minority rights, and cultural membership of these groups should therefore be protected.[25] For Kymlicka, the American conception of an ethnicity-blind constitution cannot be applicable to other countries.

In defense of minority rights, Kymlicka attempts a compromise between liberalism and communitarianism. On one hand, he accepts some claims of the weak version of communitarianism. On the other, he rejects and criticizes three strong claims promulgated by communitarians.[26] The first is Walzer's idea of membership-defining communal value. Cultural membership is seen by Walzer as the fundamental value because it defines the shared understanding of social groups in a given culture.[27] The problem with Walzer's argument, Kymlicka points out, is identifying the community that is the bearer of cultural membership. Here Walzer faces a challenging boundary problem: how do two different historical communities in a country work out the shared meanings of all citizens? Walzer offers an answer—that politics establishes its own bonds of commonality. For Kymlicka, this is unsatisfactory because it is precisely on that basis that politics in Canada has been binding Native Canadians in bonds of commonality with other citizens, for which the Native Canadians have consistently resisted.[28]

The second communitarian argument holds that cultural community shapes the identity of individuals within it, providing their sense of self. Cultural community also assumes a common perspective and attitude, thereby establishing social norms and standards. These norms and standards will be internalized so that we can expect the same behavior from members of the community. Kymlicka rejects the above argument, for the reason that two persons in a cultural community are likely to have two different life plans. Here Kymlicka defends an individualist position and rejects the cultural determinist view.

Kymlicka dismisses the third communitarian argument, put forward by Charles Taylor, that special protection of historical communities is based on some independent claim by the community itself to equal treatment. Kymlicka relies on the fact that the value of community must be assessed by individual members. A community has no moral claim to well-being independent of its members.[29]

As to the question relating to the relationship between minority rights and the stability of liberal democracy, there are two opposing arguments concerning the effects of minority rights on order and peace. Some nineteenth-century liberals felt that minority rights exacerbated the problem of developing a national political consensus, and protecting the minority culture would just prolong inevitable injustice by inhibiting the creation of a homogeneous national culture.[30] In contrast, many liberals before and after World War I, for example, Lloyd George at Versailles in 1918, believed that it was the refusal to meet the legitimate claims of minority cultures that created a danger to domestic and international peace.

Will group-differentiated rights for minority cultures inhibit the development of a shared identity necessary for a stable order? Kymlicka's answer is that both polyethnic (or multicultural) rights and special representation rights demand inclusion. To him, "Groups that feel excluded want to be included in the larger society, and the recognition and accommodation of their 'difference' is intended to facilitate this [integration]."[31] This differs from the classic liberal view that while cultural homogeneity contributes to stability, cultural heterogeneity creates instability. For Kymlicka, a state can maintain unity through plural identities,[32] though he does recognize that self-government rights raise profound problems for integration. Demands for self-government reflect a desire to weaken the bonds with the larger community, and to question the existing state. Self-government rights may divide people into separate "peoples," each with its own state, territories, and power of self-government.[33]

2. Should East Asia Adopt a Nonassimilation Policy?

Essential to the issue of minority rights is the question concerning assimilation and the basic standards of fairness. Minorities have often been unjustly treated through the modernization process, during which assimilation has been widely practiced. However, assimilation policies have, in general, failed to achieve full assimilation and have had negative consequences. Today, many states are revising assimilation and adopting multicultural policy positions. In Europe demanding for citizenship has become a big issue in France, Germany, and other countries faced with the difficulties of implementing an effective assimilation policy and grappling with the immigrants question.

Where assimilation was the main policy in the past, it is now deemed to be inappropriate. Accommodation of the aspirations of minorities without resorting to assimilation seems to be the current international trend. Thirty years ago, the Canadian government favored assimilation as evidenced in the "Just Society" policy which recommended the end of the special constitutional status of Native Canadians on the grounds that the reservation system had protected Native Canadians communities from assimilation. This position is definitely not taken now, for assimilation is today widely repudiated in Canada.

We may distinguish three types of identities in relation to the practice of assimilation. *Ethnic* identity is exclusive, although it allows other peoples to "marry in." This is a strong version of assimilation which forces minorities to adopt the ethnic culture at the cost of their own. *Civil* identity allows foreigners to live as new members of the national community, on the condition that they keep their cultures in the private realm and respect public culture, for example, speaking French in public. This is a weak version of assimilation, which allows minorities to maintain their cultures but absorbs them into a mainstream culture. *Plural* identity celebrates different cultures if individuals from those cultures subscribe to the common law, constitutions, and a common language. It does not necessarily imply the acceptance of the idea and practice of assimilation.

Kymlicka's theory of minority rights contains the idea of plural identities. While Kymlicka supports a kind of assimilationist policy for immigrants, he advocates a nonassimilation model for national communities in his justification of a reservation system for separate cultural communities.[34] He rejects the idea of assimilation of national minorities at the cost of obliterating their cultures, and makes a theoretical effort to defend the enterprise of national minorities that wish to maintain themselves as distinct societies alongside the majority culture. Kymlicka adopts the perspective of the least advantaged group, as a key element of justice, and sees assimilation as irrational and immoral. Internal communal boundaries, reinforced by a reservation system, will do justice for national minorities, although this may discomfort members of a larger community who may feel unjustly treated.

Likewise, should East Asia adopt the right of minority communities to not be assimilated into the larger community? In East Asian countries, like their counterparts in Europe in the past, assimilation has been an ideal model for national integration. Japan, for instance, has adopted an assimilation policy toward Koreans living in Japan. Second and third generation Koreans are being Japanized.[35] In Indonesia, the Chinese were encouraged or required to adopt Indonesian names and give up their Chinese names. In Thailand, the Chinese minority has been assimilated into the Thai nation through their adoption of Thai names and through intermarriage. In Taiwan, the Kuomintang (KMT) adopted the assimilation policy toward the local peoples and the aboriginal community by imposing on them the Chinese culture.

In modern China, Sun Yat-sen advocated and promoted the assimilation policy to achieve national unity, using both the terms *ronghe* (intermingling) and *tonghua* (assimilation).[36] Today, the Beijing leaders prefer the word *ronghe* to the term *tonghua*. The former assumes equality between two parties, while the latter assumes a superior position of one party over the other. Nevertheless, *ronghe* still implies a practical sense of assimilation, as Sun Yat-sen defined it as a process of all nationalities melting into one Chinese people. In practice, an assimilation rooted in Chinese tradition is still carried out in daily life although its methods and features are subtle. It should also be pointed out that the prejudice of some Han Chinese against the minorities is an unspoken psychological basis for the assimilation policy.

In the official Chinese theory of minority rights, the term *minzu zizhuquan* is used to express the right to self-government by the minority nationality, but such a term does not accept the idea of nonassimilation, nor does it tolerate the attempt to institutionalize the internal boundary through a special right embodied in a reservation system. This position is different from that of Kymlicka.

Given the predominant practice of assimilation in East Asia, a variety of ideas and traditions in supporting assimilation can be found. Therefore, we need to examine the assumptions of these assimilation ideas. Do they still hold today? Do they provide some critique of Kymlicka? Here, I will only outline one version of a Confucian criticism of Kymlicka's idea of nonassimilation. While such a choice omits other versions, it will present the Confucian response with its most forceful arguments. What follows is a summary of this conservative Confucian argument against Kymlicka's idea of nonassimilation.

2.1. The Confucian Argument for *Ronghe*

Many East Asian countries share the Confucian legacy that emphasizes the Great Way, the harmony of minorities and the majority, and the necessity of cultural assimilation. Confucianism stresses the idea that diverse minorities should merge into a unified harmony, coexisting peacefully in mutual respect and interdependence. It assumes that in the end all peoples should be unified and live harmoniously under one "heaven" as a harmonious organism. The key notion is *ronghe*, the fusion or amalgamation of majority and minorities in a process of Confucian cultural diffusion. In an ideal Confucian world, to harmonize the relations between different ethnic and cultural groups and communities is a top priority. This harmonization approach recognizes differences while not imposing conformity, and minimizes conflicts while not undermining autonomy. It stresses mutual respect and responsibility.[37] At the same time, it is also opposed to forced assimilation, calling for "a policy of non-violent assimilation through the imposition of Han-Chinese values rather than through a policy of extermination."[38]

Also, under the umbrella of *ronghe*, minorities are encouraged to maintain and develop their cultures insofar as they do not constitute a political threat towards the unity of the state and contribute to diversity, aesthetics, and tourism. *Ronghe* was expected to occur during the development of the Socialist state. More recently, the Chinese Communist Party (CCP) has stressed modernization as the precursor to amalgamation.

2.2. Rejecting Kymlicka's Historical Argument

Kymlicka supports the idea of nonassimilation on the historical grounds that national minorities have historically valid claims to a homeland and self-government. Confucian followers would reject this kind of historical argument by citing the example of the intermingling between the Manchu and the Han. When the Manchu established its empire, both Manchu and Chinese were official languages. After more than three hundred years, both ethnic groups had integrated. The Manchu language had influenced Beijing's vocabulary and pronunciation, but today only about 2,000 people can speak this language. It should be pointed out that the key elements of this successful intermingling include the ruler Manchu adopting Confucianism as an official ideology, and the Han Chinese, albeit subject to "foreign" political rule, maintaining a cultural leadership role in sustaining and developing Confucianism.

Another example is Yunnan Province, where many minorities live. Among them, the Yi ethnic group have lived there for around one thousand years. Today's younger generations of the Yi nationality know nothing about one huge tomb where 10,000 Han Chinese were buried. They had been killed by the Yi in one battle that took place during the Tang Dynasty. Looking back, we can see that intermingling and cultural assimilation did occur.[39]

The preceding examples demonstrate that the essence of Chinese civilization has been a process of assimilation, making a success of the Chinese diffusionist model. It is no exaggeration to say that without assimilation, there would have been no such thing as a Chinese cultural community today.[40] From this point of view, Confucian cultural and societal diffusion has an historical depth that is grossly lacking in Kymlicka's theory that seems very thin in historical terms. Part of the reason could be because his idea of assimilation is built on the very limited case of the Native Canadian peoples and Quebecois culture in Canada.

His ideas cannot even apply to most Western European nation-states where assimilation has been, and is still now, practiced.

2.3. The Consequentialist Argument against Nonassimilation

Pragmatic considerations have come into play in the Confucian rejection of the self-government right defended by Kymlicka. Institutionalized boundaries promote "independent kingdoms" within nation-states, and promote secessionist movements in the end. Thus the internal boundary problem of cultural communities is linked to the territorial boundary problem. Politicians in East Asia seek to secure the domination of one nationality or ethnic group (for example, the Japanese in Japan, the Han Chinese in China, the Malay in Malaysia, and the Chinese in Singapore) and force all the other ethnic and cultural communities to stay within a common territorial entity. Accordingly the right to refuse to assimilate is seen negatively because it could undervalue and even threaten the majority culture. Assimilation dissolves the ethnic problem,[41] while the right to refuse to be assimilated could intensify it. Historical records suggest that the recognition of separate collective rights leads to separate identities and claims for separate government. These notions serve as the rationale for China and other countries that reject the right to self-government. It should be noted that China's rejection of the self-determination principle fits well with a nearly universal trend described by Mayall: "It (national self-determination) has been accepted as a synonym for West European decolonization in Asia, Africa, the Caribbean and the Pacific, and the transition to majority rule in South Africa. It cannot be invoked—at least not with any hope of securing widespread support—by dissatisfied minorities within existing states."[42]

Moreover, in the eyes of Confucian practice, any institutionalization of an internal boundary will delay the process of assimilation, which usually needs at least a century or a time span of several generations. It was precisely the historical element that has delayed the process of assimilation of Native Canadians and which now poses a problem for the Canadian government. In this context, the Confucian idea of assimilation makes it difficult for the nation-states of East Asia to accept Kymlicka's notion of nonassimilation.[43]

While favoring intermingling and cultural assimilation, Confucianism also rejects any attempt to politicize past injustices which may create hatred today among ethnic groups and contribute to ethnic conflict. According to Confucianism, it is unjust for any theory or action to promote ethnic conflict. In Singapore the White Paper on Shared Values, which was tabled in Parliament in January 1991, insisted on "resolving major issues through consensus instead of contentions, and stressing racial and religious tolerance and harmony." The core values include "nation before community and society above self," and "community support for the individual."[44] During the 1997 Singapore general election, the Workers' Party candidate Tang Liang Hong was accused by the ruling People's Action Party (PAP) of being a "dangerous man" for voicing his view on Chinese culture and education which could potentially jeopardize ethnic harmony in Singapore.[45]

China has also depoliticized ethnicity. Any emphasis on ethnic conflicts is immoral, and is neither desirable nor feasible in overlapping communities. For example, Uighurs had their own state, which was destroyed by a combination of Russian and Chinese forces in the nineteenth century. Do Uighurs have the right to rebuild their state? Do the Miao minority,[46] living in the borders between China, Thailand, and Burma, have the right to establish an ethnic-based nation-state?[47] Does Tibet have the right to refuse being assimilated into a Chinese community?[48] A Confucian answer is no. The CCP has somewhat learnt the lesson that the internal boundary and the right of secession had laid the foundation for the disintegration of the Soviet Union. Moreover, minority rights, in particular the right of self-governance, are seen as institutional mechanisms which will perpetuate internal boundaries without achieving ethnic intermingling.

2.4. The Marxist Argument

The assimilation policy in China is consistent with both the Marxist and Leninist schools, which look forward to the inevitable assimilation of all people and, in turn, to the elimination of all national differences. For Marx, as well as Lenin, the historical forms of human identity, as expressed in inherited cultures, should not be viewed as authentic.[49]

Marxist historical materialism can be used to justify an assimilation policy. The upshot of the argument is that the interconnected world makes it difficult to resist assimilation, and that cultural change, caused by economic development, is a central human condition. All cultures have undergone great transformation. Some historical communities have been extinguished, while others have survived. The traditions and customs of those which have survived have been changed and for some partly lost. In today's interconnected world, reservation systems cannot work in the long term. Such systems may strengthen the closeness of a cultural community, but they in turn weaken the community's ability to survive, because its survival largely depends on special treatment, such as financial support. The survival of a historical community depends on its ability to adapt to and accommodate modern life. It is ironic that an institutional protection may actually weaken the ability of historical communities to survive.

2.5. A Liberal Rejoinder

However, from a liberal perspective, the above views are not convincing. Confucian *ronghe* is a nice ideal, but the Confucian emphasis on harmony often leads to suppression, and its success in achieving harmony often lies in paternalistic authority, of which Western liberalism is very skeptical.

Confucian rejection of Kymlicka's historical argument is not persuasive and misses the point because Kymlicka's argument is a legal argument, that is, the government has the duty to comply with the historical treaty. Moreover, to appeal to a few historical examples of assimilation is not good argument, because the key question is whether assimilation can still work in the contemporary condition.

The Confucian pragmatic argument is contingent, lacking intellectual coherence, and the direction of argument can be changed according to different situations and conditions. It therefore cannot convincingly reject Kymlicka's deontological position, in which rights triumph over utilitarian thinking. Nevertheless, the liberal cannot dismiss the political influence of this kind of thinking given the domination of pragmatism and utilitarianism in East Asia and in particular in China.

The Marxist argument is problematic in the sense that it has failed in the Soviet Union and China. Take China as an example. The Marxist class approach empowered the CCP to implement a radical program to promote a new socialist national identity in Tibet. However, rather than reducing ethnic conflicts, it intensified them. It forced a change in the structure of religious politics in Tibet; it also endangered Tibetan culture, which prompted a Tibetan separatist movement. The failure of the Marxist class approach reflects a deeper weakness in its doctrine, that is, its insistence that working people have no country.[50]

Moreover, from a liberal point of view, Confucian assimilation has happened in an unequal way. Confucianism always looks down on minorities and regards them as barbarians who should be assimilated into a higher culture.[51] Confucianism would never allow itself to be assimilated by "barbarians." It was Confucian centrism that propagated ethnic killing at the end of the Yuan dynasty; and it was Confucianism that supported Sun Yat-sen's call for the expulsion of Manchu-Mongol barbarians from China.

More importantly, to implement an assimilation policy in China, Taiwan, Japan, and Singapore one has to confront numerous difficulties. In Singapore, the policy that no Malay Singapore citizen is allowed to join the air force has already caused tension between Singapore and Malaysia. If the Chinese assimilation of the Malay groups were carried out, it would certainly worsen relations between the two countries. No wonder the Singapore government wisely adopts a multicultural approach to the minority question. In Taiwan, with the rise of the Democratic Progressive Party and Taiwanese nationalism, the whole question of minorities has been reconsidered and taken in a new direction. A few years ago, the registering of ethnic identity was abolished in order to blur sub-ethnic boundaries, as a way of managing the sub-ethnicity question. In China, minorities such as Tibetans resist the assimilation policy, and the Chinese government has adopted multiculturalism and minority rights to deal with minority question. That is why the political term widely used is *ronghe*, not *tonghua*. Of course, the assimilation process is still there but it has become more subtle and hidden. In Japan, the Meiji state had forced Ainu to be assimilated into Japanese society. Then in 1991, the Japanese government was pressured into recognizing the Ainu as an ethnic minority; but it still refused to recognize it as an indigenous people. Today, the Ainu people demand ethnic rights, in particular, special seats for Ainu representatives in the National Diet.[52] Also, imported Korean, Chinese, or Filipino cultures, and even indigenous Okinawan and Ainu cultures are recognized as having their places alongside "mainstream Japanese" culture.[53] From these cases, it is obvious that East Asian states face enormous difficulties in implementing assimilation.

An alternative approach is to abandon the ideology of assimilation and to adopt a notion of global justice. The idea of global justice is to highlight the perspective of the least advantaged groups and this would include minority groups. It criticizes Rustow's sequence of the resolution of national identity necessarily preceding democracy, for such a sequence implicitly justifies the weakening or even the disappearance of minority cultures. It also criticizes the Hobbesian world order in which the domination of one ethnic group is a necessary condition for the maintenance of stability and peace within the nation-state system. Global justice and cosmopolitan democracy intend to construct a new world order in which the perspective of the most disadvantaged groups such as minority groups is presented and stressed. From this perspective, ethnic, national, regional, and other cultural identities can coexist, with no hierarchical relation between them. Thus, the cultures of minorities should not be sacrificed for national integration or assimilation. A just international order should allow minorities to exist as "independent kingdoms" within national boundaries, and it should encourage the development of mutual or integrated borderlands for minority ethnic groups that are divided by nation-states.[54] The idea of global justice certainly will not accept the argument that "the majority nationality has an interest in making a nation state secure, and its institution stable, even at the cost of obliterating minority cultures and imposing enforced homogeneity upon the population."[55]

Kymlicka's notion on nonassimilation can be employed to challenge the Confucian notion of assimilation and offer an alternative perspective. Following Kymlicka, one may argue that Confucian scholars should recognize, as Western liberals do, the limit of an assimilation policy. A well-ordered society should allow for nonassimilation. Confucian culture should continue its cultural tolerance toward minority cultures, and allow them to survive and develop alongside the culture of the larger society, with the right to refuse to be assimilated into that larger society. Historically, Confucian culture had tolerated and incorporated different cultures; why should it not then celebrate the idea of nonassimilation so as to create an extensive just world? Is it unjust for the Chinese state to interpret those who refuse to be assimilated as ones who undermine the state's stability?

If the idea of nonassimilation is a universal trend, why should China not adopt it now as a new way to manage its internal boundary question? If assimilation is not the best solution to the nationality question, and neither is secession, then China ought to accept a special self-governing right for certain historical nationalities, as an alternative strategy for managing the national boundary question. If the seemingly conservative version of Confucianism discussed in this paper can be distinguished from a more liberal version of Confucianism, the conservative and exclusive version of Confucianism should be rejected. Meanwhile, a liberal Confucianism should be able to celebrate tolerance and diversity, and endorse Kymlicka's nonassimilation policy.[56] It is the task of more liberal Confucian scholars to develop a more appropriate response to Kymlicka's idea of nonassimilation. The upshot of the argument is that assimilation is not a solution to the minority problem, but the very core of the problem.

3. Comparative Political Philosophy

How can we understand the different attitudes towards nonassimilation outlined above? Perhaps the best way is to compare the different normative structures and political philosophies of liberalism and Confucianism, or more precisely, of the liberal rights-based theory of minority right and Confucian duties-based theory. In doing so, a better strategy is to polarize the two doctrines in order to understand their crucial differences, and therefore to help us grasp the intellectual frameworks within which the assimilation question is approached.

Before the comparison, let me justify my strategy of polarization. So far, numerous attempts have been made in Japan, Singapore, China, Taiwan, and South Korea to reconcile Confucianism and liberalism, and indeed some aspects of compatibility between Confucianism and liberalism have been detected.[57] For instance, what Kymlicka advocates — polyethnic rights and special representation rights — have already been partially or completely implemented in China, Singapore, Taiwan, and other countries. It should also be noted that in recent years, Chinese scholars like Yang Houdi, Wang Ping, and Sui Qing have developed a "Chinese-styled" theory of minority rights shaped by the Chinese theory of collective rights. They argue that China has developed a model of protecting and guaranteeing minority rights such as the rights to minority autonomy, to political consultation, to the use and development of minority languages, and to the preservation and development of minority cultures and customs.[58] It thus seems that Chinese scholars have "rightized" every official policy towards the minority, grouping them under the "minority right" umbrella. Nevertheless, behind the rhetorical claim about the minority rights, particularly in the case of Tibet, at work is a Confucian pragmatism towards the minority question. This calls for an examination of the unspoken assumptions of Confucianism, even among Chinese scholars, in dealing with Western minority rights theory, and of the tension between Confucianism and liberalism.

The polarization strategy of comparative philosophy can be also justified by the Confucian appropriation of human rights discourse in China. Interestingly Beijing has adopted a very broad concept of human rights, and even places the right to development within this broad conception.[59] As a result, economic modernization is seen as an equivalent to human rights, and the success of economic development is regarded as evidence of improved human rights. Actually, such an approach towards human rights dilutes the original and authentic meaning of human rights, redirects attention from civic and political rights to economic development, and deems the actual violations of civic and political rights as necessary for economic development. The Chinese approach to human rights demonstrates that although some efforts are genuinely for the purpose, others are just very Confucian, such as the emphasis on duty, stability, harmony, and the people's duty to obey the law and government. Such a Confucian appropriation of human rights reveals the underlying Confucian idea that rights *per se* are not essential; rather, rights must be based on duty and promotion of daily material life. This simplified comparison through the polarization strategy is aimed at showing the sharp contrast and the huge difference behind the apparent reconciliation of Confucianism and liberalism. What follows is a comparison of political philosophy.[60]

3.1. Competing Notions of Justice

A Confucian conception of fairness stresses *ren* (variously translated as love, benevolence, compassion, humanity, and man-to-man-ness) and reciprocity. The Confucian framework is characterized by duty, goodness, compassion, and the principle of humanity, which teaches love for all peoples regardless of ethnicity. A Confucian notion of justice prioritizes order and stability, and values collectivity, political authority, and the unit of the nation. Confucian policies dealing with the minority question feature paternalistic benevolence, cultural assimilation, autonomy, and intermarriage. (In practice, Chinese minority policies fail to meet Confucian ideals and theory.)

By contrast, Kymlicka's conception of justice adopts the perspective of the least advantaged group and takes seriously the value of cultural diversity. Kymlicka's normative structure of justice is based on three main ideas: the idea of equality, the honoring of historical agreements, and the value of cultural diversity.

3.2. The Different Traditions

The Confucian tradition has been associated with an emphasis on great unity, statism, and centralism and the absence of the idea of rights and political autonomy. The Confucian notion of great unity holds that all under Heaven are unified under one monolithic ruler who exercises absolute power. Confucianism does not tolerate the idea that one local region can make a law that is capable of overriding the law from the center. Confucian concepts of law do not allow inclusion of any concept of the right of self-determination, largely because the concept of rights is inimical to Confucian concepts of power.[61] Within a Confucian culture, with its emphasis on family, minorities may be regarded not as enemies but as occasionally disobedient younger brothers. Confucian obedience involves minority groups conforming to Confucian norms, maintaining unity and correct relations.

Moreover, Confucianism appeals to the rule of benevolent leaders, relies on a paternalistic authority, and does not have a system of individual rights, although some Confucian ideas can be interpreted as supporting human rights. By contrast, Europeans have been developing the idea of individual rights for a long time. Western liberalism has always deeply distrusted government, and rights are regarded as a check on the power of government.

3.3. The Starting Points and Centrality of Theories

The starting point of Kymlicka's theory of minority rights concentrates on individuals and minority groups. Kymlicka stresses individual value and human dignity as a fundamental reason to respect and protect minority cultures. His theory of minority rights talks more about rights than obligations, making them duty-less rights. It is ultimately a matter of self-love. It implies a conformity to social contract theory where human beings are deemed as equal and free. By contrast, Confucian compassion (or *ren*) is a duty-based theory which stresses love for others. From duty, one looks to others, and to serving families and communities. Confucianism stresses the freedom to choose good, disapproves of the idea of the right to do wrong, and requires that human rights must promote *ren* or humanity.[62] The Confucian idea of compassion (or *ren*) also implies a paternalistic government whose duty is to look after the weak and the poor.

While the principle of human rights occupies an essential place in Kymlicka's theory of minority rights, rights are not considered essential and play a minor role in Confucian theory. Lee Kuan Yew said clearly that good government is much better than human rights and that the West cannot impose its human rights principles on Asia.[63]

Moreover, within the Confucian theoretical framework, the state and paternal authority assume and oversee the common good. The state has a legal right to defend the unity of the state, which is more important than the right to self-government. By contrast, liberalism is skeptical of the state, sees the state as a source of evil, and does not allow the state to dictate the common good.

Not only did traditional Confucianism lack rights thinking, but contemporary Confucian scholars have also felt that rights were becoming a burden—too many rights, but too few duties and obligations.[64] For them, gay or lesbian rights will undermine the stability of heterosexual marriages and destroy family values;[65] the right to claim welfare will eventually dry up the state's revenue;

and the right to self-government will split the existing nation-state. All these rights are seen as "negative"—not good for society and the community and which will ultimately lead to the collapse of civilization.[66]

3.4. Different Interpretations and Their Consequences

According to Confucian duty-based theory, an affirmative action is interpreted as an act of paternalist goodness, not as one based on, or justified by, liberal right-based theory. The state also has the right to protect minorities on the grounds of promoting assimilation and stability, but not on the ground of rights.

Confucian doctrine sees states' provisions for minorities as "sweets," while Kymlicka's liberalism sees them as entitlements. This theoretical distinction has considerable implications. Very few members of minorities in the West have a feeling of gratefulness towards the state for the provision of material benefits, because it is seen as a matter of entitlement within the liberal theoretical framework. By contrast, members of East Asian minorities must be grateful to the state because the benefits they have are *given* by the state within the Confucian paternalist framework. With such different attitudes towards the state, Confucian paternalism tends to support political authority, while the liberal theory of minority rights is often very skeptical of political authority. Moreover, within the Confucian duty-based theory, it is expected that such paternalism (in the form of state benefits) be reciprocated with obligation and obedience from minorities. Where minority rights are seen as an entitlement, they do not guarantee obligation and obedience in return.

Take the example of the paternalist benevolence of the government in Singapore. It provides citizens the option of purchasing and living in government-subsidized housing. By 1994, more than 85 percent of the 2.7 million population lived in public flats, of whom more than 70 percent were owner-occupiers. The Government has adopted a quota system that mingles multi-ethnic groups in the subsidized housing. This policy is intended to prevent the development of racial enclaves, promote cross-cutting communities and reduce the polarization of ethnic groups. Some evidence shows that the level of interracial neighborliness has increased over the years.[67] And this policy is praised as promoting ethnic harmony.

The Confucian theoretical framework would not question this benevolent policy. By contrast, within the liberal theory of minority rights, people could criticize the repressiveness of the quota rules and charge that minorities are unable to defend racial enclaves. Individuals can defend their interests and criticize the government only if they are empowered with the right discourse. They are less likely to defend their interests if they have only the duty-based theory available to them.

Kymlicka regards the paternalist approach to the minority question as problematic. Paternalist policies towards Inuit and other Native Canadians were adopted in the 1970s in Canada, but are now seen as a disaster and repudiated by both the minorities and the central government. They are seen as a failure because they did not ensure ethnic equality. However, this can be so only if one adopts a liberal theory of minority rights. From the perspective of Confucianism, it is debatable whether paternalist policies have failed in either this Canadian or the earlier Singapore example. The policies in Singapore are seen as successful, in Confucian terms, because they help to contain potential ethnic conflicts. Both liberal theory and Confucianism have different criteria and theoretical structures to judge policies such as these. In the eyes of Confucianism, minority rights theory recognizes the legitimate conflict of interests and rights, and will thus institutionalize ethnic conflicts. In the eyes of liberal theory, Confucian duty-based theory, by containing ethnic conflicts, may lead to suppression, conformity and the imposition of restriction. In short, liberalism recognizes that conflict is a basic human condition, and that conflict is important and positive, while in Confucianism there is a denial of legitimate conflict.

4. Individualism and Confucian Communitarianism

The above comparative study of political philosophies of liberalism and Confucianism can be further pursued through an examination of their social ontology: individualism of liberalism and communitarianism of Confucianism.[68]

While Kymlicka couches his argument within a liberal and individual framework, Chinese understandings of minority rights are framed within a communitarian tradition. From an Asian perspective, Kymlicka wastes time drawing on the liberal tradition and in making the case that liberalism can provide a theory of minority rights, and he moves uneasily between individualism and communitarianism. The central problem Kymlicka faces—how to balance liberal and communitarian claims—is not the key issue in East Asia. In fact, the dichotomy between liberalism and communitarianism is not central in Asian thinking on the minorities issue.

The Chinese Confucian concept of what constitutes a Chinese community is essentially a cultural one, that is, anyone can be a member of the Chinese community as long as he or she accepts the Chinese culture. This concept of cultural community plays down ethnic criteria, and holds that a greater Confucian cultural community can embrace different political communities. Moreover, to harmonize the relationship between ethnic groups is another feature of the Confucian communitarian approach. Community should be ruled by morality, in particular, family-based moral principles. The Confucian communitarian approach towards the minority question is thus an extension of the family principle to the larger cultural and ethnic community. Confucianism holds that the government should be impartial toward all nationalities and ethnic groups like parents are towards their children, that big ethnic groups have a duty to love and look after smaller ones, like elder brothers do to their younger ones.

This line of thinking is reflected in the view that Mainland China and Taiwan should not fight each other; rather, both should conduct their behavior like brothers. What is absent in the East Asian context is purely individualistic thinking; for example, no one will make a claim for Taiwan's independence purely on individualist grounds.

While the individualist doctrine may be used to criticize some forms of state affirmative action for minorities in the West, the legacies of Confucianism and socialism make it easier for the Chinese to accommodate Kymlicka's argument for state provision for minorities. If, as Kymlicka suggests, communitarianism in the West weakens the argument for minority rights,[69] East Asian communitarianism[70] seems to provide strong support for state provision to protect minorities. It is often much easier to implement such provisions because people are required to make some kind of sacrifice according to Confucian communitarianism. For example, although some Han Chinese feel they are being discriminated against by the state's minorities policies, they cannot mobilize their discontent into a political force. This contrasts with the case of India, where the Hindu majority can develop into a political force against the state's affirmative action.

However, communitarianism plays dual roles: while it can support the state's provision for the protection of minorities, it can also be used to justify the suppression of minorities, or to camouflage the exercise of majority power. Today's Chinese communitarianism equates the existing political community with the Chinese nation-state. Such a version of communitarianism emphasizes that the state has a duty to defend the political community and to maintain the unity of the nation. To do so, the state is required to protect disadvantaged groups or cultural communities in order to ensure harmony among different ethnic groups. The state is also required to look after minorities in a paternalistic way.

Across all East Asian countries, and especially after the end of the Cold War, there has been an upsurge of cultural nationalism. Cultural nationalism assumes that historical communities have an intrinsic value independent of other values. The extinction of some historical communities, as well as of some animal species, is viewed as tragic. In modern times, Japanese, Korean, and Chinese intellectuals have voiced the concern that East Asian cultural communities may perish in the face of modernization and globalization. They have made great efforts to defend traditional values and customs. For them, the right to protect the cultural community should be prioritized, and they put the value of cultural community above that of the individual.[71] Liang Qichao, a great reformer in modern China, summarizes this well: if the community cannot survive there is no individual value.

Kymlicka's theory of minorities insists on some external protection for ethnic groups and national minorities, but is very skeptical of internal restrictions.[72] It argues against the use of collective rights to deny, limit and violate individual rights, and against the suppression of one group by another.[73] According to

Kymlicka, external protection should be provided in order to ensure that minorities have the capacity to maintain their culture. At the same time internal restriction should be rejected in order to ensure that people have the ability to revise their culture. Kymlicka is opposed to internal restriction of individual liberties and holds the position that individual members should be free to decide which parts of their cultural heritage are worth preserving and passing down to the next generation. People are not slaves of their culture, and they are free to revise their cultural heritage. Kymlicka's theory aims to achieve a balance between the provision of external protection and the rejection of internal restriction, in particular to reduce the internal violation of individual rights when external protection is provided.

Here Kymlicka's criticism of communitarianism is useful in a critique of East Asian communitarianism. The first problem associated with Confucian communitarianism is its repressive nature; it is often used to deny and violate individual rights. It gives high priority to the value of community, but fails to provide a mechanism against the abuse of communal power. The most serious problem of Confucian communitarianism is its blind trust in paternalist government. It fails to recognize that state and governments are sometimes part of the problem. For example, it was the central government of the PRC that forcibly asserted state power in Tibet, which has traditionally been autonomous, and as a result upset stable arrangements that have existed for centuries.

Second, while Confucian communitarianism rejects the right to secede, it supports the right of annexation and the enterprise of expanding Confucianism. This is a logically contradictory position which fails to recognize that it is often annexation that is the cause of ethnic conflict and the demand for the right to secede by certain national minorities.

Third, one fundamental limit of Confucian communitarianism in East Asia is that it fails to recognize equality between different cultural communities. Wang Fuzhi, a great Confucian scholar, argued a long time ago that Confucian moral principles would not apply to barbarians and could only exist within the Han Chinese community. He therefore did not regard the killing of barbarians as immoral.[74] Likewise, Chinese cultural nationalists do not respect Tibetan or Mongolian cultures, and often see minority self-rule as returning to either a federal system or despotism. In a similar manner, when Japanese cultural nationalists defend their culture, they do not accord any respect to the minority culture of Koreans in Japan.

Nevertheless, the practices of East Asian communitarianism make it difficult for Kymlicka's theory to be applied in China. Despite its theoretical soundness, it cannot work in practice. As an example, the liberal policy of internal restriction (no internal violation of human rights) may be seen as a violation of the self-governing principle by minority groups because such internal restrictions may reduce the power of minority communities to maintain their cultures. It might be argued further that Kymlicka's idea of internal restriction is a sort of liberal imperialism which does not take seriously the desire of some minorities to maintain their illiberal elements and customs.

Moreover, a defense of cultural communities, collective liberty, and communal fate involves a concession to individual liberty and requires the reduction of individual freedom. In defending a cultural community, individual rights are always sacrificed or at least seen as second-order. This is evidenced by the numerous violations of individual rights and liberties that have occurred in the history of the Chinese struggle for full independence in modern times. External protection implies and involves a kind of internal violation of individual rights. This is inherent not contingent logic. So if one protects the Yi cultural custom, the practice of prohibiting intermarriage between the Black Yi (masters) and the Yellow Yi (slaves) will continue. Another example is that of the elites of the Yi minorities, who would resist democratization because their positions are guaranteed by a quota system. If they became subject to the vote, they might lose their privileged position.[75] Similarly, some younger generations of minorities are "forced" to go to mosques on the insistence of their parents although they do not believe in Islam in their hearts, or in other cases, the older generations of minorities might interfere with their children's marriages. In the final analysis, a reservation system strengthens a system whereby the old generation makes life choices for the younger generation. There is thus no way certain individuals in the community can exercise their rights without Kymlicka's "no internal violation."[76]

Conclusion

Some aspects of Kymlicka's theory of minority rights can be used to deal with minority issues as demonstrated by the fact that it is useful in a critique of East Asian communitarianism. In particular his idea of nonassimilation can be employed to challenge Confucian assimilationist policy. The application of some elements of Kymlicka's minority theory in Confucian societies may overcome some deficiencies of Confucianism. Human rights in general and minority rights in particular are indeed relevant not only to China but also to other East Asian countries. They offer a possible solution to the minority question, or at least a way to reduce ethnic conflict.

On the other hand, the legacies of Confucianism make it easy to accommodate Kymlicka's argument for state provision for minorities. And Confucian scholars would argue that Confucianism constitutes a counterbalance to the neoliberal theory of minority rights, for the latter has practical problems such as the misuse of minority rights to maximize self-interests,[77] the institutionalization of separate community, the violation of individual rights, and the intensification of ethnic conflicts, such as in India.

In the Confucian communitarian approach to the minority rights issue there are four basic elements which are not in total consonant with Kymlicka's approach. First, according to Confucian understanding, the right to self-government should not, as Kymlicka suggests, institutionalize and strengthen an internal boundary. The Confucian communitarian approach will accept autonomous rights but these rights will not create an internal boundary. Second, in criticizing Kymlicka's idea of nonassimilation for national minorities, Confucianism celebrates the idea of intermingling: cultural exchange, economic integration, and political sharing between ethnic and cultural groups. It is the idea of intermingling that challenges the idea of the institutionalization of an internal boundary. For Confucianism, all parts (majority and minorities) should be united into one harmonious community. Third, it is this idea of one harmonious community that stipulates that all small cultural and ethnic communities should live harmoniously and intermingle with each other and with the majority community. It is this theoretical assumption that resists Kymlicka's idea of nonassimilation. Fourth, Confucian communitarianism advocates a paternalist approach to the minority question, of which Kymlicka is very skeptical.

Nevertheless, Confucian rejection of nonassimilation is not fully convincing. The Confucian approach towards the minority question might contain ethnic conflicts and strengthen stability, but it has certain repressive, unequal, authoritarian, and logically inconsistent features. Confucian support for paternal authority ignores the serious problem of the power question. Confucian rejection of nonassimilation constitutes a theoretical obstacle to the implementation of genuine autonomy, and may exacerbate the minority problem. A liberal version of Confucianism should take nonassimilation seriously.

Notes

1. Kymlicka's theory of minority rights is chosen for its practical implications in East Asia. The theory cannot be used to make claims for secession. All three types of rights which Kymlicka discusses are rights that exist within the nation-state. By contrast, Buchanan's moral theory of the right to secede is too radical to be accepted in East Asia, while Kukathas's rejection of minority rights theory is too individualistic to be taken seriously by East Asian communitarians.

2. It should be stressed that the Western debate largely takes place between communitarianism and individualism, but the cultural dialogue proposed in this paper takes place only between Kymlicka's weaker version of communitarianism and East Asian communitarianism. It should be noted that any East Asian can take an individualist stance in response to Kymlicka's theory. Such an approach is worth pursuing, and may prove to be much better than the East Asian communitarian one.

3. Thomas Heberer, for example, applies a liberal idea of minority rights and social justice in his study of the minority issue in China. He criticizes China's immigration policy and argues that "in the long run such a hard line and its effects may be the ultimate block to the unity of the country." See Thomas Heberer, *China and Its National Minorities: Autonomy and Assimilation* (Armonk, NY: M. E. Sharpe, 1989), 131.

4 Will Kymlicka, *Multicultural Citizenship: A Liberal Theory of Minority Rights* (Oxford: Clarendon Press, 1995), 194–95.

5. Surely, there are different versions of communitarianism. The Japanese version differs from the Chinese. And Tibetan communitarian arguments can support their demands for protection of their culture and even their demands for nationhood. Moreover, China is not purely a Confucian society. China's minority policies contain mixed elements of Confucianism, pragmatism, Marxism, and liberalism.

6. Liberal traditions have been divided on the minority issue. While Hobhouse has paid attention to minority rights, Rawls and Dworkin have entirely neglected them. See Will Kymlicka, *Liberalism, Community and Culture* (Oxford: Clarendon Press, 1989), 3–5.

7. Kymlicka, *Multicultural Citizenship*, p. 6.

8. Kymlicka charges Rawls with a failure to discuss cultural rights and membership, on the ground that Rawls assumes that a political community is culturally homogeneous. Kymlicka, *Liberalism*, p. 166.

9. *Ibid.*, p. 135.

10. Kymlicka, *Multicultural Citizenship*, ch. 2.

11. *Ibid.*, p. 10.

12. Kymlicka distinguishes collective rights, where a community itself exercises certain powers, from minority rights that refer to "special status," and concern the content and grounding of people's claims about cultural membership in culturally plural countries. See Kymlicka, *Liberalism*, p. 139.

13. Kymlicka, *Multicultural Citizenship*, pp. 27–30.

14. *Ibid.*, p. 31.

15. *Ibid.*, p. 32.

16. Kymlicka, *Liberalism*, p. 162.

17. Kymlicka, *Multicultural Citizenship*, p. 8.

18. Kymlicka, *Liberalism*, p. 162.

19. Kymlicka, *Multicultural Citizenship*, p. 116.

20. *Ibid.*, p. 119.

21. Kymlicka, *Liberalism*, p. 151.

22. By contrast, a classic liberal is discomforted by differences, while a socialist aims to eliminate differences.

23. Kymlicka, *Liberalism*, p. 4.

24. *Ibid.*, p. 162.

25. *Ibid.*, p. 4, and p. 162. When cultural rights are really in tension with equal liberty, what is a lexical order? Kymlicka endorses Rawls's idea of the priority of rights over good. See Kymlicka, "Rawls on Teleology and Deontology," *Philosophy and Public Affairs* 17, no. 3 (1988): 173–90.

26. Kymlicka, *Liberalism*, chs. 11–12.

27. Michael Walzer, *Spheres of Justice: A Defence of Pluralism and Equality* (Oxford: Blackwell, 1983).

28. Kymlicka, *Liberalism*, pp. 221–24.

29. *Ibid.*, ch. 12.

30. *Ibid.*, p. 212.

31. Will Kymlicka and Wayne Norman, "Return of the Citizen: A Survey of Recent Works on Citizenship Theory," in *Theorizing Citizenship*, ed. Ronald Beiner (NY: State University of New York Press, 1995), 306.

32 A distinction between homogeneity and unity should be made. The former refers to sameness or likeness, while the latter emphasizes that different peoples may feel themselves united even where there are different cultures.

33. Kymlicka and Norman, "Return of the Citizen," p. 307.

34. Of course, he values differences only as an instrument to achieve wider and more extensive equality. Equality is the goal.

35. The number of Koreans married to Japanese has rapidly increased. In 1952, there were 21,000 mixed families; in 1963 there were more than 30,000. See Richard H. Mitchell, *The Korean Minorities in Japan* (Berkeley: University of California Press, 1967), 159–60.

36. Yang Houdi, Wang Ping, and Sui Qing, *Equality, Autonomy and Development: the Chinese Model of Protecting Minority Rights* (Beijing: Xinhua chubanshe, 1998), 11.

37. Also see Derk Bodde, "Harmony and Conflict in Chinese Thought," in *Studies in Chinese Thought*, ed. Arthur Wright (Chicago: the University of Chicago Press, 1967), 46–47.

38. See Herberer, China and Its National Minorities, p. 18.

39. This depends on how minorities see their belonging, and their perceptions of the relationship between national and minority identities. Some minority people have feelings for the fate of their political community. Ma Chunwei, whom I interviewed on 23 January 1996 in Kunmin, said he was clearly conscious of being a member of the Chinese community and a member of a minority when he was an undergraduate. He thought both could coexist. Also, as a Korean who lives in north China, he says that he does not want to see the breakdown of China because he is now a Chinese citizen who will bear the suffering caused by any such eventuality. When he wants to travel abroad, he is required to have a visa. This imposes or reinforces the sense of national boundary and the communal bind.

40. This is true of German, French, and English cultures although the British colonial policies were much less assimilationist than French ones. China has a lot in common with Germany, France, and England who insist on the necessity of assimilation.

41. This is debatable. One may argue that assimilation policy has exacerbated the ethnic problem in Sri Lanka.

42. James Mayall, "Non-intervention, Self-determination and the 'New World Order,'" *International Affair* 67, no. 3 (1991): 421–29, 424; also see *The New Interventionism 1991–1994*, ed. James Mayall (Cambridge: Cambridge University Press, 1996), 6.

43. Surely, minority groups in East Asia would welcome and endorse Kymlicka's idea of nonassimilation to protect their cultures and ways of life. Kymlicka's theory, if well translated into minority languages, will contribute to the continuing battle between government assimilation policies and minority resistance against assimilation in East Asia.

44. Beng-Huat Chua, *Communitarian Ideology and Democracy in Singapore* (London: Routledge, 1995), 32. The last was a concession to public concern that Confucianism has historically bred authoritarianism. I would like to see this concession as an important step towards the synthesis of Confucian collectivism and some elements of Western individualism.

45. Kevin Y. L. Tan, "Economic Development, Legal Reform, and Rights in Singapore and Taiwan," in *The East Asian Challenge for Human Rights*, ed. Joanne R. Bauer and Daniel A. Bell (Cambridge: Cambridge University Press, 1999), 283.

46. They have a much stronger sense of their ethnicity across borders than that of the nation-state which is arbitrary for them. Here is an injustice issue arising from the nation-state system.

47. There is an international association of Miao. China rejected the attendance of its delegates at one conference held by the association for fear that such trans-national activities may encourage an independence movement by Miao.

48. Liu Suxin, whom I interviewed on 15 January 1996 in Beijing, asserted that the Tibet issue is not an ethnic conflict between Han and Tibet, but rather a conflict between unionists and secessionists. The very concept of ethnic thinking is "selfish." The key issue is the public, which goes beyond ethnicity.

49. John Gray, *Post-liberalism: Studies in Political Thought* (New York: Routledge, 1993), 159–60.

50. The failure of Chinese Marxism has led China into the direction of nationalism and the market to solve the minorities issue.

51. Writing after the fall of the Mongol Yuan dynasty, Fang Xiaoru (Fang Hsiao-ju), a great Confucian scholar, asserted that: "to elevate them [barbarians] to a position above the Chinese people would be to lead the world to animaldom. If a dog or a horse were to occupy a human's seat, even small boys would be angry. . . . why? Because the general order would be confused." Fang insisted on the importance of the distinctions between Chinese and barbarians and that a barbarian should not hold the Chinese throne. See John Fincher, "China as a Race, Culture, and Nation: Notes on Fang Hsiao-ju's Discussion of Dynastic Legitimacy," in *Transition and Permanence: Chinese History and Culture*, ed. David C. Buxbaum and Frederick W. Mote (Hong Kong: Cathay Press, 1972), 59.

52. Hanazaki Kohei, "Ainu Moshir and Yaponesia: Ainu and Okinawan Identities in Contemporary Japan," in *Multicultural Japan: Dalaelithic to Postmodern*, ed. Donald Denoon, *et al.* (Cambridge: Cambridge University Press, 1996), 117–31.

53. See Tessa Morris-Suzuki, *Re-inventing Japan: Time, Space and Nation* (Armonk: M. E. Sharpe, 1998), ch. 9 on citizenship.

54. Such an arrangement has developed between the U.S. and Mexico. See Olivier Kramsch, "Transborder Regional Planning in the Context of Binational Economic Integration: The Case of a New Border Crossing between Mexico and the United States," in *The Americas: World Boundaries*, vol. 4, ed. Pascal O. Girot. (London, Routledge, 1994), 18–46. The preconditions for this kind of development are that neighboring countries do not threaten each other; and that the minority of the borderland does not

seek independence, and thus does not threaten the existence of nation-states. In the case of China, the Chinese state has established a good relationship with Kazakhstan whose President Nazarbayev promised that his government would not support East Turkestan separatists. However, as Dillon observes, "with the increase in cross-border trade, the isolation of Muslims in Xinjiang has come to an end, and close political and religious connections are being forged with Turkic (and Tajik) Muslims throughout Central Asia. This is reinforcing their religious and ethnic identity and their sense of separateness from the Chinese." See Michael Dillon, "Xinjiang: Ethnicity, Separatism and Control in Chinese Central Asia," *Durham East Asian Papers*, no. 1 (Department of East Asian Studies, University of Durham, 1995): 46. The actual and potential separatist movements constitute an obstacle to the development of integrated borderlands.

55. I. Claude, *National Minorities: An International Problem* (Cambridge: Harvard University Press, 1955), 80–81.

56. For a discussion of the liberal element of Confucianism, see William Theodore de Bary, *Liberal Tradition in China* (Hong Kong: Chinese University Press, 1983).

57. See Wm. Theodore de Bary and Tu Wei-ming, ed., *Confucianism and Human Rights* (Columbia University Press, 1999).

58. See Yang Houdi, Wang Ping, and Sui Qing, *Equality, Autonomy and Development*.

59. For an excellent elaboration of communal sources of human rights in China, see David L. Hall and Roger T. Ames, *The Democracy of the Dead: Dewey, Confucius, and the Hope for Democracy in China* (Chicago: Open Court, 1999), ch. 11.

60. It should be acknowledged that one can develop a different comparative model from aspects of the compatibility and reconciliation of Confucianism and liberalism. But that would be a topic for a different essay. Also, the author holds a very skeptical view of the compatibility and reconciliation of Confucianism and liberalism.

61. A. Kent, *Between Substance and Freedom: China and Human Rights* (Hong Kong: Oxford University Press, 1993), 32.

62. Joseph Chan, "A Confucian Perspective on Human Rights for Contemporary China," in *The East Asian Challenge for Human Rights*, ed. Joanne R. Bauer and Daniel A. Bell (Cambridge: Cambridge University Press, 1999), 212–37, in particular, p. 228, and p. 233.

63. Lee Kuan Yew, *Lee Kuan Yew: Selected Essays on Politics Over 40 Years* (Singapore: Federal Publishers, 1993), 567–88.

64. This line of thinking is different from a classic liberal's rejection of Kymlicka's minority rights. For instance, as Chandran Kukathas claims, "the divided nature of cultural communities strengthens the case for not thinking in terms of cultural rights." Take an example in Malaysia: the masses may be more interested in jobs and economic progress whereas the elites, who already enjoy these material benefits, have a greater interest in symbolic traditions. Another example is some individual Aborigines who argue that the land as an economic asset should be bought and sold. From a liberal point of view, cultural groups' wish to live according to the practices of their own cultural communities, as Kukathas asserts, "has to be respected not because a culture has the right to

be preserved but because individuals should be free to associate: to form communities and to live by the terms of those associations. A corollary of this is that the individual should be free to disassociate from such communities." See Chandran Kukathas, "Are There Any Cultural Rights?" in *Political Theory* 20, no. 1 (1992): 105–39, 114, and 116.

65. In his comments on my paper, Kymlicka argues that there is no compelling empirical evidence for this claim and the claim is simply based on prejudice.

66. For a return to duty discourse in the West, see David Selbourne, *The Principle of Duty: An Essay on the Foundations of the Civil Order* (London: Sinclair Stevenson, 1994). The book gives rise to a fear that government will impose moral authority and move away from the idea of reducing inequality, and become more authoritarian in the West.

67. Chua, *Communitarian Ideology*, pp. 140–41.

68. A discussion of Confucian communitarianism, see Wm. Theodore de Bary, *Asian Values and Human Rights: A Confucian Communitarian Perspective* (Cambridge: Harvard University Press, 1998).

69. Kymlicka, *Liberalism*, p. 22.

70. As for Confucian communitarianism, see Chua, *Communitarian Ideology*.

71. Lee Kuan Yew, *Selected Essays*, pp. 567–88.

72. Kymlicka, *Multicultural Citizenship*, p. 7.

73. *Ibid.*, p. 152.

74. See Ji Wenpu, *Wang Chuansan Xueshu Luncong (On Scholarship of Wang Chuansa)* (Beijing: Sanlian Press, 1978), 148. I would like to argue that Wang Fuzhi's position departs from the original doctrine of Confucius and Mencius; and his narrow Confucian communitarianism is not only morally egotistic in nature, but also inappropriate to deal with the relationship between ethnic communities.

75. Tibetan elites may welcome elections which would support their independent cause.

76. It should be acknowledged that Confucianism cannot provide a coherent solution to this problem either.

77. For example, some people in Australia apply for minority benefits through identifying themselves as aboriginal. As a result, the size of the aboriginal community has dramatically increased in recent years.

PART V

SELF: THE NARRATIVE OF THE *Analects*

Finding the Self in the *Analects:* A Philological Approach

14

Yuet Keung Lo

In the past two decades, scholars have made numerous attempts at cracking the Chinese notion of the self.[1] Virtually without exception, all these studies are philosophically oriented,[2] and justifiably so. One may wonder, however, if it may be still fruitful to examine more closely what the Chinese terms for the self are and whether they have always remained the same regardless of time and authorship. On the assumption that the notion of the self is present in the Confucian *Analects* (*Lunyu* 論語), this essay addresses this question of terminology in this small classic primarily from a philological angle. It will explore the notion of the self in this seminal classic strictly on its own terms. We will first identify what possible terms the text employs to describe and discuss the self, and then analyze what these terms actually mean and how they relate to one another. We will rely on the linguistic clues unwittingly revealed in personal pronouns such as wu 吾, *yu* 予 (I/my/me), and *wo* 我 (I/my/me) in the *Analects*. We will also venture beyond the grammatical boundaries into the analytical unraveling of other key terms such as *ji* 己 (self), *gong* 躬 (body/person), and *shen* 身 (body/person). This essay will draw two conclusions. First, the two pronouns *yu* and *wo* in the *Analects* were not quite technical terms that signify the self, even though *wo* was already going through a historical process to become one. Meanwhile, *yu* seemed to have a peculiar reference for Confucius in his self-definition that linked his identity with Heaven. Second, *ji* and *shen* constitute a holistic self in the *Analects*, signifying the inner core and its outer embodiment respectively. The inner core represents the authentic identity of the self whereas the outer embodiment gives full expression to that authenticity.

The Collective Project on Human Being

Indisputably the *Analects* as we have it today represents a composite anthology of accounts of Confucius, his disciples, and some of his contemporaries, compiled over a long stretch of time, most likely by different hands.[3] Nevertheless, in spite of its accretional nature and questionable historicity, the *Analects* presents a coherent account of how a group of early Confucians, revolving

around Confucius himself, acted, behaved, thought, and lived in a loosely organized collection of often disembodied conversations, aphoristic statements,
and explorative queries. Inasmuch as the anthology consists of different layers
of texts, it is possible that the images emerging therefrom of Confucius and
his disciples are products of retrospective construction dictated by historical
and ideological demands.

The *Analects* perhaps can be viewed as a record of collective strivings for self-
fulfillment, independence, and happiness primarily within a small community
of educated scholars who took Confucius as their teacher. The endless process
of collective strivings reveals a deep underlying concern with the problem of
human self-identity, or to put it differently, the problem of human being qua
human and qua being. We can see a concerted, if anxious, effort to define who
we are as persons. Clearly, the anthology makes human expression central to
this relentless pursuit of self-definition.

In the *Analects*, the fundamental question of human identity is seldom
explicitly articulated, but one gets the sense that there was a growing awareness
of human identity in the early Confucian community and a concomitant
eagerness to pinpoint that identity and map out an understanding of it. It is
well known that the early Confucians did not estrange themselves from their
cultural past rooted in the Zhou dynasty (ca. 1050–256 B.C.E.), but there was
not a given lexicon of referents to which they could apply a prescribed formalist
definition of human identity.[4] Instead, we see numerous attempts in the *Analects* to narrow down that elusive identity to some definition. These attempts
are given expression in the rigorous probing of the human psyche and may be
characterized as phenomenological, in that description of a particular virtue
often focuses on the virtuous person's behavior as well as the psychological
and/or intellectual impetus that motivates it.

Let us take humaneness (*ren* 仁) and filial devotion (*xiao* 孝), for example.
They appear to be two basic virtues of human identity, but their meanings seem
to be developing in the *Analects*; they are not fixed. The several definitions of
xiao given to a number of individuals in Book 2 (2.5, 2.6, 2.7, 2.8) seem to vary,
depending on the identity of the questioner and the context of the question,
but it is evident that they are meant to give behavioral instructions in a form
similar to a definition. In other words, a moral being is behaviorally constructed
and phenomenologically mapped out.

Like *ren* and *xiao*, the numerous definitions of a family of other moral terms
in the *Analects* seem to reflect the active discourse and doings of naturally expressive human beings; they are attempted conceptual descriptions of fundamental
experiences in everyday human interactions and communications. Descriptive
and often prescriptive at once, they are meant to inspire people to self-realization, which is dynamic and ever-becoming, not to bring the experiences
themselves to rest under the static categories of analytic understanding.[5] Thus,

when the early Confucians talk about humaneness and filial devotion, the terms they use and the discourse they articulate represent the reflective dimensions of the ceaseless struggle for human self-identity, a dialectical struggle which is both the source and path of Confucian phenomenology. Humaneness and filial devotion, in other words, are defined phenomenologically, not formalistically. The dianoetic analysis of the moral phenomenology can offer us a glimpse of the Confucian self, but for the signifier of the notion of self itself we will have to rely on some linguistic clues.

Linguistic Clues to the Early Confucian Self

Evidently we are not born with a self. Confucius did not quite say that himself but he asserted that "men are by nature similar and become different by practice."[6] While we do not know what prompted him to say this, it seems clear that Confucius was more interested in human nature as a cultural product which may be limited by, but cannot be completely explained in terms of, biological nature. And insofar as human nature is culturally determined, a sense of self born of human nature is inevitably constructed. How would Confucius refer to the idea of self, if he indeed entertained such an idea in the first place? We should remind ourselves that even if Confucius did entertain some notion of self, it does not necessarily mean that he must have articulated it in a precise and definite vocabulary. In fact, it is entirely possible that he did not actually conceptualize it with a well-defined term. For our purpose, let us assume at the onset that Confucius and his disciples did entertain some notion of self and they did formulate and articulate it in language. Our first job, then, is to find out if there are any terms they used in their descriptions and discussions of the self.

Whether or not the early Confucians invented a vocabulary to signify and describe it, the physical boundaries between any one individual and his environment, and everything therein, human or nonhuman, animate or inanimate, must be acknowledged. In the search for Confucian self terminology, our strategy, then, is to focus on the words in the *Analects* that signify the individual himself and/or his personal attributes, which constitute an inclusive sense of his own being. Seven terms seem to meet our criteria: *wu* 吾 (I/my), *yu* 予 (I/my/me), *wo* 我 (I/my/me), *zi* 自 (one's own or oneself, reflexive adverb), *ji* 己 (self), *gong* 躬 (body/person), and *shen* 身 (body/person).[7] The first four are fundamentally grammatical pronouns while the latter three are regular nouns. However, the meanings of the pronouns *yu* and *wo* may very well go beyond their grammatical boundaries and offer some insights into the construction of the early Confucian self.

Of the four pronouns, *wu* and *yu* appear to serve only grammatical functions. As the subject in a clause or a sentence, they function as the self-referring signifier for the speaker,[8] or when used as a possessive pronoun, they serve as the adjectival qualifier for a given possession or quality of the speaker. In these functions, the two terms seem to be interchangeable. As such, they only function in a grammatical capacity and are not imputed with any philosophical meaning.

But *yu* deserves a special note here. It seems clear that by Confucius's time, *yu* had already become a standard term for the first-person pronoun. In one passage in the *Analects*, we learn that regardless of their social stations, people in general refer to themselves by this first-person pronoun,[9] and in another passage, Yang Huo 陽貨 addresses himself by the same pronoun when he speaks to Confucius.[10] Such generality in self-referral suggests that *yu* does not signify the defining personality of the speaker. It is just a grammatical marker. In this specific grammatical function, *yu* appears to be no different from *wu*, both marking the first-person speaker in contrast to the second-person or third-person pronoun.[11] Confucius himself also follows this conventional linguistic practice. For instance, once Confucius asks Zigong 子貢, "Do you think I (*yu*) am someone who is well learned and remembers everything?" When his disciple answers affirmatively, he gives his famous response: "No, I have a single thread to bind them all" (*yu yi yi guan zhi* 予一以貫之).[12] Like three other examples,[13] this one only suggests an awareness of a personal being different from others but does not refer to an unequivocally distinct personal identity of the speaker who is Confucius. It should be noted, however, that the phrase *yu yi ren* 予一人 (I, the lone individual) was in common use prior to Confucius's time and it appears once in the *Analects*.[14] The phrase unmistakably marks off personal boundaries and acknowledges the identity of a person as a unique individual. Apparently, in all its pre-*Analects* occurrences, "the lone individual" always refers to the king as the speaker, and its usage in the *Analects* is no exception. Given that only the Shang and Zhou kings, in the capacity of the Son of Heaven, were entitled to communicate with Heaven on behalf of their subjects, it seems to make sense that the usage of *yu* might connote a sense of Heaven-linked identity, as we will demonstrate shortly.

Apart from conventional practice, the way Confucius uses *yu* also tends to display a vague ring of idiosyncrasy that intimates a sense of self.[15] Let us examine *yu* in greater detail. The graph *yu* appears twenty-seven times in sixteen different passages in the *Analects*. Of these, five occurrences refer to a proper name (Zai Yu 宰予) in two different passages;[16] three reputedly come from King Wu of Zhou 周武王 and the legendary founder, Tang 湯, of the Shang 商 dynasty;[17] and two others are quoted from a popular saying in Confucius's time.[18] Of the remaining seventeen occurrences, *yu* is used as a possessive pronoun in only one passage (two occurrences), and it reportedly comes from the mouth of Zeng Zi 曾子, one of Confucius's youngest disciples.[19] The others supposedly all come from Confucius's own utterances. Virtually all of these utterances show that Confucius is acutely aware of his unique personality and historic, if not cosmic, destiny. A few famous examples will suffice to illustrate this point.

When Confucius is trapped in the state of Song 宋, Huan Tui 桓魋, who is then the Minister of War in Song, attempts to kill him. But Confucius confidently proclaims that he is somehow bestowed with moral power by Heaven (*tian sheng de yu yu* 天生德於予) in order to perpetuate what he calls culture (*wen* 文) in the world; therefore, Huan Tui can do no harm to him.[20] Similarly, when Confucius is besieged in Kuang 匡 on another occasion, he also handles the crisis with equanimity as he declares that as long as Heaven has intended him to be the transmitter of culture, the mob in Kuang cannot hurt him.[21] It is noteworthy that in both circumstances Confucius refers to himself with the pronoun *yu*, in the dative case. These two incidents, so far as the *Analects* is concerned, offer the best evidence of Confucius's own perception of himself as a Heaven-ordained transmitter of culture. He believes he is the person who can inform and reform the present and the future with a cultural past revitalized with his own hands. In this historic sense, he knows he is a unique person. Indeed, his disciples and contemporaries are also aware of his special status.[22]

On still another occasion, Confucius goes to see Nan Zi 南子, the notorious wife of Duke Ling of Wei 衛靈公 and his disciple Zilu 子路 is displeased. Thereupon Confucius swears to Heaven, saying: "If I have done anything improper (*yu suo fou zhe* 予所否者), may Heaven's curse be on me, may Heaven's curse be on me!"[23] In this somewhat unusual emotional outburst, Confucius refers to himself as *yu* in the nominative case. When his beloved disciple Yan Hui 顏回 dies, Confucius is totally devastated and he gives his grief the most powerful expression as he exclaims: "Alas! Heaven has made me bereft (*tian sang yu* 天喪予)! Heaven has made me bereft!"[24] Again, Confucius refers to himself with the first-person pronoun *yu*, in the accusative case. In both cases of spontaneous emotional outbursts, Confucius identifies himself as *yu* and links his inclusive being with Heaven. On yet another occasion, Confucius, evidently in a state of ineffable loneliness, tells his disciple Zigong 子貢: "I am thinking of giving up speech" (*yu yu wu yan* 予欲無言). Then a moment later, he seems to compare himself to Heaven, which, as he explains, also does not speak.[25] He is clearly referring to himself as a distinct person who is denied popular appreciation but continues to maintain his personal integrity vis-à-vis Heaven. It appears that Confucius's self-perception somehow implicates the potency of Heaven and this suggests that his sense of self is personal and cosmic at once.

The first-person pronoun *wo* provides another revealing window on the early Confucian self. The Han-dynasty lexical dictionary *Shuowen jiezi* 説文解字 defines *wo* (I) thus: "by which one addresses oneself when placed among others" (*shi shen zi wei* 施身自謂).[26] It is a term of self-address. It appears forty-five times in the *Analects*, functioning as a pronoun in the first person. In the nominative case, it refers to the speaker himself, while in the genitive case it indicates the relation of possession between a given attribute or effect and the speaker himself. Unlike *wu*, *wo* can also be used in either the accusative or dative case in a sentence.[27] Besides, it can be used as a reflexive pronoun.[28] Most important, *wo* can also be used as an adjective that characterizes one's ego or egotistic thought.[29] As such, *wo* is the most versatile self-referring term in the *Analects*; it can refer to any dimension of the first person, marking its somatic boundaries as well as presenting its psychic existence.[30] Given such semantic versatility, it is no surprise that of the forty-five instances of *wo*, a significant number indicate a clear sense of personal boundary and distinct identity. For instance, Confucius describes himself as someone "who transmits without inventing" and compares himself to the venerable Peng (*qie bi wo yu lao peng* 竊比我於老彭).[31] When a high-ranking official asks one of Confucius's disciples whether Confucius, given his versatile talents, is a sage, he is clearly trying to ascertain the identity of Confucius. Upon hearing about the inquiry, Confucius reportedly comments that the official "probably knows who I am" (*zhi wo hu* 知我乎).[32] Evidently, Confucius knows exactly what the official is talking about—his personal identity. The term *wo*, in this case, clearly indicates that Confucius is aware of himself possessing a personal identity.

When Confucius talks about his personal ambitions, it is common to find him using *wo* in his self-characterization. He says, "I was not born with innate knowledge,"[33] and "it is no challenge to me (*he you yu wo zai* 何有於我哉) to memorize quietly what is knowledge, to learn without losing interest, and to teach without feeling tired."[34] Since he also says, "Wealth and honor without justice are, to me (*yu wo* 於我), nothing more than fleeting clouds,"[35] so he tells Yan Hui, "Only you and I (*wei wo yu er* 唯我與爾) have the ability to practice when employed and to retire when dismissed."[36] And on another occasion, he says, "If a ruler was to employ me (*gou you yong wo zhe* 苟有用我者), in one year things would get done and in three years there would be results."[37] When Yan Hui died and his fellow disciples gave him a lavish burial, Confucius disclaimed his responsibility by saying that "it was not I" (*fei wo ye* 非我也) who made it happen.[38] In other words, he is saying that such reproachable behavior is not me; *wo* here does not simply distinguish Confucius from his disciples grammatically. Similarly, when he wants to assert his own identity through his personal principles, Confucius also uses the term *wo* to separate himself from earlier moral heroes. He says, "I am different from them" (*wo ze yi yu shi* 我則異於是).[39]

As mentioned earlier, Confucius seems to use *yu* in a special way to indicate his self-aware connection with Heaven. As a pronoun, *wo* is also used once by Confucius in referring to himself in connection with Heaven. It may not be coincidental that this unique example is also uttered when Confucius is evidently chagrined by the apparent lack of appreciation of his true worth. And he exclaims, "It is perhaps only Heaven that understands me!" (*zhi wo zhe qi tian hu* 知我者其天乎)[40]

In the *Analects*, Confucius refers to himself nine times by using his personal name Qiu 丘. Occasionally the self-address is meant to be a gesture of courtesy or humility,[41] but in virtually all cases, he is describing his personal character, his moral judgments, or what can be characterized as who he is. He expresses his sense of shame in sympathy with Zuoqiu Ming 左丘明;[42] he confesses his frankness to his disciples;[43] and he avers that he would not attempt to change the world if the Way prevails.[44] Interestingly enough, he apparently even uses this self-address in reference to his prayer.[45] Beyond the obvious implication of humility before Heaven, one may wonder if the choice of personal name in this context might not have anything to do with Confucius's self-aware Heaven-linked identity. If this is indeed the case and we are allowed to generalize from the example of Confucius, there may be some sort of affinity between personal names and the personal pronoun *wo* in their common connection to the notion of the self.

With *wo* marking the physical boundaries of a person as well as the qualities that define his personal integrity, it seems natural that the term also takes on a psychic dimension. In the *Analects*, there is one mention of *wo* that refers to a person's psychic attributes, and it comes from Confucius when he advises that we avoid four things: second-guessing, dogmatism, obstinacy, and egotism (*wo*).[46] It is notable that Confucius is talking about four different kinds of psychic propensities. The ascription of psychic characteristics to *wo* in addition to its grammatical referentiality, in our analysis, makes it a relatively self-contained term that signifies a concept of selfhood; it demarcates personal boundaries and marks individual identity. So when Confucius declares that humaneness is not far away and it is within reach as long as I have a desire for it (*wo yu ren* 我欲仁),[47] he might be referring to himself in contradistinction to others but it is more likely that he is actually referring to *any* individual self and emphasizing it as an autonomous willing subject.

The last grammatical term we need to examine is *zi*. The graph *zi* was in use as early as the oracle bone inscriptions, where it means "from (a point of reference)" in all instances.[48] It occurs twenty-one times in seventeen passages in the *Analects*, and it is used in two different ways, with virtually equal frequency. As a preposition (eleven times), it indicates directionality and means "from a particular point of reference (which can be location, time, or agent of action)."[49] This function of *zi* is identical to its use in the oracle bone inscriptions. But in the *Analects*, *zi* can also function as a reflexive pronoun (ten times). As such, it indicates that the subject is both the agent and the recipient of its own action.[50] One could well postulate that *zi* indicates the orientation or direction of action and/or contemplation toward the subject, but it seems far-fetched to argue that such self-referentiality reflected in grammatical capacity actually betrays the Confucian awareness of a distinct personal entity that stands in contrast with people other than oneself. Even if it does, such awareness may only be grammatically implied rather than consciously philosophized. In other words, *zi*, like *wu*, is not a term with philosophical import in the *Analects*.[51]

Beyond Grammatical Boundaries:
The Early Confucian Notions of Body and Self

In the *Analects*, there are only a few terms that may signify the human person as a distinct entity, physically, psychically, or morally, but the most notable are *shen*, *gong*, and *ji*. The graph *shen* was already in use in the oracle bone inscriptions; it limns the side view of a human figure with a protruding belly, and it means "to be pregnant."[52] But there is another graph *yun* 孕 that means the same in the oracle bone inscriptions. Perhaps for this reason, *shen* began to take on the additional meaning of "the body of a human being" or "person" in time. In the *Analects*, however, *shen* is not used exclusively in this physical sense in its seventeen occurrences.[53] The human body carries a clear moral connotation. The sense of physical body is expressed with the term *ti* 體 instead.[54] This, of course, does not mean that the connotation of corporeality is completely irrelevant in the notion of *shen*.

According to the *Analects*, *shen* can be killed (*sha* 殺) in order to fulfill humaneness;[55] it can be offered (*zhi* 致) for the service of one's ruler;[56] it can be forgotten (*wang* 忘) in a fit of anger;[57] it is also the medium through which one does good or evil deeds;[58] it can be humiliated (*ru* 辱);[59] it can be examined (*xing* 省) for self-reflection;[60] it can be rectified (*zheng* 正) as a moral example;[61] it can be purified (*jie* 絜) and resists defilement.[62] It is clear from these descriptions that *shen* refers to the person of an individual which normally follows the conscious conduct of its owner. It is the agent of good deeds and recipient of self-inflicted humiliation. Only when one loses control such as in a fit of anger will one become careless with it. No doubt *shen* marks the individual person as a moral being with clearly demarcated boundaries; it is a personal domain over which one should keep constant guard. It is both physical and nonphysical; the nonphysical is expressed through the physical whereas the physical defines the nonphysical. This is one reason the Confucians are so keenly concerned with rituals, because rituals can regulate our personal expressions of what or who we are in our core of being. Once our person is properly regulated (*qi shen zheng* 其身正), people will be inspired to follow our example.[63]

Self-expression and personal appearance are important even when we are alone. Book 10 of the *Analects* draws a vivid and colorful picture of Confucius in his everyday life, and much of it is about his behavior in private. Consistently, we see Confucius unifying the physical and nonphysical, countenance and psychic states, form and substance. There is a close interrelation between the inner core and the outer form; we can almost experience the uncanny power of each to change the other. The human person is both the field of self-realization and the realization itself. As we recall, in the *Shuowen jiezi* definition of *wo*, *shen* marks the physical and symbolic boundaries that distinguish one individual from others. If we read this definition of *wo* retroactively into the notion of *shen* in the *Analects*, we may just find the perfect name for it. The inner core and the outer form that together form a person constitute the identity that is called I (*wo*).

Unlike *shen*, the graph *gong* does not appear in the oracle bone inscriptions or bronze inscriptions. It, however, is listed in the *Shuowen jiezi*, which defines it as "body" (*shen ye* 身也), and it does not attempt to differentiate it from *shen*. In the dictionary, 躬 is given as the original form of the graph while 躬 is appended as a popular form. In the original form, 呂 (*lü*) on the right depicts the spine of a human being while 身 on the left indicates the corporeal form itself. Both constituents of the original form, according to the *Shuowen*, are considered to be semantically significant, and since the composite graph is listed under 呂 in the dictionary, the point may be made that 呂 is the determinative element or focal point in this graph.

The popular form 躬 is the one that is found in the *Analects*. There, it occurs nine times in seven passages.[64] Of these, seven occurrences are as a noun[65] and two as an adverb.[66] As a noun, *gong* appears to be synonymous with its relative *shen*, and it unmistakably denotes the person of an individual, rather than a mere physical body. As such, *gong* is perceived as the physical agent of moral behavior—it is the body (hinging, as if were, on the spine) that bows in accordance with rituals;[67] it is the agent that is held accountable for moral actions.[68] The constitutive meaning of "spine" in *gong* suggests the strength of character. In a sense, a spineless person cannot be characterized as having a *gong*. Hence, Confucius regards a "straight body" (*zhigong* 直躬) highly, even though what can be considered as such is not beyond dispute.[69] The adverbial use of *gong* seems to build on its basic function as a noun. In its two occurrences, the adverbial *gong* functions much like the reflexive pronoun *zi* but it emphasizes the physical execution of actions such as planting crops[70] or the embodiment of moral actions in the person.[71] Such a person is called a *junzi* 君子 (gentleman).

The graph *ji* appears as early as in the oracle bone inscriptions. It is a pictograph that depicts a string or rope of some sort which is used for binding or bundling things together.[72] As a component in a number of graphs in the oracle bone inscriptions, *ji* adds the notion of restraint to the resultant meaning of the composite graphs. We shall see that this root meaning of *ji* turns out to be a key in unpacking a hidden connotation of *ji* as self in the *Analects*. The graph *ji* appears twenty-five times in the *Analects*. Its usage demonstrates beyond doubt that it must mean something like self, and in some cases, it is used as a general term of self-address in the accusative case that refers to the speaker himself.[73] As such, it is the counterpart of the first-person pronoun *yu* that stands, in grammatical terms, for an individual in the nominative. While *shen* carries a strong sense of corporeality, *ji* seems to be completely nonphysical.

In the *Analects*, whatever happens to *shen*, it is always its owner that creates the change; *shen* apparently is not susceptible to manipulation by others. In contrast, *ji* is a lot more versatile. The agent that creates a change in *ji* can be the subject himself or other people. As far as the subject himself is concerned, *ji* can be conducted (*xing* 行);[74] it can be purified (*jie* 絜);[75] it can be restrained (*ke* 克);[76] it can be followed (*you* 由);[77] it can be cultivated (*xiu* 修);[78] and it can be made to be respectful (*gong* 恭).[79] With the exception of *jieji* (purifying the self), the various purposes for the change created in *ji* indicate that *ji* as self is not tangible like *shen*. *Jieji* is an exception because, as we have seen, *shen* can also be purified (*jieshen*). In the case of *jieshen*, it is clear that the subject, a hermit who has withdrawn from society and its attendant ritual order, wants to keep his person unsullied (18.7). On the other hand, the young boy from Hu 互 village who wants to seek audience with Confucius purifies himself before the meeting. Of course, the attempt, in the former case, to protect one's person from defilement must come from an inner core that has been purified. Similarly, the purified inner core, in the latter case, most likely would lead to the purification of the person as well (7.29).[80] In both cases, the ultimate trigger that motivates the subject to resist defilement or present himself in a dignified and respectful manner comes from the inner core that defines what the subject authentically is.[81]

Nevertheless, there is a remarkable emphasis on a different dimension in each case, as reflected by the choice of the differentiating term. The hermit insists that his inner core cannot be compromised and he is concerned about keeping his person unsullied. On the other hand, the young boy from a village notorious for its recalcitrancy to teaching impresses Confucius most probably because of his purified spirit, even though his tidy person must have embodied and manifested the purified inner self. It may be fair, then, to say that *ji* signifies the inner psychic self that makes the decisions that define what and who we are, and the endless process of decision-making ultimately constitutes our personal identity, while *shen* performs all the self-defining decisions from the inner self and ultimately embodies the inner self and gives it a personal, bodily expression. But self and person form an organic holism; the inner-outer dichotomy is a heuristic one that can only fool the purely analytical mind.

One might argue that *ji* is not entirely restricted to the inner core. Once, when Yan Hui asked about humaneness, Confucius recommended "returning to the observance of ritual by overcoming one's self" (*keji fuli* 克己復禮). And when the disciple inquired about the details, Confucius enumerated the following steps: don't look at what violates the proprieties; don't listen to what violates the proprieties; don't say anything that violates the proprieties; and don't act in anyway that violates the proprieties (12.1). True, looking, listening, talking, and moving your body (*dong* 動) are all physical activities. However, it is far from clear that *ji* would mean all these bodily movements or the body itself. Evidently, "overcoming the self" in this context would mean taking control of the inner self that ultimately determines how and what one might choose to look at, listen to, say, or act.[82] As will be demonstrated, *ji* indeed controls how and what we desire and will to do.

If our analysis of self and person is tenable, a question may arise as to which of the two is actually considered in the *Analects* to be the self stamped with personal identity. It should be noted that inasmuch as the person (*shen* 身 or *gong* 躬) is a manifested self, it has personal meaning and significance only to its owner. To others, it is just a physical body (*ti* 體). Though the idea of sacred body is not explicitly articulated in the *Analects*, it is well known from the *Xiaojing* 孝 經 (Classic of Filial Devotion) that the body (*shenti* 身體) we inherit from our parents is sacred and therefore cannot be violated or compromised in any way. In this famous dictum, the body is sacred only to its owner, so it is the owner's moral responsibility to protect it. Strictly speaking, it is the person (*shen*) that is the key concern in this dictum and the body as the material constitution of the person evidently is a later addendum; hence we have the new compound term *shenti*. As we have seen in the *Analects*, only the subjects of *shen* can create a change to their person, and that is certainly consistent with the *Xiaojing* formulation. On the other hand, *ji* as self in the *Analects* is open to outside influence and vulnerable to external impact. It can be treated harshly (*li* 厲); it can be slandered (*bang* 謗);[83] and finally, it can be understood or appreciated (*zhi* 知).[84] All of these external impacts aim at an individual's psychic life, and therefore they can be imposed on or related to his person. Thus it seems that when someone is keen on impugning our integrity, his primary interest would be, as the *Analects* informs, in our inner self (*ji*), not our person. In other words, *ji* stands for who we are.

Of all the possible external impacts on our inner self mentioned in the *Analects*, the Confucians put a particular premium on personal appreciation; they dwell on the idea of *zhiji* 知己 (having someone understand who you are) almost obsessively. The famous opening of the *Analects* advises us, through the mouth of Confucius, not to take offense when someone fails to appreciate our worth.[85] This peculiar Confucian obsession with personal appreciation suggests that our personal identity and true self and everything that is authentically us are all sublimated into a curious word *ji*. As such, *ji* stakes a personal universe of self-worth that stands in contrast with everybody else's. In this crucial connection, we may recall that when personal appreciation is in question, *wo*, the identity couched in a first-person pronoun is at stake (9.6, 14.35). The convergence of the first-person pronoun *wo* and the regular noun *ji* on the elusive definition of self seems evident.

Metaphorically, *ji* is formed around personal boundaries much like *shen*. In the *Analects*, the term *ji* is often used in contrast with *ren* 人 (people, or other)[86] or sometimes more specifically with *you* 友 (friends).[87] In contrast, *shen* is never juxtaposed with any term that refers to a human subject other than oneself.[88] Moreover, although both *shen* and *ji* can represent, linguistically, a freestanding object in the *Analects*, only *ji* is used when self-identity is in question. For instance, the gentleman would not befriend someone who cannot compare to himself (*wuyou buru ji zhe* 無友不如己者);[89] and in the old days people studied for their own good (*weiji* 為己).[90] The implication is clear: if I want to tell people who I am, I will tell them about my *ji*, not my *shen*.

If *ji* is indeed the personal self in the *Analects*, the text tells us very little about its intrinsic nature. All we know is that *ji* as self has the power to desire (*yü* 欲) or perhaps to will (*zhi* 志).[91] While it may be true that *yü* "seems to serve as the most common, generic term for indicating one's reference," as Fingarette has observed,[92] it should be noted that in the three occurrences of *yü* in conjunction with *ji*, what is being desired is almost always morally positive.[93] In fact, it is no simple desire; it is the desire to fulfill one's ultimate virtue, humaneness. We are told, for example, in the golden rule not to impose on others what we ourselves do not desire (*ji suo bu yü* 己所不欲). It is a rule that we can observe throughout our entire life.[94] By virtue of this power to desire, the gentleman seeks what he desires within himself (*qiu zhu ji* 求諸己),[95] and he takes the realization of humaneness to be an impelling mission on himself (*ren yiwei ji ren* 仁以為己任).[96] Similarly, our will is often perceived as the signature of our self, and in the *Analects*, whatever it wills is almost invariably morally positive.[97] Both *yü* and *zhi* imply that *ji* is self-motivated toward ends, and it may freely choose and be capable of some forms of "knowledge" (*zhi* 知) such as knowledge of the selves of others,[98] knowledge of words of others (*zhiyan* 知言)[99] and knowledge of the mandate of Heaven,[100] through "participation" in the actual conduct it wills or dictates. Such participation in effect embodies *ji* in *shen*, rendering the latter not merely physical. It is clear that whatever we desire or will to achieve or fulfill, we seek it in our self (*ji*), not in our person. As Confucius says, our desires come from our heart.[101]

Evidently the self controls how we turn out to be a unique individual. It is like a commander that guides our desires, our behavior, and our person. We may recall that in the oracle bone inscriptions *ji* is a pictograph that depicts a string or cord that can provide restraint. One cannot help but wonder if this original meaning of *ji* might not have contributed to the evolved meaning of *ji* as self.[102] Isn't it possible that the eponymous self, working as a thread just like its ancestor in the oracle bone inscriptions, ultimately controls, as it were, the directions, movements, and actual conduct of the person? Some of the verbs used in conjunction with *ji* reveal that *ji* as self can indeed be manipulated or controlled so that the self will behave in such a way as to achieve a desired purpose. For example, in *jieji* 絜己 and *zongji* 總己 (literally, tie the self together),[103] the verbs are ostensibly constructed with a semantic component that means "refined silk thread." According to the *Shuowen jiezi*, *jie* denotes "a bundle of hemp but it also takes on the connotative meaning of "to set a template, "to provide restraint, and "to purify while *zong* means "to assemble and tie together." Even for the other verbs that are not etymologically related to the root meaning of thread, we can still see how it can shape our understanding of some of them. Let us take the famous example of *keji fuli wei ren* 克己復禮

為仁. This sentence literally means "to overcome (*ke*) one's self and return to the observance of rituals constitutes humaneness." Although the verb *ke* is not etymologically related to the root meaning of "thread," early commentators on the *Analects* unanimously gloss it as *yue* 約 (to restrain), a verb that is indeed linked to it.[104] It is perhaps no coincidence that the *Analects* often recommends self-control in the form of restraint through rituals.[105]

In light of our foregoing discussion, it may be fruitful to imagine the thread which symbolizes the self as the string (*ji*) that is tied to a puppet. A master puppeteer is someone who by conducting the thread (*xingji* 行己) can manipulate a puppet such that it aspires to become a human being. Perfect manipulation comes from the restraint applied to the thread; no movements will be amiss (*yi yue shi zhi zhe xian yi* 以約失之鮮矣).[106] In this sense, humaneness is indeed dependent upon one's thread (*wei ren you ji* 為仁由己), and certainly not upon anybody else's. If we want to know and learn to appreciate how a puppet works, we should look at the thread. And if we want to maneuver a puppet or bring about an impact on it, the best way is to aim at the thread. In fact, it is this unique thread of each individual puppet that distinguishes it from others. In the end, the Confucians recommend us to follow the example of people in the old days, to study for the sake of their own "thread" (*weiji* 為己). The thread enlivens a puppet and defines what it is. Without the skills of manipulating the thread, the puppet will be paralyzed.

Concluding Remarks

Our mapping of personal pronouns in the *Analects* reveals that a cluster of first-person pronouns is used in overlapping and sometimes confusing ways. Since the anthology is a product of many hands over a long period of time, it is not clear how much linguistic homogenization went into the text, if that process actually took place. It is therefore hard to ascertain whether the use of different pronouns actually reflects the possible different regional backgrounds of the compilers or they simply represent a quiet evolution toward a taxonomy of pronouns with greater conceptual precision. As has been noted, many moral concepts were still quite unstable in the *Analects*; they were going through a process of conjunctural definition between Confucius and his disciples and successors. It is not entirely impossible that the search for conceptual precision in linguistic terms and the struggle to pin down the elusive moral concepts were parallel phenomena in the *Analects*, and they converged in the common pursuit of a conscious definition of the self. Just as the regular noun *ji* began to take on the functions of personal pronouns, the first-person pronoun *wo* had acquired the new denotation of egotism. In this unusual historical confluence, we see the term *ji* emerging as the candidate for the inner self. The range of its semantic meanings no doubt recommends it as such, but its ability in doubling as pronouns is noteworthy. Similarly, the first-pronoun *wo* can serve in virtually all pronominal roles. Its newly acquired meaning of psychic dimension makes it versatile enough to become a signifier for the self. While the Confucian notion of self is not given an independent name in the *Analects* to indicate that it is an organic whole integrating the inner core and the outer form, never limited to its physical, visible constituent within time and space, it might in fact call for one, and by all indications, *wo*, the personal pronoun cum adjective of psychology would seem to be the best candidate. From the vantage point of historical hindsight, we know that *wo* was indeed adopted to translate the Buddhist concept of *atman* (self) in post-Buddhist China.

Notes

1. Some of the earlier attempts can be found in a special issue of *The Monist* on "Conceptions of the Self: East & West," vol. 61, no. 1 (January 1978) and Herbert Fingarette, "The Problem of the Self in the *Analects*," *Philosophy East and West* 29, no. 2 (April 1979): 129–40 (reprinted in this volume as chapter 16). More recent studies include most notably David L. Hall and Roger T. Ames, *Thinking from the Han: Self, Truth, and Transcendence in Chinese and Western Culture* (Albany: SUNY Press, 1998) and Thomas P. Kasulis edited with Roger T. Ames and Wimal Dissanayake, *Self as Body in Asian Theory and Practice* (Albany: SUNY Press, 1993). The collective effort to explore the Chinese self in literary writings can be found in Robert E. Hegel and Richard C. Hessney, *Expressions of the Self in Chinese Literature* (New York: Columbia University Press, 1985).

2. Fingarette's essay makes some efforts in combining a philosophical analysis with philological explication of some key terms that he has identified as relevant to the notion of self.

3. The most formidable advocacy for this position can be found in E. Bruce Brooks and A. Taeko Brooks, *The Original Analects: Sayings of Confucius and His Successors* (New York: Columbia University Press, 1998). The view that the *Analects* is a book consisting of discrete strata was proposed at least since the Tang dynasty (618–906). See John Makeham, "The Formation of *Lunyu* as a Book," *Monumenta Serica* 44 (1996), esp. 6ff.

4. Even if there were existing conceptual terms for loan, Confucius would tend to redefine and transvaluate them. A case in point is the fundamental concept of *ren* 仁 (humaneness). Prior to Confucius's time, the term referred to the manly bearing of a hero rather than a moral concept of universal significance. See Lin Yü-sheng, "The Evolution of the Pre-Confucian Meaning of *Jen* and the Confucian Concept of Moral Autonomy," *Monumenta Serica* 31 (1974-75).

5. *Analects* 2.7. Confucius is evidently interested in the essential reverential attitude that defines filial devotion, rather than the mere show of food offering. The citations from the *Analects* in this essay are based on *A Concordance to the Lunyu* (The ICS Ancient Chinese Texts Concordance Series, Classical Works No. 14), ed. D. C. Lau and Chen

Fong Ching (Hong Kong: The Commercial Press, 1995). Translations are the author's own.

6. *Analects* 17.2.

7. The term *qie* 竊 is also used once in the *Analects* to refer to the speaker himself in a humble manner and it does not seem to have any philosophical significance. See *Analects* 7.1. *Yu* 余 appears in the oracle bone inscriptions and it is used as a first-person pronoun. See Li Xiaoding, 李孝定, *Jiagu wenzi jishi* 甲骨文字集釋 8 vols., 2nd ed. (Taibei: Academia Sinica, 1970), 2:277–79. However, *yu* is not used in the *Analects*, in fact, it appears very infrequently in most pre-Qin texts. For instance, it appears only once in the *Shijing* 詩經 and the *Mengzi* 孟子. The *Zuozhuan* 左傳 and *Guoyu* 國語 seem to be two exceptional texts in this regard.

8. *Yu* appears only once in the oracle bone inscriptions, where it seems to be used as a first-person pronoun. See Li Xiaoding, *Jiagu wenzi jishi*, 4:1437.

9. *Analects* 13.15 (two occurrences). Cf. *Zhongyong* 中庸: Everybody claims they are wise (literally, I am wise) 人皆曰予知.

10. *Analects* 17.1.

11. For the use of *wu* as first-person nominal pronoun, see, for instance, *Analects* 3.9, 5.9, 11.23, 16.11, 17.8.

12. *Analects* 15.3.

13. *Analects* 3.8, 9.12, and 11.11.

14. *Analects* 20.1. The phrase *yu-yi-ren* was commonly used in Shang and Zhou times; it appears frequently in the *Shangshu* 尚書 (Book of Documents).

15. It is possible that Confucius's contemporaries also used *yu* in a similar way but the *Analects*, being a record of the conversations mostly between Confucius and his disciples, leaves us no such evidence.

16. *Analects* 5.10 and 17.21.

17. *Analects* 8.20 and 20.1.

18. *Analects* 13.15.

19. See *Analects* 8.3.

20. *Analects* 7.23.

21. *Analects* 9.5.

22. The official in charge of the border at Yi 儀 commented that Heaven was going to use Confucius as the wooden tongue for a bell (*Analects* 3.24) and Confucius's disciple Zigong told people that Heaven had sent his master on the path to sagehood (*Analects* 9.6).

23. *Analects* 6.28

24. *Analects* 11.9.

25. *Analects* 17.19.

26. *Wo* appears in the oracle bone inscriptions; its original graph seems to depict a weapon of some sort, but in the oracle bone inscriptions *wo* is always used a first-person pronoun. See Li Xiaoding, *Jiagu wenzi jishi*, 12:3797-99.

27. The pronoun *wu* can also function in all four cases—nominative, accusative, genitive, and dative, even though it appears only twice in the accusative case in one single

passage in the *Analects*, and in both occurrences, it is used in inversion for the express purpose of emphasis. In other words, the use of *wu* in the accusative case seems to be somewhat unusual. See *Analects* 11.26. Further, *wu* and *wo* often appear in tandem. In such cases, *wu* is invariably used in the nominative case and *wo*, without exception, either in the accusative or the dative case. Based on his investigation of early texts prior to the first century B.C.E., Wang Li 王力 concludes that *wu* can be used in the nominal case and the genitive case while *wo* can be used in the nominative case and the objective (accusative and dative) case. Never can *wu* be used in the objective case following the verb in the sentence. See his *Hanyu shi gao* 漢語史稿, new ed. (Beijing: Zhonghua, 1980), 260.

    28. *Analects* 7.1.

    29. *Analects* 9.4.

    30. In the notorious dialogue (17.21) between Confucius and his disciple Zai Yu who refused to observe the three-year mourning ritual, we can see that Confucius acknowledged a psychological existence in ourselves. The only concern he expressed is whether Zai Yu could feel at ease without observing the conventional ritual. When Zai Yu answered affirmatively, Confucius concluded that he was not humane (*buren* 不仁). On another occasion, Confucius claimed that as long as "I" (*wo*) wish for humaneness, humaneness is within at hand (7.30). Evidently it is Zai Yu's self that did not want to be humane.

    31. *Analects* 7.1.

    32. *Analects* 9.6.

    33. *Analects* 7.20.

    34. *Analects* 7.2. Confucius defined other dimensions of his personality in a similar way (namely, using the term *wo*) in *Analects* 9.16.

    35. *Analects* 7.16.

    36. *Analects* 7.11.

    37. *Analects* 13.10. In another context, Confucius, in looking for the right ruler to offer his political advice, compared himself to a pearl seller who was waiting for the right offer to sell his goods, and he said, "I am someone who is waiting for the right offer" (*wo dai gu zhe ye* 我待賈者也). *Analects* 9.13.

    38. *Analects* 11.11.

    39. *Analects* 18.8.

    40. *Analects* 14.35.

    41. *Analects* 7.31 and 10.16.

    42. *Analects* 5.24 and 11.25.

    43. *Analects* 7.24.

    44. *Analects* 18.6.

    45. *Analects* 7.35. According to this passage ("Qiu has been praying all along," *Qiu-zhi-dao-jiu-yi* 丘之禱久矣), Confucius might or might not refer to himself by his personal name when he prayed, but in 6.28, he evidently referred to himself by using the first-person pronoun *yu* 予 in his prayer.

    46. Literally, not to be egotistical. *Analects* 9.4.

47. *Analects* 7.30. In another context, Confucius asked rhetorically, "Is it one's own effort (*ji* 己) or somebody else's that realizes humaneness?" See *Analects* 12.1. So it seems certain that *wo* in *Analects* 7.30 also refers to the individual self.

48. Li Xiaoding, *Jiagu wenzi jishi*, 4:1207–1208. Even though the graph originally depicts a human nose but we have yet to find any textual evidence to prove its actual usage in this sense.

49. *Analects* 1.1, 3.10, 6.10, 9.15, 12.7, 14.38, and 16.2.

50. *Analects* 4.17, 7.7, 12.23, 14.17, 14.28, 15.15, 16.14, 19.17, and 19.24.

51. Livia Kohn recently has argued that *zi* refers to a self that is "a spontaneous, independent organism" in contrast to *ji* (self) and *shen* (body), which she interprets as "an object-oriented, organized self," but she does not offer any valid textual evidence. While *zi* in unusual contexts can function as a noun which means "beginning" (but Kohn apparently is not aware of this), it never means "self" in any native Chinese text we know of today. See Kohn, "Selfhood and Spontaneity in Ancient Chinese Thought" in *Selves, People, and Persons: What Does It Mean to Be a Self?*, ed. Leroy S. Rouner (Notre Dame, Ind.: University of Notre Dame Press, 1992), 123–38.

52. Li Xiaoding, *Jiagu wenzi jishi*, 6:2719-2720.

53. According to Wang Yinzhi 王引之 (fl. eighteenth century), *shen* refers to the human torso (below the neck and above the hip) and in *Analects* 10.6, *shen* is used in this sense but only metaphorically as a reference for length. Cited in D.C. Lau and Chen Fong Ching, *A Concordance to the Lunyu*, 24.

54. The term *ti* appears only once in the *Analects* (18.7), where it reads *si-ti bu qin* 四體不勤 (literally, the four limbs are not toiled). Thus *ti* in this context does not actually refer to the body itself, though it is certainly used as a metonym for the body.

55. *Analects* 15.9.

56. *Analects* 1.7.

57. *Analects* 12.21.

58. *Analects* 17.7.

59. *Analects* 18.8. In contrast with *rushen* 辱身 (humiliate one's person), the text says *jiangzhi* 降志 (literally, lower one's purpose), so it seems clear that *shen* has the connotation of corporeality as opposed to *zhi*, which is psychological.

60. *Analects* 1.4.

61. *Analects* 13.6, 13.13.

62. *Analects* 18.7, 4.6.

63. *Analects* 13.6.

64. *Analects* 4.22, 7.33, 10.4, 13.18, 14.5, 15.15, and 20.1 (three occurrences). It is certain that 20.1 belongs to a layer of later date.

65. *Analects* 4.22, 10.4, 13.18, 15.15, 20.1 (three occurrences).

66. *Analects* 7.33, 14.5.

67. *Analects* 10.4.

68. *Analects* 4.22, 20.1.

69. *Analects* 13.18.

70. *Analects* 14.5.

71. *Analects* 7.33.

72. Li Xiaoding, *Jiagu wenzi jishi*, 8:4261–4264.

73. *Analects* 1.8, 1.16, 4.14, 9.25, 12.1, 14.39, 14.40, 15.19.

74. *Analects* 5.16.

75. *Analects* 7.29.

76. *Analects* 12.1. My reading of *ke* follows the early commentators on the *Analects*. See n. 104.

77. *Analects* 12.1.

78. *Analects* 14.42. Interestingly, the well-known Confucian term, if not the concept, *xiushen* 修身 (cultivation of the person) is absent in the *Analects*. It should be noted that the term *xiu* originally means "ritual cleansing of the human body," and as such, the ritual was meant to cleanse both the physical body and the mind. For an excellent discussion of the genealogy of the meaning of the term *xiu*, see Zang Kehe 臧克和, *Shuowen jiezi de wenhua shuojie* 説文解字的文化説解 (Wuhan: Hubei renmin chubanshe, 1995),114–25. That the *Analects* only talks about *xiuji* 修己 is, therefore, not surprising. And when later Confucian texts promoted the idea of *xiushen*, it should be clear that *shen* in this context does not mean so much the physical body itself as the human person that is both the field and consummation of moral cultivation. It should be also pointed out that the presence of the terms *xiu* and *jie* 絜 in the *Analects* was no coincidence; both terms refer to a process of purification and cultivation that integrates the inner self and its outer embodiment. The dual usage (for the physical body and for the inner self) of the two terms substantiates our claim about the inner-outer division of *ji* and *shen* as well as their forming a holistic unity.

79. *Analects* 15.5.

80. In *Mencius* 2B.11, we learn that while Mencius was about to leave the state of Qi, someone wished to persuade him to stay on behalf of the king. Before he sought audience with Mencius, he observed a day's fast. And when he finally met Mencius, he "sat upright and conducted himself courteously." However, Mencius paid him no attention and did not even make a reply. And he even leaned on a couch. Understandably, the visitor was offended and complained to Mencius. In this incident, it is clear that the visitor purified himself prior to the meeting with Mencius, and at the meeting he conducted his person properly to show his respect to Mencius. A two-step process of purification of the person and the self is evident.

81. According to the *Shuowen jiezi*, *jie* means "a bundle of hemp" (*ma-yi-duan* 麻一耑), and Duan Yucai's 段玉裁 (1735–1815) commentary, the standard reference on the Han-dynasty lexical dictionary, elaborates on this terse definition as follows: when bundling hemp, both ends must be even (*qi-qi-shou* 齊其首) so that they will be tidy and neat without loose threads, and from the idea of evenness comes the notion of "template" (*weidu* 圛度), which further gives rise to the derivative meaning of "cleanliness" (*jiejing* 潔淨). See *Shuowen jiezi zhu* 説文解字注, 4th ed. (Taibei: Lantai shuju, 1974), 668. Thus, our philosophical interpretation of *jieshen* as being an inner-outer continuum can be fully justified on philological grounds.

82. It is interesting to note that the Ming Neo-Confucian Wang Yangming 王陽

明 (1472–1529) had explicitly discussed *Analects* 12.1 with his disciple and he came to the same conclusion as ours. While Wang acknowledged that the "four don'ts" of "overcoming the self" pertained to the physical body, he said, "But if we want to cultivate the bodily person (*shen*), how can we do so by applying the effort to the body? The mind is the master of the body. Although the eye sees, what makes it see is the mind. Although the ear hears, what makes it hear is the mind. Although the mouth and the four limbs speak and move, what makes them speak and move is the mind. Therefore to cultivate the bodily person lies in the realizing through personal experience the true substance of one's mind and always making it broad and extremely impartial without the slightest incorrectness." See Wang Yangming, *Chuanxi lu* 傳習錄 (Instructions for Practical Living). My translation is modified from Wing-tsit Chan translated with notes, *Instructions for Practical Living and Other Neo-Confucian Writings by Wang Yang-ming* (New York: Columbia University Press, no date), 247. It should be noted that in his discussion Wang Yangming was referring the passage in question to the *Daxue* 大學 (Great Learning) but it actually comes from *Analects* 12.1.

83. *Analects* 19.10.

84. *Analects* 1.16, 4.14, 14.39, 15.19. The self can be observed too, if only through its personal manifestations. In *Analects* 2.10, even though the term *ji* is not used in the passage, but it is clear that what is being observed and examined is the inner self.

85. *Analects* 1.1.

86. *Analects* 14.24, 14.42, 14.30 (1.16), 6.30, 15.19.

87. *Analects* 1.8, 9.25.

88. It should be noted that *gong* is used in contrast with *ren* once. See *Analects* 15.15.

89. *Analects* 1.8, 9.25.

90. *Analects* 14.24.

91. Herbert Fingarette has done a perceptive analysis of the idea of *zhi* 志 (will) in the *Analects*, see his "The Problem of the Self in the *Analects*," pp. 129–40.

92. Fingarette, "The Problem of the Self in the *Analects*," p. 132.

93. *Analects* 6.30 (two occurrences) and 12.2. One may argue that the Confucian golden rule stated in 12.2 is neutral rather than positive in a moral sense.

94. *Analects* 12.2 and 15.24.

95. *Analects* 15.21.

96. *Analects* 8.7.

97. *Analects* 1.11, 2.4, 4.4, 4.9, 4.18, 5.26, 16.11, 18.8, 19.6.

98. *Analects* 1.16.

99. *Analects* 20.3.

100. *Analects* 2.4.

101. *Analects* 2.4.

102. It is of course entirely possible that the evolution of the root meaning of *ji* into self represents a phonetic loan rather than a connotative transformation, just like the case with *wo* (from weapon to self).

103. *Analects* 14.40.

104. For instance, Ma Rong 馬融 (79–166) interprets *keji* to mean "*yueshen*" 約身 (to restrain the person) and Huang Kan 皇侃 (488–545) glosses *ke* as *yue*. See Huang Kan, *Lunyu jijie yishu* 論語集解義疏, 2 vols. (Taibei: Guangwen, 1968), vol. 2, *juan* 6, 21b–22a. For a study of commentaries on this particular passage in the *Analects*, see John Kieschnick, "*Analects* 12.1 and the Commentarial Tradition," *Journal of American Oriental Society* 112, no. 4 (1992): 567–76.

105. *Analects* 6.27 (12.15), 9.11.

106. *Analects* 4.23.

Autonomy in the *Analects*

15

Kim-chong Chong

Introduction

The term "autonomy" means "self-rule," "self-government," "self-directedness," being widely used in different contexts. Thus, we have "political autonomy," meaning the independence of a political unit or entity. On the other hand, "personal autonomy" is used to refer to the individual's ability and freedom to realize projects that are important to his or her own identity. It is sometimes distinguished from "moral autonomy," often identified with Kant, which refers to the agent's exercise of his or her rational will to make universal moral laws. In this essay, although I shall be talking about personal autonomy as distinct from political autonomy, I make no distinction between "personal" and "moral" autonomy, for to do so unnecessarily assumes an antagonism from the outset, which is alien to my subject of discussion, the *Analects*. The term "autonomy" has no equivalent in the *Analects*. But I hope to show that certain features of Confucius's ethics, for example, the expression and development of aims and aspirations, their establishment and maintenance throughout one's life, an integral sense of self, and the effort required for self-directedness, are essential aspects of autonomy. In order to bring out these features, I shall first investigate three concepts in the *Analects* that are relevant to the discussion. These are *zhi* (志), *li* (禮), and *ren* (仁). Arising from the description of these concepts and their interrelations, questions about what constitutes choice and autonomy shall be discussed.

Zhi: Setting Aims and Directions

In the *Analects*,[1] the word *zhi* 志 is used several times in conjunction with the preposition *yu* 於, for example, *zhi yu dao* (way 道 4.9, 7.6), *zhi yu xue* (learning 學 2.4), *zhi yu ren* (benevolence 仁 4.4). In these cases, *zhi* means setting one's heart/mind (*xin* 心) upon the way, learning, or benevolence. It is orienting oneself toward something, giving oneself an aim or direction.[2]

There are at least two occasions in which the participants are asked to "speak" (*yan* 言) their *zhi* (5.26, 11.26). Here, the sense seems to be to express what is close to one's heart/mind. The context in each case is one where Confucius is in a relaxed mood, accompanied by some of his disciples. The setting encourages uninhibited answers. We shall see what these are shortly.

There is a close connection between the *Odes* (*shi* 詩) and *yan*. The person who fails to study the *Odes* will be unable to *yan*, and this intimates not just speaking *per se*, but speech informed by general knowledge, subtleties, nuances, sensitivities, and deep-seated aims and feelings. In addition, it is said that knowing *yan* enables one to know people (20.3). The term here probably means "words," and one is said to know the person behind the words.

The Odes stimulate imagination, heighten observation, give rise to harmonious socialization, and enable one to complain (17.9). Music was inseparable from the *Odes*,[3] and we find Confucius distinguishing between the tones and nuances of different forms of music, saying for instance that the music of Cheng was licentious (*yin* 淫), and associating this with glibness (*ning* 佞 15.11, 17.18, 3.20).

Thus, although the word *zhi* can be translated as aim or direction, or what the individual sets his heart/mind upon, it presupposes a background of education in order to form and express one's *zhi*. The expression of *zhi* seems to have been a shared practice. Such expressions allow for exploration of one's aspirations and affiliations, knowledge of self and others, exchange of ideas, criticism, contemplation, and self-examination. We know that the ability to interpret the *Odes*, to discover new or hidden meanings, and to use it to illuminate some aspect of the rites, was highly praised by Confucius (3.8). This ability must have been part and parcel of the determination of one's *zhi* and the development of character.

It is interesting to compare the *zhi* expressed by Tzu-lu, Yen Yüan, and Confucius in 5.26. Tzu-lu is known for being brash, reckless, and immodest. His sentiment to share things with friends, and "have no regrets even if they become worn," perhaps unwittingly reflects not just generosity but bravado. Yen Yüan's resolve not to "boast" of his own good points or to make a display of his efforts in helping others shows a moral concern that is, at the same time, somewhat self-conscious. In contrast to these two, Confucius's *zhi*, namely, to "bring peace to the old, to have trust in my friends, and to cherish the young," has a tone of composure. Bringing peace to the old and cherishing the young are concerns of *ren* or benevolence. Cherishing the young is also consistent with Confucius's educational mission. Trustworthiness (*xin* 信) is one important subject of his teaching (7.25), and perhaps he is voicing a concern here about himself, that he should be more worthy.

In 11.26, four disciples express their *zhi*. First, Tzu-lu followed by Jan Yu say how they would each administer a state. Their statements seem to repeat a certain formula, "If I were given a state of such and such size, in three years I would do such and such," for we find Confucius making a similar statement elsewhere (13.10). Next, Kung-hsi Hua states: "I do not say that I already have the ability, but I am ready to learn. On ceremonial occasions in the ancestral temple or in diplomatic gatherings, I should like to assist as a minor official in charge of protocol, properly dressed in my ceremonial cap and robes." And finally, Tseng Hsi states: "In late spring, after the spring clothes have been newly made, I should like, together with five or six adults and six or seven boys, to go bathing in the River Yi and enjoy the breeze on the Rain Altar, and then to go home chanting poetry."

Confucius exclaims his approval of Tseng Hsi, and by implication, disapproval of the other three. Later, Confucius explains to Tseng Hsi that "it is by the rites that a state is administered, but in the way he spoke Yu (Tzu-lu) showed a lack of modesty." As for Jan Yu, although he showed administrative concern, he had also added that he would leave the rites and music to "abler gentlemen." But in doing so, he has apparently missed the essential role of the rites and music in government. Kung-hsi Hua is known for his grasp of the details of the rites,[4] and yet offered to take a minor role. Confucius comments that if he "plays only a minor part, who would be able to play a major role?" Perhaps Confucius was disturbed by what he thought was a touch of overmodesty and the glib diplomatic language. By contrast, Tseng Hsi's spontaneity probably symbolized the perfect integration of the ceremonial aspects of the rites with the attitudes that they embody.[5]

The above examples indicate that one's *zhi* can reveal something about one's character. It can also be more or less mature or committed, and may require modification and instantiate self-reflection. Thus, the expression of one's *zhi* is only the first stage in the training of the gentleman, requiring development and consolidation. We know all these from the above comparisons and from Confucius's remarks on his own development: "At fifteen I set my heart on learning; at thirty I took my stand" (*li** 立) . . . (2.4).

*Li** and *Li:* Establishing Rituals and Attitudes

Between setting one's heart on learning and being able to take a stand is a period of fifteen years. Although we should not take this literally, it does indicate the need for prolonged effort before one can be said to *li** or "stand." The word occurs in several contexts. In 1.2, we have *ben li** *er dao sheng* (本立而道生): once the root is *established*, the way will grow. In 5.8, Confucius says of someone that he can *li** *yü chao* (立於朝): he can take his place at court, meaning that he has the *requisite ability and qualifications* to be able to hold (diplomatic) conversations with guests at the court. Related to this last usage, in 4.14 we have *bu huan wu wei, huan suo yi li** (不患無位, 患所以立): do not worry that you have no position, worry about whereupon you stand. Here, we have the sense of getting one's priorities right, of *establishing* oneself first. As we shall see, this also implies a sense of self-worth, independent of the opinions of others.

From the above, we gather that *li** or "stand" means establishing oneself on the basis of certain qualities. In 16.13 and 20.3, we are told that *bu xue [zhi]* *li wu yi li** (不學 [知] 禮無以立): unless you study [know] the rites you will not be able to take your stand. In other words, the rites have to be studied and understood before one can be said to have established oneself.

Besides religious sacrifice, ancestor worship, ceremonies of mourning, and courtly and diplomatic affairs, the rites or *li* (禮) make up a repository of rules pertaining to relationships between ruler and minister, family members, elder and younger, and so on. Of course, the rites cannot govern every aspect of behavior in all circumstances. Nonetheless, they assume the central idea of maintaining a certain hierarchical order, both within and outside the family. In 1.2, the disciple Yu Tzu attributes the basis of social order to *xiao ti* (孝弟), filial feeling toward parents and respect for elders. It is rare, he says, for one who is *xiao ti* to like rebelling against superiors, adding emphatically that there has never been a case of such a person liking to create disorder. He concludes, "The gentleman devotes himself to the root, for when the root is established, the way is formed. *Xiao ti* is the root of *ren*, is it not?" Insofar as *xiao ti* involves feelings of love, affection, reverence, and respect, the statement tells us that these are at the root of *ren*.[6]

It is generally recognized that there are two senses of *ren*. In its narrower sense, it "emphasizes the part of the ethical ideal having to do with affective concern for others," while in the broader sense, it refers to "an all-encompassing ideal for human beings," which involves attitudinal aspects of *li*.[7] I shall largely be using *ren* in its broader sense, to mean the overall perspective of one who has imbibed the attitudinal components of *li*, to be specified below. The term "benevolence" will be used instead, to refer to the narrower sense of *ren*, meaning affective concern.

We can therefore identify two aspects of what it means to have established oneself upon the rites, namely, understanding the hierarchical relations and roles specified by the rites on the one hand, and imbibing certain attitudes on the other. Let us call these the formal and the attitudinal aspects of *li*. The formal aspect provides the form or the grid for social intercourse, specifying certain core values, especially filial piety, and serves as the institutional and educational means for both training and expressing certain attitudes. These include reverence, respect, seriousness, dignity, harmony, sincerity, humility, frugality (versus ostentatious display), genuine expression of feeling (for example, grief), benevolence, trustworthiness (*xin* 信), earnestness or doing one's best (*zhong* 忠), and empathetic concern (*shu* 恕). The last four, especially, are more specifically linked with *ren*. Closely related aspects of *ren* are also revealed through the insistence that speech should be cautious, congruent with action, and not glib (see next section).

These attitudes can be invoked to balance and adapt existing practices, as well as to judge the performance of these practices. For instance, mechanical performances of the rites are criticized for going against the spirit of the rites (17.11). In addition a person's character, or more specifically, the level of commitment to his aspirations, can be judged. This is especially prominent in the context of the relation between word and action. For instance, when Tzu-kung says, "While I do not wish others to impose on me, I also wish not to impose on others," Confucius comments, "Ssu, that is quite beyond you" (5.12). We do not know the context of Tzu-kung's statement, but he can be said to be expressing his *zhi*. Evidently, Confucius thinks he is lacking in some way, and his comment is an admonishment designed to wake him up to self-examination. D. C. Lau has noted that "perhaps Tzu-kung was more given to protesting about his desire for benevolence than to the actual practice of it, for when he asked about the gentleman, the Master said, 'He puts his words into action before allowing his words to follow his action'" (2.13).[8] This is one example of Confucius tailoring his replies to particular disciples, and addressing their shortcomings.

Appreciation of this fact allows us to understand, for instance, why he is somewhat harsh toward Tsai Wo, when the latter questions the long mourning period of three years, adducing the neglect of other rites and music as a result. Although replying that if he feels at ease with a shorter period (wear finery, eat fine food, and so on) he may proceed, Confucius complains afterward that he is "unfeeling" (*bu ren* 不仁 17.21). Qian Mu has observed that Tsai Wo intended to discuss the system of rites and there is no evidence that the three-year mourning was universally practiced. He states that he does not understand why Confucius treats Tsai Wo as harshly here as he does in another passage (5.9).[9] Qian Mu is taking Tsai Wo's question at face value, as a serious and legitimate question about a particular rite which perhaps requires change. However, we learn something about Tsai Wo's character, in 5.9. Tsai Wo seems to have been in the habit of sleeping during the day. By implication, he is lazy and does not put in any effort toward his studies. Confucius likens him to a piece of "rotten wood that cannot be carved," and "dried dung that cannot be trowelled," and must have distrusted Tsai Wo's motives in questioning the long period of mourning, for he adds that he has learnt from Tsai Wo to watch a person's actions after listening to his words. A corollary of this is to see where *he* is coming from, that is, his whole orientation. In Confucius's view Tsai Wo's rottenness gives him no credentials, so to speak, with which to raise doubts about the period of mourning.[10]

Ren: Self and Life-Process

This suggests a deeper sense of misalignment between self on the one hand, and word and action on the other. The focus here is on the self and its relation to both word and action. The vocabulary of self is variously put, in terms of the pronoun *zi* (自) meaning self or oneself, and also in terms of the nouns *shen* (身) and *gong* (躬), which, though literally meaning "body," are another way of referring to the self-entity or person. These words are used in conjunction with words like *xing* (省) "reflect," *song* (訟) "criticize," *chi* (恥) "shame." Thus, we have "inwardly examining self" (*nei zi xing* 內自省 4.17), "inwardly criticizing self" (*nei zi song* 內自訟 5.27), and "daily reflecting upon my person on three counts" (*wu ri san xing wu shen* 吾日三省吾身 1.4). In addition, there is the idea of reprimanding oneself more strictly than others (*gong zi hou* [*ze*] 躬自厚 [責] 15.15), and feeling ashamed if one's person fails to keep up with one's words (*chi gong zhi bu dai ye* 恥躬之不逮也 4.22).[11]

This vocabulary indicates what we may call a concern for the wholeness of the self. What is at stake here is not just action conforming to words, but integrity. Integrity is sustained by a sense of self-worth, which is independent of the opinions of others. We find this in the frequent admonitions not to be troubled by the failure of others to appreciate oneself, but by the lack of one's own abilities (14.30, 15.19, 4.14). In sum, "The gentleman seeks within himself, the small man seeks from others" (15.21).

This concern with the integrity of self *is* the concern of *ren*. For instance, Confucius says in 1.3 that "it is rare, indeed, for a man with cunning words and an ingratiating face to be *ren*." *Ren* thus involves an integral sense of self that can be discerned and distinguished from speciousness or dissemblance, as we learn in various places in the text (2.10, 12.20). To Confucius, these imply a state of unease in contrast to the man of *ren*: "One who is not *ren* cannot remain long in straitened circumstances, nor can he remain long in easy circumstances. The *ren* man is attracted to *ren* because he feels at home in it" (4.2).

Maintaining integrity, self-worth, and independence require not just congruence of self, words, and action. In addition, it requires a sense of right, and courage. Confucius says as much when asked about the complete man: "If a man remembers what is right (義) at the sight of profit, is ready to lay down his life in the face of danger, and does not forget sentiments he has repeated all his life (*bu wang ping sheng zhi yan* 不忘平生之言) even when he has been in straitened circumstances for a long time, he may be said to be a complete man" (14.12). The reference to *yan*, so eloquently translated by Lau as "sentiments ... repeated" reminds us of the *zhi* that the gentleman has expressed and formed. And indeed the same point is made in relation to scholars (*shi* 士) who have set their *zhi* and men of *ren*, that "they do not seek life at the expense of *ren*, and may have to sacrifice their lives to complete *ren*" (15.9). It is also said that "when faced with the opportunity to practise *ren* do not give precedence even to your teacher" (15.36). This combines courage with independence. In fact, the language of integrity, self-worth, courage, and right all contrast an awareness of self with externalities, such as material things, profit, wealth, rank, and the opinions of others, and to remain independent of such things.

We learn from Confucius's continued description of his own development in 2.4 that the quest for *ren* is a life-long process. Thus, beyond establishing himself upon the rites, there is the stage of "not being in doubt" (*bu huo* 不

惑), at the age of forty. The fact that Confucius consistently links learning with ethical development means that freedom from doubt is an ethical stage. There are two passages (9.29, 14.28) which place this together with (the man of *ren*) not being worried, and not being afraid. In other words, Confucius had a sure grasp of the path which he had chosen and also consolidated his aspirations. Still, he has to deal with contingencies which may afflict his life, for example, the early death of his favorite disciple Yen Yüan, among other things. We can only surmise that things like this are what he is referring to, when he next mentions that at fifty he understood the Decree of Heaven, that is, the contingencies of life, and his resignation to such contingencies. The next stage "at sixty my ear was attuned," is obscure.[12] The word translated as "attuned" is *shun* (順), that is, (affairs going) smoothly, or being frictionless. Confucius could be referring to the ability to live in harmony with others. The final stage, "at seventy I followed my heart's desire without overstepping the line," perhaps refers to the fact that his desires are such that they have been integrated with the attitudes of the rites, and they come naturally and spontaneously to him, not as demands or requirements, but as a central part of himself. A question may arise here as to which of the last three stages is the stage of *ren*. If we equate *ren* say, with equanimity, is it the stage of ceasing to have doubts? But it is consistent with the overall dispositional stance of *ren* that there is no end stage (8.7, 9.11). Perhaps we should not regard the five stages too discretely. Together they imply the effort required to orient oneself toward the overall stance of *ren*, development and maintenance of this stance, and the integration of one's desires with the attitudes and values definitive of this stance.

Choice

It is time to raise certain issues. Firstly, the relation between formal and attitudinal aspects of the rites: how, and to what extent, is revision of the formal rules possible? As we have seen, the formal aspect serves to regulate and maintain hierarchical relations between people in different roles, with the aim of ensuring a harmonious social order. The attitudinal aspect emphasizes the appropriate feelings and attitudes to be expressed in these relations. In practice, these two aspects are inseparable, that is, one cannot be said to be expressing, say, the attitude of grief if one does not participate in a rite of mourning for one's parents, or show respect without going through the appropriate ceremonial ritual. But there is room for flexibility and choice in Confucius's ethics, insofar as the formal aspect of the rites is the institutional basis for the training and expression of attitudes like reverence, respect, grief, and benevolence. We have seen that Confucius criticizes mechanical performance of the rites (17.11). He also asserts, for instance, that in mourning it is better to "err on the side of grief than on the side of formality" (3.4). Existing ceremonial rules may be revised in the spirit of these attitudes, or if they do not inhibit or eliminate the underlying attitudes.[13] There is no saying how such revisions come about, and we can only make some general remarks here.

Ethical decisions call for considered choice. The choice must be based on some system of concepts within the language of one's tradition, and articulated through shared practice. One advantage of viewing an ethical system as being an entwinement of language and practice is that it allows for fluid interpretation of the system. This does not mean one can interpret the rules any way one likes, but to recognize, for instance, that changing circumstances can give rise to new requirements, challenges can arise from different views of what is appropriate, and as a result, practices may come to differ over time. Alternatively, changes in practice may themselves lead to new perspectives on a concept. Confucius is of course aware of such changes. Witness his comments on differences of the rites between the Yin, the Xia, and the Zhou, that "What was added and what was omitted can be known" (2.23). We learn too from the example of Tsai Wo above that challenges to existing practices like the three-year mourning period were already taking place. Although Confucius is displeased with Tsai Wo, the latter nonetheless raises an important issue: the three-year mourning period requires absence and abstinence from certain affairs, and leads to the neglect of certain other rites. The mourner therefore faces conflicting requirements. We can only surmise that a choice of priorities will have to be made.

The formal aspect of *li* seems to have led Herbert Fingarette to conclude that there is no room for "genuine choice" in the ethical system of the *Analects*. One example in particular stands out. Someone informs Confucius that in his region there is a "straightbody" who reported his own father for stealing sheep. Confucius's reply is that in his region, "straightness" is different: father and son would cover up for each other (13.18). Fingarette comments: "We could have no better proof than this that the problem of genuine choice among real alternatives never occurred to Confucius, or at least never clearly occurred to him as a fundamental moral task."[14]

Note that in this example, Confucius states the difference in practice straightforwardly. This is a bald declaration of filial piety as a core value. It is unclear that Confucius fails to see that there could be moral conflict here, as Fingarette also asserts.[15] If filial piety is a core value in Confucius's ethical system, then it does mean that he will have to take that course of action which best fulfills that value. Unless there is some expedient way to resolve the conflict,[16] it does not mean that there will be no agony or tragedy here. In any case, the notion of a "genuine" choice dramatizes the issue. It seems to point to a scenario of situating oneself outside of the ethical system, and to rethink one's options as a radical self with one's own agenda of authenticity. This may not be a realistic option, whether one is talking of Confucianism or any other ethical tradition.

Insofar as Confucius looked backward to a golden age of ritual harmony, and lamented the fact that during his time, the ritual order of political hierarchy was breaking down, it might be argued that he tends to be conservative in his defense and maintenance of the ritual rules. This is the case, let us say, not only with reference to diplomatic and political ceremonies, but with other practices such as the three-year period of mourning, covering up for one's father if he had committed a crime, or even, say, the subordinate status of women. Nevertheless, the fact that autonomous choice may be limited by the conservativeness of the ritual rules does not mean that there is no room for autonomy. This is especially so if the focus of autonomy is self-directedness, instead of the area of choice. This distinction brings us directly to the question of what constitutes autonomy.

Autonomy

Following Isaiah Berlin's distinction between the "negative" and the "positive" conceptions of liberty,[17] there are two corresponding senses of autonomy. Under the former conception, autonomy is the absence of constraints on individual action. This freedom is only to be curbed when it causes harm to others, or in certain cases, to oneself. Much debate has focused on what constitutes harm, private versus public domains of action, the circumstances under which interference or coercion may be justifiable, and the sociopolitical arrangements which would best protect freedom of action, and at the same time minimize harm. Whereas the negative conception of liberty is concerned with the *area* of control, the positive conception is concerned with the *source* of control.[18] As moral agents, we have a deep-seated desire for directing our own lives. This gives rise to a sense of autonomy called self-directedness, self-mastery, or self-control, which can stand independently of institutional arrangements, no matter how wide the area of freedom they may allow.[19]

This last point is worth emphasizing. Autonomy as self-directedness is not necessarily equivalent to liberation from institutional arrangements. The liberal conception of autonomy as absence from constraint and noninterference on the part of others is insufficient to guarantee self-directedness. For self-directedness to obtain, strength of character and effort are required to maintain an integral sense of self together with the ideals which form an important part of this self. In this sense, autonomy is an achievement concept. This allows us to make sense of the fact that although choices can be severely restricted by poverty and adversity, paradigmatic individuals are still able to express their autonomy.

The effort and commitment required to live a life according to a moral ideal comes from a conception of a self which is oriented toward the ideal conceived through a shared ethical practice with a set of like-minded individuals. The ideal may be elusive for various reasons: perfection may never be achieved; there may be pitfalls in one's understanding; weaknesses of character may intrude, and so on. Nevertheless, the ideal is a goal which sustains one throughout one's life, especially when there is the guidance and influence of a charismatic teacher who is at the same time a paradigmatic individual. One learns from the teacher and the social practices, the ideals of which he exemplifies, clarifies, and extends. Commitment to a goal and its maintenance, leading to identification of one's self with the goal, can come about only through a process of socialization. The social and developmental process is therefore necessary for acquiring self-direct-edness. One cannot become a Confucian gentleman without the moral language, concepts, and rituals of Confucianism. In other words, one can only become a certain kind of person *through* the language one has imbibed. However, the very same language and practice allows one to distinguish between a hypocriti-cal gentleman, and a genuine one. The language and its related practices must have the critical resources to allow for such distinctions.

Zhi, Li, Ren, and Autonomy

We are now in a position to join the earlier account of the three concepts in Confucius's ethics with the notion of autonomy. It is evident that *zhi*, *li*, and *ren* together allow for autonomy in the sense just discussed. As we have seen, the articulation of one's *zhi* is an initial stage in a developmental process, the goal being attainment of the ideal of *ren*. One's *zhi* could be in a state of uncertainty or doubt (*huo* 惑) (14.36), or formed to the extent that it cannot be wrested (*duo* 奪) from one (9.26).[20] Such determination may well be a function of one's effort and progress in learning *li*, and an indication of this is whether there is commitment toward learning in the first place. This is precisely what is lacking in Jan Ch'iu, for instance, who gives the excuse that it is not that he is unhappy with the master's way, rather, his strength is insufficient. Confucius notes that the person whose strength is insufficient "collapses along the course." Pointedly referring to Jan Ch'iu, he adds: "Now you draw the line" (*jin ru hua* 今女畫), that is, Jan Ch'iu has *refused* to go forward (6.12). Elsewhere, Confucius uses the analogy of aborting the building of a mound, with one basketful of earth remaining. He expresses this as, *zhi*, wu zhi** (止吾止) or "Stop, I stop." *Zhi** also means "rest," or "resting." Thus, *zhi*, wu zhi** has the sense of the stop-page (literally) resting in me (9.19). The stoppage or progress is deemed to be entirely and directly within my control.

Ren, like autonomy, is therefore an achievement concept. As the disciple Tseng Tzu says, "A gentleman must be strong and resolute, for his burden is heavy and the road is long. He takes *ren* as his burden. Is that not heavy? Only with death does the road come to an end. Is that not long (8.7)?" This reaf-firms an earlier point too, that the achievement of *ren* is a life-long process with the added stricture that it is not easy. In this regard, some commentators have found the following statement of Confucius's paradoxical: "Is *ren* indeed so far away? As soon as we want it, we should find that it is at our very side" (7.29).[21] However, we should bear in mind Confucius's role as a teacher who exhorts and admonishes his students toward self-cultivation. Since *ren* concerns the orientation of the self, it *is* "near." As Confucius says rhetorically in 12.1, "the practice of *ren* depends on self (*you ji* 由己) how can it depend on others?"

It is one aspect of this that imitation is frowned upon. Remember that Confucius disapproves of the imitative and stilted responses of some of his disciples when asked to state their *zhi* (11.26). As part of the educational process, creative, imaginative, and intelligent responses were highly praised. Confucius did not expect his disciples to agree with him and he valued the intelligent development of his teachings through practice. In 7.8 he says: "I never enlighten anyone who has not been driven to distraction by trying to understand a difficulty or who has not got into a frenzy trying to put his ideas into words. When I have pointed out one corner of a square to anyone and he does not come back with the other three, I will not point it out to him a second time." (See also 1.15, 2.9, 3.8, 5.9.)

Critical resources for self-development are therefore available in Confucius's ethical system. We have already dealt with the issue of choice in an earlier section. Any lingering dissatisfaction with the limits of choice under this system could well be based on a tendency to compare it with a liberal Millian position of allowing for a proliferation of views so as to promote the cultivation of a certain type of character: critical, original, imaginative, independent, nonconforming to the point of eccentricity, and together with this, the flowering of truth. Berlin notes that these aspects of character and truth are not necessarily found only under liberal conditions, although it may be argued that (empirically speaking) liberal conditions are more conducive to their development.[22] But more importantly, any such comparison would be ill-conceived, for as Berlin also points out, this liberal position has served as a conscious political ideal of individual rights only in recent history, its developed form being scarcely older than the Renaissance or the Reformation.[23] In reply, it might be argued that this is merely an observational point of no logical relevance. However, it does indicate the need to be aware of the historical, social and political circumstances under which conceptions of the liberal individual arose.

It is beyond my purview to discuss this, but apart from liberalism, there is an older source of the emphasis on individual rights in the Western tradition that we should be aware of. One major tendency in Western moral, social, and political thought has been to view the relations between individuals as naturally antagonistic, calling for the establishment of a social contract to safeguard individual interests, and to ensure penalties against noncompliance. From this perspective, the order of social relations is reflective of the need to compromise, so as to maximize one's satisfaction and to minimize frustration and harm. This view is older than Hobbes, going back to Book II of Plato's *Republic*, where Glaucon describes the nature and origin of justice as a compromise between suffering from the injuries others inflict on one, and being able to injure others with impunity. But if one had the absolute power to do as one liked, for example, with the magical Ring of Gyges, it would be considered the height of stupidity to act justly or morally. Instead:

> There is no one, it would commonly be supposed, who would have such iron strength of will as to stick to what is right and keep his hands from taking other people's property. For he would be able to steal from the market whatever he wanted without fear of detection, to go into any man's house and seduce anyone he liked, to murder or to release from prison anyone he felt inclined, and generally behave as if he had supernatural powers . . . no man is just of his own free will, but only under compulsion . . .[24]

This is a bleak picture of the basic human disposition: that there is a natural tendency to trespass, steal, seduce, murder, and so on. Although not shared by all in the Western tradition, the model of social relations as a compulsion or imposition has been an influential one, depicting morality as a bargaining process between individuals in an uneasy relation of compromise, so as to avoid being harmed.[25]

I have introduced the above picture because by comparison, it enables us to appreciate better the social presuppositions of Confucius's ethics. A notable characteristic of the *zhi* expressed by Confucius and his disciples is their friendly social orientation. In 5.26, Confucius and his disciples talk about generosity toward friends, moral concern, trustworthiness, and bringing peace to the old and cherishing the young. Similarly in 11.26, the *zhi* of the four disciples mention bringing peace to a troubled state, giving the people courage and a sense of direction, attention to the rites, and spontaneous relations with friends in the celebration of a spring rite. All these indicate a self which is not set over and above these social orientations but instead, defined in terms of them through a process of articulating and sharing aims and aspirations, establishing oneself upon the rites, commitment toward and identification with the ideal of *ren*. Given that one's *zhi* expresses what is close to one's heart/mind, their various expressions tell us that for Confucius and his disciples harmonious social relations is a natural state of affairs. The socialization process therefore is not just concerned with instilling or imposing the obeisance of hierarchical ceremonial rules, but involves the autonomous development of basic social sentiments, a point later to be developed by Mencius in a theory of human nature.

Notes

1. Or *Lun-yü* (論語). I have consulted D. C. Lau's translation, *Confucius: Analects* (Harmondsworth: Penguin, 1979). I have adapted some of his translations. Passage numberings in the text follow Lau. I shall use *hanyu pinyin* romanization. However, names of cited characters in the *Analects* remain as Lau has transliterated them under

the Wade-Giles system, so as to avoid confusion. For the Chinese text, I have consulted the commentaries of Yang Bo Jün 楊伯峻, *Lun-yü yi-zhu* 論語譯注 (台中: 藍燈文化事業公司 1987), and Qian Mu (Ch'ien Mu) 錢穆, *Lun-yü xin jie* 論語新解 (台北: 東大圖書公司, 1988).

2. The translation of *zhi* as aim or direction follows Kwong-loi Shun, *Mencius and Early Chinese Thought* (Stanford: Stanford University Press, 1997).

3. According to Zhu Zi Qing 朱自清, *Shi yan zhi bian* 詩言志辨 (上海: 華東師範大學出版社, 1996), p. 1.

4. For details about Confucius's disciples, see Lau, *Confucius: Analects*, Appendix 2.

5. I have discussed this passage in "The Aesthetic Moral Personality: *Li, Yi, Wen* and *Chih* in the Analects," in *Monumenta Serica* 46 (1998). Julia Ching notes that the Rain Altar by the River Yi was "a place to go in late spring in proper seasonal robes and in the company of a group of young men and children—presumably trained in the music of rain dances. There, they would bathe in the river, follow the airs of the rain dance, and return home singing, after sharing in a sacrificial meal." See Julia Ching, *Mysticism and Kingship in China* (Cambridge: Cambridge University Press, 1997), 19. She cites Wang Chong (Wang Ch'ung) 王充, *Lun-heng* 論衡, 15.9b.

6. In the last sentence of this passage, *wei ren zhi ben* 為仁之本 could mean that *xiao ti* is either (1) the root of *ren* or (2) the root of (practicing) *ren*. This was a problem which exercised the Song philosophers Cheng Yi and Zhu Xi. See my discussion in "The Practice of *Jen*," in *Philosophy East and West* 49 (1999).

7. Kwong-loi Shun, *Mencius and Early Chinese Thought*, p. 23. See also his paper "*Jen* and *Li* in the Analects," in *Philosophy East and West* 43 (1993): 457.

8. Lau, *Confucius: Analects*, p. 206.

9. Qian Mu, *Lun-yü xin jie*, p. 641.

10. But Confucius does not as a general principle dismiss the words of someone on the basis of his character. As he says, "The gentleman does not recommend a man on account of what he says, neither does he dismiss what is said on account of the speaker." (15.23)

11. See Kwong-loi Shun, "Self and Self-Cultivation in Early Confucian Thought," in *Two Roads to Wisdom?*, ed. Bo Mou (Chicago: Open Court, 2001), 229–44, for an account of the various terms for "self" in Confucianism.

12. As Lau states in a note to his translation. He spells "attuned" as "atuned."

13. According to Kwong-loi Shun, "possession of the attitude 'transcends' participation in the actually existing sacrificial rites, and thereby provides a sense in which participation in such rites is a means to cultivating and expressing the attitude." This transcendence "provides a perspective from which revision of the existing ritual practices can be assessed. For example, having come to acquire the attitude through having been brought up to participate in such rites, members of the community can propose revisions in the rites on the basis of economic consideration, as long as this does not affect the efficacy of the revised practices in cultivating and expressing the attitude." (Shun is referring to 9.3, where Confucius approves the use of a ceremonial cap made of black

silk instead of the prescribed linen, on the ground that it is more frugal.) However, a conservative attitude toward changes has to be maintained, since it is the existing practices which give rise to the attitude, and these practices have to be relatively stable in order to perform their function. See Shun, "*Jen* and *Li* in the Analects," pp. 471–72.

14. Herbert Fingarette, *Confucius: The Secular as Sacred* (New York: Harper Torch-books, 1972), 23.

15. With reference to the same example, Fingarette refers to Confucius's "failure to see or to mention the problem of internal moral conflict in such a case as this . . . " Fingarette, *Confucius*, p. 24.

16. Compare *Mencius* 7A.35, where according to Mencius, if the Emperor Shun's father has (wrongly) killed someone, although Shun would not (as Emperor) forbid his arrest, he "would have carried the old man on his back and fled to the edge of the Sea and lived there happily, never giving a thought to the Empire."

17. Isaiah Berlin, "Two Concepts of Liberty," in *Four Essays on Liberty* (Oxford: Oxford University Press, 1969), 118–72.

18. Berlin, "Two Concepts of Liberty," p. 129.

19. A point made by Robert Young, *Personal Autonomy: Beyond Negative and Positive Liberty* (London: Croom Helm, 1986), 9: "While institutional arrangements of various kinds may *undermine* autonomy, it does not follow that the adjustment of these arrange-ments will necessarily *confer* autonomy."

20. The full statement of 9.26: "The Master said, 'The Three Armies can be deprived of their commanding officer, but even a common man (*pi fu* 匹夫) cannot be deprived of his purpose (*bu ke duo zhi* 不可奪志).'" Although the statement refers to the "common man," there is no reason why it cannot apply to the gentleman as well.

21. For example, Yü-sheng Lin, "The Evolution of the Pre-Confucian Meaning of *Jen* and the Confucian Concept of Moral Autonomy," in *Monumenta Serica* 31 (1974-75): 185.

22. Berlin, "Two Concepts of Liberty," p. 128. Berlin also criticizes the abuse of the positive conception of liberty by authoritarian regimes. There is a slide from paternalistic concern of what is good for the individual, to what the "real" self wants, and finally the "real self" is identified with a higher organic entity such as the state.

23. Berlin, "Two Concepts of Liberty," p. 129.

24. Desmond Lee, trans., *Plato: The Republic*, rev. ed. (Harmondsworth: Penguin Books, 1974), 106.

25. Some communitarians would argue that with slight modifications, this contrac-tual model is also a liberal one: individuals come together, under a "veil of ignorance," to choose the principles which would govern their future interaction. This assumes the notion of an "unencumbered self" which lacks any social identity. See the critiques of Alasdair MacIntyre, *After Virtue* (Notre Dame, University of Notre Dame Press, 1981), and Michael Sandel, *Liberalism and the Limits of Justice* (Cambridge: Cambridge University Press, 1982).

The Problem of the Self in the *Analects*

16

Herbert Fingarette

My specific topic here is "the problem of the self in the *Analects*." Now "the problem of the self" is a phrase that, of course, can have various connotations. The phrase can allude to logical analysis of the concept of the self, or to psychological theories about the self, or to moral or religious prescriptions of what the ideal self would be like. The "problem of the self" may also be taken to amount to the quest to identify some specially central element of personhood—the soul, or (beneath the façade) the "true" or "real" self. The "problem of the self" may refer not to an intellectual question but to a task for the person: the task of actualizing one's "true self" and so achieving fulfilment. Or, by contrast, the phrase may refer to the task of losing or surrendering the self, and so achieving liberation from a delusion that is the seat and source of our deepest suffering.

I mention only a few possibilities, and only roughly describe them. Even so, one sees readily that the different "problems" of the "self" that I have mentioned are not unrelated. Understanding one may bring better understanding of others. However in my remarks here I shall specifically concern myself with the last of the "problems of the self" that I mentioned: the task of becoming selfless. And I do so specifically in connection with the *Analects*.[1] Nevertheless, though the *Analects* is my focus, the intended larger context is that of Asian thought in some of its major variants.

Asian thought (if I may risk a truly enormous generalization about so global a notion as "Asian thought") is perfused—not entirely, but very widely—with the teaching that the individual self or ego is the source and the seat of delusion and suffering, of frustration and bondage. Our great task is to let go of the self. The specific doctrines, differing as they do, nevertheless are significantly akin in their use of bywords, which, whatever their ultimate meaning, are at least on their face predominantly negative and passive: "*neti-neti*,"[2] "emptiness,"[3] "non-ego,"[4] "nonaction."[5] The literature of orthodoxy in India, of Buddhism, and of Taoism is as we know replete with such language regarding the individual self.

There is one major seeming exception—the thought whose source is Confucius. Confucius seems to be a yea-sayer. His language and his imagery are generally positive, affirmative, active. To read the *Analects* is inevitably to become aware how central is the concern on Confucius's part that each of us dedicate ourselves with utmost vigor and unqualified commitment to making something of ourselves personally. We must vastly develop our learning and our skills,[6] cultivate proper demeanor,[7] develop appropriate attitudes and motives,[8] and strive always to act on right principles.[9] Effort, commitment, determination, persistence, diligence[10]—these are key necessities if one is to become a truly noble person, a *junzi* 君子. There is a reasonable sense in which one may say that for Confucius the great task is self-cultivation, and not self-loss.

It is true that the phrase "cultivate oneself" (*xiu ji* 脩己) is used explicitly in only one passage in the *Analects*, though it is there repeated three times in a formulaic[11] way. The idea of self-cultivation does become a key tenet, a technical term of importance, in later Confucian thinking. An early important example is the *Great-Learning*, where we are told that "the root is self-cultivation" expressed as *xiu shen wei ben* 脩身為本.[12] But I am interested here in the *Analects* and not in the meanings the phrase takes on in later Confucian thought. In the passage in the *Analects* where it does appear, the word "cultivate" in "cultivate oneself" does not really seem to have "oneself" as the object, but has instead a more specific aim such as "one's capacity to pacify the people." Waley's translation is suggestive of this: "Cultivate in himself the capacity to ease the lot of other people (*xiu ji yi an ren* 脩己以安人)."[13] Moreover, the fact that the formula occurs in only one passage is evidence that we do not have here a self-conscious, crystallized idea of portentous significance, an idea around which Confucius himself centered his own thought. What he himself teaches us explicitly to value and to cultivate are certain *specific* traits, aims, principles, and skills.

It is the *commentator*, rather than Confucius, who is tempted to generalize these teachings by focusing on the "self" as an overarching or basic rubric, and summing it all up in terms of "self-cultivation." But of course there is more than one way to generalize from, or to characterize as a whole, a collection of particulars. Would Confucius himself have generalized on his own teachings, or summarized them, by taking the consummately cultivated self as his focal concept? The fact is, of course, that he did not. Why not? He surely had no antipathy to highly general concepts, for he explicitly used a number of general concepts as central. Why did not "self-cultivation" constitute one of these? My answer is that he did not say it because he did not mean it. And yet one cannot read the *Analects* without having the impression that for Confucius there is something focally important, in a constructive way, about the role of the individual in bringing himself to be as he should be, and thereafter in living as such, as a man of true humanity (*ren* 仁), a truly noble man (*junzi*). Is this not self-cultivation? So here we have a puzzle.

Turning to the larger Asian context, there is another way of seeing the question I want to raise. It would be agreed generally that Confucius was teaching an unselfish, unegoistic way of life, as did his principal disciples and followers. Why, then, does the Confucius of the *Analects*, in his tone as well as his language, evoke an impression that so strongly contrasts with the immediate impression produced by the *neti-neti*, the emptiness, the nonaction, and the analogous ideas and images so suggestive of self-negation and passivity that permeate major non-Confucian lines of thought in Asia? To what extent, if any, and wherein, precisely, is there really a shared approval of selflessness, and wherein lies the contrast? It is the nature of the agreement, and the nature of the contrast, that I want to track down.

There have been many discussions of these interrelations—comparisons of Confucians with each other, and with teachers in such other schools as Daoism and Buddhism. These comparisons are very often conducted within the frame of the terminologies and the distinctive larger doctrines found in the texts that are being compared, and the terms of reference are therefore in the traditions of those texts. But, in varying ways and degrees, recent studies move more independently. I propose here to try a more independent approach to identifying the respects in which Confucius is radically affirmative as to the self and its role, and the respects in which he teaches a radical selflessness. I propose to do this by inquiring particularly into the role of the will in the *Analects* by showing how there are different dimensions to willing in Confucius's usage, and how, depending on which dimensions we take as our standpoint, we get a different view of the individual self and its significance.

I will lay the foundation for my own theses by examining in some detail four terms that are used with frequency in the *Analects* that seem explicitly to refer to self and willing: *ji* 己, *shen* 身, *yu* 欲, and *zhi* 志. Of course there are passages where these terms do not occur, but where the sense of the passage presupposes such ideas. However, for brevity, and also to avoid premature interpretation, I will restrict my analysis to actual uses of these frequently used terms.

The terms in the *Analects* referring to what in English we would appropriately render as "self" are: *shen* and *ji*. *Shen* is used some seventeen times;[14] *ji* is used some twenty-five times.[15] The term *zi* 自 is used to mean "self" far less[16] than are *ji* and *shen*, and its use in this sense introduces nothing significantly different from what we will learn by examining *ji* and *shen*. Therefore I do not discuss it further.

Ji is used as a term for self-reference, often emphatic. The emphatic reference may be to oneself as *subject*: "himself wishing to be established, establishes others."[17] The reference may be to oneself as object—"I do not care that none know *me*."[18] Or the reference may be to oneself as *agent*—"I conduct myself humbly," "to cultivate oneself so as to be respectful."[19] There is a certain reflexiveness here—the person is self-observing and self-regulating, rather than merely being, or merely doing, in an unselfconscious way. It is the difference between "I am opening the door," and "*I myself* am opening the door." That is, the more ordinary personal pronoun, such as *wu* 吾 or *wo* 我, distinguishes me as subject, or agent, or possessor, or object; but it does so in an unemphatic way, in an unselfconscious, unreflective way.[20]

Ji is used repeatedly as an emphatic contrast with the others (*ren* 人). The suggestion is that oneself, *ji*, may have interests or aims conflicting with, or in some way contrasting with, the interests of the *other*.²¹ But there is also the equally plain suggestion that the interests of oneself *ought* ideally to harmonize with those of others, or even perhaps to defer to them. And finally there is also the suggestion that if there *is* due respect for others, it is the self, *ji*, that is in some crucial way the source of this.²²

Turning now to the character *shen*—though not ceasing to take into account *ji*—we can find the following major uses in the *Analects*. It seems to embody a reference to the self more as an objective phenomenon than as subject. This is consistent with the use of *shen* to mean "body." The capacity for self-observation is again manifest: Master Tseng says, "I examine my self (*wu shen* 吾身) daily as to whether I have shown loyalty, good faith, and diligence in my dealings."²³ One should not allow what is not *ren* to affect or impinge on one's self.²⁴ One should not allow one's self to become tainted.²⁵ And *shen* is used to refer to self-regulation, self-government—"govern the self rightly (*zheng qi shen* 正其身)."²⁶ One's *shen* is one's "life"—that is, one's self viewed as having a limited extension through space and time. So in this sense one can "devote" one's life or one can "disregard" one's life.²⁷ Here "one's life" is one's total potential as the individual existent self that one is. Or we say, "all my life" (*zhong shen* 終身), meaning "during all that period in which I as a person exist."²⁸ The truly human person will even sacrifice the self (*shen*) to bring what is truly human (*ren*) to perfection.²⁹

Shen adds a bit, then, to what we learned from *ji*; and it also confirms much. The main addition is that we have here an explicit conception of the self as associated with body and temporal existence. Beyond that, we have usage in which what is explicit, as with *ji*, are the self-observing and the self-regulating powers of the self.

Regarding the notions of "will" in the *Analects*, I shall focus attention on two terms in particular: *zhi* and *yu*. Since *yu* is both less interesting and more easy to discuss, I will take it up first.

Yu is translatable into English as "wish" or "desire." It is used quite frequently in the *Analects*³⁰—about forty times—and seems to serve as the most common, generic term for indicating one's preference, as is done in English by use of such words as "wish," "want," and "desire." Though it can take on specific nuances or connotations, *yu*, in itself, as used in the *Analects*, need convey no special implication as to whether we have to do with bodily appetite, or spiritual need, or social ambition; nor need it connote anything special as to intensity, source, or aim. It is available as a term that can be neutral regarding the kind or quality or intensity of the wish or desire.³¹

The word "*yu*" merely commits one to what is perhaps as truistic—and so, as basic—as anything can be about the concept of a person. Persons are conceived as beings of whom it can characteristically be said that they want this or that; every actual wanting being ascribed to some individual person as subject.

The character *zhi* presents somewhat more interesting information. *Zhi*, used about seventeen times in the *Analects*,[32] is often translated specifically as "will."[33] Among the other English words or phrases used by translators are "bent,"[34] "wish,"[35] "set on,"[36] "determined,"[37] "aim."[38] It is plain from the contexts that the sense of the term does lie somewhere within the range of such English words, and perhaps of others such as "purpose," "intention,"[39] "resolve."[40] But, whereas the intensity and persistence of *yu* may be entirely unspecified, *zhi* seems to be used in contexts where strong and persistent purpose is at issue.[41] As with *yu*, the *zhi* is always the *zhi* of a particular person. Indeed, it is inseparable from the person—no one can take away the *zhi* of even the meanest man.[42] Regarding the scope of the conduct, the ground or reason of it, or its specific aim—*zhi* seems as indefinite as *yu*.

Zhi is intimately related to action. *Zhi* can motivate and direct action,[43] yet it is not in itself action. In itself it can even be contrasted with overt behavior. For example, Confucius contrasts it with *xing* 行;[44] and he remarks that the *zhi* can be, and perhaps in its clearest form must be, discovered in retirement (rather than in action).[45]

I feel I should add at this point that Confucius's usage reveals no explicit doctrines of a metaphysical or psychological kind about the details of structure of will, or the processes internal to the individual's control of the will. There is, for example, no reification of a faculty of the will, no inner machinery or equilibrium of psychic forces, no inner theater in which an inner drama takes place, no inner community with ruler and ruled. This absence of an elaborate doctrine of an "inner psychic life" is consistent with theses I have argued elsewhere.[46] But I mention it here more particularly to emphasize that, in focusing on Confucius's use of "willing" and "wanting," I am not proposing any special philosophical or psychological doctrine of "the will." My point is simply that Confucius does often explicitly characterize persons as willing and wanting. His usage, when taken in its context in the *Analects*, is internally consistent and allows one to draw certain general conclusions about Confucius's views of human nature, real and ideal.

Let me summarize, then, the conclusions I would draw up to this point and then develop their implications.

We have the concept of the self as a self-observing and self-regulating individual, a self sharply distinct from others, a self with interests that may in fact conflict with those of others but that ought ideally to be brought into accord with or even yield to the interests of others. From this self there arises a kind of directed dynamism—wanting, willing—that characteristically is what mediates the orientation of the self and the actual conduct of the self. This intermediary dynamic may take on various degrees of intensity and persistence, and various directions, and may arise on various occasions. All these variations are contingent. But what is necessary is that, in each instance, this dynamic is generated and controlled by the self; its locus is the particular self, as distinct from all other selves.

In this summary characterization of the self as having will, there is nothing new or startling to the Western mind; but there *is* something important to our inquiry. What is important is that on the basis of this portrait we can see quite specific respects in which Confucius is affirmative, rather than negative, about the role of personal will and the self it expresses. Specifically, Confucius appeals to us to activate our will—something only we as individuals can do—as a prime means of realizing the ideal life. As we know, he repeatedly emphasizes that we should commit ourselves unflaggingly to learning and then following the Way (*dao* 道),[47] that is, to such specific commitments as learning and abiding by *li* 禮,[48] clinging to *ren*,[49] following the principles of *zhong* 忠 and *shu* 恕[50]—all this adding up to the will to become and then the will to remain a *junzi*. As Creel has said, "Confucius demanded the utmost zeal of his followers."[51]

Now, when it comes to control over activating the will, regulating its intensity and persistence, and selecting its direction, everything depends upon the *use* of powers uniquely and distinctively controlled by the self. So in achieving the ideal life, it is the self whose zealousness of will must be relied upon, and that unceasingly plays a crucial role. Confucius, as I mentioned at the outset, is the great yea-sayer when it comes to the affirmation of oneself, as an individual self, through one's own will. His conception of human nature, real and ideal, is rooted in such affirmation.

Another way in which I would like to express this is by saying that, in the respect just mentioned, our will is inherently a *personal* will. In saying this I mean that in these respects the concept of a particular will makes necessary reference to a particular person. I mean that will can only be identified and described in those aspects by identifying the individual self whose will it is. What is *personal* to me, then, in the sense at issue, is what makes essential reference to me as the unique individual I am. The will, in regard to its locus, its generative source, and control over its arousal, intensity, and direction, and thus in turn its power over conduct, is personal. This way of putting the issue presents us with a more specific integration of what is implicit in saying that Confucius is "affirmative" in his attitude to the self. He is insisting that in the respects in which the will is inherently personal it is for us to affirm that will, to exercise it, assert it—and in so doing, of course, to affirm, to assert our self as individual, as unique.

We can now in this context identify with more precision the negative aspects, the respects in which Confucius teaches, as central to his Way, that we must have *no* self and *not* impose our personal will. We can begin to see this by recalling Confucius's emphatic rejection of certain kinds of motives and goals. He tells us that we ought to abjure the quest for personal profit,[52] personal fame,[53] or personal gratification of the senses.[54] It is not that there is anything intrinsically wrong with fame, wealth, honor, or even sensual pleasure—*if* such things arise as incidental effects of a will directed to the Way (*dao*) for its own sake. But better to have poor food and shabby clothes and be unknown, and to will the *dao*, than to depart from the *dao* even for a moment.[55]

This contrast of motives brings to our attention dimensions of will that may be but that are not inevitably and distinctively *personal*. It will be recalled that my will, in respect to its generative source, control over its arousal, intensity, and direction, and its power in turn over conduct, is inherently personal. For in all these respects *my* will can only be identified and described by identifying me personally.

But the *ground* for willing a certain act is distinguishable from any of these, and it need not be personal. It is true that I and only I can will *my* will but it may be that *what* I will is called for by the *li*, or by *ren* or *zhong*, or *shu*, or *yi* 義,[56] or—to put it most generally—by the *dao*, and that my reason for so willing is precisely that this *is* what the *dao* calls for.

In respect to the ground of my will in such cases, my will is *not* personal. For neither *dao* nor its subsidiary aspects are defined by reference to me uniquely. The *li*, for example, is expressible in terms of guidelines for conduct of persons of certain kinds of status and role—the emperor, the father, the minister, the son, the friend[57]—finding themselves in certain kinds of situations, and having to deal with other people identified by reference to their own kinds of status and role. The *dao* says that *any* person in my present position should do thus and so—my proper name is not built into the *dao*, or the *li*. In all aspects of the *dao* there is an inherent generality, an absence of essential reference to a unique individual. My personal existence is contingent; not so the *dao*. The *dao* is not only intelligible independently of such reference, its moral authority is surely independent of reference to me as the unique existent that I am. So, while the will that I direct to the *dao* is personal regarding its initial locus of energy, and control over the arousal, intensity, direction, and persistence, when it comes to the *ground* on which I choose and justify the direction for my will, and on which I elect to maintain that will vigorously and wholeheartedly, that ground—the *dao*—is in no way one that has reference to me personally.

Egoists are those who have their will rooted in themselves personally as ground. The egoist wants to be famous or wealthy—and here the wealth or fame must be this person's *only*, uniquely, or it is not an adequate ground of will for the egoist. To look at the ground of an egoist's will is thus necessarily to look at that ego; whereas to look at the ground of a *junzi*'s will is to look not at the person but at the *dao*. If one seeks to understand deeply the content of an egoistic will one must necessarily understand that particular person, the motives, anxieties, hopes, and other personal data that go to make intelligible the conduct of that person. But the more deeply one explores the *junzi*'s will, the more the personal dimensions are revealed as purely formal—the individual is the unique space-time bodily locus of that will; it is *that which* controls, but it is nonsignificant regarding why, specifically, or in what specific direction, the control shall be exercised. To understand the content of the *junzi*'s will is to understand the *dao*, not the *junzi* as a particular person. The ego is present in the egoist's will. The *dao* is present in the *junzi*'s will.

The egoist's will *imposes* the egoist on affairs. The *junzi*'s will imposes nothing, but it manifests or actualizes the *dao*. I say that the *junzi*'s will does not *impose* itself, because I mean to emphasize that the *de* 德,[58] the peculiar power of the *dao*, is *not* itself *will*power. The will is directed to *li*, to being *ren*; and this means that the *junzi* intends no one to respond to him by virtue of his affirming his personal will as such. The reason people are to do as they do is because this *is* the *li* of human affairs, and ideally all participate *of* their own will, but in spontaneously harmonious ways regarding each other. The egoist, by contrast, intends that *his* will shall govern: the fact that *he* has willed thus and so is to be *my* decisive reason for action. Thus, the egoist orders or commands me how to act. Not so the *junzi*. The *junzi* accomplishes by "yielding" (*rang* 讓) — he yields his will to the *dao*, and never imposes by means of will on others; as Confucius tells us, the *junzi* gives no orders.[59]

It is out of this total exclusion of the imposition of personal will that is generated the atmosphere that pervades and distinguishes the *Analects* — the atmosphere of an ideal community in which there is no coercion or imposition of one person's will upon another. Indeed, from the standpoint of the ground of the will, there is no imposition of personal will at all, whether by physical, psychological, legal, or political means. Instead, all cooperate spontaneously in a mutually respectful harmony defined by the *dao*.

Since the *junzi*'s will is thus ideally the medium by which, and through which, the *dao* is allowed and enabled to work and to be actualized, the "I" of the *junzi*, as purely personal, has become, as it were, transparent. It is a generative space-time locus of will without content. This way of looking at matters is reminiscent of things Laozi says, as for example, that the sage has no heart of his own,[60] that he does not put himself forward,[61] that he does not seek to dominate,[62] that people do not know him,[63] that he is dark,[64] and simply rides the *dao*.[65] One gets still another perspective on this view of the *junzi* by recollecting teachings in the *Bhagavad Gita*, teachings to the effect that *I* am not the actor,[66] that Krishna or Brahman is the true ground of all.[67] The *junzi*'s will, grounded in the *dao*, is a will that in an important way is unconcerned — unconcerned *personally* — with the "fruits of action."[68] Where he acts, it is the space-time power of will unique to him that acts, but he personally is not the *ground* of the action.[69] Is this not "inaction in action?"[70] And where consequences have no *personal* relevance to the will, can *karman* any longer have significance for that person? The idea at issue here is more culturally catholic yet — for it is a way of expressing, less pregnantly but in one respect more precisely, the spirit of the phrase, "Not my will, but Thine be done."

I must now qualify my formulation by pointing out that there is an important level at which the unique personality can and must have its play. Confucius loved music, and gave it a very high place in the hierarchy of the forms of self-cultivation.[71] To cover much ground briefly in these last few words of mine, I will resort to a single extended image, that of the musical performance.

Consider a fine violinist's presentation of the Bach Chaconne, or consider *Zhi*, the Chief Musician, and his performance of the "Ospreys."[72] Plainly what governs—especially when this is an artistic performance and not an excuse for mere showmanship—is the musical conception brought forth by Bach, the poetic-musical conception of the "Ospreys." It is this musical concept, corresponding to the *dao*, that transcends the individual will, and that constitutes the ground of the will for each ideal performer. The essential conception is *encoded* in the musical score, or in the *Book of Songs*; but the musical concept itself is embodied, actualized, in the developing structure of sound, or word-in-sound, through time. Ideally, the performer's willed conduct is the medium *through* which the musical concept gets embodied, becomes actual.

Yet we know that there are legitimate personal aspects of the musical performance, aspects that are irreducible and valuable. Without the wholehearted and unwaveringly diligent will to follow through properly, there is *no* performance, or it simply breaks down. Beyond this, the personal dimensions of style, temperament, and interpretation shine in and through the embodied Chaconne. *Zhi*'s performance is singled out by Confucius for its special brilliance. Yet, although style and interpretation may be unique to the performer, that is, personal, it remains basic that the true artist's style *serves* the work; the personal interpretation is a genuine interpretation *of* the work. Style and interpretation must not dominate, obscure, or distort the concept of the Chaconne or the "Ospreys." Confucius remarks that though the musicians in ancient times were given a certain liberty, the tone remained harmonious, brilliant, consistent, right to the end.[73]

Unique personality has a role because, no more than any concept, even that of the *dao*—the musical concept cannot resolve unambiguously *every* aspect of the concrete reality to be actualized. No concept embraces the fullness of the reality. And so the performer, the one who makes *actual*, cannot be denied the office of creating a reality that is denser and richer than any concept, and that therefore is necessarily personal in important ways—even though the personal only serves and enhances the governing and pervading concept, which is nonpersonal.

It would be enlightening to explore the ways in which this conception of Confucius's significantly differs from conceptions of selflessness peculiar to other streams of Asian thought. Obviously there are differences of importance. But if we keep in view his teaching as centered, specifically, on the *dao* as ground of the will, and on the implications of this grounding, we see clearly a fundamental respect in which he shares in the pan-Asian ideal of selflessness as crucial to salvation.

Notes

Editors' Note: This paper was originally published in *Philosophy East and West* 29, no. 2, April 1979.

1. Unless otherwise indicated, all the references herein are to the *Analects*, and will be given by chapter and paragraph number without further identification.

2. See, for example, *Brhadaranyaka Upanisad*, II 3.6; III 9.26; IV 2.4.

3. Examples of the doctrine of *sunyata* in Chinese Buddhism can be found in Wing-tsit Chan, *A Source Book in Chinese Philosophy* (Princeton, N. J.: Princeton University Press, 1963), chs. 22–26. For examples from Indian Buddhism, see Edward Conze, *Buddhist Texts Through the Ages* (New York: Philosophical Library, 1954), especially selections 149–56. The *Heart Sutra* exemplifies this notion as found in the Prajnaparamita literature (see: Edward Conze, trans., *Buddhist Wisdom Books* [London: G. Allen and Unwin, 1958]).

4. The doctrine of *annata* (no-self) is distinctive of much Buddhist teaching. See, for example, the *Lankavatara Sutra*, trans. By D. T. Suzuki (London: Routledge and Kegan Paul, 1932), sections 44–45, and the *Diamond Sutra*, in *Buddhist Wisdom Books*, *supra* note 3. For an example of a Hinayana text with this idea, see selection 66 in *Buddhist Texts Through the Ages*, *supra* note 3.

5. The teaching of *wu wei* appears early in Chinese thought as a central idea in the *Dao De Jing* and *Zhuangzi* texts. The idea of "inaction in action" plays a key role in the great Indian text, *Bhagavad Gita*.

6. For example, 1.1, 6.25, 7.8, 7.19, 7.33.

7. For example, 7.36, 13.26, 15.21.

8. For example, 2.10, 2.14, 6.3, 8.2.

9. For example, 4.5, 4.6, 4.10, 12.4, 14.1, 15.17.

10. For example, 4.16, 7.8, 8.13, 15.23.

11. 14.45.

12. The *Great Learning* (*Da Xue*), ch. 6. See also ch. 4.

13. 14.45 (A. Waley, trans., [New York: Random House, 1938]). Note, too, that the term for "self" used by Confucius (*ji*) is not the one usually used in the later texts (*shen*).

14. *Shen* will be found at least once in each of the following passages: 1.4, 1.7, 4.6, 9.26, 12.21, 13.6, 13.13, 15.8, 15.23, 17.7, 18.7, 18.8.

15. *Ji* will be found at least once in each of the following passages: 1.8, 1.16, 4.14, 5.15, 6.28, 7.28, 8.7, 9.24, 12.1, 12.2, 13.20, 14.25, 14.32, 14.42, 14.43, 14.45, 15.4, 15.18, 15.20, 15.23, 19.10.

16. *Zi* is used in the sense of "self" in the following passages: 4.27, 5.26, 12.23, 14.18, 14.30, 16.14, 19.17, 19.24.

17. 6.28. See also 12.23, 15.23.

18. 14.32. See also, for example, 1.16, 12.1, 14.42, 15.18.

19. 5.15, 14.45. See also 7.28, 13.20.

20. For example, "At fifteen I [*wu*] was bent on learning . . ." (and in the remainder of this well-known sequence the personal pronoun is omitted entirely) [2.4]. In 4.6 *wo* is used as nonemphatic subject. In 5.11 one finds *wo* used as subject and as object; followed immediately by *wu* used as subject. Thus, in general, though *wu* is used more frequently than *wo*, they can be interchanged in various uses, and they take various grammatical roles. But consistently they remain used to unambiguously identify the person referred to in the sentence as the speaker, but to do so without throwing the emphasis in a reflexive way on the person. However Waley says that *wo* as nominative is more emphatic than *wu* (*supra*, note 13, p. 103, n. 2).

21. 1.8, 6.28, 9.24, 12.2, 14.25, 15.20, 15.23, 19.10.

22. 12.1, 15.20.

23. 1.4.

24. 4.6.

25. 18.

26. 13.6, 13.13.

27. 1.7, 12.21.

28. 9.26, 15.23.

29. 15.8.

30. *Yu* is used at least once in each of the following passages: 2.4, 3.10, 3.17, 4.5(1), 4.24, 5.11, 6.4, 6.28, 7.29, 9.10, 9.19, 9.13, 11.10, 12.2, 12.10, 12.18, 12.19, 13.17, 14.2, 14.13, 14.26, 14.47, 15.9, 15.23, 16.1, 17.1, 17.5, 17.19, 17.20, 18.5, 18.7, 19.24, 20.2.

31. The term seems to be used in a "neutral" way, for example, in the various versions of the golden rule to be found in the text, for example, at 5.11, 12.2, and 15.23.

32. *Zhi* is used at least once in the following passages: 1.11, 2.4, 4.4, 4.9, 4.18, 5.25, 7.6, 9.25, 11.25, 14.38, 15.8, 16.11, 18.8, 19.6.

33. Legge, for example, translates this way in *Chinese Classics*, vol. 1 (Hong Kong: Hong Kong University Press, 1960), 7.6, 9.25, and 18.8.

34. For example, Legge uses "bent" in 2.4.

35. For example, Legge uses "wish" in 5.25.

36. For example, Legge combines "will" and "set on" in 4.4.

37. For example, Legge uses "determined" in 15.8.

38. For example, Legge uses "aim" in 19.6.

39. Waley (*supra* note 13) uses "intention" in 1.11.

40. Waley uses "high resolve" in 18.8.

41. For example, 4.4, 4.18, 15.18, 18.18(2), 19.6. There are a few cases where a weaker purposiveness can be read into the passage, but where a strong purpose is also consistent with the text. Thus, in 9.25 Waley uses "opinion," but Legge uses "will." In 4.18, Waley uses "opinion" and Legge uses, as the effective verb, "incline"; but on the other hand Leslie uses stronger language here (*ne l'écoutent pas et ne changent point*," Daniel Leslie, *Confucius*, Editions Seghers, 1962).

42. 9.25.

43. 2.4, 4.9, 7.6(1), 19.6.

44. 1.11. See also 5.25, 11.25, 16.11.

45. 16.11(2).

46. Herbert Fingarette, *Confucius: The Secular as Sacred* (New York: Harper Torch-books, 1972), especially ch. 3.

47. For example, 8.13.

48. For example, 12.1.

49. For example, 4.5.

50. For a full discussion of Confucius's emphasis on these two principles as the "one thread" that runs through his teaching, see Herbert Fingarette, "Following the 'One Thread' of the *Analects*," *Journal of the American Academy of Religion* Thematic Issue 47, no. 35 (Sept. 1979): 373–415.

51. H. G. Creel, *Chinese Thought from Confucius to Mao Tse-tung* (New York: Mentor, 1953), 36.

52. For example, 4.5, 4.16, 14.1, 15.31.

53. For example, 1.1, 4.5, 4.14, 8.13, 14.32, 15.18.

54. For example, 4.9, 9.17.

55. For example, 8.13, 14.13.

56. For passages and comment on *li, ren, zhong,* and *shu,* see notes 48, 49, and 50 *supra.* For reference to *yi,* see, for example, 4.10, 4.16, 15.17, 17.23.

57. 12.11.

58. 2.1; and see 15.4. Full discussion will be found in Fingarette, note 46 *supra,* ch. 1.

59. 4.13, 12.19, 13.16.

60. *Dao De Jing,* ch. 49.

61. *Ibid.,* ch. 7.

62. *Ibid.,* ch. 22, 34.

63. *Ibid.,* ch. 17.

64. *Ibid.,* ch. 20.

65. *Ibid.,* ch. 14.

66. *Bhagavad Gita,* 5.8.

67. *Ibid.,* 5.10.

68. *Ibid.,* 4.18–20, 18.23, 18.45–47.

69. *Ibid.,* 4.16–21.

70. *Ibid.,* 4.18–20.

71. See: 3.3, 3.20, 8.8, 8.15, 11.1, 14.13, 16.5.

72. 8.15.

73. 3.23.

Contributors

KIM-CHONG CHONG is Associate Professor in the Department of Philosophy at the National University of Singapore. His research interests are ethics and Chinese philosophy. His publications include "Egoism, Desires, and Friendship" (*American Philosophical Quarterly*, 1984), *Moral Agoraphobia: the Challenge of Egoism* (1996), "The Practice of *Jen*" (*Philosophy East and West*, 1999), *Altruistic Reveries: Perspectives from the Humanities and Social Sciences* (coedited with Basant Kapur, 2002), and "Xunzi's Systematic Critique of Mencius" (*Philosophy East and West*, 2003). He is writing a book on *Early Confucian Ethics: Concepts and Arguments*, and researching a Daoist text, the *Zhuangzi*.

DEAN COCKING is Senior Research Fellow with the Centre for Applied Philosophy and Public Ethics, Charles Sturt University, Canberra, Australia. He has written extensively on friendship and moral theory and is coauthor of *Virtue Ethics and Professional Roles* (2001).

C. A. J. (TONY) COADY is an Australian Research Council (ARC) Senior Research Fellow in Philosophy at the University of Melbourne, Australia. He is Deputy Director (and Head of the University of Melbourne division) of the ARC Special Research Centre for Applied Philosophy and Public Ethics. He has published extensively in both academic and more general venues. His book, *Testimony: A Philosophical Inquiry*, was widely and enthusiastically reviewed internationally.

MARGARET M. COADY is Program Manager in Professional Ethics for the Australian Research Council Special Research Centre for Applied Philosophy and Public Ethics, and a Senior Lecturer in the Centre for Equity and Innovation in Early Childhood at the University of Melbourne, Australia. Her areas of specialty are professional ethics and children's and families' rights. She has held research fellowships at the Center for Human Values at Princeton University, the Rockefeller Center at Bellagio, Italy, and the Kennedy Institute for Ethics at Georgetown University.

HERBERT FINGARETTE is Emeritus Professor of Philosophy in the University of California, Santa Barbara. He is the author of *Confucius: The Secular as Sacred* and numerous other studies in Chinese and in Indian philosophy. His philosophical research has focused on the theme of personal responsibility, and in this connection he has also authored books and articles in the fields of law, psychiatry, philosophical psychology, and ethics.

JOHN D. GREENWOOD is Professor of Philosophy and Psychology at City College and the Graduate School, City University of New York, and Executive Officer of the Ph.D./M.A. Program in Philosophy at the City University of New York Graduate School. During 1999-2000 he was a Visiting Senior Fellow in the Department of Philosophy at the National University of Singapore. He is the author of various books and articles on the philosophy and history of social and psychological science. He recently completed a history of social psychology entitled *What Happened to the "Social" in Social Psychology*, to be published in the series *Cambridge Studies in the History of Psychology*. He is currently working on a conceptual history of psychology entitled *The Tangled Web*.

BAOGANG HE (B.A. Hangzhou University 1981; M.A. People's University of China, Beijing 1986; Ph.D. Australian National University 1993) is currently Senior Research Fellow, East Asian Institute, National University of Singapore; and Reader at the School of Government, University of Tasmania, Hobart, Australia. He is the author of *The Democratization of China* (1996), *The Democratic Implication of Civil Society in China* (1997), and *Nationalism, National Identity and Democratization in China* (2000, with Yingjie Guo). He has coauthored and cotranslated several books in Chinese (including John Rawls's *A Theory of Justice*), and has published many book chapters and articles in a variety of journals.

JOHN KEKES is Professor of Philosophy, State University of New York at Albany. He is the author of many books and articles on moral and political philosophy. His most recent book is *The Art of Life* (2002).

JEANETTE KENNETT is Senior Lecturer in Philosophy at Monash University, Australia. She is the author of *Agency and Responsibility: A Common-sense Moral Psychology* (2001). She has coauthored a number of articles on friendship with Dean Cocking.

KARYN LAI is a lecturer at the School of Philosophy, University of New South Wales in Sydney, Australia. She has published in the areas of Chinese philosophy and environmental ethics. Her publications include articles in *Philosophy East and West* and *Journal of Chinese Philosophy*. She has also contributed an entry entitled "Chinese Attitudes to Nature" to *A Companion to Environmental Philosophy*. She is the author of the book *Moral Cultivation, Self, and Community: Learning from Confucian and Daoist Philosophies* (2003).

YUET KEUNG LO teaches Chinese philosophy in the Department of Chinese Studies at the National University of Singapore. His research interests cover early Chinese thought as well as early medieval Chinese philosophy and religions. His recent publications include "To Use or Not To Use: The Idea of *Ming* in the *Zhuangzi*" in *Monumenta Serica* and "The Formulation of Early Medieval Confucian Metaphysics: Huang K'an's (485–545) Accommodation of Neo-Taoism and Buddhism" in *Imagining Boundaries: Changing Confucian Doctrines, Texts, and Hermeneutics*, ed. Kai-wing Chow et al. (1999). He is currently completing an annotated translation of an eighteenth-century anthology of Chinese Buddhist laywomen's biographies.

ALAN MONTEFIORE is an Emeritus Fellow of Balliol College, Oxford, having retired several years ago after more than thirty years there as Fellow and Tutor in Philosophy. For the following three years he was an Academic Visitor in the Department of Philosophy, Logic and Scientific Method at the London School of Economics, and is now Visiting Professor in the Centre for European Philosophy at Middlesex University. He is President both of the Wiener Library in London and of the Forum for European Philosophy and is a past Chairman of the Froebel Educational Institute, of which he remains a member of its Research Committee. He has published numerous articles, as well as books, either as author, editor or a combination of the two, on moral philosophy, philosophy and education, the University and political commitment, contemporary French philosophy, the political responsibility of intellectuals, and the relationship between the causal description and explanation of goal-directive behavior and that in intentional and normative terms. He is currently working on aspects of the relations between personal and cultural identity and hopes one day to produce a book on his own no doubt somewhat offbeat reading of Kant.

MARTHA NUSSBAUM is Ernst Freund Distinguished Service Professor of Law and Ethics at the University of Chicago Law School. She has taught at Harvard, Brown, and Oxford Universities. In November 2002, she delivered the Tanner Lectures at Australian National University in Canberra, Australia, under the title *Beyond the Social Contract: Toward Global Justice*.

A. T. NUYEN received his Ph.D. from the University of Queensland, Australia, where he was Reader in Philosophy. He is currently Associate Professor at the National University of Singapore. His research interests include the philosophy of Hume and Kant, contemporary Continental philosophy, ethics, and Chinese and comparative philosophy. His publications have appeared in *American Philosophical Quarterly*, *History of Philosophy Quarterly*, *Southern Journal of Philosophy*, *Kant-Studien*, *Hume Studies*, *Journal of Religion*, *Journal of Chinese Philosophy*, *Asian Philosophy*, and many others. He is the 2002-2003 President of the Australasian Society for Asian and Comparative Philosophy.

SOR-HOON TAN teaches philosophy at the National University of Singapore. She has published works on pragmatism, Chinese philosophy, and cross-cultural philosophy. She holds degrees from Oxford University and the University of Hawaii. Her forthcoming book, *Confucian Democracy: A Deweyan Reconstruction*, is being published by the State University of New York Press.

C. L. TEN is Professor of Philosophy, National University of Singapore. He was previously Professor of Philosophy (Personal Chair) at Monash University, Australia. He is the author of *Mill on Liberty* and *Crime, Guilt, and Punishment*, and the editor of *The Nineteenth Century* and *Mill's Moral, Political and Legal Philosophy*, and is working on a *Historical Dictionary of John Stuart Mill's Philosophy*. He has published in journals of philosophy, law, politics, and the history of ideas, and is a fellow of both the Australian Academy of the Humanities and the Australian Academy of the Social Sciences.

BRYAN W. VAN NORDEN is an Associate Professor in the Philosophy Department and in the Asian Studies Program at Vassar College. He received his B.A. in philosophy from the University of Pennsylvania in 1985, and Ph.D. in philosophy from Stanford University in 1991. He has written numerous articles on early Chinese philosophy, especially Confucianism and Daoism, edited and contributed to *Confucius and the Analects: New Essays*, coedited (with Philip J. Ivanhoe) and contributed to *Readings in Classical Chinese Philosophy*, and is currently at work on a book that will examine the philosophical positions of Confucius, the early Mohists, and Mencius on virtue ethics and consequentialism.

CECILIA WEE is an Assistant Professor with the National University of Singapore. She works primarily in Descartes and early modern philosophy, but has some interest in Chinese philosophy and environmental ethics. Her papers include "Descartes's Two Proofs of the External World" (*Australasian Journal of Philosophy*, forthcoming); "Has Aristotle's Mind Been Changed?" (*Archiv fur Geschicte der Philosophie*, forthcoming); "Descartes on Self, Other, and Community" (*History of Philosophy Quarterly*, 2002); "Cartesian Environmental Ethics" (*Environmental Ethics*, 2001). She is currently looking into how Mencius's views can help illuminate the (alleged) polarity between feminine care ethics and an impartial perspective.

Index